JESUS, SALVATION AND THE JEWISH PEOPLE

Papers on the Uniqueness of Jesus and Jewish Evangelism
Presented at a conference conducted
by
the WEA Theological Commission
18–22 August 2008
Woltersdorf, Berlin, Germany

Edited by
David Parker

Paternoster:
thinking faith

17 16 15 14 13 12 11   7 6 5 4 3 2 1

This edition first published 2011 by Paternoster
Paternoster is an imprint of Authentic Media Limited
Presley Way Crownhill, Milton Keynes, MK8 0ES
www.authenticmedia.co.uk

British Library Cataloguing in Publication Data

A catalogue record for this book is available from the
British Library

ISBN 978-1-84227-669-3

Cover design by Phil Houghton
Printed and bound in the UK

Contents

Author Information

Henri Blocher is honorary Dean of the Faculté Libre de Théologie Evangélique, Vaux-sur-Seine, France where he still teaches; he was formerly Knoedler Professor of Theology at Wheaton College Graduate School, Ill., USA. He was a participant in the Willowbank Consultation (1989).

Darrell Bock (PhD, Aberdeen, UK) is Research Professor of New Testament Studies and Professor for Spiritual Development and Culture at Dallas Theological Seminary, Tex., USA. He serves on the board of Chosen People Ministries.

Michael L. Brown (PhD, New York University, USA) is founder and President of the FIRE School of Ministry, N.C., USA, as well as an adjunct professor at The King's Seminary, Calif., USA; Denver Theological Seminary, Colorado, USA; and Gordon-Conwell Theological Seminary (Charlotte branch, N.C., USA). He is the author of the five-volume series *Answering Jewish Objections to Jesus* and is considered an expert in Jewish apologetics.

David Dowde, (PhD, Vanderbilt University, USA) is Professor of German Language and Literature at Pepperdine University, Calif., USA. He has published and presented on such German-Jewish figures as Moses Mendelssohn and Leo Baeck. His most recent publication is the book *Jewish-Christian Relations in Eighteenth-Century Germany: Textual Studies on German Archival Holdings*, 1729–42.

Richard Harvey (PhD, University of Wales, UK) teaches Hebrew Bible and Jewish Studies at All Nations Christian College, Herts., UK, where he is also Academic Dean and Director of Postgraduate

Studies. He is the author of *Mapping Messianic Jewish Theology: A Constructive Approach* (Paternoster, 2009).

Rolf Hille (ThD, Munich, Germany) is Director of Doctoral Studies at Albrecht Bengel Haus, Tübingen, Germany, where he served as Rector from 1995–2009. He is also Chairman of the Fellowship of German Evangelical Theologians (AfeT).

Kai Kjær-Hansen (DD, Lund University, Sweden) is a freelance theologian and former general editor of *Mishkan*. He serves as Chairman of the Danish Israel Mission and International Coordinator of the Lausanne Consultation on Jewish Evangelism (LCJE).

Andreas J. Köstenberger (PhD, Trinity Evangelical Divinity School, USA) is Professor of New Testament and Director of PhD Studies, Southeastern Baptist Theological Seminary, N.C., USA, founder of Biblical Foundations and editor of *Journal of the Evangelical Theological Society*.

Michael McDuffee (PhD, Brandeis University, USA) is a professor of History and Historical Theology at Moody Bible Institute, Ill., USA.

David Parker (PhD, University of Queensland, Australia) spent many years as a pastor and theological educator in Australia. He also served with the Theological Commission of the World Evangelical Alliance for more than twenty years, was its Executive Director and edited its journal, *Evangelical Review of Theology*.

Eckhard J. Schnabel (PhD, Aberdeen, UK) is Professor of New Testament at Trinity Evangelical Divinity School, Ill., USA.

Berthold Schwarz (ThD, Erlangen, Germany) is Professor of Systematic Theology at the Giessen School of Theology and rector of the Institute for Israelogy, Giesson, Germany. He spent several years as missionary in Japan and has published in the areas of Christology, the doctrine of Israel, Salvation History and eschatology.

Tuvya Zaretsky (DMiss, Western Seminary, USA) is Director of Staff Training and Development with Jews for Jesus, Los Angeles, USA and serves as President of the Lausanne Consultation on Jewish Evangelism. He was a participant in the Willowbank Consultation (1989).

Preface

The relationship between Jesus, salvation and the Jewish people has been a controversial, but important, subject over a long period of time, as the writings of the New Testament, Christian history and Christian-Jewish dialogue indicate. For this reason, the Theological Commission of the World Evangelical Alliance (WEA) conducted an international consultation on 'The Uniqueness of Jesus and Jewish Evangelism' at Woltersdorf, near Berlin, 18–22 August 2008. This volume contains the papers presented at that conference and the Declaration which it issued. As Chapter One explains, this conference was a follow-up to the Willowbank Declaration on the Christian Gospel and the Jewish People (dated 1989, also sponsored by WEA and with the support of the Lausanne movement). The 2008 conference addressed developments in the two decades since the Willowbank conference met and assessed current realities.

Berlin was chosen for the location of the conference to highlight the contrast between the recent notorious anti-Semitic history associated with this city and its earlier days as the centre of a dynamic philo-Semitism, which reached out to Jewish people in Germany and beyond with the love of God and the gospel of Jesus Christ. It is hoped that, in some small way, this conference and publication can restore appreciation for the people who witnessed so faithfully to the goodness of the gospel in that area, and to explain why many evangelicals still consider the relationship of Jesus to Judaism and salvation to be an important topic.

The papers in this volume cover biblical, historical, theological and pastoral aspects of the topic, and form a foundation for the Declaration. The authors, who are from several different countries, represent a range of backgrounds, including German Christians and Messianic Jews, with varied experience in Christian ministry among Jewish people and in the scholarship appropriate for the topic.

Much of the material was specifically prepared for the conference. However, some papers are updated versions of earlier publications; we are grateful for permission to use this material, and draw attention to the notes in the relevant chapters acknowledging the details. We also draw attention to the note referring to the dialogue which has taken place elsewhere between one of the authors, Eckhard Schnabel, and Mark Kinzer, with whose work he interacts extensively in this volume. We are also grateful to Andreas Köstenberger who, although not able to be present at the conference, supplied his paper for publication; to Michael Brown who was not able to participate but whose paper was presented *in absentia*; to Michael McDuffee whose paper was specially written for this publication, replacing the one originally presented. The authors also wish to thank Paternoster for agreeing to publish this material. We acknowledge with gratitude the cordial assistance of the staff at the EC Begegnungs-und Bildungszentrum (CE Conference Centre), Woltersdorf, and others who helped in various ways to facilitate the conference.

We appreciate those who have received the Declaration in the spirit in which it was intended. It is our prayer that this volume, and the Declaration itself, will help to provide deeper and stronger foundations for the important ministry which, following the example of the Apostle Paul, believes the gospel is 'first for the Jews, and also for the Gentiles' (Rom. 1:16 [GNB]).

The Berlin Declaration on the Uniqueness of Christ and Jewish Evangelism in Europe Today

An international task force of the Theological Commission of the World Evangelical Alliance met on the issue of the uniqueness of Christ and Jewish evangelism in Berlin, Germany, from August 18–22, 2008. We met to consider how our community might express genuine love for the Jewish people, especially in Europe. Participants included Christians from Germany and Messianic Jews.

1. Love is not Silent: the Need for Repentance

We deeply regret the all too frequent persecution of Jewish people in Jesus' name. We do not for a second deny the evil it represents. During the genocide of the Holocaust, when the Jewish people were in their greatest peril, most Christian believers were silent. Many, such as The Stuttgart Confession of Guilt right after World War II, have apologized for the failure to speak out and for not doing more to demonstrate genuine Christian love to the Jewish people. Some of our brothers and sisters in the European Christian community suffered as well for resisting the anti-Semites and perpetrators of the atrocities. Many more today feel embarrassment and shame for the general failure to protest. As a result, there is an evident insecurity about relations with Jewish people. Also, there is a tendency to replace direct gospel outreach with Jewish-Christian dialogue.

We believe that genuine love cannot be passive. Jesus taught that authentic love could not be unfeeling when other human beings are in misery and need. Honest love must include an expression of Christ's good news in word and deed. Therefore, Christians everywhere must not look away when Jewish people have the same deep need for forgiveness of sin and true *shalom*, as do people of all nations. Love in action compels all Christians to share the gospel with people everywhere, including the Jewish people of Europe.

2. Beyond Genocide: the Problem of Sin

We acknowledge within the sad record of European Christian history the "teaching of contempt," intolerance toward Jewish people and Judaism, abhorrent acts of coercion, anti-Semitism in attitude, word and deed. The historical events of the Holocaust developed within a climate of anti-Semitism. The German Evangelical Alliance out of concern for that history has expressed shame and responsibility for Christian silence and too few attempts to stop the horror.

Jewish people interpret Christian failure to speak out as complicity in their genocide during World War II. However, there were some valiant Christians who did speak up, risking and sometimes losing their own lives to save Jews.

In light of rising European anti-Semitism and anti-Israelism vigilance is necessary now. Jewish people are not the only victims of genocide as evidenced today. The Holocaust survivor, Primo Levi, warned, "It has happened. Therefore, it can happen again." The source of all genocide is sin. This sin affects all humanity, both the persecutor and the sufferer. God's response to sin is the gospel. Therefore, this grace must be proclaimed to every human being.

3. The Solution for Sin: the Uniqueness of Christ

We recognize that genocide illustrates the enormity of sin. God is not responsible for genocide; we humans are. God has provided the solution.

It is often seen as unacceptable to challenge another's religious views. Nevertheless, we regard failure to share the gospel as ignoring the problem of sin. No one should ignore Jesus' assessment of human sin. Everyone needs what God offers by his grace: forgiveness of sin and a transforming divine presence in those who respond. Jesus did not seek to dominate, but gave himself on the cross as sacrifice for sin. His death cleanses from the guilt of sin and provides a new relationship with God. This benefit is neither earned nor entered into by birth. It is received through acknowledging our deep need for God to supply what we lack.

Confessing Jesus as Messiah affirms Jesus' uniqueness as a person, especially to Jews, because Messiah (or Christ) is a Jewish concept. He is sent as the Word, anointed as Messiah and vindicated by God to sit at his right hand. Through resurrection Jesus shares in the divine glory, task and authority. Jesus of Nazareth is more than a prophet or a religious teacher. Rather, he is the unique Son of God, mediating and administering God's promise. By his divine authority, Jesus extends his offer to all. He exercises the divine prerogatives of forgiving sin and receiving worship. This is why we confess Jesus as both human and divine.

God calls believers to take the gospel to the world. Everyone needs to hear this message including the Jewish people. Proclamation to Israel was Jesus' priority. It also reflects the apostles' practice of going to the Jew first. Nothing has occurred since Jesus came that changes the need for Israel and the nations.

4. The Call to Action: Jewish Evangelism

Christians are called to share this good news, with sensitivity and humility. Witness to the gospel should be motivated by heart-felt love and expressed in practical ways. So, we stand in solidarity with the Jewish people, opposing anti-Semitism, prejudice and discrimination. This sinful behavior is irreconcilable with the calling of Christ's disciples.

Most of all, we invite Jewish people and all others to consider the claims of Jesus. We share this gospel with Israel and all nations, not as an attack on the integrity of others. We uphold everyone's right to freedom of speech, freedom of religion and an open forum for all. While respecting the views of others, we still challenge them to consider the message of the Messiah.

Christians have much to learn from the Jewish people. We recognize our need to hear Jewish concerns. We affirm the importance of dialogue in promoting mutual understanding and sympathy. Dialogue provides an opportunity to share deeply held beliefs in a context of mutual respect. Dialogue and evangelism are not mutually exclusive. We reject the notion that evangelism is deceptive in claiming that Jews can believe in Jesus. We also reject the accusation that evangelism is the equivalent of spiritual genocide. We affirm the right of Jewish believers in Jesus to practice those traditions that affirm their identity, reflect God's faithfulness to his people and uphold the messiahship of Jesus.

We recognize the important role of Messianic Jews in the work and witness of the Church. Their special contribution gives testimony to the Jewish origins of Christianity and brings understanding of our Jewish roots. They remind us of the Jewishness of Jesus and of the first Christians. They also point to the fulfillment of God's promises to save his people. We encourage them to stand firm in their identification with and faithful witness to their people. The Lord is also glorified in the visible demonstration of reconciliation of Jew and German in the body of Christ.

The Next Step

Therefore, as Christians concerned for the well-being and salvation of the Jewish people, we call for:

- Respect for religious conviction and liberty that allows frank discussion of religious claims
- Repentance from all expressions of anti-Semitism and all other forms of genocide, prejudice and discrimination.
- Recognition of the uniqueness of Christ as the crucified, resurrected and divine Messiah who alone can save from death and bring eternal life
- Reconciliation and unity amongst believers in Jesus
- Renewed commitment to the task of Jewish evangelism

This statement was developed by a World Evangelical Alliance Task Force meeting on the Uniqueness of Christ and Jewish Evangelism in Berlin, Germany • Adopted August 22, 2008 • Participants: Henri Blocher (France), Michael L. Brown (USA), Darrell Bock (USA), David Dowdey (USA), Richard Harvey (UK), Rolf Hille (Germany), Kai Kjær-Hansen (Denmark), Michael McDuffee (USA), David Parker (Chair, Australia), Eckhard Schnabel (Germany/USA), Berthold Schwarz (Germany), Bodil Skjøtt (Denmark) and Tuvya Zaretsky (USA).

1

The Call to Jewish Evangelism

David Parker

This volume contains the papers presented at a consultation held at Woltersdorf, near Berlin, Germany on 18–22 August 2008, sponsored by World Evangelical Alliance Theological Commission.[1] Its purpose was to consider the uniqueness of Jesus in relation to Jewish evangelism from an evangelical biblical, theological, historical and missiological perspective. The conference produced a statement, 'The Berlin Declaration on the Uniqueness of Christ and Jewish Evangelism in Europe Today', reasserting the importance of and the rationale for presenting Jesus Christ to Jewish people as Saviour, Messiah and Lord.[2] The papers are being published with the hope that they will be useful in strengthening the cause of Jewish evangelism and the lives of Jewish believers and churches in the light of current issues. Such a need exists because of developments since the publication of the Willowbank Declaration in 1989 (see below).

In this introduction,[3] we set out some of the context for the consultation, in particular the background which has led up to it. There is also a brief survey of the current position of churches and other Christian groups in regard to the call to present Jesus Christ to Jewish people.

---

[1] Note that A. Köstenberger (chapter 4) was unable to be present at the conference but supplied his paper later for publication. M. Brown (chapter 9) was also unable to be present but his paper was read *in absentia*. Michael McDuffee's paper (chapter 8) published here is a replacement for the one he presented at the conference.

[2] The text of the Berlin Declaration immediately preceeds this chapter; it is also available online at http://www.worldevangelicals.org/commissions/list/tc/49.htm.

[3] This is an edited version of the author's Opening Statement to the Consultation.

The papers which follow will cover some of this material in much more detail, but it is helpful to have an overall perspective at the outset.[4]

The Willowbank Declaration

Although most regrettably there has been a sad history of anti-Semitism on the part of some Christians over many centuries, there has also been long and meritorious history of Jewish evangelism, commencing at the day of Pentecost. For example, the story of nineteenth-century Jewish missions by British and European churches of the Reformed/Presbyterian, Anglican and Lutheran traditions makes inspiring reading as we learn of the enterprising, faithful and sacrificial work of missionaries, their families and their supporters.[5] Their converts often faced extreme difficulties as they maintained their faith to the glory of God and for this we give humble honour.

However, during the twentieth century, there were several developments which created a completely new situation for Jewish missions. These include the horrors of the Holocaust/*Shoah*, the establishment of the State of Israel and changes in theology and church practice in the post-World War II period in both Catholic and Protestant churches, including influences stemming from and subsequent to the Second Vatican Council. After World War II, Protestant churches in Europe and elsewhere began to issue statements revealing new approaches to the evangelism of and relations with the Jewish people. These included statements and policies on evangelism, including Two Covenant Theology[6] in particular, which were antithetical to the formerly accepted views.[7] The result was that any form of direct evangelism of Jewish

---

[4] I am greatly indebted to Dr Zaretsky and Dr Richard Robinson for considerable assistance in locating resources and information which I have used in the preparation of this paper. In addition to personal correspondence and conversation, I would point to Dr Robinson's resource book, *The Messianic Movement: A Field Guide for Evangelical Christians* (San Francisco: Purple Pomegranate Productions, 2005), and his article, 'Jewish Mission' in *Dictionary of Mission Theology: Evangelical Foundations* (ed. John Corrie; Nottingham/ Downers Grove: IVP, 2007).

[5] For example, George H. Stevens, *'Go, tell my Brethren': A short popular history of Church Missions to Jews (1809 to 1959)* (London: Olive Press, n.d.); see also chapters 6 and 7.

[6] See also chapter 10.

[7] Isaac C. Rottenberg, 'Opening the Covenant: A Jewish Theology of Christianity by Michael S. Kogan – A Review' (online: http://www.isaacrottenberg.com/ uploads/pdf/www.isaacrottenberg.com/a_review.pdf refers to a Reformed

people was considered theologically invalid, religiously offensive and ethnically scandalous.

The Holocaust/*Shoah*,[8] in particular, is widely regarded as creating a completely new situation, not only for Jewish people but also for Christian theology, touching such areas as the nature of God, guilt, suffering and triumphalism. In particular, in the view of many, it demands the complete eradication of previous supersessionist or Replacement Theology with its allegedly negative views of Jews and Judaism. Such views are said to be responsible for the long history of anti-Semitism and ultimately the Holocaust. Thus, the First Symposium of Christian Theology sponsored by the Confraternidad Argentina Judeo Cristiana held in Buenos Aires on the topic of 'Holocaust-Shoah: Its Effects on Christian Theology and Life in Argentina and Latin America'[9] stated in its Final Declaration, dated 17 May 2006:

> A long history of Christian antijudaism and of Christian violence against the Jews prepared the road for Nazi ideology. The fundamental weakness, and even the failure, of the Christian vision before the Shoah resided basically in a declaration of the uselessness or irrelevancy of the Jewish people.

It therefore concluded:

> [T]heologians must critically re-examine the whole of their own traditions in light of the Shoah. Theology has to ask itself in what way do the theological roots of this event still continue to be present, and put all its efforts into extirpating them, so that no one can in any manner base his or her anti-Jewish statements on any supposed Christian doctrine, and so that any Christian that listens to anti-Jewish statements can energetically respond. Otherwise, theologians become accomplices of those who tolerate Nazism, or of those who continue to believe that Christian faith and antijudaism are compatible.

This meant that 'the Jewish people in their concrete historic and religious reality, in our present day and at all times, has (sic) an irreplaceable

---

Church in the Netherlands statement in 1947, the 'Ten Points of Seelisburg' issued by the International Council of Christians and Jews in 1947 (http://www.ibilby .info/CHU395/Scans/ICCJ%20Ten%20Points%20of%20 Seelisburg.pdf) and the Bossey Consultation of 1949. Accessed 19 May 2008.

8 See chapter 9 for more discussion.

9 Online: http://www.jcrelations.net/en/?item=2683. Accessed 19 May 2008.

mission, and that Christians are in permanent need of Judaism's contribution'.

By the late 1980s, this mood was making a direct impact on some of the denominations that had previously been to the fore in Jewish evangelism. Furthermore, the theological atmosphere in relations between Christians and American Jewish leaders was becoming somewhat strained. Three high-level interfaith dialogues had taken place, but Jewish believers in Jesus were either excluded, permitted to attend but marginalized at the end, or participated but were disrespected in the process.

At the same time, two major US denominations, at the urging of American Jewish leaders, had renounced evangelization of the Jewish people. In the spring of 1989, the Presbyterian Church USA was considering a white paper that advocated the same conclusion by calling into question the uniqueness of Christ for salvation to the Jewish people. In these circumstances, action was needed in support of Jewish evangelism, Messianic Jews and in affirmation of the uniqueness of Christ for salvation among Jews and Gentiles. As Kenneth Myers wrote a short time later: 'many church leaders and theologians had not only "retreated from embracing the task of evangelizing Jews," they had vehemently condemned the traditional understanding of the person and work of Christ that undergirds evangelicalism'.[10]

So in 26–29 April 1989, a consultation was held in Willowbank, Bermuda, to consider the 'Christian Gospel and the Jewish People.' It was sponsored by the World Evangelical Fellowship (now World Evangelical Alliance) and officially endorsed by the Lausanne Committee for World Evangelization. Fifteen scholars, churchmen and missiologists from Europe, Africa, Asia and North America met to deal with questions confronting the church, which arose from the existence of a growing body of Jewish believers in Jesus. Vernon Grounds served as the chairman, while James I. Packer and Kenneth Kantzer agreed to help write the consultation statement known as 'The Willowbank Declaration on the Christian Gospel and the Jewish People'.[11]

This statement was widely circulated and came to be regarded as a pivotal expression for evangelicals on this issue. It noted at the outset

---

[10] Kenneth A. Myers, 'Adjusting Theology in the Shadow of Auchwitz', *Christianity Today* (8 Oct 1990): 41. Some theologians he mentioned were Paul Van Buren on Christology; Rosemary Radford Ruether on Jewish–Christian relations; Roy Eckhardt on the resurrection.

[11] For the full text of the Willowbank Declaration, see http://www.worldevangelicals.org/commissions/list/index.php?com=tc&id=52.

that Christians have generally recognized the unique role of the Jews in the prehistory of Christianity, as well as the Jewishness of Jesus and the primitive church. However, due to the prevailing theological and historical climate, there was a definite trend away from the earlier conviction that Jews needed to be evangelized so that they could have the opportunity to come to faith in Jesus as their Messiah and Saviour.

The statement laid a biblical foundation by stressing the centrality of the person and work of Christ, especially in terms of the new covenant which brings both Jew and Gentile together in God's saving plan and into the one new community of God's people. But it said that Jewish believers are not thereby forced to lose their particular distinctiveness, nor are Gentile believers to ignore the history of the Jews and their place in God's present and future plan.

Willowbank emphatically agreed that anti-Semitism is wicked and shameful, and it repudiated the view that Jewish people were specially responsible for the death of Jesus. At the same time, however, it asserted that to acknowledge these realities was no reason to prohibit evangelism of Jews. Indeed, Christianity has been charged with the responsibility of sharing the gospel with all people, irrespective of who they are or of any other actions of service that may be carried out in the name of Christ. This mandate is considered even more urgent in this case because of the biblical pattern, 'to the Jew first'. Not even the older covenant relationship between God and Israel seen in the Old Testament can negate this mandate, which should nevertheless be carried out with respect and integrity. In fact, to withhold the gospel of Jesus the Messiah from Jewish people for any reason and, therefore, to deprive them of its blessing, could be considered a serious form of anti-Semitism.

At the practical level, Willowbank declared that it was appropriate for specialized ministries to be developed for Jewish evangelism and nurture, even while interfaith dialogue was carried out for the purposes of better mutual understanding and cooperation in matters of common concern.

The statement concluded by supporting the idea of a secure homeland for the Jewish people, but it also warned that biblical links between Jewish people and the land could not justify unethical practices by those who worked to implement such links.

The Willowbank Declaration circulated at the General Assembly of the Presbyterian Church USA, but any move to condemn Jewish evangelism did not eventuate. The Willowbank document was also available at the Second Lausanne Congress on World Evangelisation held in July 1989 in Manila, Philippines; the essence of its message was included in Section 3 of the Manila Manifesto:

> It is sometimes held that in virtue of God's covenant with Abraham, Jewish people do not need to acknowledge Jesus as their Messiah. We affirm that they need him as much as anyone else, that it would be a form of anti-Semitism, as well as being disloyal to Christ, to depart from the New Testament pattern of taking the gospel to 'the Jew first...'. We therefore reject the thesis that Jews have their own covenant which renders faith in Jesus unnecessary.[12]

As might have been expected, the Declaration was attacked by some Jewish leaders as 'a blue print for spiritual genocide'.[13] It fared no better in some Protestant circles where one scholar responded: 'It gives the impression that the Jewish people are devoid of any spiritual vocation.'[14] However, in reality, as Kenneth A. Myers wrote in *Christianity Today*,[15] it was not 'the Willowbank Declaration, but the development of two-covenant theology . . . that drafts a blueprint for spiritual genocide. To withhold the gospel from any people is to ensure their spiritual death.'

As Stan Guthrie explained recently, 'Such a statement, attacked when it was released, remains politically incorrect. Voices both inside and outside the church say that evangelizing Jewish people – calling them to repent of their sins and trust in Jesus Christ as their Lord, Savior, and Messiah – is inappropriate.' However, 'God's chosen people need Jesus as much as we do.' Like many other supporters of Jewish evangelism who refer to the Willowbank Declaration as a reliable guide, he concluded: 'let's renew our commitment to also sensitively but forthrightly persuade them to receive the Good News.'[16]

---

[12] Online: http://www.lausanne.org/manila-1989/manila-manifesto.html. Accessed 19 May 2008.

[13] Myers, 'Adjusting Theology', 41.

[14] M.R. Wilson, Gordon College, in *New York Times*, 21 May 1989.

[15] Myers, 'Adjusting Theology', 43.

[16] *Christianity Today*, 'Why Evangelize the Jews? God's chosen people need Jesus as much as we do' http://www.christianitytoday.com/ct/2008/march/31.76.html by Stan Guthrie, posted 3/25/2008 08:35AM. Accessed 19 May 2008.

Willowbank and After

Mainline Protestant churches

The situation in the Protestant churches in regard to Jewish evangelism has not been reversed since the 1980s. In fact, some churches still look back to material produced in this period as the norm, apparently believing that the issues have been resolved and that no further discussion is necessary.[17]

For example, Presbyterians Concerned for Jewish and Christian Relations (PCJCR), an 'informal group of members, ministers, and congregations of the PC (USA)', states that it is 'committed to positive, constructive and respectful, and meaningful relationships with Jews' working 'in the spirit of the 1987 statement of principles approved for study by the General Assembly of our Church: "A Theological Understanding of the Relationship Between Christians and Jews."'[18] That document articulated seven principles, including those that affirmed that 'The Church's identity is intimately related to the continuing religious identity of the Jewish people', the commitment to 'ponder with Jews the mystery of God's election of both Jews and Christians to be a light to the nations' and the acknowledgment 'that Jews are in covenant relationship with God' which called for consideration of the 'implications of this reality for evangelism and witness'. From this perspective, evangelising or proselytising Jews was completely inappropriate. Instead, the aim was to engage in 'honest dialogue between Christians and Jews', and deepening 'theological understanding of and appreciation for both Judaism and Christianity'.

A statement of the United Church of Canada (UCC)[19] can be taken as typical of mainline Protestant churches. It refers to the common roots of Judaism and Christianity in the Old Testament era and the Jewishness of Jesus and of the early church; it asserts that NT texts have often been misinterpreted because their Jewish context has been ignored. It goes on to affirm the call of the UCC as a Christian church to 'bear faithful witness concerning God's reconciling mission in Jesus

---

[17] Online: http://www.pcjcr.org/missionstatement.htm. Accessed 18 May 2008.

[18] Online: http://www.pcusa.org/oga/publications/christians-jews.pdf.

[19] 'Bearing Faithful Witness Statement on United Church-Jewish Relations Today' (approved at the thirty-eighth General Council of The United Church of Canada, August 2003). Online: http://www.united-church.ca/partners/interfaith/bfw/finalstatement. Accessed 19 May 2008.

Christ,' but it believes that 'In Jesus Christ, God has opened the door in a new way to those previously outside the covenant.'

Basing its view on adherence to 'faithfulness of God', it holds that 'the gifts and calling of God to the Jewish people are irrevocable' and, therefore, rejects the views that 'God has abolished the covenant with the Jewish people' and 'that Christians have replaced Jews in the love and purpose of God'. It also rejects 'proselytism which targets Jews for conversion to Christianity.' Instead it supports dialogue and 'ongoing worship opportunities within the church for highlighting the importance of the Jewish–Christian relationship' which would lead, as well, to 'growth in Christian self-understanding.' Christians should recognize 'our common calling with Jews and others to align ourselves with God's world-mending work'. Faithful obedience to the call of Jesus Christ for love of neighbour should be exemplified especially in positive attitudes towards Jewish people.

Roman Catholic

For the Roman Catholic Church, the decisions of the Second Vatican Council are generally regarded as decisive for its new approach, reinforced strongly by subsequent statements and papal actions such as visits to Nazi death camps, synagogues and other places of high significance for Jewish people.[20] The Council's decisions on this topic, which were strongly debated, were enshrined in the document *Nostra Aetate-Declaration on the Relationship of the Church to Non-Christian Religions* (28 Oct. 1965)[21]

It stated:

> Since Christians and Jews have such a common spiritual heritage, this sacred council wishes to encourage and further mutual understanding and appreciation. This can be achieved, especially, by way of biblical and theological enquiry and through friendly discussions.

It denied that

---

[20] Documents prepared by the Pontifical Commission for Religious Relations with the Jews included *Guidelines and Suggestions for Implementing the Conciliar Declaration, Nostra Aetate* No. 4 (1974); Notes on the Correct Way to Present Jews and Judaism in Preaching and Teaching in the Roman Catholic Church (1985); and We Remember: A Reflection on the Shoah (1998). Other documents appeared in various countries.

[21] Online: http://www.jcrelations.net/en/?item=2552. Accessed 19 May 2008.

all Jews indiscriminately at that time [first century], nor Jews today, can be charged with the crimes committed during his [Jesus Christ] passion. It is true that the church is the new people of God, yet the Jews should not be spoken of as rejected or accursed as if this followed from holy scripture.

Accordingly, it deplored 'all hatreds, persecutions, displays of anti-semitism directed against the Jews at any time or from any source'. Nevertheless, it also held to the traditional christological view and the implications of this for the church's evangelistic mission:

> The church always held and continues to hold that Christ out of infinite love freely underwent suffering and death because of the sins of all, so that all might attain salvation . . . It is the duty of the church, therefore, in its preaching to proclaim the cross of Christ as the sign of God's universal love and the source of all grace.

Despite these concessions, *Nostra Aetate* recognized the historical reality that 'Jews for the most part did not accept the Gospel; on the contrary, many opposed its spread (see Rom. 11:28).' Yet it spoke of God's continuing grace to the Jewish people and their place in the divine plan, so that 'together with the prophets and that same apostle, the church awaits the day, known to God alone, when all peoples will call on God with one voice and serve him shoulder to shoulder.' In the same vein, it said: 'The church believes that Christ who is our peace has through his cross reconciled Jews and Gentiles and made them one in himself.'

This tension between the new approach and the traditional position on the Jewish people and the claims of Christ was continued in the *Guidelines and Suggestions for Implementing the Conciliar Declaration Nostra Aetate* (1 Dec. 1974).[22] This document said that, in view of the history of poor relations between Christianity and Jewish people, 'From now on, real dialogue must be established', even though 'In virtue of her divine mission, and her very nature, the Church must preach Jesus Christ to the world (*Ad Gentes*, 2).' The tension appeared very starkly concerning teaching about Jesus. On the one hand, his Jewish background (and that of the early disciples) was to be recognized, but 'when he revealed himself as the Messiah and Son of God

---

[22] Online: http://www.sacredheart.edu/pages/1930_guidelines_and_suggestions_1974_vatican_statement_.cfm. Accessed 19 May 2008.

(Matt. 16:16), the bearer of the new gospel message, he did so as the fulfillment and perfection of the earlier Revelation.' This unresolved tension at the theological level has been overcome to a considerable extent by the actions and statements of various popes which have been welcomed by Jewish people as welcome signs of a softening in the age-old hard line of the Catholic Church.

But the tension is still in existence. As recently as February 2008, changes were made to the reinstated Good Friday prayer in the Latin Mass to delete references to the 'blindness' of the Jews and those asking God to 'remove the veil from their hearts.' Yet the prayer still says, 'Let us pray for the Jews. May God our Lord enlighten their hearts so that they recognize Jesus Christ saviour of all men . . . Almighty and everlasting God . . . graciously grant that with the fullness of peoples entering into your Church all Israel may be saved.'[23] Jewish spokesmen such as Abraham Foxman, US national director of the Anti-Defamation League, were reported as saying that while the removal of 'some of the deprecatory language' was welcome, the changes were only 'cosmetic'. He declared that the prayer was 'a major departure from the teachings and actions of Pope Paul VI, Pope John Paul II, and numerous authoritative Catholic documents, including Nostra Aetate'.[24]

Throwing some light on the situation is a well received, but unofficial, document, *Reflections on Covenant and Mission Consultation of The National Council of Synagogues and The Bishops Committee for Ecumenical and Interreligious Affairs*.[25] The report by Catholics attending this event acknowledged the closer relationships between Jewish people and Christianity since Vatican II. It linked this with a belief in the 'permanence of the Jewish people's covenant relationship with God'. This, the document stated, raised questions about Christian evangelization, which was clearly understood in Catholic teaching to be the church's primary task. However, it went on to say that 'It should be stressed that evangelization, the church's work on behalf of the kingdom of God, cannot be separated from its faith in Jesus Christ', thus, highlighting the central problem for Catholics to the new approach. The conclusion to be drawn was that 'the Catholic

---

[23] Online: http://www.bc.edu/research/cjl/meta-elements/texts/cjrelations/news/Prayer_for_Jews.htm. Accessed 19 May 2008.

[24] Online: http://blogs.reuters.com/faithworld/2008/02/06/popes-prayer-change-disappoints-jews-some-traditionalist-catholics. Accessed 19 May 2008.

[25] Online: http://www.bc.edu/research/cjl/meta-elements/texts/cjrelations/resources/documents/interreligious/ncs_usccb120802.htmUSCCB, 12 August 2002. Accessed 19 May 2008.

Church has come to recognize that its mission of preparing for the coming of the kingdom of God is one that is shared with the Jewish people, even if Jews do not conceive of this task christologically as the Church does.'

The conclusion that follows is important missiologically. Quoting a lecture by Professor Tommaso Federici, it declared that 'on historical and theological grounds . . . there should be in the Church no organizations of any kind dedicated to the conversion of Jews.' Then it quoted Cardinal Walter Kasper who said that 'mission' in its 'proper' sense referred to 'conversion from false gods and idols', which was not the case for the Jews; hence, 'the Church believes that Judaism, as the faithful response of the Jewish people to God's irrevocable covenant, is salvific for them, because God is faithful to his promises.' Thus, 'we both [Jews and the Church] therefore have missions before God to undertake in the world.' Because 'the Jewish people's mission *ad gentes* continues' (and is one which 'the Church also pursues in her own way'), then the call in Matthew 28:19 of making disciples 'of all nations' is a reference to the Gentile world only. This renders any kind of evangelistic outreach to Jewish people invalid because the Catholic Church 'no longer includes the wish to absorb the Jewish faith into Christianity and so end the distinctive witness of Jews to God in human history.'

According to Michael Kogan,[26] this represents 'an extraordinary expression of the new spirit of openness towards Jews and Judaism animating the Catholic Church and the mainline churches of the Protestant world.' This 'new openness' undercuts any mission to Jews; as the former Cardinal Joseph Ratzinger (Pope Benedict XVI) has said: 'God's providence . . . has obviously given Israel a particular mission in this "time of the Gentiles."'

Jews and Christians

These developments towards recognition by Christians of the place of Jewish people in the scheme of divine salvation have found a complementary response among some Jewish people as well, especially in the document, *Dabru Emet: A Jewish Statement on Christians and Christianity*, which was published in the *New York Times*.[27] This too is

---

[26] Michael Kogan, *Opening the Covenant: A Jewish Theology of Christianity* (Oxford: Oxford University Press, 2008), 180f.

[27] Online: http://www.jcrelations.net/en/?item=1014. Accessed 19 May 2008.

not an official statement but one which has been endorsed by various individual rabbis and Jewish scholars. It follows the same line as many recent Christian statements, but goes one step further by arguing that if 'Jews and Christians worship the same God' and even though 'Christian worship is not a viable religious choice for Jews, as Jewish theologians we rejoice that, through Christianity, hundreds of millions of people have entered into relationship with the God of Israel.' While the 'humanly irreconcilable' differences between Jews and Christians can only be resolved eschatologically,[28] each side can in the meantime respect the other knowing that they both serve God in their own divinely appointed way.

This initiative by Jewish scholars was in turn welcomed by Christian scholars who published *A Sacred Obligation Rethinking Christian Faith in Relation to Judaism and the Jewish People: A Statement by the Christian Scholars Group on Christian-Jewish Relations.*[29] These scholars assert that 'revising Christian teaching about Judaism and the Jewish people is a central and indispensable obligation of theology in our time.' Following closely the same line as many other Christian documents, they conclude that 'Affirming God's enduring covenant with the Jewish people has consequences for Christian understandings of salvation', because if 'God's covenant with the Jewish people is eternal, Christians can now recognize in the Jewish tradition the redemptive power of God at work.'

Evangelicals and the Evangelization of Jewish People

These developments in the Roman Catholic and mainline Protestant churches raise profound theological challenges for evangelicals. But while they have been unfolding, evangelicals, both denominational and parachurch, have continued to go about the task of presenting the message of Jesus as Messiah and Son of God to Jewish people in various ways – often encountering considerable opposition in the process. The most prominent part of this work has been the vigorous activity by specialist organizations, mainly those who are members of the Lausanne Committee on Jewish Evangelism (and previously through

---

[28] As Kogan suggestively notes, both Jews and Christians are 'incomplete' (or fulfilled) since both 'await the complete knowledge' to be revealed at the End (*Opening the Covenant*, 177).

[29] Online: http://www.bc.edu/research/cjl/meta-elements/sites/partners/csg/Sacred_Obligation.htm, 1 September 2002. Accessed 19 May 2008.

comparable groups that preceded it).[30] The type of work carried out by these organizations ranges from direct evangelism, sometimes of a highly enterprising kind, through to mercy ministries covering a wide range of need, especially in Israel and countries of high Jewish population (which is reminiscent of earlier missions which worked incessantly among the poor of European Jewry).

A direct outcome of this work is the existence of a considerable number of converts in mainline evangelical and other churches. There are also congregations composed mainly of Jewish believers comprising the messianic church movement in Israel (where there was significant growth in the 1990s), USA and many other countries as well.[31]

There has also been a rise in interest by non-Jewish believers in the Jewish background of Christianity, exemplified in demonstrations of Jewish religious practices as an educational tool in mainline churches, typically at times like Easter with the Passover celebration. There does not seem to be much connection, if any, between this trend and the remarkable recent growth of interest in academic circles about the Jewish background to the New Testament. However, concern should be expressed in cases where non-Jewish messianic Christians are aggressively pushing their own particular views on other Christians on the basis that traditional Christianity must recover its Jewish origins which it has illegitimately rejected or which have been paganized through the course of its later history.[32] It is one thing to recover the Jewishness of Jesus and the early church in terms of understanding its nature by studying its cultural context as biblical scholarship has done, but another thing entirely to suppose that the church today must be Judaized in order to be authentic. There are also concerns in regard to some philo-Semitic groups which tend to give more priority to their love for Israel than witnessing to Jesus as Messiah.[33]

There are also analogous problems for mainline Christianity arising from the equally aggressive Christian Zionist stream which aligns itself apparently uncritically with the State of Israel in the strongly held belief that the re-establishment of this nation in 1948 is a highly significant episode in the fulfilment of prophecy. This is even more of a concern because of the risky political and strategic potentialities that are

[30] Robinson, *Field Guide*, #1.4, 'Umbrella Organisations', 51–60. See also chapter 14.
[31] Kai Kjaer-Hansen and Bodil F. Skjøtt, 'Facts and Myths about Messianic Congregations in Israel', *Mishkan* 30–31, 1999 (Jerusalem: UCCI/ Caspari Center, 1999). See also chapter 14.
[32] Robinson, *Field Guide*, #2.3, 'The Hebrew Roots Movement', 107–20.
[33] Robinson, *Field Guide*, #1.6, 'Philo-Semitic Organisations', 73–85.

bound up with this approach, the complex nature of political issues in the Middle East and the consequences it has for attitudes towards Palestinian Christians in the region. The impact of these political concerns can result in the diminution of interest in Jewish evangelism and support of Jewish believers in Jesus; it can also hinder Arab evangelism out of uncritical support for one group of people over another. Therefore, many Christians are extremely cautious in their statements and general approaches to the issue of Israel and Jewish/Christian relationships.

Efforts for Jewish evangelism, church planting and pastoral care undertaken by evangelicals are supported by study and training programmes for potential workers and other interested people in various locations, mainly in North America and Israel.[34] However, it is very noticeable that in the general seminary context, missiological studies rarely, if ever, treat missions to Jews, which contrasts starkly with the extensive attention which is given to other specialized areas of missiology and to the study of other religions.[35]

The general level of interest by evangelical Christians in Jewish evangelism varies considerably (even in areas where there is high level of Jewish population) but it is generally in decline since World War II. Baptistic groups seem to be more interested than Reformed, a reversal of the situation in earlier times. Anecdotal evidence suggests that there is greater interest by dispensationalist believers than others, although the apparently conflicting relationship between loyal support of the State of Israel, which is typical of many dispensationalists, and the evangelization of Jewish people is a complex subject.

The Southern Baptist Convention (SBC) is one denomination actively involved in Jewish evangelism.[36] SBC interest in this field began more than a century ago, and it has had work in Israel for more than eighty years. However, considerable controversy has emerged from its determination to respond in a simple and straightforward manner to the biblical pattern indicated in the example of Jesus Christ and texts

---

[34] Robinson, *Field Guide*, #1.5, 'Educational Institutions', 61–72. See also Chapter 14.
[35] A recent exception to this situation is Richard Robinson's article on 'Jewish Mission' in *Dictionary of Mission Theology*. See also Martin Pakula, 'First for the Jew: The urgency of Jewish mission today: The Leonard Buck Lecture 2007' (Melbourne: Bible College of Victoria, 2007). Online:http://www.bcv.vic.edu.au/Resources/AudioDownloads/LeonardBuckMissiologyLecture.aspx.
[36] Others include the Lutheran Church Missouri Synod and the Presbyterian Church in America which recognize the 'CHAIM Reformed Ministry to Jewish People'. Online: http://www.chaim.org.

like Romans 1:16, 'I am not ashamed of the gospel, because it is the power of God for salvation of everyone who believes: first for the Jew, then for the Gentile.' Thus, there was strong Jewish reaction to its 1996 statement, which spoke of a directing 'our energies and resources towards the proclamation of the gospel to the Jewish people' (in response, *inter alia*, to a confession that 'our evangelistic efforts have largely neglected the Jewish people, both at home and abroad'). Support of the same policy by way of official recognition of the Southern Baptist Messianic Fellowship (a loose organization for fellowship and encouragement of those interested and involved in Jewish ministry) in September 2005 caused A.H. Foxman, National Director of the Anti-Deformation League, to say, 'The idea of the Southern Baptist Convention using a so-called Jewish messianic group – which misrepresents two faiths – to target Jews for conversion is disgraceful, insulting and dangerous. We are outraged over the continuing efforts by the Southern Baptist Convention to target Jews for conversion.'[37]

The SBC position was not shared by all evangelicals, not even by all Baptists. For example, in 1995, the 'Alliance of Baptists' rejected 'negative stereotypes and myths concerning Jews' and complained that Jewish-Baptist dialogue has been reduced to a 'theology of conversion'. They called on all Baptists to engage in 'dialogue built on mutual respect and the integrity of each other's faith' and affirm 'the teaching of the Christian Scriptures that God has not rejected the community of Israel, God's covenant people (Rom. 11:1–2), since the gifts and calling of God are irrevocable (Rom. 11:29).'[38]

However, few evangelicals would have been prepared to go down the line of dual covenant theology. Most would have been happier with the approach of Dr Richard Mouw, President of Fuller Seminary, one of the most prominent and influential evangelical spokespersons for the cause.[39]

---

[37] Online: http://sacredheart.edu/pages/12644_southern_baptist_convention_resolution_on_jewish_evangelism_june_1996_.cfm. Accessed 19 May 2008. http://www.adl.org/PresRele/ChJew_31/4798_31.htm. Accessed 19 May 2008. Dr J. Sibley, Pasche Institute of Jewish Studies, Criswell College, personal correspondence, 1 Jan 2009.

[38] Online: http://www.sacredheart.edu/pages/12647_alliance_of_baptist_statement_on_jewish_christian_relations_march_4_1995_.cfm.

[39] Richard J. Mouw is president of Fuller Theological Seminary, Pasadena, California. This excerpt is condensed from a chapter in *The Smell of Sawdust: What Evangelicals Can Learn from Their Fundamentalist Heritage* (Grand Rapids: Zondervan, 2000), which is an expansion of an editorial in *Christianity Today*, 'To the Jew First' (11 August 1997), 12. http://www.christianitytoday.com/ct/2001/march5/5.70.html?start=1. Posted 5 March 2001. Accessed 19 May 2008.

In a 1997 *Christianity Today* article, he wrote, 'As an evangelical I have a non-negotiable commitment to evangelism – and this includes witnessing to Jewish people about my firm conviction that Jesus is the promised Messiah.' But he refused to treat the Jews 'as if they were only "targets" for evangelism' and advocated not only witnessing to Jews but also 'learning from' them (in areas such as justice and suffering) and 'cooperating with' them in key areas of responsibility in public life. However, referring to the criticism levelled at the SBC, he said:

> I hope this controversy will at least serve to inform the larger world that some of us really do believe we have an obligation to present the claims of Christ to non-Christians. We evangelicals need to keep reminding our Jewish friends that if they are really serious about having better relations with us – and I sense many Jews are indeed serious in this intention – they cannot demand that we think and act like liberal Protestants or Roman Catholics. This is a price of admission we cannot pay. We are evangel people. Our proclamation that Jesus is the promised Messiah cannot be silenced for the sake of interreligious civility.

As a Reformed theologian, Mouw also disputed some aspects of the position taken by dispensationalism, indicating that there is no simple consensus among evangelicals on the topic. Indeed, views on the topic are often strongly held and there is a considerable body of literature now available, including significant works by participants at our consultation.[40]

The Present Situation

So now, in a new context almost twenty years after Willowbank, the need to restate the case for Jewish evangelism is clear. Many of the relevant theological issues which have become evident in the foregoing

---

[40] For example, Darrell Bock and Mitch Glaser, eds., *To the Jew First: The Case for Jewish Evangelism in Scripture and History* (Grand Rapids: Kregel, 2008); Kai Kjær-Hansen, ed., *Mishkan: a Forum on the Gospel and Jewish People*; Kai Kjær-Hansen, ed., *LCJE Bulletin*; Tuvya Zaretksy, ed., Jewish Evangelism: a Call to the Church, Lausanne Occasional Paper No. 60, (LCWE, 2005). See also R.T. Kendall and David Rosen, *The Christian and the Pharisee* (New York: Faith Words, 2006); Stephen Sizer, *Zion's Christian Soldiers: The Bible, Israel and the Church* (Nottingham: IVP, 2007); David W. Torrance and George Taylor, *Israel God's Servant: God's Key to the Redemption of the World* (Edinburgh/London: Handsel Press/Paternoster, 2007).

brief discussion are discussed in the papers that follow. In the broader context, attacks by rabbinical leaders, Jewish theologians, authors, scholars, sociologists and demographers on the legitimacy of Jewish evangelism and Jewish Christian identity have persisted. Though a growing body of Messianic Jews is present in Israel and messianic congregations are flourishing in every Jewish community in the world, their legitimacy and the ethnic linkage of Jewish believers in Jesus are undermined by Jewish community leaders.

On the level of faith, there is still the need for Christians to present the significance of Jesus as the Messiah of Israel, despite the fact that, as David Rosen indicates, the feeling of most Jewish people towards missionary activity by Christians is 'Leave us alone' and 'Get off my back'. For them, the claims of Jesus are irrelevant or designed to demean them and their heritage.[41] It is, therefore, not surprising that some evangelicals, including well-known leaders, have decided not to place any special focus on Jewish people in their evangelism. However, this policy of treating Jewish people in 'the same way as anybody else' can be seen as obviously inconsistent with the common practice of con-textualizing Christian witness to particular groups of people and, thus, avoiding the issue of Jewish evangelism or even discriminating against them.

There are also new issues which are a cause of concern. The resurgence of anti-Semitism in Europe can be documented, while neo-Nazi groups like the Magyar Garda in Hungary can now be observed. Their anti-Semitic statements are on the record and represent a serious challenge to the Jewish presence in Europe.

In the political realm, some Christian Zionism has become an unexpected opposition force to Jewish evangelism. There are those who would, for eschatological reasons, extend unqualified support to the State of Israel while excluding gospel proclamation from the relationship and, in the process, ride roughshod over the needs of other Christians in the Middle East, including fellow evangelicals.

The 1989 Willowbank Declaration addressed the situation which existed at that time with an emphasis on covenant and salvation. Then in early 2008, the World Evangelical Alliance sponsored a statement on 'The Gospel and the Jewish People.'[42] It was a brief message expressed in a way that was appropriate for its publication in a newspaper advertisement;

---

[41] Kendall and Rosen, *The Christian and the Pharisee*, 106, 124.
[42] Published in the *New York Times*, 28 March 2008, with fifty-four signatures. Online: https://www.worldevangelicals.org/commissions/tc/wp_ad_lo-res.pdf.

furthermore, it was directed to an American audience. However, it clearly affirmed:

> If Jesus is not the Messiah of the Jewish people, He cannot be the Savior of the World . . . we are compelled by our faith and commitment to the Scriptures to stand by these principles. It is out of our profound respect for Jewish people that we seek to share the good news of Jesus Christ with them, and encourage others to do the same, for we believe that salvation is only found in Jesus, the Messiah of Israel and Savior of the World.

Our consultation, on the other hand, concentrated on the uniqueness of Christ and addressed a much broader global context although focused on Europe and particularly Germany. The location, near to Berlin, was selected to highlight strongly the contrast between the grim anti-Semitic memories associated with this city and the history of Christian community and of compassionate and dedicated missionary outreach to Jewish people for which it was known in earlier times. For example, in 1822, the 'Berlin Society for the Promotion of Christianity among the Jews' was founded as the first Jewish mission organization in recent times on continental Europe. This was the start of a work which included not only Berlin but other places in Germany and Eastern Europe, resulting in many converts and a significant academic and literary production on Jewish mission and other related topics associated with names such as Hermann L. Strack. It was also in Berlin, in 1885, that the Russian Jesus-believing Talmudic scholar, Joseph Rabinowitz, was baptized – a person who, in many ways, set the agenda for the discussion of the identity of a Jesus-believing Jew.[43] Today there are again Messianic Jews in Berlin and in Germany.

Participants at the 2008 Consultation included Germans, Messianic Jews and people from other countries with scholarly and personal experience of the biblical, theological, historical and practical issues covered in their papers. The Declaration they produced represents their heartfelt convictions concerning the uniqueness of Jesus Christ in relation to the presentation of the gospel to Jewish people, together with a firm declaration of their principles and priorities. This Declaration provides a theological rationale for the mission to and evangelism of Jews. It also shows the theological imperative that should empower and energize all Christians in their mission and

---

[43] See also chapter 7.

evangelism, focused on recognizing the necessity and priority of presenting Jesus 'to the Jew first' as Messiah and Saviour. The statement is also aware of the practical realities and missiological issues of Jewish evangelism, including the personal element involved. Importantly, it also confesses wrongs and serious omissions by the church in the history of Jewish-Christian relations. It is the expression of a group broadly representative of global evangelicalism. Our hope and prayer is that it will be able to speak for other evangelicals and, in so doing, support the task of Jewish evangelism and Jesus-believing Jewish people as they too fulfil their missionary and evangelistic role as 'a light to the Gentiles.'

2

The Uniqueness of Christ for Salvation with Implications for Jewish Missions

Rolf Hille

The Question of Salvation as the Specific Characteristic of Religions

Anthropologically, there is deeply rooted knowledge about a 'paradise lost', that is, the existential experience that the world in its real, present condition is not how it could be and how it should be. From intuitive knowledge of the experience of lostness and that of a complete endangerment of the world and humanity arises a longing for happiness, for the fulfilment of purpose and meaning, and for salvation.

In distinction to the instrumental knowledge in the respective sciences, which should serve the worldly improvement of human life conditions, and the basic question of knowledge in philosophy, religions are characterized by their attempt to take up and answer the question of happiness and salvation. When we consider in the context of this paper 'The Uniqueness of Christ for Salvation with Implications for Jewish Missions', it is reasonable to talk briefly about the uniqueness of Jesus in the greater horizon of the history of religions as a contrast and to define the contours of our topic.[1]

---

[1] Quotations in this paper are occasionally taken from German translations of original works.

The understanding of salvation in the important religions besides Judaism and Christianity

Taoism in China, as described by Lao Tze, takes as a starting point a cosmic harmony that is based on the balance of polar entities – for example, male and female, day and night, etc. In the way they deal with nature and how they live in society, people must be careful to keep this cosmic harmony in balance or there must be some way for it to be restored. As a religious figure, Lao Tze was a prominent Chinese sage who discussed and lived out the principle of Yin and Yang.

As a very ancient and many-faceted religion of Indians, Hinduism starts out primarily with the ritual duties of man which must be fulfilled according to the social status and age of the person in different ways. The gods of the pantheon are pacified or are made favourably disposed by the rituals and are, therefore, relied on for the temporal well-being and the post-mortem salvation of people. There is no special person who can be pointed to as the founder of Hinduism. In the end, it is the national religion of the people who live on or around the Indus River.

At its beginning, Buddhism was a very philosophical and subtle reform movement within Hinduism, without any explicit concept of God and, instead, representing a form of religious psychology. Salvation is found, first of all, in the illumination about the causes of suffering and how to overcome it. The way to salvation consists of the eightfold path of virtue, that is, by overcoming morally the individual thirst for life through meditation (for example, in the form of Zen) and asceticism. The historical founder of Buddhism, Sidharta Gautama, has no direct redeeming function. Through his illumination that was tied to exemplary meditation and asceticism, Sidharta only pointed to the way that all living beings must find for themselves and follow through innumerable cycles of reincarnations.

As a post-Christian religion, Islam goes back, in part, to ancient Arab traditions and, especially, to Old and New Testament narratives. As a theologically based system of laws, it points to ritual and moral commandments that people must keep if they want to stand before Allah at the final judgement. Whether or not a person has fulfilled the law enough cannot be said with certainty, but it rests ultimately on the sovereign will of the judgement verdict of Allah. Muhammed plays a dominant role as Prophet of God, more precisely, as seal and conclusion of all prophecy of scripture. The Qu'ran, which was verbally inspired according to Islamic tradition, was revealed to him. But, as Prophet, Muhammed still has no meaning with regard to salvation.

Judaism and Christianity in the horizon of the interreligious search for salvation

Modern liberal theology of religions presumes that the different religions in their search of salvation all strive for a common goal and even attain this, though in different ways. Judaism and Christianity, including the person of Jesus, are brought into this universalist concept of redemption. When there are differences between the world religions with respect to the final redemption of the world and of humanity, then these are only differences in degrees and not of an essential nature.

Conservative evangelical theology of religion has a fundamentally different assessment of world religions. While it recognizes in them the human longing for salvation, it considers the ideas of God, worship and ways of salvation held by these religions to be idolatry. Nevertheless, the missionary proclamation of the gospel can connect with the ethical values and cultural truths and, last but not least, with the longing for salvation of the 'pagan' religions but, at the same time, reject their answers to the question of salvation as false ways.

In distinct contrast to the 'Gentiles' in the biblical sense, Judaism has another position. Israel is and remains God's chosen people. Throughout its history, salvation in Christ is prepared for and, through its history as recorded in the Hebrew Bible, it has a part in God's eternal revelation. Nevertheless, Israel is also dependent on Jesus as her Messiah and Saviour. This is true regardless of the fact that Israel's way to salvation is accomplished on the basis of the covenant and the promises in a different context with respect to the history of redemption than the Gentile peoples.

Peter's confession of Christ before the Jewish Sanhedrin states what is valid for Israel in the circumstances mentioned, in which he says: 'He (Jesus) is "the stone you builders rejected, which has become the capstone." Salvation is found in no one else, for there is no other name under heaven given to men by which we must be saved.' (Acts 4:11–12).

Biblical evaluation

To be able to present properly and effectively the testimony of Christ for the salvation of the Jews, it must first be clearly explained where the difference and the continuity lie between Israel, the people of God in the Old Testament and the phenomenon of Judaism in the history of religions. Then, it must be shown briefly how Judaism deals with the person and messianic claim of Jesus. Finally, this implies the question of the importance of the Torah as the Jewish way to salvation in significant contrast to salvation in Christ, which is manifest in the cross and in the resurrection of Jesus.

The mission to bear witness concerning Christ to the Jews implies two trajectories, the first being the biblical history of revelation up to the first coming of the Messiah Jesus of Nazareth. This goes from the call and election of Abraham to the giving of the Torah to Moses on Sinai, then to the royal house of David all the way to Jesus the Jew. He is from the seed of Abraham, he fulfils the Torah of Moses and is, as a son of David, the Anointed One (Messiah/Christ) of God.

As far as their ideas of salvation are concerned, no other world religion is even remotely comparable to the prehistory Israel received regarding salvation. Therefore, the fact is even more painful and worse that Israel, by and large, did not recognize the time of salvation that began with the birth of Jesus (Gal. 4:4) and rejected Christ. The rejection of the Messiah Jesus marks the transition from the biblical Israel of redemptive history to post-Christian Judaism.

In this religious historical sense, Judaism represents the history of Israel in the almost two thousand years of Diaspora. It is the epoch of the synagogue and the rabbinate in which the Talmud, the Midrash and the Halacha define the typical Jewish exposition of the Hebrew Bible. Rabbinic exegesis and tradition rejects Jesus as Messiah and waits for the appearance of the coming Messiah who will gather the people from the Diaspora and establish the Davidic kingdom. It applies the legal ordinances of the Torah for the Jewish community in very different, and even contradictory, historical and cultural contexts.

During this time, most of the Jewish Diaspora has lived under the dominance of Christian churches. In the best case, the relationship, from the Christian side, was characterized by dialogue and tolerance, but very often by discrimination against and persecution of the Jews. As a result, the latter distanced themselves in their faith and in their lifestyle consciously and clearly from the claim to truth and the offer of salvation of the Christian churches. Under these conditions, despite individual attempts at rapprochement and occasional conversions, Judaism must always, and essentially, be understood as a religion in counterpoint and opposition to Christianity. Missiologically speaking, this makes the history of Judaism significantly different from the major religions of Asia. On the other hand, the promises concerning biblical Israel are still valid, without restriction, for Israel under the conditions of 'Judaism' 'God's gifts and his call are irrevocable.' (Rom. 11:29).

The following remarks will now reflect briefly on the messianic understanding and the soteriology of Judaism in view of the claim of the uniqueness of Jesus Christ and his way of salvation.

Jesus in the Horizon of Jewish Messianic Expectations and Disappointments

For the Christian church, the entire biblical message is centred in the person of Jesus as the Christ. Thus, Matthew structures his gospel as proof of the fulfilment of Old Testament messianic promises in the life story of Jesus, whose way is marked out even into the details in the writings of Moses and the prophets and who is attested to and confirmed by the prophecy preceding it in detail. The view of Judaism concerning the Messiah who is to come is very different. The term 'Judaism', however, has already been defined more precisely in the context of our analysis above. For our context, Judaism is to be understood as that epoch of Israel's history, which begins with the New Testament and extends all the way to the present.

In this age spanning many centuries, messianism is interpreted anew in clear contradistinction to Jesus and is even reconceived anew for an open future, without giving up its basic biblical substance. This Jewish concept will be briefly sketched below.

The expectation of the Messiah and its crisis

The history of Israel must be understood as one providentially guided in time, which proceeds to a final, time-ending and world-transcending completed goal. The inner movement of the historical existence of Israel is most essentially defined by the expectation of the Messiah, because the Messiah will bring about the kingdom of Israel as the true kingdom of God. As an inner motivation of a believing Jew, the expectation of the Messiah even points beyond death. Thus, Rabbi Jeremiah, for example, orders in his last will:

> Dress [i.e. Bury] me in clean white [i.e. linens], dress me in my socks [i.e. lined with pockets and in a tunic with a collared cap], put my shoes on

my feet and a walking stick in my hand, lay me on my side, when the Messiah comes I shall be ready.[2]

And, full of pleading desire are the words of the Kaddish Prayer (Prayer for the Dead):

Exalted and sanctified is God's great name
in the world which He has created according to His will
and may He establish His kingdom
may his salvation blossom and his anointed near
in your lifetime and your days
and in the lifetimes of all the House of Israel
speedily and soon; and say, Amen.[3]

Yet until the Messiah can come, Israel passes along in the Diaspora on a thorn-filled path of disappointing messianic hopes again and again. Martin Buber talks in his work, *Tales of the Hasidim*,[4] about how God fears that his people could fall throughout the centuries into a dulled stupor and give up the hope of the Messiah. Therefore, the Almighty decides to wake them up from their slumber from time to time through the appearance of false messiahs, until one day, in the first light of dawn, the true Messiah appears. In fact, the temptation occurs again and again on Israel's path through world history to give up faith in the coming of the Messiah completely out of despair. This temptation to give it up is, on the one hand, because it is said that the Messiah had already appeared and Israel had not recognized him. Rabbi Hillel comments, for example, here: 'There shall be no Messiah for Israel because they have already enjoyed him in the days of Hezekiah.'[5]

On the other hand, the argument from despair appears even more profoundly for Rabbi Yochanon, who ties the appearance of the

---

[2] *The Jerusalem Talmud, (Kil'ayim* IX, 32a), Edition, Translation and Commentary by Heinrich W. Guggenheimer (Berlin/New York: de Gruyter, 2001), 303. See here Guggenheimer's note 83 also. Translation from a German translation uses the words included in brackets [].

[3] English translation of the Kaddish Prayer (Prayer for the Dead) found at: http://en.wikipedia.org/wiki/Kaddish.

[4] Martin Buber, *Die Erzählungen der Chassidim* (Zurich: Manesse Verlag, 1949), 364 of the German edition. Quotation translated here by James Louis Kautt, but consult the English translation of this work: *Tales of the Hasidim*, which was not available to the translator.

[5] *Sanh.* 99a. See *The Babylonian Talmud*, online translation, edited by Rabbi Dr Isidore Epstein at http://www.come-and-hear.com/sanhedrin/sanhedrin_99.html.

Messiah to conditions, which in fact do not exist in reality: 'The son of David will come only in a generation that is either altogether righteous or altogether wicked.'[6]

Yet one can also find long, in-depth discussions among the rabbis on whether or not it is possible to calculate the arrival of the Messiah from the dates given in the biblical chronologies:

> (Rabbi) Elijah said to Rab Judah, the brother R. Salia the pious: 'The world shall exist not less than eighty five jubilees, and in the last jubilee the son of David will come.' He asked him, 'At the beginning or at the end?' – He replied, 'I do not know.' Shall [this period] be completed or not?' – 'I do not know,' he answered. R. Ashi said: He spoke thus to him, 'Before that, do not expect him; afterwards thou mayest await him.'[7]

Besides these, apocalyptic scenarios are portrayed which either precede or accompany the age of the Messiah. These descriptions talk about the desolation of the land, the moral decay of the people and the chaotic human relationships between people.[8] It will come down to a final battle between the Messiah and his opponents. Yet the important thing in these threats is the very fact that the massive apocalyptic afflictions and confusion will announce the imminent messianic age.

The harsh rejection of Jesus in Judaism and the modern appreciation of the 'Jesus' Brother'[9]

Two basic streams of Old Testament messianic prophecy flow together in view of Judaism's horizon of expectation. One is the hope of an anointed one from the Davidic dynasty, who will raise anew the political kingdom of David, the conqueror and founder of the great Israelite empire. Along this line, for example, Rabbi Judah comments in the Talmud on Jeremiah 30:9 as follows:

> The Holy One, blessed be He, will raise up another David for us, as it is written, *But they shall serve the Lord their God, and David their king, whom I will raise up unto them*: not 'I raised up', but '*I will raise up*' is said.[10]

---

[6] *Sanh.* 98a.
[7] *Sanh.* 97b.
[8] See, for example the Mishnah *Sfota* IX, 15.
[9] See Hans Küng and Pinchas Lapide, *Brother or Lord? A Jew and Christian talk together about Jesus* (Glasgow: Collins, 1977).
[10] *Sanh.* 98b.

In referring back to David, messianism gets its indispensable political orientation. This is a feature which definitely becomes clear in the claims and failures of numerous pretenders to messiahship who fought as freedom fighters. The Jewish historian Josephus, thus, describes the founding of the party of the Zealots alongside the already existing Sadducees, Essenes and Pharisees.[11]

More specifically, Josephus recounts, as an example of this, the story of a man who travelled from Egypt to Jerusalem during the days of the Roman governor Felix between the years of AD 52 and AD 60. He proclaimed himself to be the Messiah and surrounded himself with a large number of armed Jews on the Mount of Olives to attack the Romans. Josephus ends the war story with the comment that, after the defeat of the Jews, the same Egyptian escaped and 'then it happened – he became invisible'.[12]

It is understandable that Judaism at the time of Jesus was not, under these conditions, very open to the preacher who preached the Sermon on the Mount and the Suffering Servant of God. Fed instead by messianic visions, the readiness for revolutionary struggle in Judaism has survived even into modern times. In this regard, the French state attorney Cahier-de-Gerville explained the involvement of the Jews in the French Revolution on 30 January in the year 1790:

> Of all the districts of the city of Paris, it is the Carmelite District which has the largest number of Jews. More than any other district, this one had, therefore, since the beginning of the Revolution, the possibility to observe the position of Jewish residents . . . No other category of citizenry showed greater zeal in the fight for freedom than the Jews; no one panted so much for the uniforms of the national guard than they did

---

[11] But of the fourth sect of Jewish philosophy, Judas the Galilean was the author. These men agree in all other things with the Pharisaic notions; but they have an inviolable attachment to liberty, and say that God is to be their only Ruler and Lord. They also do not value dying any kinds of death, nor indeed do they heed the deaths of their relations and friends, nor can any such fear make them call any man lord. And since this immovable resolution of theirs is well known to a great many, I shall speak nor further about that matter; nor am I afraid that anything I have said of them should be disbelieved, but rather fear, that what I have said is beneath the resolution they show when they undergo pain. And it was in Gessius Florus's time that the nation began to grow mad with this distemper, who was our procurator, and who occasioned the Jews to go wild with it by the abuse of his authority, and to make them revolt from the Romans. (Josephus, *Antiquities of the Jews*, 18,1,6, trans. William Whiston).

[12] Josephus, *Ant.* 20,8,6.

> ... Although the Jews living in Paris have still not reached the status of Frenchmen, we can still assure you that they are most definitely worthy of this name. I would even dare to say that they are already counted as Frenchmen in our midst.'[13]

The political expectation is strengthened by – and this is the second stream that has flowed into Jewish messianism – chiliastic, or millennial, that is, prophetic statements of the Old Testament such as Isaiah 11:1–2, which the church later related to the so-called 'Millennial Reign of Christ'.

In view of this background of expectations, the crucifixion of Jesus could only be considered as a failure of any claim to messiahship. This is why the curse of the Nosrim, that is, the Nazarenes or the Christians, is found in the Eighteen Benedictions Prayer (Birkat al-Minim), which was so important to early Judaism in the early period of conflict between the church and Judaism. The prayer states:

> May the apostates have no hope and may the malicious empire be speedily uprooted, and may it be destroyed and vanquished in our days. And may the Nazarenes and the heretics perish instantly, and may all the enemies of your people and their foes be quickly cut off. And break the yoke of the nations from upon our necks. Blessed are you, O Lord, who destroys the wicked and vanquishes the infidels.[14]

This harsh attitude was later given up in part. Yet even with a moderate Jewish thinker like Moses Maimonides (1135–1204), this definite critical conflict with the person and history of Jesus can still be found. Typically, though, only indirect reference is made to Jesus. Maimonides writes, for example:

> Do not think that King Messiah will have to perform signs and wonders, bring anything new into being, revive the dead, or do similar things. It is not so . . . If there arise a king from the House of David who

---

[13] Quoted in J. Höxter, *Quellenbuch zur jüdischen Geschichte und Literatur* (5.Teil, Frankfurt, 1930), 8f. The official proclamation of equal rights for all Jews was announced on 28 September 1791 by the French National Assembly.

[14] From the Eighteen Benedictions (Shemoneh Esreh), Benediction 12 (Birkat al-Minim – The Heretics). See Yechezkel Luger, trans., 'Palestinian Versions of the Eighteen Benedictions', in *The Weekday Amidah in the Cairo Genizah* (Jerusalem: Orchot Press, 2001). Online: http://www.ucalgary.ca/~elsegal/RELS_601/18Blessings.html.

meditates on the Torah, occupies himself with the commandments, as did his ancestor David, observes the precepts prescribed in the Written and the Oral Law, prevails upon Israel to walk in the way of the Torah . . . and fights the battles of the Lord, it may be assumed that he is the Messiah. If he does these things and succeeds, rebuilds the sanctuary on its site, and gathers the dispersed of Israel, he is beyond all doubt the Messiah.[15]

Martin Buber (1878–1965) is one of the most important representatives of Judaism who made an effort to achieve a new appreciation for the person of Jesus in the sense of a philosophy of dialogue. Nevertheless, in spite of all of his esteem for the Jewish rabbi Jesus, even he noted the christological confession of the church only with critical displeasure, when he remarked:

I am more certain than ever before that he deserves a great place in the history of Israel's faith and that this place cannot be rewritten by one of the traditional categories. As history of faith, I mean the history of the human part known to us, what has happened between God and man. Yet, Thomas believes and makes his faith known: Jesus, whom he recognizes as the risen one, is his God. We do not learn what brought him to believe that and we don't get any further explanation for it. There is no other choice for us but to imagine anew that the resurrection of a single person does not belong to the body of ideas present in the Jewish world of faith. Because no individual person can rise from the dead, this one here is no human being, but a god, and because he had been for him the man, his man, he is therefore his god. But, with this, the Jewish world of faith, which knows no other god than God, collapses all at once for the Thomas of the narrative. Among all Jesus disciples, he is the first Christian in the sense of Christian dogma.[16]

Pinchas Lapide is recognized as a Jewish author who stands for a new level of dialogue between Judaism and Christianity in the present.

---

[15] Maimonides, *Mishneh Torah (Yad Chazaka), Book Shoftim, Section Melachim (Kings)*. The English translation here is taken from the Yale Judaica Series of the Mishneh Torah, Book 14, *The Book Of Judges, Treatise Five: Kings and Wars, XI*, 3–4, 239–40 (trans. Abraham M. Hershman, 1949).

[16] Martin Buber, *Zwei Glaubensweisen* (Heidelberg, 1986), 93. Passage translated by James Kautt from the German text quoted. For a published English translation of this work, see *Two Types of Faith*, trans. by Norman P. Goldhawk (London: Routledge and Paul, 1951). This translation was not available to the translator.

Even the title of his book on Jesus, 'Jesus the Jew',[17] makes his new perspective clear. In his work, Jesus is brought back home to the Jewish family as 'Brother Jesus'. In the summary of his work, Lapide starts out by
pointing to historical-critical research done on the life of Jesus, that Jesus
did not understand himself to be the Messiah and, therefore, he also
could not have been rejected by Israel. However, Lapide recognizes, from
a Jewish standpoint, Jesus as a teacher of Israel and as a righteous person.
His special significance consists, however, in the fact that he called the
Gentile peoples to faith in the God of Abraham, Isaac and Jacob.

Lapide even quotes the church hymn: 'Come now, Redeemer of the
Gentiles' (the lyrics were written by Ambrosius of Milan before AD 397
and translated by Martin Luther into German in 1524; the melody is
from a medieval melody adapted by Luther in 1524) and concludes: 'I
believe, Ambrosius and Luther both are right. In the inscrutable ways
of God, Jesus of Nazareth has become the redeemer of the world.'[18] The
common faith in the only one true God and Creator, as well as the hope
of his salvation, strengthen Lapide's certainty that the still deeply controversial questions of faith between Christians and Jews compel us to
a real dialogue, 'which will begin tomorrow'.[19]

In view of the Jewish conflict with Jesus of Nazareth and how he is
perceived in Judaism, we must remember the following: The longer it
goes, the more the history of Israel is complexly interwoven with the
question of the Messiah. Basic to it is the idea of the Son of David, who
exercises the rule of king, commissioned by God. Out of political
oppression and centuries of deportation, hope for liberation by the
Messiah has increasingly grown in Judaism. By contrast, Jesus directs
his claim to truth to the question of sin, reconciliation with God and the
forgiveness of sins. The signs and wonders he performs point to
the dawning of the approaching kingdom of God. But it is, in fact, not
the political-military expansion of power of the Messiah, but rather the
'suffering Servant' of the prophet Isaiah who is evident in the person
and saving work of Jesus. In this respect, in view of the widely differ-

---

[17] Pinchas Lapide and Ulrich Luz, *Der Jude Jesus: Thesen eines Juden, Artwort eines Christen* (Düsseldorf: Benziger, 2nd edition, 1986), 47ff. Quotation translated by James Kautt from the German text. See the published English translation, Pinchas Lapide and Ulrich Luz, *Jesus in Two Perspectives: A Jewish-Christian Dialog* (Minneapolis: Augsburg, 1985). Original from the University of California, digitized 15 December 2006, ISBN 0806621710, 9780806621715, 174 pages. This transla-tion was not available to the translator.

[18] Lapide, *Der Jude Jesus*, 121.

[19] Lapide, *Der Jude Jesus*, 123.

ing messianic expectations between Israel and Jesus, a chasm has
opened up which is only deepened throughout the history of Jewish
suffering among the peoples of the so-called Christian West.

Jewish-Christian dialogue and the positive welcoming home of
Jesus, as a son of Israel, back into Judaism are good approaches to start
from. Yet, in this dialogue, Christians can and must make clear by
means of the Old Testament that, while Christology has a relationship
to messianic promises, it is not exhausted by it; rather, it goes beyond
these promises in the sense of atonement through the cross and the better righteousness which Jesus himself brought. The unlimited rule of
Jesus as Messiah King still remains to be seen for Jews and Christians
in expectation of the second coming of Christ. The testimony of Christ
to the Jews in this context consists in helping the Jews realize that the
Messiah they are expecting is the one who has already come.

This is unique with Jesus that, in Christianity, everything depends
on the person of Jesus. In no other world religion, including Judaism,
no founding or leading figure has ever had the same status as Jesus of
Nazareth has in Christianity. Salvation depends exclusively on him.
Without his personal cross and resurrection, Christianity is nothing
more than a moral system and has no salvific power.

The True Fulfilment of the Torah as the Way to Salvation in Judaism

The relationship of Christology and soteriology

The expectation of a coming Messiah described above and the rejection
of Jesus of Nazareth as Israel's Messiah at the same time leads necessarily to a differing understanding of salvation and, especially, to a
completely contradictory way to salvation. This fundamental difference between Judaism and Christianity becomes evident already in the
New Testament, especially through the letters of the Apostle Paul. This
is very clearly expressed both in the conflict he had, for example, in the
Epistle to the Galatians with the so-called Judaizers, as well as in the
great systematic-theological arguments advanced concerning the question of the justification of the sinner in Romans.

If one takes the Jewish position as the starting point, i.e. that the
Torah, as God's law, is the way of salvation both for Israel and the
Gentiles, a completely different soteriological conception results from
Christianity. In the latter, God reconciles the world with himself

through Christ – as Paul writes in 2 Corinthians 5:19: 'God was reconciling the world to himself in Christ, not counting men's sins against them. And he has committed to us the message of reconciliation.'

Reconciliation with God (i.e. soteriology) is inseparably tied to the essence of God in Christ and, therefore, also to Christology in the sense of divine sonship. Beginning with the fact that God is present in personal unity in Christ opens the possibility of universal atonement for Jews and Gentiles.

The Torah is fulfilled in Christ and, thus, there is justification by grace alone through faith. This fact is also still connected in an eschatological sense with the promises of the pilgrimage of the Gentiles to Zion and, therefore, remains unaffected. It is, then, a pilgrimage of Israel and the nations to the Zion of Jesus, the Son of David, the *telos* (end) of the Torah (Rom. 10:4) in the dual sense of the Greek term: He is the *end* of the validity of the Torah as the way of salvation through works and the *goal* of the Torah, namely, as obedience of faith in a new life through Christ in the Holy Spirit.

In the following, we will now briefly present the perspective of the Jewish way of salvation in a few aspects and comment on them theologically from a Christian viewpoint.

The pattern of blessing and curse in Deuteronomy

The basic understanding of the Torah is the conviction that the gift of the law, given to the chosen people Israel through Moses, shows itself to be good instruction. By fulfilling the commandments, one finds peace (*shalom*) and succeeds in life under God's blessing. Psalm 119 praises the gift of the Torah in a hymnic fashion. The pattern of blessing and curse is the basis for this, as we read, in Deuteronomy 28:1–9, 15–16:

> 1 If you fully obey the LORD your God and carefully follow all his commands I give you today, the LORD your God will set you high above all the nations on earth.
> 2 All these blessings will come upon you and accompany you if you obey the LORD your God:
> 3 You will be blessed in the city and blessed in the country.
> 4 The fruit of your womb will be blessed, and the crops of your land and the young of your livestock – the calves of your herds and the lambs of your flocks.
> 5 Your basket and your kneading trough will be blessed.

6 You will be blessed when you come in and blessed when you go out.

7 The LORD will grant that the enemies who rise up against you will be defeated before you. They will come at you from one direction but flee from you in seven.

8 The LORD will send a blessing on your barns and on everything you put your hand to. The LORD your God will bless you in the land he is giving you.

9 The LORD will establish you as his holy people, as he promised you on oath, if you keep the commands of the LORD your God and walk in his ways.

15 However, if you do not obey the LORD your God and do not carefully follow all his commands and decrees I am giving you today, all these curses will come upon you and overtake you:

16 You will be cursed in the city and cursed in the country.

However, the inner certainty of this connection between moral behaviour and happiness in the world is apparently contradicted by the massive experiences of just the opposite in life. Israel expressed this problem of theodicy when confronted with the unjust suffering of the righteous in the book of Job and the apparent happiness of the ungodly in Psalm 73: 'They are free from the burdens common to man; they are not plagued by human ills . . . This is what the wicked are like – always carefree, they increase in wealth.' (Psalm 73:5–12).

The spiritualization and the universalizing of the Torah

The fulfilment of the Torah as external obedience to the commandment does not, though, grant one salvation automatically as such. A reaction to this crisis in Judaism is the spiritualizing of the command as an expression of true love for God. Thus, it says in the Talmud:

> Ben Azzai (6) said, 'Hasten to do even a slight precept (7), and flee from transgression; for one virtue leads to another, and transgression draws transgression in its train; for the recompense of a virtue is a virtue, and the recompense of a transgression is a transgression' (8).[20]
>
> Antigonus of Soko (12) received (the tradition) from Simon, the Just. He used to say, 'Be not like hirelings who work for their master for the sake of receiving recompense; but be like servants who minister to their

---

[20] Pirqe Avoth, *Sayings of the Fathers*, trans. by Joseph I. Gorfinkle. Online: http://www.ultimasurf.net/bible/pirkeavot/pirke-avot-1.htm. Pirqe Aboth, IV, 2.

master without any thought of receiving a reward; and let the fear of Heaven (13) be upon you.'[21]

R. Joshua b. Levy explained it: Happy is he who over-rules his inclination (7) like a 'man'. That delighteth greatly in His commandments, (8) (Psalm 112:1) was explained by R. Eleazar thus: 'In His commandments,' but not in the reward of His commandments. (9) This is just what we have learnt. 'He used to say, Be not like servants who serve the master on the condition of receiving a reward; but be like servants who serve the master without the condition of receiving a reward.' (10)[22]

Maimonides writes:

[T]hen what is it that is written in throughout the Torah, that if one listens, one will receive such-and-such, and that if one doesn't listen such-and-such will happen to one, as well as all earthly matters such as plenty, famine, war, peace, monarchy, humility, living in Israel, exile, success, misfortune and other covenantal matters? All these matters were true and always will be. Whenever we fulfil the commandments of the Torah we will receive all good earthly matters, and whenever we transgress them, all the mentioned evils will befall us. Nevertheless, the goodness is not all that the reward for fulfilling commandments consists of, and the evils are not the entire punishment received by transgressors. This is how all matters are decided: The Holy One, Blessed Be He, gave us this Torah, which is a support of life, and anybody who does what is written in it and knows that everything contained in it is complete and correct, will merit life in the World To Come. He will merit [a portion] in proportion to the magnitude of his actions and to the extent of his knowledge. The Torah assures us that if we fulfil it with joy and pleasure and always act according to it, then all things such as illness, war, famine, et cetera, which could prevent us from doing so will be removed, and all things such as plenty, peace, richness, et cetera, which will aid us in fulfilling the Torah will be influenced to come our way so that we will not have to occupy ourselves all day in [obtaining] bodily needs, but that we will be free to sit all day, learn and gather knowledge and fulfil commandments, in order to merit life in the World To Come.[23]

---

[21] Pirqe Avoth, *Sayings of the Fathers*, I,3.

[22] Babylonian Talmud, *Aboda sara* 19a, transl. by A. Mishcon. Online: http://www.come-and-hear.com/zarah/Zarah_10.htm/.

[23] Maimonides, *Mishneh torah hilchot teshuba* IX, 1, transl. by Immanuel M. O'Levy, 1993. Online: http://www.panix.com/~jjbaker/rambam.html.

In the interpretation of Maimonides, it is important to emphasize that the well-being of man only creates the conditions so that one can devote oneself inwardly and entirely to the study of the Torah. This view finds support in Judaism even into the Modern Age. Even among enlightened modern Jews one can find similar statements such as:

> When the rabbis speak of paradise and hell, describing vividly the delights of the one and the torments of the other, these are only metaphors for the agony of sin and the happiness of virtue. True piety serves God neither from fear of punishment nor from desire for reward, as servants obey their master, but from pure love of God and truth.[24]

Leo Baeck also emphasizes this idea:

> The Bible, when it often and emphatically speaks of the punishment of sin and the reward of piety, is referring to tangible and earthly rewards and punishments. In the education of the Jewish people this was necessary and valuable. But as the goal and outcome of the development of Judaism, we find that freedom and unselfishness are categorically demanded as essential to the deed of which the only reward is the continuation of the work of goodness. That this idea became the possession of the entire Jewish community is shown by the religious literature of the Middle Ages which unanimously states that only a deed intended and carried out for its own sake is esteemed a good deed. Only it, as the ancient saying goes, is done from the 'love of God.'[25]

As much as the gift of the Torah means salvation first and foremost for Israel, the perspective still remains, in the sense of a universal call of Israel for the Gentiles, that all people should study the Torah:

> R. Meir used to say, Whence can we learn that even where a Gentile occupies himself with the study of the Torah he equals [in status] the High Priest? We find it stated: . . . *which if a man do he shall live in them;*

---

[24] Kaufmann Kohler, *Grundlagen einer systematischen Theologie des Judentums*, p. 231 of the German edition. English version: K. Kohler, *Jewish theology: systematically and historically considered* (New York: KTAV, 1968; 1st pub. 1918), XLVI. This quotation is found on page 308.

[25] Baeck, *Das Wesen des Judentums*, p. 192f. of the German edition. The English translation quoted here: Leo Baeck, *The Essence of Judaism* [Rendition by Irving How, based on the translation from the German by Victor Grubenwieser and Leonard Pearl]. (Rev. ed; New York: Schocken, 1948), 180.

it does not say 'priests, Levites and Israelites', but *'a man'*, which shows that even if a Gentile occupies himself with the study of the Torah he equals [in status] the High Priest.[26]

Rabbi Eleazar also said: The Holy One, blessed be He, did not exile Israel among the nations save in order that proselytes might join them, for it is said: And I will sow her unto Me in the land; 20 surely a man sows a se'ah in order to harvest many kor! While R. Johanan deduced it from this: And I will have compassion upon her that hath not obtained compassion.'[27]

The rejection of a substitutionary atonement – in particular, by Jesus

In the discussion about the possibility of a substitutionary atonement, it becomes clear how much Judaism is a post-Christian religion, i.e. a community that intends to critically call into question the gospel. This leads decidedly to the rejection of New Testament soteriology. The bases for this criticism are already found in the Palestinian Jewish Apocryphal writings, such as 4 Ezra 7:104f:

> Just as now a father does not send his son, or a son his father, or a master his servant, or a friend his dearest friend, to be ill or sleep or eat or be healed in his stead, so no one shall ever pray for another on that day, neither shall any one lay a burden on another; for then everyone shall bear his own righteousness and unrighteousness.[28]

In the many expressions of modern Judaism, Christian dogma is then very explicitly rejected along with the theology of atonement:

> The other things they believe in, that the Messiah, their God redeemed the souls of the dead from Hell through His death, even this tenet makes no sense, for how would it be possible that one sin, namely, the putting to death of the body of their God, would be atoned for? According to their tenet He, Jesus, redeemed through his death the souls of the fathers and children of those who lived before as well as those who lived later, redeeming them from Hell. So then, whose souls have his disciples, apostles, and followers, who were also killed by the

---

[26] Babylonian Talmud, *Baba Kamma* 38a, trans. E.W. Kirzner. Online: http://www.come-and-hear.com/babakamma/index.html.

[27] Babylonian Talmud, *Pesachim* 87b. Complete Soncino English translation of the Babylonian Talmud at http://wilkerson.110mb.com/index.htm.

[28] 4 Ezra 7:104–5 [RSV].

judgment sentence of the Romans and others, redeemed through their deaths?[29]

The sinner himself is to turn to God, since it is he who turned away; it was his sin and it must be his conversion. No one can substitute for him in his return, no one can atone for him; no one stands between him and God, no mediator or past event, no redeemer and no sacrament.[30]

No divine event concerning the essence of God is necessary to affect peace to a Jew's soul through his peace with God. No priest, as the representative of a God, and no God-man himself may say here: I am the way to God. The soul wrestles here without any mediator and it achieves its redemption in personal repentance, in prayers, and in the resolve to live morally upright.[31]

In these statements, it is clear that the Jewish authors have understood quite precisely the connection between Christology and soteriology in Christianity, have reflected on it and, in the end, consistently rejected it.

It is characteristic that Moses is deeply rooted in the Jewish conscience as 'Moses, our teacher.' He is not our Revelator, but our teacher. Even his role in mediation between God and the people is understood purely as teaching. All spiritual mediation is veneration.[32]

The difference between Judaism and Christianity with regard to the relationship to the Father should be pointed out here. Jesus certainly preferred calling God Father and taught His disciples to use this same form of address, but He also claimed to have a very special relationship to 'His Father' and made this dependent for His disciples upon His own relationship towards the Father. Jesus' statement: 'No one knows the Father except the Son and to whom the Son reveals Him' (Mt. 11:27), is a statement that Judaism can never approve of. It only knows a *direct* relationship between God and man, *the same for all*, for which no mediator is necessary and it recognizes no person who has the 'uniqueness of the relationship of the Son' so that He could become the mediator between man and His Father in Heaven.[33]

---

[29] Isaak Abraham Troki, *Chissuk Emuna* I ch. 11; quotation translated by James Kautt.

[30] Leo Baeck, *Das Wesen des Judentums*, 182f.

[31] Hermann Cohen, *Die Bedeutung des Judentums für den religiösen Fortschritt, in Protokoll des 5. Weltkongresses für freies Christentum*, II, 566f. Quotation translated by James Kautt.

[32] Hermann Cohen, *Streiflichter über jüdische Religion und Wissenschaft, in Neue jüdische Monatshefte*, Jg. 2, S. 282. Quotation translated by James Kautt.

[33] Ismar Elbogen, *Die Religionsanschauungen der Pharisäer in 22. Bericht über die Lehranstalt f. d. Wiss. des Judts.*, 63. Quotation translated by James Kautt.

The necessity of preaching salvation in Christ despite all rejection

The Gospels make clear in their references to Jesus' many disputes with the Jews how deep the controversy really was, from the very beginning, between Jesus and the Jews of his time concerning the question of the Messiah and salvation. Particularly John's Gospel is, in its own way, Jesus' own intense struggle with his people with the goal that they recognize him as the Son of God and Saviour.

After Paul's call as the apostle to the Gentiles, it becomes clear, both missiologically and theologically, that Israel still remains the first and preferred recipient of the gospel, even before the Gentiles (cf. here particularly Romans 9 – 11).

The whole Torah and atonement theology of the former Pharisee Saul takes as its starting point the fact, deeply rooted in the Torah, that atonement demands sacrifice and that ultimately sacrifices of the Old Testament find their eschatological validity and fulfilment once and for all in Jesus' death on the cross.

It is quite clear that Israel could not fulfil, by its own strength and moral will, the requirements of the Torah. This is the argumentation of Paul as we find it in Romans 2:17–29, where he states that Israel did not meet the standard of the Torah and, therefore, stands accused by the commands of the Torah itself.

To wish to exclude Israel today from the preaching of the gospel, by saying that the Jews have their own different way to salvation apart from their Messiah Jesus and his act of atonement, turns the New Testament upside down.

After a long period of rabbinic exposition of Scripture, by which the veil is laid over the Old Testament (see 2 Cor. 3:14f.), Israel needs the message of the New Testament anew. Then the promise will be fulfilled: 'But whenever anyone (Israel) turns to the Lord, the veil is taken away' (2 Cor. 3:16).

3

Irreconcilable Views of Salvation in Early Christianity and Early Judaism

Eckhard J. Schnabel

Before we look at the differences between Jews and Christians with regard to their views on salvation, it is important to note that Jews and Christians share fundamental convictions. The extent and significance of these commonalities become particularly obvious when we compare the common views of Jews and Christians with the convictions and practices of polytheistic pagans. When I speak of 'Jews' in this essay, I include proselytes (Gentiles who converted to Judaism through circumcision and commitment to the Torah), and when I use the term 'Christians', I include both Jewish followers of Jesus and Gentile followers of Jesus. Both Jews and Christians agreed about convictions such as the existence of one true God, the non-existence of the pagan deities, the significance of God's revelation in the works of creation, the greater significance of God's revelation in the Scriptures and in the history of Israel, the reality of God's future judgement, the need for repentance of sins, the need for obedience to the will of God, the hope of the restoration of creation in a new world.

The disagreements between Jews and Christians concern details of the proper interpretation of Scriptural texts (e.g. Can Gentile believers in Israel's God call themselves 'children of Abraham' and, thus, be full members of God's people?) and of personal behaviour (e.g. related to the food laws). Even more importantly, Jews and Christians disagree concerning basic questions linked with the procurement and the reality of salvation. The disagreements in these areas were so fundamental that John calls the Jews' rejection of Jesus the Messiah and the result-ant Jewish animosity towards the followers of Jesus 'satanic' (Rev. 3:9),[1] while Jews cursed Christians in synagogue prayers from the late first or early second century onwards.[2]

This essay focuses on the differences of Jewish and Christian views regarding salvation since this is a fundamental aspect of the question whether Jews need to hear and accept the message of Jesus, whom the apostles proclaimed as Israel's Messiah and Saviour. I will present the evidence regarding these disagreements for the Jews of the Second Temple period and Jesus and the apostles Peter and Paul. I will focus on the fundamental questions of the presence of God, the forgiveness of sins and the nature of the people of God. We will see that Jews, in agreement with the Scriptures, connect the forgiveness of sins with the grace and mercy of Israel's God as well as with the observation of the law, which includes the offering of sacrifices and ritual immersions as expressions of repentance and as the means by which God atones for sin. However, for Christians the forgiveness of sins is focused on Jesus of Nazareth, who is accepted and affirmed as the crucified, risen and exalted Messiah and Lord. The believers in Jesus of the first century emphasized that only Jesus, as Israel's Messiah and Saviour, has the authority to forgive sins as he has been revealed as the 'place' of God's saving presence on earth. As God grants forgiveness through Jesus' death on the cross, all people stand equally in need of this forgiveness, both Jews and Gentiles.

I present and discuss the evidence as a New Testament exegete explaining first-century texts and realities, aware of the terrible legacy of Christian, and especially German, anti-Semitism which used and misused New Testament texts and realities to justify the oppression and elimination of the Jewish people. At the same time, as an exegete who interprets historical texts and as a Christian for whom the New Testament is authoritative Scripture just as much as the Old Testament, I resist attempts to take post-Holocaust realities and sensibilities as the norm for what first-century texts can be allowed to mean.

---

[1] Cf. Peter Hirscherg, 'Jewish Believers in Asia Minor according to the Book of Revelation and the Gospel of John', in *Jewish Believers in Jesus: The Early Centuries* (ed. O. Skarsaune and R. Hvalvik; Peabody: Hendrickson, 2007), 217–38; 223.

[2] Cf. Philip S. Alexander, '"The Parting of the Ways" from the Perspective of Rabbinic Judaism', in *Jews and Christians: The Parting of the Ways A.D. 70 to 135* (ed. J.D.G. Dunn; WUNT 66; Tübingen: Mohr Siebeck, 1992), 1–25, 11, with reference to Justin, Dialogue with Trypho 47, 137; I Apology 31; and 1 Cor. 12:3; Acts 26:11.

Salvation in Second Temple Judaism

The following description of central beliefs of the Jewish people during the period of the Second Temple assumes that there was a commonality of conviction in these areas, notwithstanding the diversity of various groupings and movements such as the Sadducees, Pharisees and Essenes.[3]

The presence of God

Jews believed that there was only one God, the Creator of the heavens and the earth, who was the God of Israel. As there was only one God, there was only one temple in which he could be worshipped. As God was sovereign and holy, access to the place of his presence was restricted. This reality explains the increasing sanctity of the areas surrounding the temple. When Herod rebuilt Zerubbabel's temple, he trained 1,000 priests as masons and carpenters because laymen were not allowed to enter the court of the priests or the sanctuary itself.[4] The temple was holy 'not only because the holy God was worshipped there, but also because he was there.'[5] Jesus' comment that 'whoever swears by the sanctuary, swears by it and by the one who dwells in it' (Matt. 23:21 [NRSV]) reflects this conviction.

The Pharisees believed that national renewal must begin with the worship of Yahweh in the temple, which had been threatened by syncretistic transformation through pagan Hellenistic values and traditions during the time of Antiochus IV. They were convinced that the most effective protection of the temple required the collective effort by all Jewish people: if the entire nation kept the ordinances related to purity in analogy to the requirements of the priests, 'the nation guarded the purity of the temple by being given a share in its holiness.'[6]

Jews believed that God had revealed his will to them in the Holy Scriptures, focused on the law given through Moses. The martyrs of

---

[3] Cf. Jeff S. Anderson, *The Internal Diversification of Second Temple Judaism: An Introduction to the Second Temple Period* (Lanham: University Press of America, 2002); E.P. Sanders, *Judaism: Practice and Belief 63 BCE – 66 CE* (London: SCM, 1992).

[4] Josephus, *Ant.* 15.390.

[5] Sanders, *Judaism*, 70.

[6] Roland Deines, 'The Pharisees between "Judaisms" and "Common Judaism"', in *Justification and Variegated Nomism. Vol. 1: The Complexities of Second Temple Judaism* (ed. D.A. Carson, et al.; WUNT 2.140; Tübingen/Grand Rapids: Mohr Siebeck/Baker, 2001), 443–504; 496.

the Maccabean period were willing to give their lives for 'the holy God-given law' (2 Macc. 6:23, 28). The seer Ezra exclaims after the catastrophe of the destruction of the temple in AD 70 that 'we who have received the Law and sinned will perish, as well as our heart which received it; the Law, however, does not perish but remains in its glory' (4 Ezra 9:36:37). In the Qumran texts, citations from the Law or the Prophets can be introduced with the formula 'which God said', ascribing the words of Scripture to God.[7] Thus, God is present in the reading and hearing of the Scriptures.

Jews observed holy days 'which functioned either to renew their covenant with [God], to celebrate great moments of the nation's past, to mark the seasons of the agricultural year and give thanks for them, or to atone for sin.'[8] Jews who travelled to Jerusalem to attend the festivals would sing, among others, Psalm 84 which begins with these lines:

> How lovely is your dwelling place, O LORD of hosts!
> My soul longs, indeed it faints for the courts of the LORD;
> My heart and my flesh sing for joy to the living God (Ps. 84:1–2 [NRSV]).

At Passover, probably all of Exodus 12 was recited during the meal, recalling God's presence which had judged the Egyptians and saved the Israelites:

> The blood shall be a sign for you on the houses where you live: when I see the blood, I will pass over you, and no plague shall destroy you when I strike the land of Egypt (Exod. 12:13 [NRSV]).

The nature of the people of God

A fundamental feature of Jewish self-identity is the conviction that Jews are descendants of Abraham, members of God's covenant with the fathers, obedient to the Mosaic law as the expression of God's covenant with Israel *par excellence*. Ben Sira begins his description of Abraham in the 'praise of the fathers' with a passage which contains a reference to the basic 'privileges' of which the Jews were proud – Abraham as their father, glory, law, covenant, circumcision, faithful obedience to the will of God:

---

[7] Moshe J. Bernstein, 'Scriptures: Quotation and Use', in *Encyclopedia of the Dead Sea Scrolls* (ed. L.H. Schiffman and J.C. VanderKam; Oxford: OUP, 2000), 2:839–42, 840. Cf. CD VI, 13; VIII, 9; 1QM X, 6.

[8] Sanders, *Judaism*, 48.

Abraham was the great father of a multitude of nations, and no one has been found like him in glory. He kept the law of the Most High, and entered into a covenant with him; he certified the covenant in his flesh, and when he was tested he proved faithful. (Sir. 44:19–20).

When Josephus describes the episode of the erection of an altar beyond the river by the trans-Jordanian tribes of Israel (Josh. 22), he clarifies that 'ethnic descent from Abraham is subservient to obedience to the Mosaic law when it comes to membership in the commonwealth of Israel.'[9]

The three major Jewish movements of the first century – Pharisees, Sadducees and Essenes – all focused on the Torah (and the Prophets) as the centre of life of the individual Jew and of the nation as a whole. It was the Pharisaic movement in particular which emphasized the tradition of the Deuteronomistic view of history: 'obedience to the revealed will of God brings salvation and blessing; disobedience, on the other hand, leads to exile and loss of the land.'[10] These convictions continue to characterize the rabbis of the Tannaitic period who produced the Mishnah and the early rabbinic commentaries.[11] In their theology and practice, Torah was both central and binding. They were convinced that Israel achieves righteousness by keeping the commandments of the Torah – the righteousness is worthy of Israel's God and the righteousness that God demands. This is a works-righteousness, however, which is moderated by the mercy and grace of God who forgives the repentant sinner and who has provided means of the atonement of sins in sacrifices, ritual immersion and redress of the consequences of sinful actions.

Many Jewish groups of the Second Temple period, represented by documents such as *Jubilees*, the *Testament of the Twelve Patriarchs*, *1 Enoch*, the *Psalms of Solomon*, and the Qumran texts had a 'remnant theology'. Many Jews believed in the election of the faithful remnant within Israel which faces God's judgement on account of the nation's apostasy. Numerous Jewish theologians and writers believed that

Israel, God's chosen people, is in danger of judgment and in this regard has been placed on a par with Gentiles; that the historical covenants are

---

[9] Paul Spilsbury, 'Josephus,' in *Justification and Variegated Nomism* (ed. D.A. Carson et al), 241–60, 251.

[10] Deines, 'Pharisees', 495.

[11] For the following summary cf. Philip S. Alexander, 'Torah and Salvation in Tannaitic Literature,' in *Justification and Variegated Nomism* (ed. D.A. Carson, et al.), 260–301.

not unqualifiedly valid for all who consider themselves participants in them; that the normal rites of maintaining the covenant have become ineffective; that an individual soteriology *apart from* previous divine acts of deliverance on behalf of Israel has now become necessary.[12]

The forgiveness of sins

In many Jewish texts of the Second Temple period, forgiveness of sins is connected with obeying the commandments of the law on one hand and with God's covenantal mercy and grace on the other hand. This combination of the causes of forgiveness can be seen in Ben Sira. He writes:

> Those who fear the Lord do not disobey his words, and those who love him keep his ways. Those who fear the Lord seek to please him, and those who love him are filled with his law. Those who fear the Lord prepare their hearts, and humble themselves before him. Let us fall into the hands of the Lord, but not into the hands of mortals; for equal to his majesty is his mercy, and equal to his name are his works. (Sir. 2:15–17).

The *Rule of the Community* is another example.[13] The Qumran community had a keen sense of sin. It knew that only God could atone for sins, which he did on account of his righteous character and his righteous acts. We read in 1QS XI, 2–5:

> As for me, my justification lies with God. In His hand are the perfection of my walk and the virtue of my heart. By His righteousness is my transgression blotted out. For from the fount of His knowledge has my light shot forth; upon his wonders has my eye gazed – the light of my heart upon the mystery of what shall be. He who is eternal is the staff of my right hand, upon the Mighty Rock do my steps tread; before nothing shall they retreat. For the truth of God – that is the rock of my tread, and His mighty power, my right hand's support. From His righteous fount comes my justification, the light of my heart from His wondrous mysteries.[14]

---

[12] Mark Adam Elliott, *The Survivors of Israel: A Reconsideration of the Theology of Pre-Christian Judaism* (Grand Rapids: Eerdmans, 2000), 664.

[13] For the following comments cf. Markus Bockmuehl, '1QS and Salvation at Qumran,' in *Justification and Variegated Nomism* (ed. D.A. Carson, et al.), 381–414.

[14] Translations from Emanuel Tov and Noel B. Reynolds, *The Dead Sea Scrolls Electronic Library* (rev. ed.; Provo/Leiden: Brigham Young University/Brill, 2006).

At the same time, the priests of the Qumran Community emphasized that atonement for sin was not available for people who did not repent or for the people outside the Community. They connected the appropriation of the atonement for sins which God procured with the worship and praxis of the Community which functioned in deliberate analogy to the sacrificial cult of the temple.[15] In 1QS III, 2-9, ritual purity is connected with the atonement for sins:

> His knowledge, strength, and wealth are not to enter the society of the Yahad. Surely, he ploughs in the muck of wickedness, so defiling stains would mar his repentance. Yet he cannot be justified by what his willful heart declares lawful, preferring to gaze on darkness rather than the ways of light. With such an eye he cannot be reckoned faultless. Ceremonies of atonement cannot restore his innocence, neither cultic waters his purity. He cannot be sanctified by baptism in oceans and rivers, nor purified by mere ritual bathing. Unclean, unclean shall he be all the days that he rejects the laws of God, refusing to be disciplined in the Yahad of His society. For only through the spirit pervading God's true society can there be atonement for a man's ways, all of his iniquities; thus only can he gaze upon the light of life and so be joined to His truth by His holy spirit, purified from all iniquity. Through an upright and humble attitude his sin may be covered, and by humbling himself before all God's laws his flesh can be made clean. Only thus can he really receive the purifying waters and be purged by the cleansing flow.

In one important passage, the awaited 'Messiah of Aaron and of Israel' is said to atone for the sins of the people:

> And this is the exposition of the regulations by which [they shall be governed in the age of] [wickedness until the appearance of the Messi]ah of Aaron and of Israel, so that their iniquity may be atoned for. Cereal [offering and sin-offering . . .] (CD XIV, 18–19).[16]

---

[15] 11QT and 4QMMTa suggest that the quasi-cultic atonement of sin of the Qumran Community is not meant to replace the sacrificial cult of the temple in Jerusalem but functions in deliberate analogy to it; cf. Bockmuehl, '1QS and Salvation', 401.

[16] Cf. Joseph. M. Baumgarten, 'Messianic Forgiveness of Sins in CD 14:19 (4Q266.i.12–13)', in *The Provo International Conference on the Dead Sea Scrolls. Technological Innovations, New Texts, and Reformulated Issues* (ed. D.W. Parry and E. Ulrich; STDJ 30; Leiden: Brill, 1999), 535-44.

It should be noted that in the Qumran Community, only the true Israel is saved, never the Gentiles.[17] According to the War Scroll (1QM) and the Messianic Rule (1QSa), there will be a battle between 'Israel' and the Gentiles, and the Community Rule (1QS) and the Hodayot (1QH) include the Israelites who are not members of the Community among the enemies of 'Israel'. The redactional history of 1QS suggests 'a tightening religious practice in which atonement and forgiveness were increasingly limited to the sect itself, and religious authority was concentrated in the hands of Zadokite priests.'[18]

Philo asserts that God alone can forgive sins (*Somn.* 2.299) because sin represents a violation of God's law. But human beings receive God's forgiveness only if and when they repent, when they confess their sins, when their conscience exposes the evil thoughts in the soul and seeks divine judgement and forgiveness and divine help in distinguishing good and evil.[19] And forgiveness is possible only when the sacrifices for sin which Moses prescribed are offered. The most appropriate means of divine forgiveness are those sacrifices for sin which are offered daily in the temple in Jerusalem as well as during the festivals, particularly the sacrifices offered on the Day of Atonement when forgiveness is granted both for voluntary and involuntary sins, not just for legal impurity (*Spec.* 2.180–93, 234; 2.193–6).[20]

Jews believed that there was only one temple in which God was present and, thus, they believed that there was only one place of sacrifice, one place of forgiveness, linked with the hereditary priesthood. While Jews living in the Diaspora could visit the temple in Jerusalem only occasionally, 'their awareness of daily sacrifices there for sins may have given them a sense of God's mercy and grace for themselves, wherever they lived.'[21] After the destruction of the temple in AD 70, the rabbis believed that there were many means at the disposal of the Jewish people to call forth God's grace, to make atonement for sins and to mitigate divine justice which punishes sinners – repentance

---

[17] Cf. Katell Berthelot, 'La notion de GER dans les textes de Qumrân', *Revue de Qumran* 19 (1999), 171–216; Bockmuehl, '1QS and Salvation', 392 n. 40.

[18] Bockmuehl, '1QS and Salvation', 411.

[19] Cf. Philo, *Abr.* 17–26; *Praem.* 15–21; QG 1.82. Cf. David Winston, 'Philo's Doctrine of Repentance', in *The School of Moses: Studies in Philo and Hellenistic Religion* (In Memory of H.R. Moehring; ed. J.P. Kenney; Brown Judaic Studies 304; Atlanta: Scholars, 1995), 29–40.

[20] Cf. David M. Hay, 'Philo of Alexandria,' in *Justification and Variegated Nomism* (ed. D.A. Carson, et al.), 357–79; 377, with reference to Jean Laporte, *Théologie liturgique de Philon d'Alexandrie et d'Origène* (Liturgie 6; Paris: Cerf, 1995), 93–5.

[21] Hay, 'Philo', 377 n. 62.

(*teshubah*) which involved confession of sin and supplication of the mercies of God, restitution if restitution was possible, performance of good deeds if it was not, punishment which atoned for wrongdoing and restored communion with God, fasting and praying on Yom Kippur which expiated the sins of the community as a whole, and the sufferings which the righteous underwent gratuitously.[22]

Salvation in Early Christianity

It is quite obvious for anyone who reads through the New Testament that salvation, i.e. atonement for sin, forgiveness of acts of disobedience, reconciliation with God, transformation of personal behaviour, are all linked with Jesus, whom his followers confess to be the crucified, risen, and exalted Messiah, Lord and Saviour of both Jews and Gentiles. This conviction is not an innovation by the Apostle Paul, but can be traced back to Jesus of Nazareth himself. We will look again at the three main areas which helped us understand the Jewish understanding of salvation – the presence of God, the forgiveness of sins, the nature of the people of God – and present the evidence for Jesus, Peter and Paul.

The presence of God

The presence of God in Jesus' proclamation

Jesus' proclamation is summarized by Matthew, Mark and Luke with his call to repentance on account of the arrival of the kingdom of God (Matt. 4:17; Mark 1:15; Luke 4:43; 8:1).[23] The kingdom of God refers to God's rule and, thus, to the presence of God. The announcement of the arrival of God's kingdom sometimes refers to the future, when the present world would be transformed into paradise restored in which God's will would be perfectly realized (Matt. 6:10 = Luke 11:2; Matt. 8:11 = Luke 13:28–29; Mark 14:25). But the announcement of the arrival of God's kingdom also refers to the present, to a new reality which characterizes the ministry of Jesus and his followers. The presence of the kingdom of God and, thus, of God himself, is seen in the fact that Jesus casts out demons by the Spirit of God, a reality which proves that

---

[22] Cf. Alexander, 'Torah and Salvation', 287–8.
[23] Cf. George R. Beasley-Murray, *Jesus and the Kingdom of God* (Grand Rapids: Eerdmans, 1986).

the kingdom of God has come (Matt. 12:28 = Luke 11:20). The new and powerful presence of God in the ministry of Jesus, of which the ministry of the disciples is a part, signifies Satan's fall from heaven, i.e. his defeat (Luke 10:18). In Jesus' ministry, the 'strong man' is bound (Mark 3:27), which means that, in his ministry, God's kingdom is being established, rendering Satan powerless to oppose his will or to harm his people.[24]

When John the Baptist enquires whether Jesus is the promised Messiah (Matt. 11:2-6 = Luke 7:18–23), Jesus gives an answer which connects the miracles which happen in his ministry with passages in Isaiah which speak of healing of diseases, of the raising of the dead and of the good news being proclaimed to the poor (Isa. 26:19; 29:18–19; 35:5–6; 61:1). As these passages describe God's ultimate deliverance in the time when paradise would be restored, Jesus' answer to John's enquiry implies that the messianic age has arrived.[25] As Isaiah's prophecies are fulfilled in the miracles which Jesus performs, God himself is at work in Jesus' ministry. This is the reason why Jesus can claim that he has greater significance than father or mother (Matt. 10:37 = Luke 14:26), than Solomon (Matt. 12:42 = Luke 11:31) and than Moses (Matt. 5:21, 27, 38). The parables about old and new cloth, and old and new wine (Matt. 9:16–17 = Mark 2:21–22 = Luke 5:36–38) illustrate the impossibility of containing Jesus and the reality of the arrival of the kingdom of God within the existing forms of encountering God.[26]

The consummation of God's revelation, which the prophets and the righteous longed to see, has become a reality in Jesus' ministry (Matt. 13:16–17 = Luke 10:23–24).[27] When Jesus asserts: 'Whoever welcomes one such child in my name welcomes me, and whoever welcomes me welcomes not me but the one who sent me' (Mark 9:37 [NRSV]; cf. John 13:20), he emphasizes that he represents God and that to receive him is to receive God.[28]

---

[24] R.T. France, *The Gospel of Matthew* (NICNT; Grand Rapids: Eerdmans, 2007), 173–4.

[25] This is supported by the parallels with 4Q521 Frag. 2 II, 1–13, a messianic text which also alludes to Isa. 61:1–2; cf. Darrell L. Bock, *Luke* (BECNT; Grand Rapids: Baker, 1995/1996), 1:665–9; Martin Hengel and Anna Maria Schwemer, *Jesus und das Judentum* (Geschichte des frühen Christentums Band I; Tübingen: Mohr Siebeck, 2007), 330–3.

[26] R.T. France, *The Gospel of Mark* (NIGTC; Eerdmans: Grand Rapids, 2002), 140–2.

[27] William D. Davies and Dale C. Allison, *The Gospel According to Saint Matthew* (ICC; Edinburgh: T & T Clark, 1988–97), 2:394.

[28] Cf. France, *The Gospel of Mark*, 375.

When Jesus explains his demonstration in the Court of the Gentiles on the temple platform with a reference to Jeremiah 7 (Matt. 21:13 = Luke 19:46: 'den of robbers'), he uses Jeremiah's great sermon in which the prophet denounced the temple, warned against trusting in it and announced its destruction on account of the refusal of the people and their leaders to listen to God's message'.[29] A few days later, in his discourse on the last days and the end of the present world, Jesus explicitly announces the destruction of the temple (Matt. 24:1–2 = Mark 13:1–2 = Luke 21:5–6). The Jewish leaders believed that they could indict Jesus on a capital charge with witnesses who claim to have heard Jesus plotting the destruction of the temple (Matt. 26:59–61 = Mark 14:55–58). If we link these statements with the geographical focus of Jesus' ministry in Galilee, the conclusion is difficult to avoid that Jesus' proclamation of the arrival of the kingdom of God evidently did not require the temple as the place of God's atoning and sanctifying presence.

Jesus' cryptic statement: 'Destroy this temple, and in three days I will raise it up' (John 2:19 [NRSV]),[30] if it indeed referred to the resurrection of his body as John asserts (John 2:21), implies that he claimed to be the true temple and that the expectations of a restored messianic temple would be fulfilled, not in a future temple, but in his own resurrection 'after three days'.[31] Jesus claimed to embody the temple and thus the presence of God, in his own person. This is confirmed by the promise to the apostles, 'I am with you always, to the end of the age' (Matt. 28:20 [NRSV]), a reality that expresses the presence of God among his people.

The presence of God in Peter's preaching

As Peter explains the dramatic events of the speech miracle in which the followers of Jesus were caught up on the day of Pentecost, he argues that Joel's prophecy of God granting his Spirit, i.e. his saving presence, in the last days to all flesh (Joel 2) has been fulfilled in the ministry and in the death of Jesus (Acts 2:22–24). He argues further that Jesus has been raised from the dead and he is, therefore, the Son

---

[29] Cf. David Pao and Eckhard J. Schnabel, 'Luke', in *Commentary on the New Testament Use of the Old Testament* (ed. G.K. Beale and D.A. Carson; Grand Rapids: Baker, 2007), 251–414; 359.

[30] Cf. Matt. 27:61; Mark 14:58; Acts 6:14.

[31] Peter W.L. Walker, *Jesus and the Holy City: New Testament Perspectives on Jerusalem* (Grand Rapids: Eerdmans, 1996), 281.

of the last days of whom David spoke in Psalm 16 (Acts 2:25–32). He also argues that, since Jesus has been exalted by God, the person whom David calls 'my Lord', who is addressed by the LORD (i.e. by God) and who received dominion (Ps. 110:1) is nobody else but Jesus himself – Jesus the Messiah has become Lord, God's coregent (Acts 2:33–36).[32]

The Spirit of God, who has come upon the followers of Jesus, is the Spirit of Jesus – Jesus is 'Lord' of the Spirit as he has granted God's Spirit to his disciples. According to Jewish conviction, only God can pour out the Spirit, since the Spirit of God is the active presence of the one true God, revealing himself personally to his creation. Jesus' claim that he would send the Spirit (Luke 24:49) has been fulfilled.[33]

If Luke's description of the pouring out of the Spirit on the day of Pentecost was formulated on the background of Jewish traditions about the giving of the law at Sinai,[34] Peter's sermon implies three additional points:

First, the pouring out of God's Spirit as the gift of Jesus the exalted Lord to his followers is the fulfilment of the promised new climax of God's saving revelation, consummating God's revelation at Sinai.

Second, as the Festival of the Firstfruits of the Wheat Harvest (Exod. 34:22) had become the festival when Israel remembered God's giving of the law on Mount Sinai, Jewish exegesis inferred from Exodus 19:1–4 that the day of the giving of the law was the same day as the day of the exodus from Egypt. The Festival of Weeks (Pentecost) was, therefore, the festival of the renewal of God's covenant with Israel. As Jesus' death and resurrection had inaugurated the promised new covenant, the law of the old covenant is transformed through the gift of the Spirit who had been promised for the new covenant (Jer. 31:31–4) and who now helps the new covenant community to do God's will.

Third, just as Moses ascended Mount Sinai and received the law from God, which he passed on to Israel, accompanied by visible signs of God's presence, so Jesus ascended to God's right hand and poured out the gift of God's Spirit upon the people of the new covenant. The events of Pentecost mark the beginning of the fulfilment of God's promises and the renewal of God's covenant with Israel in which the

---

[32] Max M.B. Turner, *Power from on High: The Spirit in Israel's Restoration and Witness in Luke–Acts* (JPTSup 9; Sheffield: Academic Press, 1996), 275–6.

[33] Turner, *Power from on High*, 277–9.

[34] Cf. Philo, Decal. 33–7, 46–7. Cf. Alexander J.M. Wedderburn, 'Traditions and Redactions in Acts 2.1–13', JSNT 55 (1994): 27–54.

presence of God's Spirit, as the gift of his Son, transforms the followers of Jesus.[35]

The presence of God in Paul's theology

Paul was convinced that God revealed himself in and through Jesus Christ. An important passage is 1 Corinthians 1:30 [NRSV] where Paul emphasizes that God 'is the source of your life in Christ Jesus, who became for us wisdom from God, and righteousness and sanctification and redemption.' The saving action of God who, in his mercy, grants righteousness, holiness and redemption to sinners is bound up with Jesus the Messiah who is the power of God and the wisdom of God (1 Cor. 1:24). Jesus Christ is the power of God, because it is through Jesus, and only through him, that God declares felons to be righteous, sinners to be holy and convicts to be redeemed. Jesus Christ is the wisdom of God, since it is through Jesus' death and resurrection that God creates life where people had been dead in their sins.

Another significant passage is 1 Corinthians 8:6 [NRSV]: 'for us there is one God, the Father, from whom are all things and for whom we exist, and one Lord, Jesus Christ, through whom are all things and through whom we exist.' In the context of his discussion of the question of whether Christians can accept invitations to banquets in pagan temples, Paul emphasizes that, while the people of Corinth have many deities and many lords, believers in Jesus Christ have only *one* God and only *one* Lord. The statement that 'there is *one* God' corresponds to the fundamental confession of God's people (Deut. 6:4).[36] Paul explains the confession that there is only one God with the point that God is Father. As all creation and all human beings owe their existence to God, there can only be one God. The phrase 'for whom we exist' expresses the conviction that God is the First and the Last (Isa. 41:4; 44:6; 48:12). The one true God is the Lord of history which moves towards the consummation of God's salvation on the promised new earth.

---

[35] Cf. Turner, *Power from on High*, 280–9; see also idem, 'The "Spirit of Prophecy" as the Power of Israel's Restoration and Witness', in *Witness to the Gospel: The Theology of Acts* (ed. I.H. Marshall and D. Peterson; Grand Rapids/Cambridge: Eerdmans, 1998), 327–48.

[36] For monotheistic texts in the Old Testament and in the Jewish tradition cf. Exod. 20:3; Deut. 4:35, 39; 5:7; 32:39; 1 Kgs 8:60; Isa. 43:10; 44:6; 45:5–6; *Sib. Or.* 3:11–16; *Sib. Frag.* 1:32–5; *Let. Aris.* 132; Ps.–Phoc. 54; Josephus, *Ant.* 4.201; 5.112; 8.335; Philo, *Legat.* 115.

The second part of Paul's confessional formulation represents a new understanding of Jewish monotheism in terms of a christological monotheism.[37] He includes Jesus the Messiah who is Lord within the identity of the one true God in whom the members of God's new covenant people believe. He identifies Jesus with the 'Lord' whom Israel's confession of faith proclaims as the only God. The two phrases which follow the reference to Jesus Christ the Lord – 'through whom are all things and through whom we exist' – state realities that are true of Israel's God. After having described the one true God as the effective cause and as the ultimate goal of creation, he now describes Jesus as the instrumental cause of creation. Jesus' identity as mediator of creation presupposes his identification with the sovereign and powerful word of God the Creator[38] and/or with the personified wisdom of God the Creator,[39] presupposing Jesus' pre-existence.[40] God the Creator, who saves his people, is present in Jesus, the mediator of creation and the Saviour of sinners.

As Paul explains the revelation of the saving righteousness of God[41] in Romans 3:21–6, he describes Jesus' death as the new place of God's atoning presence. The term *hilastērion* in Romans 3:25 is best understood against the background of its Old Testament usage where it designates the gold plate on the ark of the covenant in the Holy of Holies (Exod. 25:17–22) above which God was thought to be present and where blood was sprinkled on the Day of Atonement to cleanse the

---

[37] Cf. Richard Bauckham, *God Crucified: Monotheism and Christology in the New Testament* (Grand Rapids: Eerdmans, 1999), 36–40.

[38] Cf. Gen. 1:3–26; Ps. 33:6; cf. Exod. 15:1–18; Ps. 107:20; Isa. 55:1; Philo, *Migr.* 6.

[39] Cf. Prov. 8:22–31; Job 28:25–27; Sir. 24:9; Wis. 7:22; 78:4; 9:9; Bar. 3:32–37. Cf. Eckhard J. Schnabel, *Law and Wisdom from Ben Sira to Paul: A Tradition Historical Enquiry into the Relation of Law, Wisdom, and Ethics* (WUNT 2/16; Tübingen: Mohr-Siebeck, 1985), 244–6; Hermann von Lips, *Weisheitliche Traditionen im Neuen Testament* (WMANT 64; Neukirchen-Vluyn: Neukirchener Verlag, 1990), 290–317.

[40] Cf. Col. 1:16–17. Cf. Larry W. Hurtado, *Lord Jesus Christ: Devotion to Jesus in Earliest Christianity* (Grand Rapids: Eerdmans, 2003), 123–4.

[41] The genitive 'of God' in the phrase 'the righteousness of God' (*dikaiosynē tou theou*) has been understood as (1) a possessive genitive – the righteousness or covenant loyalty of God himself; (2) a genitive of source or origin – the righteousness that sinners receive from God, as new and undeserved legal status in view of the last judgment, and/or as the transformation of the sinner effected by God; or (3) a subjective genitive – God's righteousness as his saving action. These interpretations are not mutually exclusive, especially the latter two meanings. The interpretation in terms of an objective genitive, in the sense of a righteousness that the sinner demonstrates to God in order to be accepted, has been rejected by Martin Luther as contrary to what Paul argues.

temple from sin and, thus, facilitate the atonement for Israel's sins (Lev. 16; cf. the reference to 'blood'). Jesus' death on the cross is the eschatological Day of Atonement for the sins of all sinners who come to faith in Jesus, whether Jews or Gentiles. The cross is where God has revealed his saving righteousness which inaugurates the new covenant in which Jews and Gentiles are liberated from his wrath and from the death sentence of the law. God is present in Jesus' death on the cross, procuring the ultimate atonement for sin.[42]

Paul's convictions regarding Jesus, the Messiah and Lord, transformed his traditional views regarding the temple. Inasmuch as the temple 'symbolized the reality of God's presence on earth, it was countered by the teaching that God had been 'in Christ' (2 Cor. 5:19), fully 'dwelling' in him (Col. 1:19; 2:9), and that the Spirit of God now dwelt in God's people (Rom. 8:11).'[43]

The forgiveness of sins

The forgiveness of sins in Jesus' proclamation

When Jesus heals a paralyzed man in the synagogue in Capernaum, he asserts not only the power to heal but the authority to forgive sin (Matt. 9:1–8 = Mark 2:1–12 = Luke 5:17–26). The claim to have the authority to forgive sin – apart from the temple and without sacrifices – provokes the first reaction from Jewish leaders who believe that Jesus' claims are blasphemy (Mark 2:7). Jesus' challenge to the scribes: 'But so that you may know that the Son of Man has authority on earth to forgive sins' (Matt. 9:6 [NRSV]) probably formulates Jesus' claim to exclusivity: he is '*the only one* on earth with the power and the right to forgive sins. On this interpretation Jesus has replaced the temple in Jerusalem and its priests.'[44]

During the anointing of Jesus' feet by a sinful woman, Jesus declares the woman to be in a state of forgiveness, demonstrated through her actions which testify to her love in gratitude for having been forgiven (Luke 7:47, 48).[45]

---

[42] Wolfgang Kraus, *Der Tod Jesu als Heiligtumsweihe. Eine Untersuchung zum Umfeld der Sühnevorstellung in Römer 3.25-26a* (WMANT 66; Neukirchen-Vluyn: Neukirchener Verlag, 1991), 189–90.

[43] Walker, *Jesus and the Holy City*, 125.

[44] Davies and Allison, *Matthew*, 2:93. Davies and Allison regard Matt. 9:6 as an editorial aside to the reader; for a defense as a statement made by Jesus cf. France, *Matthew*, 347.

[45] The verbal form *apheōntai* (*sou hai hamartiai*) is perfect tense. Cf. Bock, *Luke*, 1:703, 705.

During his last supper with his disciples, Jesus' pronouncement over the cup links his impending, voluntary death with the forgiveness of sins: 'Drink from it, all of you; for this is my blood of the covenant, which is poured out for many for the forgiveness of sins' (Matt. 26:27–28 [NRSV]). Sins are no longer forgiven in the context of the Sinaitic covenant (Exod. 24:8) which followed the exodus, celebrated in the Passover. Sins are now forgiven in the context of the new covenant (Luke 22:20, referring to Jer. 31:31–4) which is now being inaugurated with Jesus pouring out his blood as God's Suffering Servant (Isa. 53:11–12) whose death achieves the forgiveness of sins (Isa. 53:5–6, 8, 10–12). Jesus' statement recalls the original description of Jesus' mission in Matt. 1:21: to 'save his people from their sins'.

The forgiveness of sins in Peter's preaching

After Peter's explanation of the language miracle at Pentecost, when the people experienced the fulfilment of Joel's prophecy that God would pour out his Spirit on all flesh in the last days, he advises listeners who enquire as to what they should do: 'Repent, and be baptized every one of you in the name of Jesus Christ so that your sins may be forgiven; and you will receive the gift of the Holy Spirit' (Acts 2:38 [NRSV]). The nature of Jesus' exaltation and the gift of God's Spirit which results from Jesus' exaltation 'involves such a close identification with "the Lord" of Joel's citation that Jesus may be presented as the Redeemer upon whose name men should call for salvation (2:38–9).'[46]

Salvation is now linked with calling upon the name of the 'Lord Jesus the Messiah', i.e. with the acknowledgement of Jesus' messianic dignity, with the understanding that his death on the cross achieved atonement for sins, with the recognition that his resurrection from the dead and his exaltation to the right hand of God inaugurated the new covenant for which God had promised his Spirit. Repentance is linked with an act of purification, which demonstrates personal repentance and acknowledgement of Jesus as the crucified Messiah and risen Lord. The confession of Jesus as Messiah and Lord is the reason why the immersion in water is linked with 'the name of Jesus Christ'. Salvation through repentance and public confession of the need for purification entails reception of God's Spirit and the integration into the people of God's new covenant.

---

[46] Turner, *Power from on High*, 273. For the following points cf. Eckhard J. Schnabel, *Early Christian Mission* (Downers Grove: IVP, 2004), 1:404–5.

The forgiveness of sins in Paul's theology

For Paul, Jews need forgiveness of sins just as much as Gentiles do.[47] Paul begins his exposition of the gospel in his letter to the Christians in Rome with a succinct statement about the revelation of God's wrath on account of human sinfulness (Rom. 1:18), followed by a description of the nature of human sin (1:19–23) and the consequences of sin (1:24–31), thus confirming the legitimacy, the severity and the scope of God's judgement (1:32). He then argues that Jews are not exempt from the revelation of God's wrath (2:1 – 3:20). While Jewish readers would agree with Paul's indictment of humankind in 1:19–32, they believed that they had a privileged position before God.

Paul argues in Romans 2 that, while pious Jews may indeed rely on God's kindness in delaying his judgement, they make the mistake of having little regard for the scope of God's kindness in view of the hopeless condition of humankind, unaware that they need as much repentance as the Gentiles do. Jews are not exempt from judgement, because they have failed to recognize that they have a hard and impenitent heart, a condition that will result in God's condemnation. The Jewish claim to covenant privileges is contradicted by the reality of the actions of the Jewish people. Paul argues with Isaiah 52:5 that, just as Israel's disobedience in the past brought shame upon God and the exile upon Israel,[48] so now the Jewish people dishonour God by their disobedience (2:17–24).

Paul concludes his exposition of the sinfulness of humankind in 3:20 with an allusion to Psalm 143:2 (and perhaps Gen. 6:12), asserting that final justification by God does not take place on the basis of obedience to the works prescribed by the law. No 'flesh' has the ability to obey the law.[49] The law may have indeed provided various mechanisms for the atonement of sin, such as the burnt offerings and the sin offerings described in Leviticus chapters 1, 4 and 5 (cf. Exod. 34:7; Num. 14:18–19). These provisions of the law can no longer compensate for sin, because God has provided a new place of atonement.

---

[47] Paul does not use the term 'forgiveness' much, but since forgiveness is connected with justification, it belongs to the centre of Paul's theology. Cf. Simon J. Gathercole, 'Justified by Faith, Justified by his Blood: The Evidence of Romans 3:21 – 4:25', in *Justification and Variegated Nomism. Vol. 2: The Paradoxes of Paul* (ed. D.A. Carson, et al.; Grand Rapids: Baker, 2004), 105–45, 159–60.

[48] Cf. the larger context in Isa. 50:1–3.

[49] In 8:3–4, Paul argues, as he did in 2:13–14 and 2:25–29, that the Spirit provides for the Christian believer the power to fulfill the law.

This is what Paul argues in 3:21 – 5:21, explaining the revelation of God's saving righteousness for Gentiles and Jews in Jesus the Messiah. In 3:21, he explains the significance of God's action in the death of Jesus Christ, providing atonement for sins and redemption. Paul emphasizes with the opening adverb *nyni de* in 3:21 ('*But now* a righteousness from God, apart from law, has been made known') a twofold contrast. He contrasts the time of Gentile idolatry and immorality with God's provision of righteousness for sinners. He also contrasts Jewish efforts to find salvation through the law in the old covenant with the revelation of God's righteousness in the new covenant. Paul asserts that now God's saving action takes place independently of the Mosaic law, both for Gentiles who do not have the law and for Jews who do not obey the law. God saves the ungodly and the disobedient, the very people who assaulted his glory and who did not obey his will. Paul clarifies that this new reality is scriptural: the law and the Prophets bear witness to it.[50] The gospel of God concerning Jesus Christ that Paul proclaims is the fulfilment of God's promises for the new covenant; it is not a new religion.

In 3:22–6, Paul explains the revelation of the saving righteousness of God as follows:

(1) The *means* of salvation is faith in Jesus Christ (v. 22). The means of salvation is not the law but trust in Jesus the messianic Saviour.
(2) The *scope* of salvation is universal (v. 22), without distinction between idolatrous polytheists and disobedient Jews, open to all who believe in Jesus Christ.
(3) The *target* of salvation is sinners (v. 23), people whose behaviour suppresses God's truth and ignores God's will, people who have lost the glory of living in God's presence.[51]
(4) The *nature* of salvation is justification (*dikaioumenoi*), which is God's acquittal of the sinner who faced condemnation on the day of judgement, but now is declared righteous and, thus, set right with God (v. 24).
(5) The *manner* of salvation is that of a free gift (*dōrean*, v. 24).
(6) The *origin* of salvation is God's grace (*charis*), the undeserved love of God (v. 24).

---

[50] Cf. Rom. 1:2; 4:1–25; 9:25–33; 10:6–13; 15:8–12.
[51] Many see in 3:23 ('all fall short of the glory of God') a reference to Adam's fall. In *Apoc. Mos.* 21:6 Adam accuses Eve, 'you have deprived me of the glory of God'; cf. also *L.A.E.* 20–21; *Gen. Rab.* 11:2; *b. Sanh.* 38b. Cf. Mark A. Seifrid, 'Romans', in *New Testament Use of the Old Testament* (ed. G.K. Beale and D.A. Carson), 607–94, 618.

(7) The *process* of salvation is redemption (*apolytrōsis*, v. 24), deliverance from the hopeless human condition which Paul had described in 1:18 – 3:20.[52]

(8) The *operation* of salvation is bound up with Jesus the Messiah (v. 24). It is in and through Jesus' death and resurrection that the new epoch of salvation has been inaugurated and both idolatrous pagans and lawbreaking Jews are delivered from sin and death.

(9) The *locale* of salvation is the cross, where Jesus Christ became the new place of God's atoning presence (*hilastērion*, v. 25). Paul emphasizes the consequences of Jesus' death for God's wrath (1:18), for humankind's sinfulness (1:18 – 3:20) and for the power of sin (3:9). Jesus' death redeems the unrighteous from God's wrath, cleanses sinners from sin and breaks the power of sin. Because Jesus is the sinless sacrifice and dies in the place of sinners, the sinners live. The phrase 'God presented him' describes Jesus' death as a public manifestation of God's grace.

(10) The effects of Jesus' death are appropriated 'by faith' in Jesus Christ (vv. 25, 26), i.e. by responding with trust and confidence.

(11) Another effect of salvation is the demonstration of God's righteousness (v. 25). God demonstrated his righteousness by providing Jesus as the sacrifice which fulfils the terms of his covenant with Israel.

(12) Yet another effect of Jesus' death is the final, ultimate forgiveness of sins (v. 25). While in the past God's forbearance had left the sins committed beforehand unpunished, Jesus' sacrificial death was God's final answer to the problem of sin, which the sacrificial system of the law was not.

In 3:27–31, Paul argues that, when Jews understand the law as commanding obedience to works which leads to justification on the day of judgement, the sequence 'works > obedience > justification > boasting' is confirmed. If the law is understood in the context of faith – in the revelation of God's saving righteousness through Jesus Christ (vv. 21–26) – now faith being the means of justification, the sequence is 'faith > justification'. This means that the pattern which leads from works to boasting is abandoned.[53] In 3:28, Paul contrasts the two ways

---

[52] The Greek term is sometimes used in a general sense, sometimes with reference to a ransom which has been paid (cf. 1 Cor. 6:20; 7:23; also Mark 10:45); many see an allusion to the OT motif of redemption in a new exodus, a new covenant and a new creation (Isa. 43:14–21; 48:20–21; 52:1–2; Ezek. 20:33–38; Hos. 2:14–23).

[53] Simon J. Gathercole, *Where is Boasting? Early Jewish Soteriology and Paul's Response in Romans 1 – 5* (Grand Rapids: Eerdmans, 2002), 224–5.

of justification: sinners are justified on the day of judgement by faith in Jesus Christ without the involvement of the law (Paul's conviction), or sinners are justified by works prescribed by the law (the Jewish conviction). Paul had argued in 2:1 – 3:20 that the latter is not possible. The truth that justification before God is not by obedience to the law applies not only to Jews (who do not obey the law), but also to Gentiles (who do not have the law).

In 3:29–30, Paul provides a theological argument for this point. God's final solution to the problem of the reality of sin among Gentiles and among Jews is not justification through obedience to the law, because then only Jews could be saved (only Jews possess the law). This is an unacceptable position since God is not only the God of the Jews but also the God of the Gentiles. The truth is that 'there is only one God' (v. 30). This formulation reflects the basic confession of Jewish monotheism (Deut. 6:4). Since there is only one God, there can be only one means of justifying sinners. This is what Paul has argued in 3:21–6, read in the context of 1:18 – 3:20: members of God's covenant people (the circumcised Jews) are justified before God by faith in Jesus Christ, and idolatrous polytheists (the uncircumcised pagans) are justified 'through that same faith' (v. 30).

Other important passages in Paul, which cannot be considered here in detail, are Romans 8:3 where Jesus' death is linked with the phrase *peri hamartias*, with the implication that Jesus is described as a sin-offering;[54] 2 Corinthians 5:18–21 where Paul describes the 'ministry of reconciliation' that he has been given, focused on the message that 'in Christ God was reconciling the world to himself' (v. 19 [NRSV]);[55] as well as Colossians 1:14 and Ephesians 1:17.

The nature of the people of God

The nature of the people of God in Jesus' proclamation

Jesus' calling of twelve disciples was a programmatic action. Since the disciples were not physical descendants of the twelve Israelite tribes

---

[54] Note the use of the formulation *peri hamartias* in Lev. 4 – 5. Cf. Ulrich Wilckens, *Der Brief an die Römer* (EKK 6/1–3; Neukirchen-Vluyn/Einsiedeln: Neukirchener Verlag/Benzinger, 1978–82), 2:126–8; J.D.G. Dunn, *Romans* (WBC 38; Dallas: Word, 1988), 1:422; N.T. Wright, *The Climax of the Covenant: Christ and the Law in Pauline Theology* (Philadelphia: Fortress, 1992), 220–5.

[55] Cf. Stanley E. Porter, 'Reconciliation and 2 Cor. 5', in *The Corinthian Correspondence* (ed. R. Bieringer; BEThL 125; Leuven: Leuven University Press, 1996), 693–705.

and, since 'Israel' consisted of mostly only two or two and a half tribes (Judah, Benjamin, the priests from Levi) after ca. 700 BC, the Twelve represent the hope for the restoration of the people of God in the last days.[56]

According to Matthew 16:13–20, Jesus speaks of his *ekklesia*, which will be built on the rock that is Peter, who has acknowledged Jesus to be the Messiah. Jesus gives Simon a new name (Peter, the rock). Of the Old Testament figures to receive a second name, the most memorable are Abram and Jacob. The former was given the new name 'Abraham' to signify that he would be the father of a multitude (Gen. 17:1–8); the latter was renamed 'Israel', by which the people that would spring from him would be known (Gen. 32:22–32). Particularly intriguing are the parallels between Genesis 17 and Matthew 16. In both cases, we are witnessing the birth of the people of God – the people of Israel and the people of those who follow Jesus. In both cases, birth is associated with one particular individual – Abraham, then Peter. In both cases, an individual has a name which symbolizes his crucial function: Abraham is taken to mean 'father of a multitude', Peter to mean the 'rock' on which the church is founded.

Jesus' demonstration in the temple (Matt. 21:12–16 = Mark 11:15–19 = Luke 19:45–8) indicts the Jewish people for their sinful disobedience, announcing the destruction of the temple with the allusion to Jeremiah 7:11. He advocates, in the Court of the Gentiles, the holiness of the entire temple platform, announcing the beginning of the conversion of the Gentiles to the one true God whom they will worship (allusion to Isa. 56:7). Jesus used his dramatic action in the temple to proclaim the end of Israel's sacrificial cult and, at the same time, the inauguration of a house of prayer for the nations. Peter, who confesses Jesus as the Messiah, is the foundation of a new 'house' which is now being established.

Jesus' words at the Last Supper, in particular his reference to the new covenant (Jer. 31:31–4; Ezek. 16:59–63) as being established through his blood which he sheds as God's Suffering Servant forgiving the sins of sinners (Luke 22:20), imply the creation of a new community – the community of the new covenant which consists of all who partake of his body and of his blood, i.e. of all who follow him and who are united with him as the messianic Son of Man whose ministry, death and

---

[56] Cf. Isa. 11:11–12; 49:6; Jer. 3:18; 29:14; 30:3; 31:7–10; 32:36–41; Ezek. 36:8–11; 37:19; 47:13; Amos 9:14; Mic. 2:12; 4:6–7; Zeph. 3:19–20; Zech. 10:8–10; cf. Sir. 36:18–21; Tob. 14:7; 2 Macc. 1:27–8; 2:18; *T. Levi* 16:6; *T. Ash.* 7:7; *T. Benj.* 9:2; *Jub.* 1:15; *Pss. Sol.* 11; 17:26–34; *2 Bar.* 77:5–6; 78:7; *Jos. Asen.* 5.6; 4Q508 Frag. 2, 2.

resurrection mark the coming of the kingdom of God and the establishment of the promised new covenant.

The nature of the people of God in Peter's preaching

When Peter calls on his Jewish listeners in Jerusalem, who have heard
his explanation of the death and resurrection of Jesus and of the coming of the promised Spirit of God, he insists that they need to repent in
order to be saved (Acts 2:38).[57] As God has poured out his Spirit, the
last days have arrived and the new covenant has been inaugurated.
This is the reason why even Jews need to be 'saved'. In view of the reality of the new covenant established by Jesus the Messiah, being born as
a member of the old covenant is no longer sufficient. The salvation of
Jews in Jerusalem signifies that the restoration of Israel has begun.

The fulfilment of the promises regarding Israel's restoration in a new
covenant occurs as the messianic community of the followers of Jesus
are gathered from among the 'house of Israel' that has proven to be a
'corrupt generation' in the crucifixion of the Messiah. Peter's designation of his Jewish contemporaries as a 'corrupt generation' (Acts 2:40)
alludes to the generation of Israel in the desert (cf. Deut. 32:5 [NRSV]:
'yet his degenerate children have dealt falsely with him, a perverse and
crooked generation'). The typology of the 'corrupt' generation of the
desert implies an announcement of impending judgement. Peter calls
on his Jewish listeners to be rescued from their rejection of God's second great act of liberation and to accept God's act of salvation which
took place in the death and resurrection of Jesus the Messiah. Peter
announces that the gathering of the new people of God in Israel is
accompanied by the promised ingathering of 'all who are far away'
(Acts 2:39), i.e. of the Gentiles to whom God's promise applies as well.

In Acts 4:11–12, Peter quotes Psalm 118:22 to make the point that
Jesus' death is the fulfilment of prophecy. Despite the fact that the
'builders', i.e. the Jewish leaders, have rejected Jesus, he is the 'stone'
which God has elevated to be the cornerstone. This means that God has
given to Jesus, whom the Jewish leaders rejected, the position of greatest prominence.[58] Jesus is the place of God's presence and the centre of
God's people as he is the only Saviour.

---

[57] For this and the following points cf. Darrell L. Bock, 'The Book of Acts and Jewish
Evangelism: Three Approaches and Once Common Thread, in *To the Jew First: The
Case for Jewish Evangelism in Scripture and History* (ed. D.L. Bock and M. Glaser;
Grand Rapids: Kregel, 2008), 53–65; 55–6.

[58] C.K. Barrett, *The Acts of the Apostles* (ICC; Edinburgh: T. & T. Clark, 1994–8), 1:230.

In 1 Peter 2:4–8, Peter quotes three Old Testament passages[59] in which Jesus is described as God's chosen cornerstone, rejected by some and believed by others. The imagery of the stone which is a cornerstone refers to a 'house' which is being built by God, specifically a temple. The believers in northern Asia Minor, evidently mostly Gentiles,[60] are described in verse 5 [NRSV] as 'a spiritual house, to be a holy priesthood, to offer spiritual sacrifices acceptable to God through Jesus Christ.' The place of God's earthly dwelling is neither the temple in Jerusalem nor the synagogues of the Jewish people, but the community of the followers of Jesus consisting of Gentile believers and Jewish believers who represent the place of true worship and acceptable sacrifice, which is the transformed lives of the believers offered to the glory of God.[61]

In verses 9–10, Peter uses Old Testament language describing Israel, God's people, drawn from Exodus 19:6; Isaiah 43:20–21; Hosea 2:25, to describe the international community of the followers of Jesus: they are 'a chosen race', 'a royal priesthood', 'a holy nation', 'God's own people', the people who have been constituted as 'God's people' by God's unmerited grace. Peter highlights the fact that the *ekklesia* of Gentile and Jewish believers in Jesus Christ are the true people of God in the new covenant, standing in a line of continuity with the people of God in the old covenant. And he emphasizes that the identity of the people of God in the new covenant is connected with God's grace in and through Jesus Christ, and with their response in faith, obedience and holiness.[62]

The nature of the people of God in Paul's theology

Paul's description of the Corinthian congregation as 'the church of God' (*ekklēsia tou theou*) provides a theological interpretation of the reality of people from different ethnic and social backgrounds who assemble to worship the one true God. The community of the followers of Jesus is not simply a gathering of like-minded people who have decided to spend time together regularly. The church is the community of God's people created by God's initiative in the last days, in the

---

[59]   Ps. 118:22–3; Isa. 8:14–15; 28:16.

[60]   Cf. the reference to the believers' 'former ignorance' (1 Pet. 1:14), to their once not being God's people (2:10) and to idolatry (4:3).

[61]   Cf. Karen H. Jobes, *1 Peter* (BECNT; Grand Rapids: Baker, 2005), 148–9.

[62]   Don A. Carson, '1 Peter', in *New Testament Use of the Old Testament* (ed. G.K. Beale and D.A. Carson), 1015–45; 1032.

death of Jesus Christ, to redeem fallen humanity – both Jews and Gentiles (1 Cor. 1:18–25, 26–31; cf. 7:18–19; 12:13).

The identity of God's people is no longer connected with ethnic origins or with circumcision and obedience to the Mosaic law, but with the sovereign power of God who sanctifies all who believe in Jesus Christ.[63] The church is the community of God's people, whose lives have been impacted and transformed by the good news of a crucified Messiah and Lord who has risen from the dead and who is present in the church through his Spirit. The church is the community of God's people, both Jewish believers and Gentile believers in Jesus Christ, who have been called to live in the world as a witness to God's saving action in Jesus Christ. Paul applies metaphors to the church consisting of Gentile and Jewish believers (field, building, temple) which in the Old Testament described the identity of Israel.

The church is a field (1 Cor. 3:6–9).The metaphor of a field (or vineyard) is a traditional description of the congregation of Israel.[64] If Paul alludes here to the song of Isaiah 5:1–7 in which Israel is described as God's vineyard,[65] he implies that the congregation of Jewish and Gentile followers of Jesus Christ constitutes the true people of God.

The church is a building under construction (1 Cor. 3:10–15). The metaphor of building construction echoes two Old Testament texts. The phrase *sophos architektōn* ('skilled master builder', v. 10) occurs once in the Greek Bible (Isa. 3:3); both 1 Corinthians 3:10 and Isaiah 3:3 speak of wisdom and of judgement with regard to the leaders of God's people. The materials gold, silver and stone (vv. 12–15) are also mentioned in connection with Bezalel who was filled with the Spirit of wisdom, skilled as an architect and appointed to build the tabernacle (Exod. 35:31–2 LXX).[66] The description of the church as God's building takes up the traditional description of Israel as God's building in the

---

[63] Cf. Wolfgang Kraus, *Das Volk Gottes. Zur Grundlegung der Ekklesiologie bei Paulus* (WUNT 85; Tübingen: Mohr-Siebeck, 1996), 160–71.

[64] Cf. Isa. 60:21; 61:3; Jer. 1:10; 2:21; 18:9; 24:6; 1QS VIII, 5; XI, 8, 1QH VI, 15; VII, 18–19; VIII, 5–26; CD I, 7. For the metaphorical use of 'planting' cf. Isa. 5:7; 60:21; 61:3; Ezek. 17:1–8; 34:29; Wis. 4:3–5; *Jub.* 16:26; *1 En.* 10:16; 84:6; 93:2–10; Matt. 15:13; 20:1–5; Mark 4:1–20; Rom. 11:16–24. Cf. Shozo Fujita, 'The Metaphor of Plant in Jewish Literature of the Intertestamental Period', *JSJ* 7 (1975): 30–45.

[65] Cf. H.H. Drake Williams, *The Wisdom of the Wise: The Presence and Function of Scripture within 1 Cor. 1:18 – 3:23* (AGAJU 49; Leiden: Brill, 2001), 243–9.

[66] Cf. Williams, *Wisdom*, 257–300; Gregory K. Beale, *The Temple and the Church's Mission: A Biblical Theology of the Dwelling Place of God* (NSBT 17; Downers Grove: Apollos/IVP, 2004), 245–52.

Old Testament and in Jewish writings.[67] The community of the followers of Jesus is the people of God.

The church is God's temple (1 Cor. 3:16–17). The hope for a perfect
temple in the last days characterizes the Old Testament and Second
Temple Jewish literature.[68] Paul reminds the Corinthian believers that
they are 'God's temple and that God's Spirit dwells in you' (v. 16
[NRSV]). The Christian believers in Corinth are the holy place of the
presence of God's Spirit, i.e. of God himself.

In 1 Corinthians 7:19 [NRSV], Paul asserts that 'circumcision is nothing, and uncircumcision is nothing; but obeying the commandments of
God is everything.' With this statement, Paul declares a crucial Jewish
identity marker as irrelevant for salvation and for the life in a mixed
community of Jewish and Gentile followers of Jesus. Paul overcomes
the dichotomy between Jews and Gentiles, since belonging to the
'church of God' through faith in Jesus Christ has priority over any distinctions which used to be important in God's prior revelation in his
covenant with Israel.[69]

This is Paul's argument in Galatians chapters 2 and 3, climaxing in
the emphatic statement:

> [I]n Christ Jesus you are all children of God through faith. As many of
> you as were baptized into Christ have clothed yourselves with Christ.
> There is no longer Jew or Greek, there is no longer slave or free, there is
> no longer male and female; for all of you are one in Christ Jesus. And if
> you belong to Christ, then you are Abraham's offspring, heirs according
> to the promise (Gal. 3:26–9 [NRSV]).

The reality of the kingdom of God, which has become a present reality
in and through Jesus the Messiah, combined with the expectation that

---

[67] Cf. Jer. 1:10; 31:4 (LXX 38:4); 33:7 (LXX 40:7); 48:7; for Qumran cf. 1QS XI, 8–9; 1QH
VI, 24–8; VII, 8–9; CD III, 19; for metaphor of God's building with the metaphor of
planting cf. Jer. 1:9–10; 24:6; 31:27–8; 42:10; 45:4; Ezek. 36:36; 1QS VIII, 4–10; 1QH
VI; Philo, *Cher.* 98–106; *Her.* 116; *Praem.* 139; *Leg.* 1.48.

[68] The basic text is Ezek. 40 – 48; cf. also Ezek. 37:26–7; Isa. 44:28; Tob. 14:5; *Jub.* 1:17,
29; 4:24–5; 1 *En.* 90:28–9; 91:13; *Sib.* 3:290; 1QM II, 3; VII, 11; 11QT XXIX, 8–10. The
Qumran Community understood itself as the true Israel and described its identity
in terms of the 'sanctuary of Aaron', the 'house of truth in Israel', the 'most holy
place for Aaron'; cf. 1QS V, 4–7; VIII, 4–10; IX, 3–9; XI, 8; 1QH VI, 24–8; 4QFlor I,
2–3; CD III, 18 – IV, 10. Cf. Georg Klinzing, *Die Umdeutung des Kultus in der
Qumrangemeinde und im Neuen Testament* (SUNT 7; Göttingen: Vandenhoeck &
Ruprecht, 1971), 50–93.

[69] Cf. Kraus, *Volk Gottes*, 168–9.

Jesus Christ would return soon, created a new eschatological and universal awareness.[70] It also produced new ecclesiological communities in which the exclusive unity of ethnic Israel as the political-religious location of God's people was transformed into the inclusive unity of spiritual Israel as the people of God's new covenant.

Paul argues in Romans 4 that faith in Jesus Christ creates the universal people of God consisting of Jews, the ethnic descendants of Abraham, and of Gentiles, the families of the earth whom God wanted to bless through Abraham. He argues in Romans 4:1–16 that Abraham was justified by God not on the basis of works but on the basis of faith. When Abraham was justified, he was an ungodly idolater who had no 'works' which God could reward. God justified Abraham who believed, not Abraham who 'worked'. This is also true with regard to David, whose sins were forgiven and who was reckoned by God as righteous apart from works (vv. 6–8, quoting Ps. 32:1–2). The blessing of justification which God pronounces on sinners such as David is valid not only for Jews such as David, but also for Gentiles such as Abraham the Chaldean (vv. 9–12). Abraham's circumcision was the 'seal of the righteousness' which God granted him on account of his faith in God's promises (v. 11). Abraham is, thus, the ancestor of the new people of God – the ancestor of the uncircumcised Gentiles who have come to faith and who are graciously granted righteousness by God on the basis of this faith (v. 11b) and the ancestor of the circumcised Jews who have come to faith (in God's saving revelation in Jesus Christ, cf. vv. 21–2).[71]

In Philippians 3:2–11, Paul responds to Jewish Christians who demand that Gentile believers need to be circumcised with the emphatic statement, 'it is we who are the circumcision, who worship in the Spirit of God and boast in Christ Jesus and have no confidence in the flesh' (v. 3 [NRSV]). This statement represents not merely a spiritualization of circumcision but the description of the identity of all followers of Jesus in the categories of Jewish identity.[72] Paul does not deny the validity of the claim which is connected with the demand for circumcision – full membership in the covenant people of God. However, he counters the demand for circumcision with the assertion that believers in Jesus the Messiah, including Gentile believers, already belong to the community of salvation. Paul asserts that Jewish

---

[70] Cf. Hengel and Schwemer, *Jesus und das Judentum*, 34.

[71] Cf. Mark A. Seifrid, ' "For the Jew First": Paul's *Nota Bene* for His Gentile Believers', in *To the Jew First* (ed. D.L. Bock and M. Glaser), 24–39; 26.

[72] Cf. Kraus, *Volk Gottes*, 338.

privileges, such as being circumcised, being a member of the people of Israel, of the tribe of Benjamin, a Hebrew born of Hebrews, are no longer 'gain' but 'loss because of Christ' (v. 7). Righteousness no longer comes from the law but comes 'through faith in Christ, the righteousness from God based on faith' (v. 9).

In Ephesians 2:11–22, Paul explains that uncircumcised Gentiles, before their conversion to faith in Jesus Christ, were 'aliens from the commonwealth of Israel', 'strangers to the covenants of promise', 'having no hope and without God in the world', being 'far off' from God and God's people. This situation has changed 'now in Christ Jesus' as a result of Jesus' sacrificial death on the cross (v. 13). Jesus the Messiah has given Gentiles access to God. God the Father has made peace between Jews and Gentiles who believe in Jesus Christ; he has integrated both groups into one new group; he has broken down the dividing wall; he has removed the hostility that existed between Jews and Gentiles (v. 14).

Jesus the Messiah has created a unified new humanity (*hena kainon anthrōpon*, v. 15) as a result of the reconciliation with God, which he procured through his death on the cross for both Gentile sinners and for Jewish sinners (v. 16). Gentiles who were 'far off' and Jews who were 'near' were all in need of reconciliation and peace with God (v. 17) as God's wrath is being revealed against idolatrous pagans and against disobedient Jews. Gentile believers and Jewish believers are united as they have received the one Spirit of the one true God who is the Father of those who belong to him (v. 18). As a result, Gentile believers are no longer strangers and aliens; they are neither homeless nor second-class citizens in the homeland of Israel. They have become 'fellow citizens' (*sympolitai*, v. 19) and 'members of God's household' (*oikeioi tou theou*, v. 19). They are an integral part of the new temple of which Jesus Christ is the cornerstone and whose foundation is described by the promises of the prophets and by the proclamation of the apostles; together with the Jewish believers they are being built into the dwelling place of God himself (vv. 20–22).

The new community, created as a result of Jesus' death on the cross, 'transcends Israel and its privileges' as it is a community in which Gentiles and Jews are on an equal footing 'in Christ'.[73] Their identity is no longer determined by ethnic realities or by stipulations of the old covenant according to which Gentiles were unclean. Their identity is

---

[73] Peter T. O'Brien, *The Letter to the Ephesians* (PNTC; Grand Rapids: Eerdmans, 1999), 191.

determined by the saving work of Jesus the Messiah, by their access to God and by their fellowship with all other believers who constitute the place of God's very presence.

Summary

It has become obvious that while Jews and Christians believe in the same God and accept the same Scriptures as God's revelation, Christians are convinced that the life, death, resurrection and exaltation of Jesus of Nazareth as Israel's Messiah and Saviour has modified the way in which people – both Jews and Gentiles – encounter God's presence, receive forgiveness of sins and live their lives as members of the people of God.

1. As regards the convictions and the patterns of behaviour of Jews and (Jewish and Gentile) Christians in the first century, there is both continuity and discontinuity. When compared to their pagan counterparts, one could argue that these two groups possess far more that unites them than separates them. However, important elements of dissonance divided Jews and Christians in the first century, provoking mutual criticism, suspicion and (lamentably) hostility. Focusing on these elements of dissonance, three basic areas are foundational: convictions and practices regarding the presence of God, regarding the forgiveness of sins and regarding the nature of the people of God. The distinct way in which each group conceives these three areas colours their understanding of salvation in general.

2. In Second Temple Judaism, *the presence of God* was tied primarily to the physical structure of the Jerusalem temple and to the worship practiced in the temple, including the offering of sacrifices and the yearly pilgrimages. The special care taken in the construction and administration of the temple reflected the Jewish belief that God revealed himself in a particular way here where sacrifices established and maintained the holiness and the purity of Israel. Any violation of this structure represented an offence against God himself. Jews in the first century also believed that God was present in the reading and hearing of the Scriptures, and in the observation of religious holy days.

In early Christianity, the presence of God was expressed through Jesus' proclamation of the kingdom of God, inaugurated by God through Jesus the messianic Son of Man in both the present and the future. This kingdom, and the presence of God which it entails, is consummated in the coming of Jesus Christ. The contrast between the local focus of the old administration is evident in Jesus' demonstration in the temple which announces the destruction of the temple and the inauguration of the last days for which the prophets had promised the conversion of the Gentiles to the worship of Israel's God.

The christocentric nature of God's presence is reinforced throughout the New Testament. Peter emphasizes that God's Spirit, whose universal presence Joel prophesied for the last days, is Jesus' Spirit. God is present among the followers of Jesus the Messiah whose ministry, death, resurrection and vindication represent the fulfilment of God's promise to pour out his Spirit on all flesh. Paul identifies Jesus with the 'Lord' whom Israel's monotheistic confession of faith proclaims as the one and only true God, the Creator who saves his people as he is present in Jesus, the mediator of creation and the Saviour of sinners. And Paul emphasizes that God revealed himself in Jesus' death on the cross, providing saving righteousness for both Jews and Gentiles.

3. In Second Temple Judaism, *the people of God* consisted of those people who stood in the line of Abraham and his descendants through Isaac and Jacob. Membership in this people was expressed most poignantly through obedience to the Mosaic law, with all the identity markers contained therein, such as circumcision, purity laws, food laws and sacrifices. The centre of the Jewish community is Torah, both at a corporate and individual level. Woven into this idea is a latent theology of retribution wherein those who follow Torah will be blessed and those who reject it fall under God's curse. Thus, although the identity of the Jewish community was based on God's grace, there is a sense in which God's favour is preserved through the practising of his commandments.

The concept of the people of God is re-envisioned in early Christianity both in its scope and its identity. While the phrase 'people of God' was primarily an ethnic designation for first-century Jews, the followers of Jesus saw continuity with the past to be tied up with factors other than biological descent. The true 'children of Abraham' are those who respond in faith to Jesus the promised Messiah. That the early Christian community understood itself to be in continuity with the 'people of God' of the old covenant is evident through the appropriation of language traditionally used of Israel and the Jews into the vocabulary describing the New Testament church (royal priesthood, temple imagery, etc.). Thus, the 'people of God' is defined not in terms of ethnicity or in terms of ritual regulations of the Mosaic law, but in terms of the universal access every individual has to the presence of God through the salvific work of Jesus Christ.

4. In Second Temple Judaism, *the forgiveness of sins* is connected both with the grace of God and with the observation of the law. While pious Jews were under no illusions that they could merit the forgiveness of God by their own deeds forcing God to forgive, there is a sense in which their own righteousness acts as a causal agent in the procuring of God's grace. Also important is the concept of atonement tied up with the sacrificial practices offered in the temple and the sacrifice of good works that replaced them after the destruction of the temple in AD 70. Salvation was essentially ethnically located, suggesting that the Gentiles were excluded from the salvific will of God, unless they became proselytes.

The forgiveness of sins in first-century Christianity is focused on Jesus of Nazareth, who is accepted and affirmed as the crucified, risen and exalted Messiah and Lord. The followers of Jesus emphasized that only Jesus has the authority to forgive sins, as he has been revealed as the 'place' of God's saving presence on earth. As God grants forgiveness through Jesus' death on the cross, all people stand equally in need of this forgiveness, both Jews and Gentiles. It is not only the Jews who have access to God's grace, but all who in repentance and faith come to believe in Jesus Christ as Messiah and Lord.

Although similarities of theological and ethical convictions and practices between Jews and Christians are abundant, the differences proved to be of such a decisive nature that substantive unity gradually evaporated, resulting in a 'parting of ways'. The earliest followers of Jesus were convinced that God was present in Jesus, that God forgives sins through Jesus' death, that God gives new life on account of Jesus' resurrection, that God bestows the Holy Spirit through the exalted Jesus and that God restores his chosen people by inviting all – Jews and Gentiles – to belong to him through faith in Jesus. These convictions explain the fact that the earliest followers of Jesus, who were all Jews – Peter and John, Stephen and Philip, and then Paul – proclaimed the message of Jesus as Israel's Messiah and Saviour to the people of Israel wherever they could find them – in the temple in Jerusalem (Acts 3 – 5), in the local synagogues (Acts 6:8–10; 13:13–43), in private houses (Acts 5:42) and even in the Sanhedrin (Acts 5:17–41).

4

John's Gospel and Jewish Monotheism

Andreas J. Köstenberger

'Jesus did many other miraculous signs in the presence of his disciples, which are not recorded in this book. But these are written that you may believe that Jesus is the Christ, the Son of God, and that by believing you may have life in his name' (John 20:30–31). That Jesus is the Messiah, the Son of God, is by itself a remarkable assertion to make. What is even more remarkable is that the same Gospel opens with the affirmation that 'In the beginning was the Word, and the Word was with God, and the Word was God' (1:1) and that this Word, in turn, became flesh in Jesus Christ (1:14, 17). Also, just prior to the above-cited purpose statement, Thomas confesses Jesus as his 'Lord' and 'God' (20:28) and, in the body of the Gospel, Jesus utters claims such as 'I and the Father are one' (10:30), drawing charges of blasphemy for violating the Jewish bedrock belief that there was only one God.

All of this raises the question of how John and other first-century messianic Jews were able to reconcile the notion of Jesus' deity with Jewish monotheism. Before turning to a discussion of this issue, it will be important to remember that John's Gospel was not written in a vacuum. One's construal of the most likely context in which the Gospel was penned will significantly affect the way in which one understands the Gospel's teaching on the present topic. What is more, it will be vital to treat the present matter within the larger framework of the notion of monotheism in the Old Testament and in Second Temple literature. In this regard, it will also be helpful to consider the most likely backdrop for John's portrayal of Jesus' pre-existence. This will enable a more accurate assessment of John's teaching in relation to notions of God in the larger Jewish and Greco–Roman world in which he lived.[1]

John's Context

The traditional view holds that the Apostle John, at the urging of some of his disciples, wrote the Gospel towards the end of the first century AD in Ephesus in Asia Minor.[2] On this view, John's Gospel, alongside the Synoptics, occupies a place well within the mainstream of first-century Christianity. The sources underlying the Gospel are not merely comprised of what may be called 'Johannine tradition' (i.e. material independent of the so-called 'Synoptic tradition'), but the Gospel is ultimately grounded in eyewitness testimony on the part of one of the key participants in the actual story and history leading to Jesus' crucifixion (cf., e.g. 19:35; 21:24).[3]

This view has recently received significant support in the important work of Richard Bauckham, *Jesus and the Eyewitnesses*, in which Bauckham furnished compelling evidence that the Gospels constitute eyewitness testimony in keeping with first-century Jewish and Greco–Roman literary and historiographical conventions. According to Bauckham, the ideal source in ancient Greco–Roman literature was not the dispassionate observer, but the eyewitness.[4] The written Gospels, Bauckham contends, contain oral *history* related to the personal transmission of eyewitness testimony, not merely oral *tradition*

---

[1] The present article is adapted from Chapter 1 in Andreas J. Köstenberger and Scott R. Swain, *Father, Son and Spirit: The Trinity and John's Gospel* (NSBT 24; Nottingham: Apollos, 2008). Used by permission.

[2] Irenaeus, *Against Heresies* 3.1.2. For a more detailed account see Köstenberger, 'The Destruction of the Second Temple and the Composition of the Fourth Gospel', in *Challenging Perspectives on the Gospel of John* (ed. John Lierman; WUNT 2/219; Tübingen: Mohr–Siebeck, 2006), 69–108.

[3] There have been many challenges to the traditional views over the course of the past two centuries, none of which has proved to provide compelling evidence to overturn it. See Andreas J. Köstenberger, 'Early Doubts of the Apostolic Authorship of the Fourth Gospel', in *Studies in John and Gender: A Decade of Scholarship* (Studies in Biblical Literature 38; New York: Peter Lang, 2001), 17–47; idem, *The Theology of John: The Word, the Christ, the Son of God* (BTNT; Grand Rapids: Zondervan, 2008), ch. 1; and the introduction to John's Gospel in Andreas J. Köstenberger, L. Scott Kellum and Charles L. Quarles, *The Cradle, the Cross, and the Crown: An Introduction to the New Testament* (Nashville: Broadman and Holman, 2008).

[4] Richard Bauckham, *Jesus and the Eyewitnesses: The Gospels as Eyewitness Testimony* (Grand Rapids: Eerdmans, 2006), 8–11.

which is the result of the collective and anonymous transmission of material.[5]

In Bauckham's own words:

> It is the contention of this book that, in the period up to the writing of the Gospels, gospel traditions were connected with named and known eyewitnesses, people who had heard the teaching of Jesus from his lips and committed it to memory, people who had witnessed the events of his ministry, death, and resurrection and had formulated the stories about these events that they told. These eyewitnesses did not merely set going a process of oral transmission that soon went its own way without reference to them. They remained throughout their lifetimes the sources.[6]

In this context, the Twelve served as 'an authoritative collegium'.[7] Especially important in this regard is the phrase 'from the beginning', which is found at several strategic points in the Gospels and the New Testament record (e.g. Luke 1:2; 1 John 1:1; cf. John 1:1). Several other literary devices are used to stress the Gospels' character as eyewitness testimony, such as 'the *inclusio* of eyewitness testimony' (see especially. Mark 1:16–18 and 16:7 for Peter; John 1:40 and 21:24 for the Beloved Disciple). According to Bauckham, the transmission process of the Jesus tradition resulting in our written canonical Gospels is best understood as a formal controlled tradition in which the eyewitnesses played an important, and continuing, part.[8]

What is more, the Gospel material was transmitted not merely in a given community's quest for self-identity but for profoundly theological reasons, in the conviction that the events of Jesus' history were of epochal historical significance when understood in the larger framework of the (salvific) activity of Israel's God. Jesus was viewed not merely as the founder of a movement, but as the source of salvation, and Christianity was not just a new movement – it celebrated the fulfilment of God's promises in Jesus the Messiah who had now come, and died, and risen. John's Gospel, for its part, like the other three canonical Gospels, is founded on apostolic eyewitness testimony. What is more, John's is the Gospel that was written by the one who was closest to Jesus during his earthly ministry, a claim that fits historically

---

[5] See esp. Bauckham, *Jesus and the Eyewitnesses*, 36.

[6] Bauckham, *Jesus and the Eyewitnesses*, 93.

[7] Bauckham, *Jesus and the Eyewitnesses*, 94 (echoing Birger Gerhardsson).

[8] Bauckham, *Jesus and the Eyewitnesses*, 264 et passim.

only with the Apostle John who, according to the unified witness of Matthew, Mark and Luke, was one of three members of Jesus' inner circle together with Peter and John's brother James.[9]

With regard to the occasion for writing John's Gospel, recent studies have focused particularly on the Johannine temple theme and explored the possible connection between the destruction of the Jerusalem temple in AD 70 and the composition of John's Gospel.[10] It has been argued that now that the temple had been destroyed, the resurrected Jesus was without peer or rival as the new tabernacle, the new temple and the new centre of worship for a new nation encompassing all those who were united by faith in Jesus as Messiah. Over against non-messianic Jewish hardening against the Christian message and the formation of rabbinic Judaism, and over against the emergence of proto-gnosis (see 1 John), John seized the opportunity for evangelizing Jews and Diaspora proselytes.

In light of this plausible reconstruction of the Johannine context, how is one to understand John's teaching on God and the deity of Jesus within the framework of Second Temple Judaism, Greco–Roman thought and early Christianity? Only the broad contours of such an approach can be sketched here. As will be seen, first-century Jews held to a strict form of monotheism rather than blurring the lines between God and other divine mediator figures. At the same time, John did not violate exclusivist Jewish monotheism by attributing divinity and pre-existence to Jesus, because he understood Jesus as belonging to the identity of God rather than as a second, separate, distinct God, resulting in his portrayal of Jesus as Son of the Father.

John's Portrayal of Jesus and Jewish Monotheism

The Jews' belief in one God was firmly grounded in the *Shema*: 'Hear, O Israel: The LORD our God, the LORD is one' (Deut. 6:4). The Decalogue, likewise, in the first two commandments forbids Israelites to have (monotheism) or worship (monolatry) any gods other than Yahweh (Exod. 20:2–6; Deut. 5:6–10). Everywhere in the Hebrew Scriptures, it is this one God who manifests his character and acts in human history both redemptively and in terms of

---

[9] It should be noted that Bauckham himself does not hold to apostolic authorship; but see the critique in Köstenberger and Swain, *Father, Son and Spirit*, 31–3.

[10] See Köstenberger, 'Destruction of the Second Temple' and the literature cited there.

revelation.[11] This includes seminal events such as the exodus (Exod. 20:2; Deut. 4:32–9; Isa. 43:15–17), the giving of the law, and the Assyrian and Babylonian exiles. This God is the Creator and sole and sovereign Ruler of all things.[12]

Not only is God recognized as the one and only God, he alone is worshipped. As Bauckham notes: 'Judaism was unique among the religions of the Roman world in demanding the exclusive worship of its God . . . Jewish monotheism was defined by its adherence to the first and second commandments.'[13] This sharp distinction between God as being alone God and worthy of worship stood in distinct contrast to Hellenistic conceptions which held that worship was a matter of degree because divinity, likewise, was a matter of degree, so that worship was to be rendered to the extent appropriate to its object. Judaism, on the other hand, viewed God as unique and, thus, uniquely worthy of worship.[14]

The belief in, and worship of, one and only one God set Israel apart from the polytheistic beliefs and practices of its pagan neighbours, including the Greco–Roman pantheon, which was made up of dozens of gods. While the Jews had lapsed into the worship of other deities in

---

[11] See esp. Peter Machinist, 'The Question of Distinctiveness in Ancient Israel', in *Essential Papers on Israel and the Ancient Near East* (ed. Fredrick E. Greenspan; New York: New York University Press, 1991), 420–42, who notes that affirmations of the uniqueness of Israel's God are found in every genre and at every stage of OT literature; similarly, Ronald E. Clements, 'Monotheism and the Canonical Process', Theology 87 (1984): 336–44; and the chart in Christopher J. H. Wright, *The Mission of God: Unlocking the Bible's Grand Narrative* (Leicester: IVP, 2006), 104.

[12] See esp. Isa. 43:11; 44:6; 45:5–6, 14, 18, 21–2; 46:9; Richard Bauckham, *The Gospels for All Christians: Rethinking the Gospel Audiences* (Grand Rapids: Eerdmans, 1998), 10–11.

[13] Richard Bauckham, 'Jesus, Worship of', *ABD* 3:816. See also Robert Karl Gnuse, *No Other Gods: Emergent Monotheism in Israel* (JSOTSup 241; Sheffield: Sheffield Academic Press, 1997); N. MacDonald, *Deuteronomy and the Meaning of 'Monotheism'* (FAT 21/2; Tübingen: Mohr–Siebeck, 2003); idem, 'Whose Monotheism? Which Rationality?' in *The Old Testament in Its World* (ed. Robert P. Gordon and J. C. de Moor; Leiden: Brill, 2005), 45–67; Richard Bauckham, 'Biblical Theology and the Problems of Monotheism', in *Out of Egypt: Biblical Theology and Biblical Interpretation* (ed. Craig G. Bartholomew et al.; Carlisle: Paternoster, 2004), 187–232 (including a critique of Gnuse); and Wright, *Mission of God*, 73–4.

[14] Bauckham, *Gospels for All Christians*, 15. Cf. Larry W. Hurtado, *Lord Jesus Christ: Devotion to Jesus in Earliest Christianity* (Grand Rapids: Eerdmans, 2003), 31, who notes: 'For devout Jews, the core requirement of Judaism was the exclusive worship of Israel's God.' Hurtado also points out that none of the 'divine agents' of God were 'treated as rightful recipients of cultic worship in any known Jewish circles of the time' (ibid.).

the period prior to the exiles,[15] post-exilic Judaism, including that of the first century AD, was committed to monotheism and monolatry.[16] In fact, this became an important distinguishing characteristic of Jewish religion in a polytheistic environment and was recognized as a hallmark of Jewish faith by Greco–Roman historians such as Tacitus, who wrote: 'The Jews conceive of one God only.'[17]

As C. Wright observes, faith in the one and only God anchored 'the theocentric, monotheistic worldview of first-century Jews' and constituted 'the assumptive bedrock of Jesus and all his first followers'.[18] 'This God', Wright continues, 'was acknowledged now by Israel, his covenant people. But the God of Israel was also the universal God to whom all nations, kings and even emperors must finally submit.'[19] As the New Testament attests strikingly, Jesus claimed, and his followers believed, that he shared the identity of YHWH, the one and only God of Israel and of the nations, indicated by the application of *maranatha* (Aram. 'O Lord, come') to Jesus (1 Cor. 16:22; Rev. 22:20) and the appellation of Jesus as *kyrios* ('Lord') in the Christian confession *kyrios Iēsous* ('Jesus is Lord'; see esp. Acts 2:36; Rom. 10:9; 1 Cor. 12:3; Phil. 2:11 cf. Isa. 45:22–3).[20]

---

[15] See Bernhard Lang, *Der einzige Gott: Die Geburt des biblischen Monotheismus* (Munich: Kösel, 1981); idem, *Monotheism and the Prophetic Minority* (Sheffield: Almond, 1983); Saul M. Olyan, *Asherah and the Cult of Yahweh in Israel* (SBLMS 34; Atlanta: Scholars, 1988); and Mark S. Smith, *The Early History of God: Yahweh and the Other Deities in Ancient Israel* (San Francisco: Harper & Row, 1990), cited in Hurtado, *Lord Jesus Christ*, 29–30, n. 5.

[16] See esp. Larry W. Hurtado, 'First-Century Jewish Monotheism', JSNT 71 (1998): 3–26.

[17] Hist. 5.5.

[18] Wright, *Mission of God*, 105.

[19] Wright, *Mission of God*, 105.

[20] See ch. 4 in Wright, *Mission of God*, 105, esp. 106–9; also C. Kavin Rowe, 'Romans 10:13: What Is the Name of the Lord?' *HBT* 22 (2000): 135–73; idem, 'Luke and the Trinity: An Essay in Ecclesial Biblical Theology', *SJT* 56 (2003); idem, *Early Narrative Christology: The Lord in the Gospel of Luke* (BZNW 139; Berlin: de Gruyter, 2006). Contra James D. G. Dunn, *Christology in the Making: A New Testament Inquiry into the Origins of the Doctrine of the Incarnation* (2d ed.; Grand Rapids: Eerdmans, 1996), 259, who claims that 'only in the Fourth Gospel can we speak of a doctrine of the incarnation'. But see, e.g. the critique by C.E.B. Cranfield, 'Some Comments on Professor J.D.G. Dunn's *Christology in the Making: A New Testament Inquiry into the Origins of the Doctrine of the Incarnation*, with Special Reference to the Evidence of the Epistle to the Romans', in *The Glory of Christ in the New Testament: Studies in Christology in Memory of George Bradford Caird* (ed. L.D. Hurst and N.T. Wright; Oxford: Clarendon, 1987), 267–80 with regard to Romans; and Gordon D. Fee, *Pauline Christology* (Peabody, Mass.: Hendrickson, 2007), 500–512. What is more, the recent works by Bauckham, Lee and Hurtado have decisively undercut Dunn's thesis.

In light of the Jewish context of John's Gospel noted above and the Jewish belief in monotheism, it is apparent that any claims to deity by an individual such as Jesus would have been fiercely opposed by pious first-century Jews. Numerous passages in John's Gospel suggest that this is, in fact, what occurred when Jesus' Jewish contemporaries repeatedly attempted to stone Jesus on account of blasphemy (e.g. 5:18; 8:59; 10:31–3; cf. 11:8). Also, at Jesus' trial before Pilate, the Jews, after initially insinuating Jesus was a political threat to Roman imperial power, eventually insist that Jesus 'must die, because he claimed to be the Son of God' (19:7). Hence Jesus died, first and foremost, because he claimed to be God (cf. Matt. 26:65).[21]

Some believe that Second Temple Judaism held to a strict monotheism that rendered it impossible to attribute divinity to anyone other than God. In this case, only a radical break with Judaism would have allowed his followers to attribute divinity to Jesus. Hence Maurice Casey contends that 'the deity of Jesus is . . . *inherently* unJewish. The witness of Jewish texts is unvarying: belief that a second being is God involves departure from the Jewish community.'[22] Others favour the view that Second Temple Judaism was more flexible, pointing to various intermediary figures such as angels, exalted humans or personified divine attributes, claiming that these provide Jewish precedents for identifying Jesus as divine.[23]

Indeed, the Old Testament and Second Temple literature feature several passages where beings other than God are called 'god'. Philo refers to Moses as 'god' (*Mos.* 1.155–8; *Prob.* 42–4; cf. Exod. 7:1).[24] Human judges are called 'gods' in the LXX (Exod. 22:27) as are angels (Ps. 8:6;

---

[21] Darrel L. Bock, *Blasphemy and Exaltation in Judaism: The Charge against Jesus in Mark 14:53–65* (Grand Rapids: Baker, 2000).

[22] Maurice Casey, *From Jewish Prophet to Gentile God: The Origins and Development of New Testament Christology* (Louisville: Westminster John Knox, 1991), 176, cited in Marianne Meye Thompson, *The God of the Gospel of John* (Grand Rapids: Eerdmans, 2001), 28. See the critique of Casey's work in Hurtado, *Lord Jesus Christ*, 43–4 and James D. G. Dunn, 'The Making of Christology – Evolution or Unfolding?' in *Jesus of Nazareth: Lord and Christ. Essays on the Historical Jesus and New Testament Christology* (ed. Joel B. Green and Max Turner; Grand Rapids: Eerdmans, 1994), 437–52.

[23] Cf. Larry W. Hurtado, *One God, One Lord: Early Christian Devotion and Ancient Jewish Monotheism* (Edinburgh: T & T Clark, 1998); idem, *Lord Jesus Christ*. Though see the important clarification in Hurtado, *Lord Jesus Christ*, 29, n. 3, where Hurtado notes that he believes Jewish 'divine agency' traditions 'were *not* by themselves sufficient to explain the emergence or distinctive character of devotion to Jesus'.

[24] Philo also calls the Logos 'a second god' (*QG* 2.62; cf. Justin Martyr, *1 Apol.* 63.15; *Dial.* 56.4).

82:1, 6; 97:6; 138:1) and the mysterious figure of Melchizedek (11QMelch 2:24–5).[25] Yet intermediary figures such as these were clearly understood as creatures, and the line between God and created beings was clearly drawn (cf. Ezek. 28:2; Hos. 11:9). Rather than blurring divine-human distinctions, in passages such as these, beings who are not God are shown to exercise divine prerogatives.[26] Hence, these instances cannot serve as genuine precedents.

Rather than pointing to Jewish intermediary figures, therefore, it is most plausible that the early Christians identified 'Jesus directly with the one God of Israel' and included 'Jesus in the unique identity of this one God.'[27] If correct, this view has revolutionary implications for understanding the Christology of the New Testament. In Bauckham's words: 'the highest possible Christology, the inclusion of Jesus in the unique divine identity, was central to the faith of the early church even before any of the New Testament writings were written . . . Although there was development in understanding this inclusion of Jesus in the identity of God, the decisive step of so including him was made at the beginning.'[28]

What is more, this high Christology was entirely possible within strict Jewish monotheism. This explains why neither John nor the other NT writers evidence any consciousness of tension between the attribution of deity to Jesus and their Jewish monotheistic beliefs. Jesus' inclusion in the unique deity was novel, but did not compromise Jewish monotheism. John's Gospel also shows Jesus appropriating the divine name *'ănî hû'* (LXX: *egō eimi*).[29] At times, the expression is used simply meaning 'I am' without indicating a claim to deity on Jesus' part. At other times, especially in the seven absolute 'I am' sayings, Jesus' deity is clearly implied.[30]

---

[25] See Jesus' citation of Ps. 82:6 per John 10:34, on which see the discussion later on in this volume.

[26] So, rightly, Thompson, *God of the Gospel of John*, 45.

[27] Bauckham, *Gospels for All Christians*, 4.

[28] Bauckham, *Gospels for All Christians*, 27. Bauckham's findings stand in sharp contrast to those of Dunn, *Christology in the Making* (except for a new foreword, unchanged from the 1980 edition).

[29] Philip B. Harner, *The 'I Am' of the Fourth Gospel* (Philadelphia: Fortress, 1970); David M. Ball, 'I Am' in *John's Gospel: Literary Function, Background and Theological Implications* (JSNTSup 124; Sheffield: Sheffield Academic Press, 1996); Catrin H. Williams, *I am He: The Interpretation of 'ani hu' in Jewish and Early Christian Literature* (Tübingen: Mohr–Siebeck, 2000); Richard Bauckham, 'Monotheism and Christology in the Gospel of John', in *Contours of Christology in the New Testament* (ed. Richard N. Longenecker; Grand Rapids: Eerdmans, 2005), 153–63.

[30] 4:26; 6:20; 8:24, 28; 13:19; 18:5, 6, 8. Both Isaiah 40 – 66 and John's Gospel feature a total of nine (seven plus two) references to God or Jesus as 'I am'.

In keeping with Isaiah's vision of a new exodus for God's people, the Gospels provide a new narrative of God's acts.[31] Just as Israel knew God as the one who delivered the nation out of Egypt and told the story of that God, the NT writers identify God as the God of Jesus Christ and tell the story of Jesus as the account of the deliverance of God's people from sin.[32] This new story is consistent with the OT account of God and his acts on behalf of his people, yet it is new in the way God now has revealed himself and provided redemption in a final and universal way (1:18; cf. Heb. 1:1–3). In Jesus, the Creator and Ruler of the world has become its universal Saviour (4:42; cf. Luke 2:1).

Jesus' inclusion in the identity of God means that God must be conceived in relational terms, uniting God as Father, Son and Holy Spirit. God, thus, transcends one-dimensional conceptions of human identity. This entails an element of novelty: 'Nothing in the Second Temple Jewish understanding of divine identity contradicts the possibility of interpersonal relationship within the divine identity, but on the other hand there is little, if anything, that anticipates it.'[33] Jesus is now 'God with us' (Matt. 1:25) and 'will be with' his people (Matt. 28:20).[34] 'The Father, the Son and the Holy Spirit' names the newly disclosed identity of God revealed in the Gospels' account of Jesus (e.g. Matt. 28:19).[35]

With this we have come full circle, and yet have come to realize a massive advance in God's self-revelation in and through his Son. As noted at the outset, OT Israel's belief in one God is grounded in the *Shema* of Deuteronomy 6:4. In 1 Corinthians 8:4–6, Paul applies this most foundational of all Jewish monotheistic texts decisively and unmistakably to Jesus, inserting Jesus into the 'one God, one Lord' formula and connecting him with the creative work of God the Father:

> We know that an idol is nothing at all in the world and that there is no God but one. For even if there are so-called gods, whether in heaven or

---

[31] Bauckham, *Gospels for All Christians*, 71; idem, *Jesus and the Eyewitnesses*, 277. See also Kevin J. Vanhoozer, *The Drama of Doctrine: A Canonical-Linguistic Approach to Christian Theology* (Louisville: Westminster John Knox, 2005), in further development of Hans Urs von Balthasar, *Theo-drama: Theological Dramatic Theory* (trans. Graham Harrison; 4 vols.; San Francisco: Ignatius, 1988, 1990, 1992 and 1994).

[32] See esp. John 1:14–18 with its repeated allusions to Exodus 33 – 34, esp. 33:18 and 34:6.

[33] Bauckham, *Gospels for All Christians*, 75.

[34] See the important monograph-length treatment by D.D. Kupp, *Matthew's Emmanuel: Divine Presence and God's People in the First Gospel* (SNTSMS 90; Cambridge: Cambridge University Press, 1996).

[35] Bauckham, *Gospels for All Christians*, 76.

on earth . . ., yet for us there is but one God, the Father, from whom all things came and for whom we live; and there is but one Lord, Jesus Christ, through whom all things came and through whom we live.

Richard Bauckham aptly draws out the implications of Paul's statement for biblical monotheism:

The only possible way to understand Paul as maintaining monotheism is to understand him to be including Jesus in the unique identity of the one God affirmed in the Shema' . . . Paul is not adding to the one God of the Shema' a 'Lord' the Shema' does not mention. He is identifying Jesus as the 'Lord' whom the Shema' affirms to be one. In this unprecedented reformulation of the Shema', the unique identity of the one God consists of the one God, the Father, and the one Lord, his Messiah (who is implicitly regarded as the Son of the Father).[36]

This shows that Paul and the early church, as well as John, included Jesus within the identity of the one God confessed in the *Shema* and believed that Jesus shared in the identity of YHWH, in keeping with Jesus' own claim that he and the Father are one. Contrary to the Jewish charge that Jesus' claim constituted a breach of their monotheistic beliefs (cf., e.g. John 10:31–3), Jesus' followers understood that Jesus' claim did not imply that he was a second God alongside, and in addition to, God the Father (ditheism), but that his deity was to be accommodated within the framework of Jewish monotheism in such a way that the one and only God affirmed in the *Shema* could accommodate the notion of Father, Son and Spirit – three in one – as God.[37]

---

[36] Bauckham, 'Biblical Theology and the Problems of Monotheism', 224 cited in Wright, *Mission of God*, 111–12. See also N.T. Wright, *The Climax of the Covenant: Christ and the Law in Pauline Theology* (Edinburgh: T & T Clark, 1991), 120–36; Hurtado, *Lord Jesus Christ*, 123–6 (with implications for Jesus' pre-existence, on which see also Douglas J. Moo, 'The Christology of the Early Pauline Letters', in *Contours of Christology* (ed. Richard N. Longenecker), 178–9 and the discussion below) et passim; David B. Capes, *Old Testament Yahweh Texts in Paul's Christology* (WUNT 2/47; Tübingen: Mohr-Siebeck, 1992); and Fee, *Pauline Christology*, 88–94.

[37] This is why there is no contradiction between the church's worship of God as the Trinity and its claim that its God is Israel's God, a question addressed by Bruce D. Marshall, 'Do Christians Worship the God of Israel?' in *Knowing the Triune God: The Work of the Spirit in the Practices of the Church* (ed. James J. Buckley and David S. Yeago; Grand Rapids: Eerdmans, 2001), 258, who notes that 'the lack of referential fixity in Christian discourse about the God of Israel teaches us . . . that the Father is the God of Israel, the Son is the God of Israel, and the Holy Spirit is the God of Israel, yet they are not three gods of Israel, but one God of Israel.'

The Background of John's Portrayal of Jesus' Pre-existence

One important question that has received considerable attention in recent years is what led the early church to conclude that Jesus pre-existed with God in eternity past. In a recent study, A.H.I. Lee demonstrated convincingly, and against the preponderance of much contemporary scholarship, that neither Jewish angelology nor the pre-existent Messiah ever exerted sufficient influence on early Christology to serve as ready-made categories for viewing Jesus as a divine and pre-existent being alongside God. Rather, the early Christian under-standing of Jesus as the pre-existent Son of God is the result of early Christian exegesis of Psalm 110:1 and 2:7 in the light of Jesus' self-understanding as the Son of God.[38]

According to Lee, Jewish wisdom traditions never issued in person-ified divine attributes that took on divine hypostases separate from God. Rather, these enabled Second Temple Jews to speak of God's activity in the world without sacrificing the notion of his transcen-dence. Viewing himself as sustaining a unique personal relationship to God as his Father, Jesus was the Messiah because he was the Son of God, and his consciousness of divine sonship played a significant role in the development of early Christology. Hence, Jesus' self-under-standing is foundational for the early Christian conception of Jesus as the pre-existent Son of God. The parable of the wicked tenants, for example, makes clear that Jesus was God's Son sent into this world from above.[39]

In particular, Jesus' consciousness of divine sonship laid the foun-dation for the early church's messianic exegesis of Psalm 110:1 and 2:7 with reference to Jesus (rooted, again, in Jesus' own usage). Through its messianic exegesis of these two Psalms and other similar passages, the early church came to confirm what it was already beginning to believe on the basis of Jesus' self-consciousness and his resurrection. In Psalm 110:1, the early church found biblical grounding for the notion of Jesus' resurrection as his exaltation to God's right hand (see especially Acts

---

[38] Aquila H. I. Lee, *From Messiah to Preexistent Son: Jesus' Self-Consciousness and Early Christian Exegesis of Messianic Psalms* (WUNT 2/192; Tübingen: Mohr-Siebeck, 2005). See already Bauckham, *Gospels for All Christians*, 29–31; and Simon Gathercole, *The Pre-existent Son: Recovering the Christologies of Matthew, Mark, and Luke* (Grand Rapids: Eerdmans, 2006) on the Synoptic material.

[39] See the important discussion of Mark 12:1–9 in Markus Bockmuehl, *Seeing the Word: Refocusing New Testament Study* (Studies in Theological Interpretation; Grand Rapids: Baker, 2006), 215–20.

2:34–5). Importantly, the early Christians did not view Jesus' resurrection as conferring on him an essentially new status but as confirming the status he already possessed.

The early Christian understanding of Jesus as Lord finds an important point of departure in Jesus' treatment of Psalm 110:1 with reference to himself as David's Lord who stands and exists before David. This implies Jesus' claim of pre-existence, which is also confirmed by his statement before the Sanhedrin in Mark 14:62. Psalm 2:7, likewise, was understood by the early church as a prophecy concerning Jesus' divine sonship, which was decisively fulfilled at his resurrection and exaltation (Acts 13:33; cf. Acts 4:25–6). Jesus did not become God's Son at the resurrection; he already was God's Son prior to the crucifixion, and his resurrection and exaltation merely confirmed his status as Son of God.

Conversely, wisdom Christology is not clearly present in Paul's writings.[40] Rather, the early Christian understanding of Jesus as the pre-existent Son of God, aided by its messianic exegesis of certain psalms, led it to express this conviction by using Jewish wisdom traditions. Hence, the church expressed the implications of its conviction that Jesus was the Son of God, namely that Jesus was active in creation and co-eternal with God the Father, in terms provided by Jewish wisdom traditions. Thus, the latter were not the *source* for the church's understanding of Jesus' pre-existence but rather one way of expressing the *implications* of this conviction at which the church had arrived on different grounds.

If Lee is correct, John did not derive his Christology from Jewish wisdom traditions,[41] but rather chose to contextualize his understanding of Jesus' pre-existence and divine sonship by couching some of the implications in Jewish wisdom categories, a different procedure altogether. This hypothesis comports well with the internal data of John's Gospel, mentioned above, regarding the grounds of Jewish opposition to Jesus during his earthly ministry, namely Jesus' implicit and explicit claims to deity. Intermittent attempts to stone Jesus on account of blasphemy throughout John's Gospel, and the Jews' remark before Pilate that Jesus deserved to die because he claimed to be the Son of God confirm that Jesus claimed to be God.

---

[40] Fee, *Pauline Christology*, 594–619.
[41] Contra, e.g. Ben Witherington, *John's Wisdom* (Peabody, Mass.: Hendrickson, 1995), following Dunn.

Christ-Devotion and Exclusivist Jewish Monotheism

In his work *Lord Jesus Christ*, Larry Hurtado argues three basic interrelated theses: (1) 'devotion to Jesus emerges phenomenally early in circles of his followers, and cannot be restricted to a secondary stage of religious development or explained as the product of extraneous forces'; (2) 'devotion to Jesus was exhibited in an unparalleled intensity and diversity of expression, for which we have no true analogy in the religious environment of the time'; and (3) 'this intense devotion to Jesus, which includes reverencing him as divine, was offered and articulated characteristically within a firm stance of exclusivist monotheism, particularly in the circles of early Christians that . . . helped to establish what became mainstream . . . Christianity.'[42]

According to Hurtado: 'the exclusivist monotheism of ancient Judaism is the crucial religious context in which to view early Christ-devotion', and this monotheism helped shape Christ-devotion 'especially in those Christian circles concerned to maintain a fidelity to the biblical tradition of the one God.'[43] Central to this exclusive monotheism is a sharp distinction between legitimate and illegitimate recipients of worship: 'Jesus is not reverenced as another deity of any independent origin or significance; instead, his divine significance is characteristically expressed in terms of his relationship to the one God.'[44] Hence, Jesus devotion was binitarian (worshipping both God and Jesus), but not ditheistic.[45]

John's claim that Jesus is 'Christ' and 'Son of God' amounts to more than asserting that Jesus is Israel's rightful king. Rather, these designations express the belief that Jesus was also divine and of heavenly origin.[46] Other than in the Synoptics, where the charge of blasphemy surfaces only at the trial of Jesus, in John's Gospel, Jesus is charged with blasphemy throughout his ministry (cf. 5:18; 8:59; 10:31–3). John's adaptation of the Isaianic 'I am' formula and of the 'glory' and 'lifted up' motifs also intimately associate Jesus with God in a way unparalleled by any other Jewish tradition of the period.[47] Remarkably, Jesus is given 'glory' by God (e.g. 17:5, 24) despite the fact that God does not share his glory with another (Isa. 42:8; 48:11).

---

[42] Hurtado, *Lord Jesus Christ*, 2–3.
[43] Hurtado, *Lord Jesus Christ*, 48.
[44] Hurtado, *Lord Jesus Christ*, 51.
[45] Hurtado, *Lord Jesus Christ*, 52–3.
[46] Hurtado, *Lord Jesus Christ*, 362.
[47] Hurtado, *Lord Jesus Christ*, 379.

On the basis of the identification of Jesus with Isaiah's Suffering Servant, which is doubtless grounded in Jesus' own self-understanding (e.g. Luke 4:18), John read Isaiah 40 – 55 as referring, not to one, but to two divine figures, God on the one hand and the Suffering Servant on the other.[48] In Isaiah, John found warrant for seeing Jesus as a figure properly identified with the 'I am' of Isaiah and the exodus (cf. Exod. 3:14), and sharing the glory of God as the one who bore the transgressions of many and who was 'lifted up' and exalted by God.[49] Indeed, the Gospel's portrayal of Jesus as the Word sent by God which, once it has accomplished its purpose, returns to the one who sent it, derives directly from Isaiah 55:11.[50]

Other startling attributions of divinity in John's Gospel are entailed by its emphasis on Jesus being given God's name (e.g. 17:11–12); the requirement of believing in Jesus' name (e.g. 1:12); and by the frequent references to prayer being rendered in Jesus' name (e.g. 14:13–14). At the same time, Jesus is portrayed by John as both obedient to the Father and yet equal to him (compare 14:28 with 10:30); and as both human and divine (compare 4:9 or 11:35 with 8:58 or 17:5).[51] Jesus is a historical, earthly, human figure who is primarily perceived by his contemporaries as a rabbi, a Jewish religious teacher though, at the same time, he is also the Son of God.[52]

Jesus' humanity (his 'flesh', 1:14) is required particularly for the efficacy of his redemptive cross-death (e.g. 6:51–8).[53] Significantly, the

---

[48] Hurtado, *Lord Jesus Christ*, 380, citing Donald Juel, *Messianic Exegesis: Christological Interpretation of the Old Testament in Early Christianity* (Philadelphia: Fortress, 1988), 119–33; and Bauckham, *Gospels for All Christians*, 47–69.

[49] On the 'I am' motif, see briefly above. Regarding the phrase 'lifted up', compare 3:14; 8:28; 12:32 with Isa. 52:13, which speaks of the Suffering Servant being 'raised and lifted up and highly exalted' in the context of a reference to the disfigured Servant 'sprinkl[ing] many nations'. On the use of Isaiah in John's Gospel, see esp. Craig A. Evans, 'Obduracy and the Lord's Servant: Some Observations on the Use of the Old Testament in the Fourth Gospel', in *Early Jewish and Christian Exegesis: Studies in Memory of William Hugh Brownlee* (ed. Craig A. Evans and William F. Stinespring; Atlanta: Scholars, 1987), 221–36.

[50] Andreas J. Köstenberger, *John* (BECNT; Grand Rapids: Baker, 2004), 27.

[51] On the former, see Christopher Cowan, 'The Father and Son in the Fourth Gospel: Johannine Subordination Revisited', *JETS* 49 (2006): 115–35; on the latter, see Marianne Meye Thompson, *The Humanity of Jesus in the Fourth Gospel* (Philadelphia: Fortress, 1988), ca. Ernst Käsemann, *The Testament of Jesus* (trans. Gerhard Krodel; Philadelphia: Fortress, 1968).

[52] See Andreas J. Köstenberger, 'Jesus as Rabbi in the Fourth Gospel', *BBR* 8 (1998): 97–128.

[53] On the nature of Jesus' work, see Andreas J. Köstenberger, *The Missions of Jesus and the Disciples according to the Fourth Gospel* (Grand Rapids: Eerdmans, 1998), 74–81.

fourth evangelist bears witness to Jesus' full humanity at the cross (19:34–5). Jesus is also shown to be endowed with the Spirit (1:32–3; 3:34) and as performing a series of startling signs confirming his messianic identity (e.g. 2:11). The Spirit's role as 'other helping presence' and as sent by both God and Jesus ties him intricately to Jesus the Son. The tri-unity of Father, Son and Spirit forms the paradigm and basis for the love and unity among Jesus' followers and for their mission to the world as they re-present his message and follow their Lord (20:21; cf. 17:18).[54]

Implications for John's Gospel

The understanding of the Jewish monotheistic framework for the characterization of Jesus in John's Gospel is relevant for a proper reading of John's prologue and for understanding the portrayal of Jesus throughout the Gospel as the Son of the Father, as one with the Father and as the 'I am'.[55] The depiction of the Word in John 1:1 and of its instrumentality in creation in 1:3 makes clear that the Word, rather than being a creature, belongs to God's own unique, uncreated identity and, thus, has life in itself (1:4; cf. 5:26). John's christological retelling of Genesis has several Second Temple precedents, though it is of course unique in its reference to Jesus as the Word.[56]

According to John, the Word, while distinct from God, is at the same time intrinsic to his own identity – it existed with God 'in the beginning' (1:1).[57] In the Gospel proper, however, the designation of Jesus as the Word is, naturally, superseded by Jesus' own way of speaking of himself as the Son of the Father. In its portrayal of Jesus as distinct from God and yet intrinsic to his identity, John's Gospel does not compromise Jewish monotheism, since, while being 'with God', the Word 'was

---

[54] See Köstenberger, *Missions of Jesus and the Disciples,* and idem, *Theology of John,* ch. 15.

[55] See esp. Bauckham, 'Monotheism and Christology', 148–66.

[56] Bauckham, 'Monotheism and Christology', 150.

[57] Note, in this regard, the thesis by Bauckham, *Jesus and the Eyewitnesses,* that the four canonical Gospels, including John, constitute eyewitness testimony and his proposal that John, like Mark and Luke, features an *inclusio* of eyewitness testimony, (see 1:40; 21:24). More importantly, 1:1, in conjunction with 1:18, indicates that Jesus himself, who was 'in the beginning' with God, serves as the ultimate eyewitness (cf. 18:37), whose testimony is foundational for the Beloved Disciple's testimony: compare Jesus' position *eis ton kolpon* (1:18) with the Beloved Disciple's position en tō kolpō of Jesus (13:23; reiterated in slightly different terms in 21:20).

God' in its own right and hence one with God (1:1–2; cf. 10:30; see also 5:26), rather than a second God, that is, a divine entity apart from the one and only God revealed in Scripture as the Creator and Ruler of all things.

Implicit in Jesus' inclusion in the identity of God is his right to receiving worship (5:23; cf. 9:38; 20:28). His inclusion in the divine identity is also indicated by the possible allusion to the *Shema* of Deuteronomy 6:4 in John 10:30 (cf. 1 Cor. 8:6).[58] As Bauckham writes: 'Without contradicting or rejecting any of the existing features of Jewish monotheism, the Fourth Gospel, therefore, redefines Jewish monotheism as christological monotheism. Christological monotheism is a form of monotheism in which the relationship of Jesus the Son to his Father is integral to the definition of who the one true God is.'[59] It is for reasons such as these that John is able to affirm unequivocally that Jesus is both the Son of God and, indeed, himself God, without finding himself in contradiction with the first commandment and the *Shema*. It is hard to overstate the relevance and implications of this fact for Jewish believers today.

---

[58] The change from masculine to neuter 'one' is a necessary adaptation of language (Bauckham, 'Monotheism and Christology', 163).

[59] Bauckham, 'Monotheism and Christology', 165.

5

Martin Luther and the Jewish People with Implications for Jewish Missions

Berthold Schwarz

To talk or to teach about 'Luther and the Jews' could be a dangerous undertaking for at least two major reasons. First, 'Luther was terribly wrong in his reasoning against Jews, so he cannot be right in other parts of his theology.' Therefore, he should not be received as an authority for the church anymore. I do not share this opinion, but it is taught in several ways, and it is often heard in the case against Luther's anti-Jewishness. Furthermore, if we do not share this judgement against Luther, we are likely to find ourselves immediately labelled as anti-Semitic as well.

Second, another danger could be that Luther's reasoning against the Jews is wrongly understood. Indeed there exist several interpretations of how Luther's anti-Jewishness should be interpreted. The popularized, non-academic extremes are either: 'Luther is all in all the believer's enemy because of his cruel words against Jews' [i.e. total condemnation], or: 'Luther has said some wrong things against Jews and erred in his understanding of the Jews, but he is still our hero of faith. Therefore, his words against Jews are of minor importance' [i.e. somehow a glorification].

Both of these extremes are taught today among Christians, Jews, scholars and in Messianic-Jewish circles, but they should both be avoided.[1]

---

[1] W. Bienert's interpretation of Luther on Jews is all in all the weakest and most inaccurate though.

Honest answers must be given as to why Luther said what he did; unfortunately, those answers do not completely free him of anti-Semitism.[2]

While I do not consider myself an expert in Luther-studies, I have tried nevertheless to present a reasonable and fair assessment, based on careful research and study of the sources.[3] According to this research, I cannot agree with either extreme. I personally do not condone Luther's anti-Jewish writings. He was deeply wrong in saying what he said. I have sadness and anger towards Luther's later anti-Jewish writings and his treatment of Jews. Neither can I accept Luther's teaching on Jews as if it was just a minor aberration (it was not!), nor can I condemn him, making him a *persona non grata* to be erased out of Christian theology.

This paper will present several crucial aspects of Luther's teaching on the Jewish people and close with selected implications for Jewish missions.[4]

Luther's Teaching on the Jewish People

Writing on the Jews relatively peripheral

Popularly speaking, Luther's ministry as a reformer begins in 1517 with the posting of the *95 Theses* at the door of Wittenberg's Schlosskirche. His 'anti-Jewish' writings span his last eight years (1538–46). Thus, for around twenty years he said little about the Jews, and what he did say was relatively positive (when judged by the standards of popular culture of his time). Therefore, we can conclude that Luther's attitude towards the Jews is somewhat peripheral to his overall life's work because, as the largest collections of his writings show, comparatively few of those pages are dedicated to his opinions on the

---

[2] Cf. Beatrice Acklin-Zimmermann, *Die Gesetzesinterpretation in den Römerbriefkommentaren von Peter Abaelard und Martin Luther. Eine Untersuchung auf dem Hintergrund der Antijudaismusdiskussion* (Frankfurt am Main: Otto Lembeck, 2004), 255.

[3] My reasoning is mainly based on the research done by Beatrice Acklin-Zimmermann, Roland Bainton, Walther Bienert, Johannes Bosseder, Martin Brecht, Eric Gritsch, Carter Lindberg, Heiko A. Oberman, Peter von der Osten-Sacken, Gordon Rupp, James Swan, Johannes Wallmann and others.

[4] 'LW' refers to *Luther's Works*, English edition (55 volumes). 'WA' refers to *Luther's Works*, Weimar edition, the official academic German version of *Luther's Works*.

Jews.[5] But there is no getting around it: *in his later years, Luther did say some awful things about the Jewish people*. Where Luther was gravely mistaken, Protestants must admit his faults.

Treatment of the Jews not racist

It is helpful to explain some of the features of Luther's treatment of the Jews and the historical context in which these writings originated. It can be shown that Luther's writings began favourably towards the Jews but, as the years progressed, he developed a deep hostility that was nurtured within the framework of the medieval stereotype and bias, as well as his own apocalyptic expectations.

It should be kept in mind that Luther's later anti-Jewish tracts were written from a position different from modern anti-Semitism. Luther was born into a society that was anti-Jewish, but it was not like today's anti-Judaic type of society which is racist and based on racist factors. As far as I understand the facts, Luther had no objections to integrating converted Jews into Christian society. He had nothing against Jews as 'Jews'. He had something against their religion because he believed it denied and blasphemed Christ.[6] As Heiko Oberman points out:

> One thing must be clearly understood: Luther was anti-Jewish in his repeated warnings against the Jews as bearers of an anti-Christian religion which had established itself both within and outside Christianity. But Luther was not an anti-Semite or racist of any kind because – to apply the test appropriate to his time – for him a baptized Jew is fully Christian. Conversely, he said that among us Christians in Germany there are horrifyingly many who in their hearts deny Christ. Those are the true Jews! Not race but belief in the law, in good works, makes Jews.[7]

---

[5] 'Much attention has been focused upon Luther's attitude toward the Jews, although they were quite peripheral to his reformatory concern, as a comparison of the very few pages on the Jews with the total output in the 110 folio volumes of his collected works suggest', in Lewis W. Spitz, *The Protestant Reformation* (New York, 1985), 357. George S. Robbert points out that 'Luther wrote some 60,000 pages, much of it later in life' ('Martin Luther's Later Years' in *Christian History 39/ XII, No. 3*, 34). The material Luther wrote in regards to the Jews probably spans some hundred pages. Of that amount, only a small percentage involves hostile rhetoric against Jews.

[6] Cf. LW 26:118.

[7] Heiko A. Oberman, *The Impact of the Reformation* (Grand Rapids: Eerdmans, 1994), 76. See also H.A. Oberman: *The Roots of Anti-Semitism: In the Age of Renaissance and Reformation* (Philadelphia:Fortress, 1984), 102, or Kenneth A. Strand, 'Current Issues

I agree with Oberman and say: Luther cannot rightly be labelled an anti-Semite.[8] In his article 'Luther's Attitudes toward Judaism', Carter Lindberg provides a good example, showing that Luther's anti-Jewish writings were not motivated by racism. Lindberg says:

> More to the point is Luther's stance on religious intermarriage. In his criticism of the medieval Catholic canonical prohibition against a Christian marrying a Jew, Luther wrote, 'Just as I may eat, drink, sleep, walk, ride with, buy from, speak to, and deal with a heathen, Jew, Turk, or heretic, so I may also marry and continue in wedlock with him. Pay no attention to the precepts of those fools who forbid it. You will find plenty of Christians – and indeed the greater part of them – who are worse in their secret unbelief than any Jew, heathen, Turk, or heretic. A heathen is just as much a man or a woman – God's good creation – as St. Peter, St. Paul, and St. Lucy, not to speak of a slack and spurious Christian'.[9]

Rather than being motivated by racist factors, Luther's criticisms were motivated by theological concerns. Luther directed intensely abusive language against Anabaptists, heretics, spiritualizers and the papacy as well as against the Jews (and even against his German fellow citizens!). Luther felt these groups were united in the conviction that men were ultimately made right before God by works of the law.[10] Anabaptism held a moralistic view of the gospel with an emphasis on the heavy burden of righteousness placed upon men in order to be accepted before God. Lawyers made their living by imposing the law. The papacy was viewed as the antichrist, which promoted a false religion with a false view of salvation through obedience to the law. The Jews had a religion based upon works righteousness. When Luther attacked these groups, he felt he was attacking the devil – the underlying spirit of works righteousness, of a ministry dealing with the works of the law.[11]

---

and Trends In Luther Studies' in *Andrews University Seminary Studies* 22/1 (Spring 1984): 141–2. Cf. LW 26:354.

[8] Cf. Eric Gritsch, 'Was Luther Anti-Semitic?' in *Christian History* 39/ XII, No. 3, 39; see also E. Gritsch, *Martin – God's Court Jester: Luther in Retrospect* (Philadelphia:Fortress, 1983), 145.

[9] Carter Lindberg, 'Tainted Greatness: Luther's Attitudes toward Judaism and their Historical Reception' in *Tainted Greatness: Antisemitism and Cultural Heroes* (ed. Nancy A. Harrowitz, Philadelphia: Temple University Press, 1994), 20–21.

[10] LW 26:9–10 (on Galatians, 1531).

[11] Cf. H.A. Oberman, *Luther: Mensch zwischen Gott und Teufel* (Berlin: Severin und Siedler, 1991) (*Luther: Man Between God and the Devil* (New York: Yale University Press, 1989)); Hans-Martin Barth, *Der Teufel und Jesus Christus in der Theologie*

In his last expositions on Genesis in 1544, Luther makes it explicit that no one has the right to boast on their race or lineage:

> Accordingly, the Jews have no grounds for boasting; they should humble themselves and acknowledge their maternal blood. For on their father's side they are Israelites; but on their mother's side they are Gentiles, Moabites, Assyrians, Egyptians, Canaanites. And by this God wanted to point out that the Messiah would be a brother and a cousin of both the Jews and the Gentiles, if not according to their paternal genealogy, at least according to their maternal nature. Consequently, there is no distinction between Jews and Gentiles, except that Moses later separated this people from the Gentiles by a different form of worship and political regime. Moreover, these things were written to make it known to all that the Messiah would gather the Gentiles and the Jews into one and the same church, just as they are joined by nature and consanguinity.[12]

In his commentary on Galatians 3:28, Luther explains that we are all equal. No particular people have any right to claim special privilege before God:

> 'There is neither magistrate nor subject, neither professor nor listener, neither teacher nor pupil, neither lady nor servant.' For in Christ Jesus all social stations, even those that were divinely ordained, are nothing. Male, female, slave, free, Jew, Gentile, king, subject – these are, of course, good creatures of God. But in Christ, that is, in the matter of salvation, they amount to nothing, for all their wisdom, righteousness, devotion, and authority.[13]

Luther's most well known anti-Jewish writing, *On the Jews and their Lies*, is often quoted and cited as the clearest example of Luther's anti-Semitism. Interestingly though, this very document proves that Luther was not a *biological* anti-Semite, he was not against the Jews as *people* nor did he seek for their extermination.[14] In that treatise, Luther launches into a long section arguing against any notion that the Jews

Martin Luthers (FKDG 19, Göttingen: Vandenhoeck und Ruprecht. 1967). Cf. C. Lindberg, 'Tainted Greatness: Luther's Attitudes Toward Judaism and Their Historical Reception', in *Tainted Greatness* (ed. Harrowitz), 22.

[12] See LW 7:14; LW 26:236.

[13] LW 26:353.

[14] Cf. Bertold Klappert: 'Erwählung und Rechtfertigung', in *Die Juden und Martin Luther – Martin Luther und die Juden: Geschichte, Wirkungsgeschichte, Herausforderung* (ed. Heinz Kremers; 2d ed.; Neukirchen-Vluyn: Neukirchener Verlag, 1987), 368–410, esp. 377. Cf. also Lindberg, 'Tainted Greatness', 30, n. 1; Oberman, *Luther: Man Between God and the Devil*, 294.

are better than anyone else. He puts forth an *alleged* popular anti-Jewish argument that they thanked God that they were not born Gentiles or women. In arguing against this 'nonsense', Luther mocks those who think any one particular people is better than another:

> [T]he Greek Plato daily accorded God such praise and thanksgiving – if such arrogance and blasphemy may be termed praise of God. This man, too, praised his gods for these three items: that he was a human being and not an animal; a male and not a female; a Greek and not a non-Greek or barbarian . . . Similarly, the Italians fancy themselves the only human beings; they imagine that all other people in the world are nonhumans, mere ducks or mice by comparison.[15]

Luther also levels the playing field in regard to gender or sexuality. He sees it as blasphemy to view women as inferior to men:

> [They] are also human beings and the image of God as well as we; moreover, they are our own flesh and blood, such as mother, sister, daughter, housewives, etc.[16]

Luther insists that, before God, we are all equal and this equality consists in the entire human race standing condemned by our sin before a holy God.[17]

Negative views on Jews by contemporary society

Having highlighted some aspects of Luther's anti-Jewishness as not being based on racist reasons, we should have a look to the society in which Luther lived. Martin Luther was born into a society (Roman Catholic and Protestant) which largely accepted an attitude of animosity towards the

---

[15] LW 47:140.

[16] LW 47:142.

[17] '[T]o strut before God and boast about being so noble, so exalted, and so rich compared to other people – that is devilish arrogance, since every birth according to the flesh is condemned before him without exception in the aforementioned verse, if his covenant and word do not come to the rescue once again and create a new and different birth, quite different from the old, first birth.' (LW 47:142); 'Oh, what do we poor muckworms, maggots, stench, and filth presume to boast of before him who is the God and Creator of heaven and earth, who made us out of dirt and out of nothing! And as far as our nature, birth, and essence are concerned, we are but dirt and nothing in his eyes; all that we are and have comes from his grace and his rich mercy.' (LW 47:154).

Jews. Since the early church the Jews were stigmatized as those who killed Christ and deserved to experience God's wrath as his rejected people. They had become – as a sad development over the centuries – the scapegoats of society, blamed for countless evils befalling the medieval age. The populace had gone as far to create fictional crimes to charge to their account. They were said to partake in ritual murders slaughtering Christian children for blood to use during Passover.[18] Mark U. Edwards explains:

> Only on rare occasions did Luther encounter Jews; he never lived in close proximity to them, but he inherited a tradition, both theological and popular, of hostility toward them. He lived within a larger community, Western Christendom, which saw Jews as a rejected people guilty of the murder of Christ, and capable of murdering Christian children for their own evil purposes. And he lived within a local community that had expelled Jews some ninety years earlier.[19]

In the earliest days of his academic career, Luther held four theological opinions on the Jews, which were to remain unchanged throughout his whole life. Gordon Rupp presents these as follows:

1. God's wrath has fallen on his disobedient people and only God can take it away.
2. Humanly speaking, the Jews are unconvertible and they cannot be saved by human action.
3. Because they reproach God and blaspheme against Christ, their faith is an actively anti-Christian religion.
4. And this one makes the difference: All these things are true not only of the Jews, but of all human beings who set themselves against God, so that unbelieving Jews and unbelieving Christians or Gentiles are comprehended within one solidarity of guilt.[20]

---

[18] See Mark U. Edwards, Jr., *Luther's Last Battles* (Ithaca: Cornell University Press, 1983), 118–19.

[19] Edwards, *Luther's Last Battles*, 121. Cf. Gordon Rupp, *Martin Luther and the Jews* (London: The Council of Christians and Jews, 1972), 10. Cf. also C. Müller, 'Luthers Haltung zu den Juden', in *Auf dem Weg zu einem Neuanfang. Dokumentation zur Erklärung der Evangelisch-Lutherischen Kirche in Bayern zum Thema Christen und Juden* (ed. W. Kraus; Munich, 1999), 135–49.

[20] Rupp, *Martin Luther and the Jews*, 9; Gritsch, *Martin – God's Court Jester*, 133. Cf. the sources analyzed by Peter von der Osten-Sacken, *Martin Luther und die Juden. Neu untersucht anhand von Anton Margarithas, "Der gantz Juedisch glaub"* (1530/31), (Stuttgart, 2002), 47–208.

Changes to Luther's View during his lifetime

Friendly Interest

Many Luther scholars say that Luther's views of the Jews underwent an extreme change in his lifetime. They claim that Luther at first showed friendly interest and compassion to the Jews, only to turn against them later on. Luther's earliest known dealing with the Jews occurred in 1510. A converted Jew named Pfefferkorn accused his former people of all kinds of cruelties and blasphemies. He then arranged to have Jewish books burned. John (Johannes) Reuchlin, the foremost Hebrew scholar of Germany, opposed Pfefferkorn's actions. Luther sided with Reuchlin. Some take this to be an indication of Luther's early pro-Jewish views. But Luther's actions, of course, were not strictly pro-Jewish but were more in support of true scholarship, especially where it would aid biblical study. But some of the Jews of the day failed to understand Luther correctly. A Jewish historian correctly notes:

> They were overjoyed that at last a famous Christian teacher spoke of them as human beings. A few enthusiasts among the Jews of Germany went so far in their misunderstanding of Luther that they actually congratulated him on the steps he was taking to come closer to Judaism.[21]

Luther apparently was not troubled by this development at this time. He was optimistic that the Jews, the true blood relatives of Christ, would be converted once the abuses of the Roman Catholic Church were removed.

Luther saw the great value of Reuchlin's *Rudiments*, the first Hebrew grammar published in Germany, and expressed his concern in 1514 for the great Hebraist: '[L]et us pray for our Reuchlin.'[22] Luther saw great value in learning the Hebrew language. When an opportunity arose in 1519 to have the learned Jewish scholar Matthias Adrian teach at Wittenberg, Luther made haste to acquire him. This is not to suggest that Luther was a defender of Judaism. Rather, his primary concern was 'the preservation of Hebrew literature for scholarly purposes, rather than the merits of Judaism or the Jews as such.'[23]

---

[21] Solomon Grayzel, *A History of the Jews* (New York: New American Library, 1968), 374.

[22] LW 48:10.

[23] LW 47:127.

In 1516, one finds Luther moving towards the position of friendliness towards the Jews that would be explicit in his work in the 1520s:

> [M]any people are proud with marvelous stupidity when they call the Jews dogs, evildoers, or whatever they like, while they too, and equally, do not realize who or what they are in the sight of God. Boldly they heap blasphemous insults upon them, when they ought to have compassion on them and fear the same punishments for themselves. Moreover, as if certain concerning themselves and the others, they rashly pronounce themselves blessed and the others cursed. Such today are the theologians of Cologne, who are so stupid in their zeal, that in their articles, or rather their inarticulate and inept writings, they say that the Jews are accursed. Why? Because they have forgotten what is said in the following chapter: 'Bless and do not curse' (Rom. 12:14), and in another place: 'When reviled, we bless; when slandered, we try to conciliate' (1 Cor. 4:12–13). They wish to convert the Jews by force and curses, but God will resist them.[24]

With Luther's proclamation of the gospel in the early 1520s, he re-evaluated the plight of the Jews against the prevailing culture of his day. For a time, he rose above cultural conformity and extended the gospel message to the Jewish people. Perhaps it was due to the persecution he received from the Roman Catholic Church. In his exposition of the *Magnificat* in 1521, Luther said: 'We ought, therefore, not to treat the Jews in so unkindly a spirit, for there are future Christians among them, and they are turning every day.'[25] In his lectures on the Psalms during the period of 1519–21, Luther chastises his 'Christian' culture that oppressed the Jews:

> The fury of some Christians (if they are to be called Christians) is damnable. They imagine that they are doing God a service when they persecute the Jews most hatefully, think everything evil of them, and insult them with extreme arrogance and contempt amid their pitiable misfortunes, whereas, according to the example of this psalm and that of Paul (Rom. 9:1), a man ought to be most heartily sorry for them and continually pray for them. These folk ought certainly see to it that they listen to Paul (Rom. 11:18): 'Boast not against the branches. But if thou boast, thou bearest not the root, but the root thee.' And again (v. 20): 'Be

---

[24] LW 25:428; cf. LW 47:126–8.
[25] LW 21:354.

not high-minded, but fear.' But by this tyrannical attitude of theirs these godless people, who are Christians in name only, are inflicting no light injury on the Christian name as well as Christian people. And they are guilty and partakers of Jewish godlessness. By the example of this cruelty they are, as it were, repelling Jews from Christianity, whereas they ought to attract them by all manner of gentleness, patience, pleading, and care.[26]

Against the spirit of his day, Luther did not singularly blame the Jews for the death of Christ. Eric Gritsch points out: 'Luther did not, however, hold Jews responsible for the death of Christ. As he wrote in a hymn, "We dare not blame . . . the band of Jews; ours is the shame." And he felt that at least a few Jews might be won for Christ'[27] It was the sins of all men that brought about Christ's death. Heiko Oberman explains:

> Though his attitude toward the Jews remained medieval, even in the last phase of his life he never took over that medieval hatred for the Jews as 'murderers of Christ' which subjected them 'in a Christian spirit' to the rage of the mob.[28]

In the early days of the Reformation, Luther placed the origin of the blame for Jewish unbelief on the Catholic Church. In 1523, his pen produced a favourable tract, *That Christ was born a Jew*. He told the Jews that he could understand why they did not want to join the Catholic Church. He writes: 'The papists have so demeaned themselves that a good Christian would rather be a Jew than one of them, and a Jew would rather be a sow than a Christian.'[29] Not only was Luther understanding towards them, he also optimistically thought that they would then become true Christians according to 'his' understanding of the gospel. Luther showed this attitude: I hope that if one deals with the Jews in a kindly way and instructs them carefully from Holy Scripture, many of them will become genuine

---

[26] Ewald M. Plass, *What Luther Says: An Anthology* Volume Two (St. Louis: Concordia, 1959), 683; cf. W.H.T. Dau, *Luther Examined and Reexamined: A Review of Catholic Criticism and a Plea for Revaluation* (St. Louis, 1917), 202–3.

[27] Gritsch, 'Was Luther Anti-Semitic?', 38.

[28] Oberman, *Luther: Man Between God and the Devil*, 296; cf. Johannes Wallmann, 'Kirche und Israel im Mittelalter und in der Reformationszeit', in *Kirche und Israel* 34 (1989): 69–90.

[29] Roland Bainton, *Here I Stand* (New York: Abingdon Press, 1950), 297.

Christians and turn to the faith of their fathers, the prophets and patriarchs.[30]

The reason Luther wrote *Jesus Christ was born a Jew* was because his enemies charged him with denying the virgin birth of Christ, promulgating the rumour that Luther held Christ was the natural son of Joseph.[31] Luther announces early in the treatise that he will exonerate himself by proving from the Scriptures that Christ was born of the Virgin Mary, and in doing so might 'perhaps also win some Jews to the Christian faith'.[32] Luther would not only prove his detractors false but, for the benefit of the Jews, he would prove the Old Testament Scriptures prophesied of the New Testament Jesus:[33]

> Let [the Jews] first be suckled with milk, and begin by recognizing this
> man Jesus as the true Messiah; after that they may drink wine, and learn
> also that he is true God. For they have been led astray so long and so far
> that one must deal gently with them, as people who have been all too
> strongly indoctrinated to believe that God cannot be man.[34]

Tolerance

Against the spirit of medieval culture, Luther took bold steps of tolerance towards the Jews. He said:

> I would request and advise that one deal gently with them and instruct
> them from Scripture; then some of them may come along. Instead of this
> we are trying only to drive them by force, slandering them, accusing
> them of having Christian blood if they don't stink, and I know not what
> other foolishness. So long as we thus treat them like dogs, how can we
> expect to work any good among them? Again, when we forbid them to
> labor and do business and have any human fellowship with us, thereby
> forcing them into usury, how is that supposed to do them any good? If
> we really want to help them, we must be guided in our dealings with
> them not by papal law but by the law of Christian love. We must receive

---

[30] LW 45:200; cf. WA 56, 436, 7–23 dealing with Romans 11:22 or WA 6, 140, 16–20 dealing with Romans 15:13f.

[31] 'Luther's writings about the Jews were all solicited by others and written out of a situation, and their intent, whatever their results, was apologetic rather than polemical', wrote Gordon Rupp, *Martin Luther and the Jews*, 11.

[32] LW 45:199.

[33] Cf. LW 45:213–22, see comments by Gritsch, *Martin – God's Court Jester*, 134.

[34] LW 45:229.

them cordially, and permit them to trade and work with us, that they may have occasion and opportunity to associate with us, hear our Christian teaching, and witness our Christian life. If some of them should prove stiff-necked, what of it? After all, we ourselves are not all good Christians either.[35]

In this treatise, Luther expresses sympathy towards the Jews saying that he would not have become a Christian either if he had been born a Jew under the papacy.[36] Against the cultural stereotype that the Jews were enemies of Christ, Luther says that the Jews are (biologically speaking) closest to Christ.[37] His hope was that a proper understanding of the gospel would bring the Jews to faith in Christ. The Jews would only be returning to the ancient faith of their fathers and prophets. They were to cease waiting for the Messiah, for he had come 1,500 years before.

Frustration with learned Jews

Luther's hope for Jewish conversion seems to have reached its zenith of dismaying frustration in 1536. Sometime previous to this year, Luther met with three learned Jews who, using rabbinic tradition, disagreed with his interpretation of messianic passages from the Old Testament. During these years, Luther had been taking great effort to expound a christological interpretation of the Old Testament. The argument centred on the christological interpretation of Jeremiah 23:6. The rabbis refused to see Christ in the passage. Luther said of this meeting:

> I myself have discussed this with the Jews, indeed with the most learned of them, who knew the Bible so well that there wasn't a letter in it that they did not understand. I held up this text to them, and they could not think of anything to refute me. Finally they said that they believed their Talmud; this is their exegesis, and it says nothing about Christ. They had to follow this interpretation. Thus they do not stick to the text but seek

---

[35] LW 45:229; cf. H. Boockmann, 'Kirche und Frömmigkeit vor der Reformation', in *Martin Luther und die Reformation in Deutschland. Ausstellung zum 500. Geburtstag Martin Luthers. Veranstaltet vom Germanischen Nationalmuseum Nürnberg in Zusammenarbeit mit dem Verein für Reformationsgeschichte* (ed. G. Bott; Frankfurt am Main: Insel Verlag, 1983), 41–72.

[36] LW 45:199–200.

[37] LW 45:200.

to escape it. For if they held to this text alone, they would be vanquished.[38]

That these learned Jews took this approach must have evoked deep frustration. Coupled with the failure of Jewish conversion since his writings from 1523, Luther vowed never to enter into dialogue with the Jews again.

However, the rabbis were not particularly interested in theological talks with Luther. They needed Luther to write them a letter which would allow them to pass safely through Saxony. Luther obliged, only to hear reports that later they spoke blasphemously of Christ, calling him merely a 'crucified bandit'.[39] Luther had now come to perceive the Jews quite negatively. They did not mind appealing to him for toleration in Saxony, but they completely ignored his theological exhortations and proclamation of the gospel. The proclamation of the gospel did not have the effect on them that Luther thought it would. Heiko Oberman describes Luther's mindset towards them:

> For Luther the Jews were doing anything but improving. What was worse, encouraged by their misreading of his own words, they had become more daring, defaming and cursing Jesus of Nazareth and regarding Christians as their 'worst enemies,' so much so that 'if you could, you would [now] rob [all Christians] of what they are and what they have.' However, the decision not to speak for the Jews in Saxony hinged on the analysis that they were appealing to religious tolerance while irreligiously rejecting their own God . . . the Father of Jesus Christ.[40]

Luther took the decision not to debate anymore with learned Jews seriously. In 1537, he refused to intercede for the Jewish official, Josel of Rosheim, who needed a guarantee of safe-conduct through electoral Saxony. Josel was said to be one of the leading spokesmen for the Jews throughout the empire. Indeed, he needed to speak on behalf of all Jews in Saxony; they had recently been driven out of the area by the decree of Johann Friedrich ('Luther's magnanimous patron and staunch defender of the Reformation').[41] Josel felt that Luther could aid

---

[38] LW 47:191.

[39] James Mackinnon, *Luther and the Reformation*, Vol. IV (New York: Russell & Russell, 1962), 196; cf. WA 20, 569 f.; WA, TR 4, 619f.; LW 47:190, n. 63.

[40] Oberman, *Luther: Man Between God and the Devil*, 293–94.

[41] Oberman, *Luther: Man Between God and the Devil*, 292.

him in his task, since Luther was known as a friend of the Jews from his writings of 1523. The plan was for Luther to help Josel change the mind of the elector. Interestingly, Rabbi Josel had earlier sided with the emperor *against* Luther.[42] Now seeing Luther's importance in political situations, he showed interest in his aid.

Luther, however, denied him any assistance. In his letter to this Jewish official, Luther reiterated his position on the Jews from his 1523 treatise *That Jesus Christ Was Born a Jew*, and also added that his influence was not to be used to further Judaism. He said:

> My dear Josel:
>
> I would have gladly interceded for you, both orally and in writing, before my gracious lord [the elector], just as my writings have greatly served the whole of Jewry. But because your people so shamefully misuse this service of mine and undertake things that we Christians simply shall not bear from you, they themselves have robbed me of all the influence I might otherwise have been able to exercise before princes and lords on your behalf. For my opinion was, and still is, that one should treat the Jews in a kindly manner, that God may perhaps look graciously upon them and bring them to their Messiah – but not so that through my good will and influence they might be strengthened in their error and become still more bothersome.
>
> I propose to write a pamphlet about this if God gives me space and time, to see if I cannot win some from your venerable tribe of the patriarchs and prophets and bring them to your promised Messiah . . .[43]
>
> For I have read your Rabbis, how they simply cry out that Christ is a crucified and damned Jew . . . so please take this as a friendly warning: for the sake of that Crucified Jew, I would willingly do my best for your people but I will not contribute to your obstinacy by my own kind actions. You must find another intermediary with my good lord.[44]

Luther's optimism clearly showed itself, but he did not go so far as to lose touch with reality. He proposed dealing with the Jews in Christian love, but even then he knew they would not all be converted. But this

---

[42] Cf. Spitz, *The Protestant Reformation*, 359. See also Walther Bienert, *Martin Luther und die Juden. Ein Quellenbuch mit zeitgenoessischen Illustrationen, mit Einfuehrungen und Erlaeuterungen* (Frankfurt am Main: Ev. Verlagswerk, 1982), 109–14.

[43] LW 47:62; cf. also Edwards, *Luther's Last Battles*, 125.

[44] Luther's letter to Rabbi Josel as cited by Rupp, *Martin Luther and the Jews*, 14. This paragraph – as far as I see it – is not available in the English edition of Luther's works.

thought did not seem to bother him, as he said: 'If some of them prove stiffnecked, what of it? After all, we ourselves are not all good Christians either.'[45] Luther's kind words and compassionate under-standing produced noticeable results. His pamphlet, *That Christ was born a Jew*, met with special favour. The Jews read and circulated his writings. One Jewish historian even said this of Luther's works: 'The Jews of Antwerp sent them to Spain, their former homeland, and even as far away as Palestine.'[46]

So Luther's writing did produce definite results. However, these were not the results that Luther was expecting. Needless to say, the Jews of Germany did not beat a path to Luther's door. Mainly for this reason Luther's views of the Jews began to change. A Jewish historian said this about Luther:

> He thought he could win the Jews with a few kind words. When this did not happen, he was bitterly disappointed. He outdid the Catholics in the vile terms which he heaped on the Jews and Judaism. A movement, hopeful in its beginning for the Jews, ended in utter disillusionment.[47]

These frustrating experiences, however, represent only a small factor in Luther's change of attitude because, at this point, he had been reading anti-Jewish works of Lyra, Paul of Burgeos, Victor of Carben and Antonius Margaritha,[48] writings which greatly influenced him. It was somehow made known to Luther that Moravia and Bohemia were gaining Jewish converts from Christianity.[49]

Reaction to reports about the Jews

The main reason for Luther's change of mind centred once again on religion. By 1538, he came to believe the popular stories about attempts by Jews to convert Christians.[50] In Moravia, Lutherans were – so was the rumour – beginning to keep the Sabbath day and enforce the rite of circumcision. Just as Paul was upset with the Judaizers in Galatia, Luther was upset that people were preaching law instead of the free-dom of the gospel. He was informed that the Jews had convinced some

---

[45] LW 45:229.

[46] Armas K. E. Holmio, *Luther – Friend or Foe* (Chicago, 1949), 18.

[47] Grayzel, *History of the Jews*, 374.

[48] See Rupp, *Martin Luther and the Jews*, 14–15.

[49] Gritsch, *Martin – God's Court Jester*, 138–9.

[50] Rupp, *Martin Luther and the Jews*, 13; cf. Mackinnon, *Luther and the Reformation*, 195.

Christians that they should be circumcised, that the Messiah had not yet come, that the Jewish law was externally valid, and that it should be observed by Gentiles. So Luther wrote the tract *Against the Sabbatarians* (1538). Luther begins this writing (an 'open letter') stating exactly what topics he will cover:

> You informed me that the Jews are making inroads at various places throughout the country with their venom and their doctrine, and that they have already induced some Christians to let themselves be circumcised and to believe that the Messiah or Christ has not yet appeared, that the law of the Jews must prevail forever, that it must also be adopted by all the Gentiles, etc. Then you inquired of me how these allegations are to be refuted with Holy Scripture. For the time being and until I am at greater leisure, I will convey my advice and opinion briefly in this matter.[51]

This letter, however, did not stop the activity. Zealous rabbis began enticing Christians away from their faith. They even began to write Jewish apologetic pamphlets in reply to Luther. Luther's patience simply ran out. The change has been described this way: from the mild and friendly call of the gospel for all to come to Jesus, he turned to the idea of chastisement through the law of God as a means of bringing them to repentance.[52] His earlier position of patience towards them proved to be wrong. There were not many converts. In his eyes, the Jews were a clear example of *hardened hearts*; they were no longer the church's responsibility, but rather needed to be given over to God's judgement.

Luther laid out a number of scriptural arguments to counter these claims. By and large, he treats the Jews in this writing as he would any group that opposed the gospel. He uses rhetoric, *argumentum ad absurdum*, and appeal to a clear exposition of the Scriptures. It is helpful to consider some of the arguments he put forth, to see that Luther's beginning polemic against the Jews was primarily theological.

Luther first blames the stubbornness of the Jewish people towards the gospel on the teachings of their rabbis (recall though, his emphasis in the early 1520s also blames the Papacy). He is also still aware of the difficult plight of the Jews through history and sees this plight as the direct anger of God towards them in rejecting the Messiah.

---

[51] LW 47:65.
[52] Holmio, *Luther – Friend or Foe*, 26.

Luther then develops the argument that either God has lied and not sent the Messiah, or the Jews have lied in saying that he has not come.[53]

Luther's next argument was that the observance of the Jewish ceremonial law had ceased. It was not the case that Christians should become Jews because God's law *endured for ever*. Luther argues that if the Messiah has come, the law is fulfilled. He then argues that if the law endures for ever, why is it that for 1,500 years Judaism has been in a state of ruin? The ceremonial law inferred the existence of an actual Jerusalem. Since the Jews were not able to fulfil the ceremonial law in its designated location, the law has not endured for ever, but has been fulfilled in Christ.[54]

Luther then launches into a long series of scriptural arguments concerning the law and its fulfilment. He then concludes with arguments concerning the inadequacy of Jewish theology claiming it has a direct claim on the Ten Commandments. This is *their* law that endures for ever. Luther though argues that the Ten Commandments are not simply the property of Israel. They were, in fact, in place before Moses ever directly received them.[55]

Luther ends this writing by admitting defeat in converting the Jews:

> If you are unable to convert the Jews, then consider that you are no better than all the prophets, who were always slain and persecuted by this base people who glory solely in the boast that they are Abraham's seed, though they surely know that there have always been many desperate, lost souls also among them, so that they might well recognize that it requires more to be a child of God than just to be the seed of Abraham . . . Because God for fifteen hundred years has failed to do this with the Jews but lets them live on and on in exile without any word or prophecy to them regarding it, it is evident that he has forsaken them, that they can no longer be God's people, and that the true Lord, the Messiah, must have come fifteen hundred years ago.[56]

Mark U. Edwards correctly summarized:

> Each of these arguments was drawn out and buttressed with careful examination of the appropriate texts from Scripture. Luther was uncompromising

---

[53] LW 47:73–8.
[54] LW 47:79.
[55] LW 47:89–90.
[56] LW 47:96.

in his insistence on the error of the Jews, but his language is still, for the most part, temperate and restrained.[57]

After this treatise, Luther decided, 'to write no more either about the Jews or against them'.[58] Had Luther kept to this decision, he would have avoided writing one of his most controversial and dismaying treatises: *On the Jews and their Lies*.

Severe Negative Reaction

Finally, in May 1542, Luther received from a Moravian friend, a certain Count Schlink, a copy of a Jewish apologetic work along with the request that he reply to it. Luther's anger boiled over; restraint could not contain his anger and the result was a lengthy tract *Against the Jews and their Lies*. This treatise of Luther's may come as a shock to many. The language is very biting; his proposals almost seem inhumane. Yet the context of Luther and his times must be kept in mind to properly understand what he really meant. Luther very thoroughly and systematically condemned the religious errors of the Jewish people. From the start, it can be seen that he was no longer writing to convert them: 'It is not my purpose to quarrel with the Jews, nor to learn from them how they interpret the scriptures, I know all that very well already. Much less do I propose to convert the Jews, for that is impossible.'[59] So the change in Luther's approach is obvious from the start.

First of all, he lashed out against the false boasts of the Jewish people. The Jews took special pride in their ancestry; they were thankful that they were God's chosen people, the physical descendants of the patriarchs. Luther replied: 'They boast of being the noblest, yea, the only people on earth. In comparison with them we Gentiles are not human; in fact we hardly deserve to be considered mere worms by them.'[60] In reply to this boast, Luther pointed out the common ancestry of all people in Adam and Eve. Another boast they flaunted was their special rite of circumcision. Luther countered this claim by pointing out that other religions have this same custom. Their third major boast centred on the promised land. But Luther asked why they would boast about a land they had not possessed for 1,500 years. He let none of their false boasts stand unscathed.

---

[57] Edwards, *Luther's Last Battles*, 127.
[58] LW 47:133.
[59] LW 47:137.
[60] LW 47:140.

Following this section, Luther proceeded to an exegesis and explanation of key OT prophecies. Using a book they too regarded as sacred, he cited several key messianic prophecies. He proved to them from God's word that *olam* need not mean 'for ever', that David's ruling house was not an earthly dynasty, and that Christ perfectly fulfilled all the messianic requirements. But Luther did not expect this to produce great results; he said:

> When I debated with them, they gave me their glosses, as they usually do. But when I forced them back to the text, they soon fled from it, saying they were obliged to believe their rabbis. The more one tries to help them, the baser and more stubborn they become. Leave them to their own devices.[61]

Nevertheless, he spent nearly one half of this lengthy treatise explaining scriptural proofs for the Jews. Luther then listed a few reasons for his dislike of them. A medieval rabbi wrote *Der gantz Juedisch glaub*, which contained this interesting sidelight; 'Jesus is a whore's son, his mother Mary was a whore, who conceived him in adultery with a blacksmith.'[62] Another matter that Luther, along with almost all Europeans, could not tolerate was the Jewish practice of usury. He found this particularly detestable. *Had Luther stopped here, his treatise probably would be of little interest to anyone.* Roland Bainton, a biographer of Luther, once wrote: 'One could wish that Luther had died before ever this tract was written.'[63]

Often, Luther's tone and method of argumentation was strongly influenced by that taken in the work to which he was responding. James Mackinnon thinks that the original pamphlet was a direct response to Luther's *Against the Sabbatarians*: 'It naturally provoked a reply in which a Jew, in the form of a dialogue with a Christian, controverted his exegesis.' Whatever was in that Jewish writing (unfortunately, this letter and attack have been lost, so we are unaware of the exact tone of argument Luther was responding to), Luther erupted in vicious polemic; he moved from his earlier writings of attacking Jewish theology to attacking Jewish people.[65] Still, Luther was not against the

---

[61] LW 47:191–2.

[62] LW 47:257.

[63] Bainton, *Here I Stand*, 297.

[64] Mackinnon, *Luther and the Reformation*, 198.

[65] Written pre-Holocaust, the Roman Catholic historian Hartmann Grisar comments 'It is clear that [Luther] was within his rights when he scourged the anti-Christian blasphemy and seductive wiles of the Jews, however much he may have been wrong in allowing himself to be carried away by fanaticism so far as to demand their actual persecution' (H. Grisar, *Luther*, Vol. IV (St Louis: Herder, 1915), 306.

Jews for being 'Jews' – he had no objections to integrating converted Jews into Christian society:

> Now, in order to strengthen our faith, we want to deal with a few crass follies of the Jews in their belief and their exegesis of the Scriptures, since they so maliciously revile our faith. If this should move any Jew to reform and repent, so much the better.[66]

Nevertheless in this work, Luther no longer holds out any hope for Jewish conversion which he had expressed in his earlier writings.[67] Nor is there to be any debate over their scriptural interpretation: 'Therefore, a Christian should be content and not argue with the Jews'[68] and, 'it is useless to argue with them about how God is triune, how he became man and how Mary is the mother of God. No human reason nor any human heart will ever grant these things, much less the embittered, venomous, blind heart of the Jews.'[69] Luther has completely given up writing for the purpose of dialogue or possible conversion; he now writes for the sole purpose of warning Christians against the Jews.

Biblical Arguments

Not all the work is violent rhetoric against the Jews. Much of it involves arguments based on the Scriptures. Luther argues for equality among groups of people (who are all in sin and condemned by God equally). He argues that circumcision is not essential to salvation, and sees that any attempt to link circumcision to giving one a special status with God is a form of works righteousness and, thus, a denial of the gospel.[70] Even though Luther comes down hard on the Jews in regard to circumcision, by analogy, he argues that the Christian church has done the same thing with the sacraments; they have turned them into works righteousness.[71]

Luther also launches into arguments concerning the law. He views the Jews as being conceited because God gave them the law, and he sees them as the disobedient wife of God, because the law that they

---

[66] LW 47:140.
[67] LW 47:137: 'Much less do I propose to convert the Jews, for that is impossible.'
[68] LW 47:138.
[69] LW 47:139.
[70] LW 47:155–8.
[71] LW 47:160.

were given is not kept.[72] He argues that the Jews delight in their special status based on the land given to them by God: 'they pride themselves tremendously on having received the land of Canaan, the city of Jerusalem, and the temple from God.'[73] However, he also believes that they were taken out of their homeland because of their disobedience.[74]

Luther defends prophecies concerning Jesus. For example, with Genesis 49:10, Luther concludes that the Bible clearly teaches that the Messiah has come.[75] He argues that the last words of David in 2 Samuel 23 proclaim an everlasting covenant in which God's house will stand eternally.[76] Only Christ proves this prophecy accurate. Luther argues from Haggai 2:6–9 that the 'consolation of the Gentiles' is Christ and he came while the Jewish temple was still standing 'in a little while'. He argues that the Jews are still waiting for Christ, although this is hardly a 'little while' and their temple is now destroyed.[77]

Thus, for Luther, the biblical record once again refutes Judaism. He argues that the seventy weeks prophesied in Daniel have been fulfilled and the Messiah has come.[78] He defended various charges against the person and work of Christ – many of which that had been part of popular medieval tradition.[79] Roman Catholics should be especially interested to find out that Luther defends Mary: in the third section, charges that Mary was a prostitute and that there was not a virgin birth were vigorously refuted. But the treatise is littered with harsh rhetoric throughout. Luther takes seriously his belief that the Jews were gross blasphemers and that to even converse with them one supports their blasphemy.[80]

Popular Prejudice

Luther now believes all the popular slanderous myths about the Jews:

> They stuff themselves, guzzle, and live in luxury and ease from our hard-earned goods. With their accursed usury they hold us and our

---

[72] LW 47:167.
[73] LW 47:172.
[74] LW 47:173.
[75] LW 47:183.
[76] LW 47:192–3, 199.
[77] LW 47:210.
[78] LW 47:229.
[79] LW 47:256.
[80] LW 47:274.

property captive. Moreover, they mock and deride us because we work
and let them play the role of lazy squires at our expense and in our
land.[81]

Because of their blasphemy against Jesus, Mary, the Trinity and the
whole of the Christian faith, Luther's understanding of the Jewish people reduces them to being murderers, blasphemers, liars and thieves.
He has stereotyped an entire group of people to be the worst of crimi-
nals. With this prejudice, Luther launches into the section of the treatise
for which *On the Jews and their Lies* is most remembered. He says:

> We must exercise harsh mercy with fear and trembling, in the hope that
> we could save some from the flames and embers. We must not avenge
> ourselves. They are under God's wrath – a thousand times worse than
> we could wish it upon them.[82]

Luther considered his early treatise from 1523 *soft mercy*: an appeal to
the Jews to convert. Now Luther attempts to use *harsh mercy*: forcing
the Jews to convert and to protect Christians from blasphemy.

Luther gives his infamous seven recommendations to the political
authorities. His 'sincere advice'[83] *consisted of seven major points*: (1) burn
their synagogues and schools; (2) raze and destroy their homes; (3)
take away their books; (4) forbid their rabbis to teach; (5) allow no safe
conduct for them on the highways; (6) prohibit usury, take their money
from them; and (7) put an axe, hoe or spindle into the hands of young,
strong Jews to let them earn their bread. As if this were not enough,
Luther was still bothered about the abusive blasphemy of the Jews. He
wrote: 'We are at fault in not avenging all this innocent blood of our
Lord and of the Christians which they shed . . . we are at fault for not
slaying them.'[84] No one can accuse Luther of understatement.

Yet one cannot concentrate only on these several pages of aggression
and anger. In this same writing, he calls on God to soften their hearts
with this entreaty: 'O God, heavenly father, relent and let your wrath
over them be sufficient and come to an end, for the sake of your dear
Son.'[85] Finally, Luther closes with this prayer for their conversion: 'May

---

[81] LW 47:266.
[82] This sentence was left out of the English translation. It can be found in WA 53, 522,
347; Oberman, *Luther: Man Between God and the Devil*, 290.
[83] LW 47:268.
[84] LW 47:267.
[85] LW 47:292.

Christ, our dear Lord, convert them mercifully and preserve us stead-fastly in the knowledge of him, which is eternal life.'[86] This was no mere cover-up for his harsh statements. Rather, it shows that Luther wrote this way out of religious considerations.[87]

Luther's last sermon

Luther's last sermon preached at Eisleben, 15 February 1546, surprisingly does not contain anti-Jewish material. Gordon Rupp also refers to Luther's last sermon and its material against the Jews:

> Probably Luther preached his last sermon within hours of his death. It is the rambling, repetitious sermon of an old, tired man and we can almost hear the pauses for breath. But it is in the main a moving and simple exposition of the great evangelical mandate 'Come unto me . . .' Yet at the end of it, he spoke about the Jews.[88]

Rupp then provides this citation from Luther's sermon:

> Now I am going home, and perhaps I will never preach to you again, and I have blessed you and prayed you to stay always close to God's Word . . . I see the Jews are still among you. Now we have to deal with them in a Christian manner and try to bring them to the Christian faith that they may receive the true Messiah who is their flesh and blood and of the seed of Abraham – though I am afraid Jewish blood has got watery and wild these days. Yet they must be invited to turn to the Messiah and be baptized in him . . . If not then we must not suffer them to remain for they daily abuse and blaspheme Christ. I must not, you must not be a partaker of the sins of others. God knows I have enough to do with

---

[86] LW 47:306.

[87] Luther went on to publish two more anti-Jewish writings, *On The Ineffable Name and On Christ's Lineage* (1543) and *On The Last Words of David* (1543). Neither of these treatises is contained in the English edition of Luther's Works. *On The Ineffable Name and On Christ's Lineage* is available, translated in English, in Gerhard Falk, *The Jew in Christian Theology: Martin Luther's Anti-Jewish Vom Schem Hamphoras, Previously Unpublished in English, and Other Milestones in Church Doctrine Concerning Judaism* (North Carolina: MacFarland, 1992). In these writings, Luther intended to show the superiority of Christian interpretation over rabbinical interpretation. In the first treatise, *On The Ineffable Name and On Christ's Lineage*, Luther picks up where he left off in *On The Jews and Their Lies*. Mark U. Edwards explains that the first part revealed Luther at his worst, in *Luther's Last Battles*, 132–3.

[88] Rupp, *Martin Luther and the Jews*, 20.

sins of my own, but if they will give up usury and receive Christ we will willingly receive them as our brethren . . . but if they call Mary a whore and Jesus her bastard still we must exercise Christian love towards them that they may be converted and receive our Lord . . . this I tell you as your Landeskind not to be partakers of the sins of others. If they turn from their blasphemies we must gladly forgive them, but if not we must not suffer them to remain![89]

Heiko Oberman notes in a similar fashion:

[I]n his final Admonition . . . the concept of tolerance that leaves room for conversion is certainly retained. But his imminent expectation of the Last Judgment lets him interpret and evaluate the 'signs of the times' so as to keep this tolerance within very narrow bounds, as it is the very last chance to avert expulsion.[90]

Luther's Eschatology and the Jews

In addition to what has already been said, it is important to note that the eschatological framework of Luther's theology is essential for understanding his attitude towards the Jews. As early as 1522, he preached that his generation was living in the last days:

I do not wish to force any one to believe as I do; neither will I permit anyone to deny me the right to believe that the last day is near at hand. These words and signs of Christ compel me to believe that such is the case. For the history of the centuries that have passed since the birth of Christ nowhere reveals conditions like those of the present.[91]

In 1542, he said, 'I think the last day [judgement day] is not far away. My reason is that a last great effort is now being made to advance the gospel.'[92]

Thus, the entirety of his Reformation career embraced an impending consummation of history.[93] Lutheran scholar Paul Althaus notes that

---

[89] These words probably are not from Luther's last sermon, but rather from his *An Admonition Against The Jews* (1546), which was added to his last sermon.

[90] Oberman, *Luther: Man Between God and the Devil*, 296.

[91] Martin Luther, *The Sermons of Martin Luther* Volume 1 (Grand Rapids: Baker, 1996), 62. Online: http://www.orlutheran.com/html/mlselk21.html.

[92] LW 54 Table Talk: 427.

[93] See also Edwards, *Luther's Last Battles*, 97.

the 'Middle Ages feared the Day of Wrath but Luther desires the coming of Jesus, because he will bring an end to the antichrist and bring about redemption. Luther can call it "the most happy Last Day".'[94]

Towards the end of his life, this expectation increased much more. Luther spoke out strongly against those groups who resisted the gospel: the Papacy, Turks, radicals and the Jews. These groups were led by the devil and were a tool for continued opposition to the gospel.[95] Early in his career, his treatise *That Jesus Christ was born a Jew* made a kind appeal for the Jews to embrace the gospel. Later in his career, the impending judgement day compelled Luther to appeal to the authorities to protect Christendom against those groups that continually chose not to convert; he believed that those who did not embrace the gospel were not indifferent to it, but rather were opposed to it. Heiko Oberman explains:

> [Luther] spoke to the Christian authorities: the Last Judgment is fast approaching, so woe to those temporal rulers who have neglected their duty to protect Christendom! Now is the time for defense against the storm troopers of the Antichrist, whether they descend upon Christendom from the outside in the form of the Turks, subvert the preaching of the Gospel and order in the empire from inside the Church like the pope and clerics beholden to him, or, like the Jews, undermine the public welfare from the inside. Luther had discovered this concatenation of Jews, pope, and Turks as the unholy coalition of the enemies of God long before he began leveling his massive assaults on the Jews. Now that the terrors of the Last Days had been unleashed, the Church and temporal authorities were forced into their own defensive battle, one without the promise of victory but with the prospects of survival. Christian rulers, you should 'not participate in the sins of others, you must pray humbly to God that he should be merciful to you and allow your rule to survive.[96]

---

[94] Paul Althaus, *The Theology of Martin Luther* (Philadelphia: Fortress, 1966), 420–21.

[95] 'As he grew older, Luther became increasingly convinced that Satan had rallied many forces against him and the gospel's cause. Papists, Turks, other Protestants (whom he called schwaermer because they were like swarming bees), and Jews were to him Satan's agents attacking the gospel he had rediscovered', E. Gritsch, 'The Unrefined Reformer', in *Christian History 39/ XII, No. 3*, 36.

[96] Oberman, *Luther: Man Between God and the Devil*, 294. See also H.A. Oberman: The *Impact of the Reformation* (Grand Rapids: Eerdmans, 1994), 56.

Luther's Anti-Jewishness and the Holocaust

On the one hand, Luther almost always argued against the 'enemies of the gospel' from a theological point of view. His attacks on Jews were, so to speak, part of his attack on legalistic ways of interpreting the relationship with God, for example, as Jesus did against the Pharisees or Paul against Judaizers in Galatia. On the other hand, we must not deny the somehow, at least, mental association of Luther's anti-Jewishness and the Nazi Holocaust. Yet, needless to say, theological reasons or not, not many are proud to identify themselves with Luther when it comes to his later pamphlet *On the Jews and their Lies*. His contemporaries were dismayed – Philipp Melanchthon and Andreas Osiander condemned it. A 1543 document of the Zurich churches reads: 'If it had been written by a swineherd, rather than by a celebrated shepherd of souls, it might have some but very little justification.'[97]

Nevertheless, for the most part, such type of pamphlets from Luther's pen against Jews stayed undisturbed until the twentieth century. 'Nobody took Luther's program seriously and the new mandate of John Frederick in 1543, though severe, was on other lines. Three years later, as we shall see, Jews were still living unmolested in the Mansfeld area.'[98]

It took a modern day dictator and tyrant to bring Luther's terrible thoughts against Jews out of oblivion. That dictator was none other than Adolf Hitler. He was able to quote the writings of Luther – often not with their original meaning – to his own advantage. Luther always remained a famous German hero. Hitler recognized this and, being no fool, played it for all it was worth. It is a rather obvious fact that Hitler was misrepresenting Luther. Yet there are many so-called scholars who claim that Luther's treatise on the Jews gave Hitler the ideas for the Holocaust. But nowhere in Luther's writings can the Nazi idea of Aryan anti-Semitism be found. However, it was to the Nazis' advantage to make Luther seem to support them. John W. Montgomery says:

> These Nazi writers were only too anxious to give some intellectual respectability to the weird hotchpotch of ideas which made up Nazi doctrine by citing great names of Germany's past in their support.[99]

---

[97] LW 47:123.

[98] Gordon Rupp, *Martin Luther and the Jews*, 18. Cf. Joseph Clayton, *Luther and his Work* (Milwaukee: Bruce, 1937), 189.

[99] John W. Montgomery, *In Defense of Martin Luther* (Milwaukee: Northwestern Publishing House, 1970), 146.

It is interesting to note that most biographies of Hitler do not even mention Luther. Also interesting is the fact that respectable Jewish histories of the Holocaust make no mention of Luther. Luther's motives for his treatise had a totally different origin. As stated above, Luther's reasons were theologically and religiously motivated. The word of God was Luther's greatest treasure. His love for the word prompted him to react violently when others showed disrespect for it. Heinrich Bornkamm writes: 'Luther's love for the Old Testament, to which he dedicated by far the greatest part of his scholarly efforts, and his rejection of post New Testament Jewry are two sides of the same thing.'[100] So Luther held no special hatred for the Jews as a race; he did not, however, have much use for their rejection of Christ.

Luther's Language

Some think that Luther's harsh language against the Jews was unique, but it must be noted that his language against the Papacy was much stronger and his words against the Turks and false brethren were almost as strong:

> Neither the vulgarity nor the violence nor the charges of satanic motivation nor the sarcastic mocking is unique to [Luther's later Jewish] treatises. If anything, Luther's 1541 *Against Hanswurst* and his 1545 *Against the Papacy at Rome, Founded by the Devil* contain more scatology, more sallies against the devil, more heavy sarcasm, and more violence of language and recommendations. The polemics of the older Luther against the Turks and Protestant opponents are only slightly more restrained. Against each of these opponents – Catholics, Turks, other Protestants and Jews – he occasionally passed on libelous tales and gave credence to improbable charges. In all these respects Luther treated the Jews no differently than he treated his other opponents.[101]

Oberman traces Luther's harsh language as far back as a sermon preached in 1515, thus proving the *young* Luther used the same type of speech as the *old* Luther. Most importantly, Oberman provides insight rather than psychological condemnation.[102] Luther's rough language was, therefore, a weapon to use against the devil:

---

[100] Heinrich Bornkamm, *Luther's World of Thought* (St. Louis: Concordia, 1958), 31.

[101] Edwards, *Luther's Last Battles*, 140. Grisar provides examples in *Luther*, Vol. 4, 287–8.

[102] Cf. Oberman, *Luther: Man Between God and the Devil*, 108–9.

[A]ll true Christians stand in a large anti-defamation league and are called upon to combat the God-awful, filthy adversary, using his own weapons and his own strategy: 'Get lost Satan.'[103]

In other words, Luther used scatological language to fight against Satan. Since Luther felt Satan was the mastermind behind works-centred religions (like Judaism), Luther attacks those religions using Satan's own weapons against him.[104] Since it is the last days, Satan must be resisted with as much energy and all the vehemence possible. By exposing Satan in these systems, Satan becomes enraged and fights harder against God. By fighting harder, the last day approaches quicker.[105] Luther also felt he was following the example of Christ. Luther asks rhetorically if the Lord used abusive language against his enemies.[106] In similar fashion, Luther responded to his opponent Latomus.[107] We can conclude, then, that the vulgarity of Luther in his tracts against Jews is of no special significance.[108]

---

[103] Oberman, *The Impact of the Reformation*, 61.

[104] Grisar, *Luther*, 286.

[105] Oberman, *The Impact of the Reformation*, 63.

[106] 'Was he abusive when he called the Jews an adulterous and perverse generation, an offspring of vipers, hypocrites, and children of the Devil? . . . The truth, which one is conscious of possessing, cannot be patient against its obstinate and intractable enemies', as cited by Gritsch, 'The Unrefined Reformer', 36.

[107] LW 32:141: 'He [Latomus] says that I lack the evangelical modesty which I enjoin, and that this is especially true of the book in which I replied to the sophists of Louvain when they condemned my teachings. Now I have never insisted that anyone consider me modest or holy, but only that everyone recognize what the gospel is. If they do this, I give anyone freedom to attack my life to his heart's content. My boast is that I have injured no one's life or reputation, but only sharply reproached, as godless and sacrilegious, those assertions, inventions, and doctrines which are against the Word of God. I do not apologize for this, for I have good precedents. John the Baptist [Luke 3:7] and Christ after him [Matt. 23:33] called the Pharisees the 'offspring of vipers.' So excessive and outrageous was this abuse of such learned, holy, powerful, and honored men that they said in reply that He had a demon [John 7:20]. If in this instance Latomus had been judge, I wonder what the verdict would have been! Elsewhere Christ calls them 'blind' [Matt. 23:16], 'crooked,' 'liars,' 'sons of the devil' [John 8:44, 55]. Good God, even Paul lacked evangelical modesty when he anathematized the teachers of the Galatians [Gal. 1:8] who were, I suppose, great men. Others he calls 'dogs' [Phil. 3:2], 'empty talkers' [Tit. 1:10], 'deceivers' [Col. 2:4, 8]. Further, he accused to his face the magician Elymas with being a 'son of the devil, full of all deceit and villainy [Acts 13:10].'

[108] Cf. Montgomery, *In Defense of Martin Luther*, 144: 'Luther was a product of his times. The writers of his day were unrestrained by modern standards. It is important to note that Luther did not use this harsh language for the Jews alone. Luther

Also, the historical setting must be considered. Luther was not the first to speak unkindly about the Jews. The Romans disliked them and the Christians slaughtered thousands of them during the Crusades. In 1290, England expelled them; thirty years later France did likewise; in 1492, they were murdered and expelled from Spain. Bainton speaks to this situation:

> If similar tracts did not appear in England, France, and Spain in Luther's day, it was because the Jews had already been completely expelled from these countries.[109]

Luther's actions are – to a certain extent – almost mild in comparison.

One last consideration centres on the fine art of quoting out of context. The critics who condemn the last writing of Luther against the Jews only quote, of course, what will promote their cause, using only a few selected passages. They quote Luther without considering the times or the context of his entire article. The following shows the need for contexts: it would be quite out of place to use Luther's and Erasmus' strongly-worded writings against the Turks as a weapon against modern Turkey or to quote the pamphlet of King Henry VIII against Luther as a weapon against present-day Lutherans.[110] Johann Eck also wrote some virulent anti-Jewish tracts, too, as Lindberg reminds us:[111]

> The absolute champion of anti-Jewish polemic in the early modern period was Luther's Catholic opponent Johannes Eck, whose 1541 *Refutation*

---

called princes, 'the greatest fools and worst knaves on earth', monks, 'tame dogs that lie on pillows and whistle with their hind ends'. He also said of his own people: 'I know that we Germans are brutes and stupid swine.' Yet no one accuses him of being anti German. This rough, graphic language was the style of the day: Luther was by no means the worst: Luther delighted less in muck than many of the literary men of his age . . . Detractors have sifted from the pitch-blende of his ninety tomes a few pages of radioactive vulgarity.'

[109] Bainton, *Here I Stand*, 297.

[110] Holmio, *Luther – Friend or Foe*, 8.

[111] Eck perpetuates some of the leading anti-Jewish propaganda prevalent in his day. His anti-Jewish treatise, 'Refutation of a Jew-book', in *Which a Christian, to the Dishonor of All Christendom Claims That Injustice is Done the Jews in the Accusation That They Murder Christian Children*, published a year before Luther's most infamous treatises, is dedicated to proving, in reply to a Lutheran sceptic, that Jews did murder Christian children for their rituals; that they did desecrate the eucharistic host; and that they did do such things as poison wells and bewitch animals and ruin crops. These were the convictions of a scholar, writing in this case for a popular audience' (Edwards, *Luther's Last Battles*, 120).

of a Jew Book was 'a summa of the anti-Jewish literature of the Middle Ages, leaving out no accusation of genocide, blasphemy, or treason'.[112]

The Roman Catholic Church (especially that of Luther's time and before) does not have a spotless record of defending the Jews and other groups against intolerance and hatred.[113] Despite this, those who are critical often insist on quoting Luther to promote ideas he never had any intention of saying. And yet we need not defend Luther too far. The words from Luther's pen were not inspired. Gordon Rupp had it right when he wrote about Luther:

> I confess I am ashamed as I am ashamed of some letters of St. Jerome [and] some paragraphs in Sir Thomas More . . ., and must say that their authors had not so learned Christ, and that, thank God, this is not the major part of what they had to say.[114]

Luther could have taken a different position. Some of his colleagues, such as his dear friend Justas Jonas, present at Luther's deathbed, and Andreas Osiander, reformer in Nuremberg, were very understanding of the position of the Jews.[115]

Thus, we must understand that Martin Luther was a sinful human being and his writings against his opponents, especially against the Jews, show this. At times we may wish that Luther would have exercised a little more tactful restraint. To reason that Luther's work is somehow nullified because of his anti-Jewish writings is an argument

---

[112] Lindberg: 'Tainted Greatness', 17.

[113] 'In 1553 all copies of the Talmud found in Rome were burned in public. Pope Paul IV (1555–1959) ordered measures to be taken against the Jews, and twenty-four men and one woman were burned at the stake. On July 12, 1555, he issued a bull that renewed all the oppressive medieval legislation against the Jews, excluding them from professions, limiting their financial and commercial activities, forbidding them to own real estate, and humiliating them by obliging them to wear yellow hats', wrote Spitz, *The Protestant Reformation*, 357. Cf. Owen Chadwick, *The Reformation* (New York: Penguin, 1964), 271.

[114] G. Rupp, *Martin Luther: Hitler's Cause or Cure?* (London: Lutterworth, 1945), 76.

[115] Cf. Spitz, *The Protestant Reformation*, 358; see also Po-chia Hsia, 'Jews as Magicians in Reformation Germany', in *Anti-Semitism in Times of Crisis* (ed. Sander L. Gilman and Steven T. Katz; New York: New York University Press, 1991), 1245; cf. also Osten-Sacken, *Martin Luther und die Juden*, 242–2; Berthold Schwarz, ' "Israelogie" als Bindeglied innerhalb der Loci Theologici. Ein dogmatischer Entwurf', in *Christen, Juden und die Zukunft Israel. Beiträge zur Israellehre aus Geschichte und Theologie*, EDIS 1, (ed. Berthold Schwarz and Helge Stadelmann; Frankfurt am Main: Peter Lang, 2009), 250–51.

that asks for the impossible: it is the same as saying that one must live a life of perfection in order for one's work to have any validity. Many examples can be drawn from Scripture to show that God uses sinful people to proclaim his truth – including the Apostle Peter, Solomon and David. The Bible also presents the Christian life as a struggle with sin (1 John 1:8–10; Rom. 7). We would stand against Peter's denial, Solomon's idolatry, David's adultery and conspiracy to murder, and against Luther's anti-Jewish writings.

Yet, at the same time, we dare not let others falsely accuse and slander a man whom God used to restore the truth. Simply because Luther was wrong at times on his attitude towards the Jews does not necessarily mean he was wrong on the need for church reform, the proclamation of the gospel of justification by faith alone (*sola fide*), the uniqueness of Christ for salvation (*solus Christus, sola gratia*), or the hermeneutical principle of *sola scriptura*. No Protestant with a clear understanding of biblical anthropology argues that Luther was an infallible interpreter or a divine authority. We realize Luther was a man of many faults. Yet when he proclaims the gospel, he is, in many cases, correct because the Bible clearly teaches what he had discovered. When he makes terrible statements about the Jews, he is not right (or wrong) because he is considered somehow a Protestant pope or the originator of Protestantism. He is wrong because a clear exposition of the Scriptures do not support such terrible statements.

Implications for Jewish Missions

In looking at Luther's attitude towards the Jews overall, believers in Jesus Christ can be challenged in several ways, learning both positively and negatively from him.

(1) In Luther's view, the 'bad' example of the papacy with its self-righteousness was an obstacle for Jews to become believers in Christ. We need therefore, instead, 'good' examples of God's love and compassion – examples of true words and godly deeds, so that Jews could become more and more open to listen to the gospel-truth of Jesus, as their Messiah and Saviour, their Lord and God (John 20:28). Compassion, endurance, kindness are necessary while sharing the good news with Jews.

(2) In proclaiming the gospel to Jews (i.e. the truth about the Lord Jesus Christ and his salvation), it is helpful to expect steps of

increasing recognition and faith: for example, the understanding of the deity of Christ, the trinity, the cross, the state of total depravity of sinners, the righteousness of Christ for believers etc. (cf. Heb. 5).

(3) As we have seen in Luther's case, each missionary to the Jews should be aware of his 'own' doctrine about Israel and Jews, and his own understanding of the biblical relationship between church and Israel in the past, the present and the future. Without a thoroughly developed, biblically based position, problems could arise in addressing Jews with the gospel.

(4) Some severe problems occurred in the days of Luther because of the *zeitgeist* (mindset) against Jews from the medieval age. Thus, the different models of Replacement Theology existing today have to be acknowledged and to be assessed on biblical grounds too. Every missionary to the Jews needs to have solid understanding of supersessionism, and how it could be avoided, and of anti-Jewish mindsets respectively.

(5) Romans 9 – 11 is a particular passage that should be clearly understood using sound hermeneutical and theological principles to undergird and inform our efforts at witnessing to the Jews about the gospel.

(6) Based on different Scripture passages, mass-conversion of Jews is not to be expected at any time but only at a specific salvation-historical time in the future (e.g. Rom. 11:25–8). Therefore, patience is to be the attitude of the Christian's heart in talking to Jews.

(7) A fundamental issue is the uniqueness of Christ and the salvation that he brings. Understanding Luther's emphasis on these central issues can be of vital importance. That means: Luther – in following the teaching of the apostles – had stressed the one way of salvation in the crucified and resurrected Christ (Rom. 3 etc.). Thus, any second or even a third way of salvation 'without faith in Christ' (as a matter of *revelatio generalis*), for example for Jews because of their covenant relationship to Yahweh from biblical times on, is not to be expected.

(8) We also have carefully to consider matters of eschatology, e.g. Israel's future in Romans 9 – 11, the eschatological fulfilment of the Old Testament promises (return to the promised land, the reign of the Messiah on the throne of David etc.) and the salvation-historical schedule mentioned and taught in the Scriptures.

(9) It is important also to reflect on a theological understanding of the relationship of church and Israel.

(10) Another important implication for Jewish missions is hermeneutics, especially in regarding to explaining the relation between OT and NT, and principle of 'progressive revelation' of God within the Bible.

(11) Reuchlin, Osiander, Justus Jonas (later Spener and other German Pietists, Franz Delitzsch, etc.) were good examples to show that the study of Judaism (Hebrew language, Hebrew texts, rabbinic literature, rituals, daily Jewish life, etc.) and the love of Jews, Judaism and their traditions is still a central issue for the dialogue with Jews today.

(12) Abusive and harsh language in criticizing the Jews' customs, theology or traditions should be avoided.

Luther is a salutary example to anybody who is active in evangelizing Jews. He started well in 1510, 1514 and 1523, and ended tragically in 1537 and in the 1540s. Today's missionaries among Jewish people should be aware that there could be frustration ahead in their ministry, because the conversion of Jews needs patience and endurance. Quick conversions are usually not to be expected.

Luther's theology is still a challenge. His teaching was not inerrant and his writings were not inspired; he was terribly wrong in his cruel teaching on Jews. But, even as a sinner, his emphasis on the uniqueness of Christ and his salvation, and his understanding of justification by faith in Christ without works or merit has to be discussed in fulfilling the task of evangelizing Jews.

6

The Early Pietistic Movement's Contribution to Jewish Evangelism[1]

David Dowdey

Pietism – its Background and Mission

A new and somewhat different, less hostile, era of relations between Jews and Christians commenced in Protestant Germany during the late Baroque and early Enlightenment times. This is not to imply that, in the preceding seventeen hundred years, there had been no encounters between Jews and Christians on the basis of faith and theology. Regrettably, though, these encounters were all too often hostile.

Since the time of Protestant Orthodoxy, it was believed that the mission commandments of Jesus were to be taken seriously, although not by individual Christians but, instead, by the secular rulers. For that reason, secular rulers compelled Jews and Muslims in their territories to hear the Christian message.[2] Furthermore, at no time in the history of European Christianity had there been a more intensive preoccupation with rabbinical and Hebrew sources than during the age of Protestant Orthodoxy.[3] From 1575 onwards, there was spirited production of theological and controversial writings on the topic of the Jews.

---

[1] This paper is based on, and quotes extensively from, the author's original study *Jewish-Christian Relations in Eighteenth-Century Germany: Textual Studies on German Archival Holdings, 1729–1742* (New York: Edwin Mellen, 2006).

[2] Karl Heinrich Rengstorf and Siegfried von Kortzfleisch, eds., *Kirche und Synagoge: Handbuch zur Geschichte von Christen und Juden* (Stuttgart: Klett Verlag, 1968), I, 487.

[3] Rengstorf and Kortzfleisch, *Kirche und Synagoge I*, 488.

Hebrew translations of the New Testament, or parts thereof, as well as various catechisms and confessions appeared.

All of this fits into the scheme of things that saw the age of God's predetermined time for the conversion of the Jews.[4] But something was amiss in the methods and it took a Jewish convert to Christianity, Christian Gerson, to raise a critical opposing voice. At the beginning of the seventeenth century, in 1613, he wrote in *Der Juden Thalmud* an account of the methods of force used to convert the Jews. Concluding a major section, he states:

> A few ecclesiastical persons, who did not have the sword of the government in their hands, preached in the pulpits and also wrote books that people should persecute, slaughter, and exterminate the blind blasphemers and devilish Jews as enemies and Christ-murderers so that the blood of Christ would be avenged. It happened numerous times that people executed them by the hundreds and thousands using fire, water, and sword.
>
> Since . . . these are not the proper means to convert one single Jew, first because in the Word of God they have neither reason nor promise and also because neither Christ nor his beloved Apostles nor the prophets in the Old Testament used such methods, it is not surprising that hitherto among them . . . so little has been accomplished.[5]

This new era has been called one of 'philo-Semitism'.[6] The eventual outcome was a zealous interest in Judaism, the Old Testament and Hebrew, unlike any interest heretofore shown. Luther, of course, in his early period may be regarded as a prototype of this stance. Luther did, however, in the years between the writing of *Daß Jesus ein geborener Jude sei* (1523) and the banning of Jews from Saxony by Johann Friedrich (1536) change his attitude. The best explanations why Luther changed his views are: (1) he saw the unyielding anti-Semitism of the Catholic Church; (2) he had unpleasant experiences in dealing with the Jews; (3) he came to believe tolerance towards the Jews made them more fixed in their errors; and (4) his strong nationalism made him suspect a Jewish alliance with the Turkish Empire.[7] It was definitely not from this late

---

[4] Rengstorf and Kortzfleisch, *Kirche und Synagoge I*, 488–9.

[5] Christianum Gerson, *Der Jüden Thalmud fürnembster Inhaltend Widerlegung* (Erffurdt: Verlag Christiani von Sabers. Druck Paul Michael, 1659), a2b-a8a.

[6] Rengstorf and Kortzfleisch, *Kirche und Synagoge I*, 15.

[7] Armas Kustaa Ensio Holmio, *The Lutheran Reformation and the Jews: The Birth of the Protestant Jewish Missions* (Hancock, Mich.: Finnish Lutheran Book Concern, 1949), 157–60.

Luther that philo-Semitism drew its inspiration. But, as Rengstorf and Kortzfleisch have accurately observed, missions among the Jews had as a goal the conversion of the Jews so there would *be* no more Jews to confront on questions of faith and theology; the Jewish community naturally viewed, and still views, such activity as a threatening and fatal form of anti-Semitism.[8]

No portrayal of the period 1650 to 1750 would be complete without first describing that influential religious phenomenon known as Pietism. Its roots reach back into the seventeenth century and the times of Philipp Jakob Spener (died 1705), whose far-reaching influence is seen in such people as August Hermann Francke, Paul Anton, Johann Caspar Schade and Johann Heinrich Callenberg.[9] It would be inaccurate to say that all Christianity or all Protestantism came under the sway of Pietism. Such was not the case. Side by side with Pietism, we find Protestant Orthodoxy, that group especially known for fostering mainly academic relations with the Jews.

Why did Pietism reach out and commence its work among the Jews? It was not primarily because of theological interests, or for academic zeal, or for theological dogmatism. Orthodox Protestantism may indeed have been motivated by these reasons. But in regard to Pietism, it cannot be ignored that, just prior to its emergence, there was a strong conviction that the 'fullness of times' had come for Gentiles and, thus, it was time to expect the conversion of Israel. As early as 1601, Johannes Molther wrote:

> Take into consideration how you want to support yourselves as Christians because you will no longer be allowed to practice that damned Jewish usury. For God will indeed support you, as he has never let anyone starve who has sought him and served him sincerely . . . May the faithful and merciful God rescue you from that evil and perverted mind so that, once the number of Gentiles has entered, likewise the fullness of the Jews may enter in.[10]

No doubt another basic reason for Pietism's missionary zeal was that Jesus had commanded his followers to teach all people of the world

---

[8] Rengstorf and Kortzfleisch, *Kirche und Synagoge I*, 15.

[9] Joh. F. A. de Le Roi, *Die evangelische Christenheit und die Juden in der Zeit der Herrschaft christlicher Lebensanschauungen unter den Völkern, Vol. I, Von der Reformation bis zur Mitte des 18. Jahrhunderts* (Leipzig: Verlag von H. Reuther, 1884), I, 200.

[10] Johannes Molther, *Theologia et chronologia judaica. Das ist: Gründliche Erzehlung der Juden Fabeln* (Frankfurt am Main: n.p., 1601), 96.

(Matt. 28:19–20). As Le Roi points out, according to the geographical knowledge of the time, the Protestant theologians believed there were no more lands without Christians; the last age announced by the Apostle Paul (Rom. 11:2–26) had dawned.[11] Pietism's real reason was a burning desire for the salvation of Jewish souls, notwithstanding the scepticism with which the Jewish community viewed this reason. 'For the time being, here the heart was dealing with the Jews and felt deeply the seriousness of the question of salvation', as Le Roi observed:[12]

> It seemed a matter of inner necessity to reach the hearts and consciences of the Jews with the Christian Gospel, seeking only what was best for the person. The Pietists sought to use warm and urgent language understandable to the Jews and to show deep, inner hurt whenever Jews turned their backs on the truth of the message.[13]

How effective were these efforts of the Pietists? If Le Roi's evaluation is valid, their effectiveness never reached beyond a certain large number of isolated Protestant Christian groups that were enthusiastic about the efforts.[14] The blame for this limited effectiveness goes to Pietism's debilitating subjectivism, and the inability to elevate in a more general way the spiritual status of the Lutheran church.

What follows is a catalogue-type summary of people and their contributions to missions among Jews in Germany of late Baroque and early Enlightenment times.[15] As mentioned, a strong impetus went forth from Spener. Quite diligent as a student to learn Hebrew and rabbinics, he travelled from his native Alsace to Basel in order to study the Talmud with a Jew. Being singularly impressed with the work of Esdras Edzardi in Hamburg, he journeyed there to observe first hand apparently well-suited techniques of winning the Jews for Christianity. Spener was convinced that it was the fault of Christians that Christianity had won so little acceptance among the Jews.[16] 'First and foremost the Jews are annoyed by the externals of the Christians,' wrote Spener in his *Pia Desideria*.[17] His voice resounded in pulpits from Frankfurt a/M to Dresden to Berlin. Sincere love, he believed, should

---

[11] Rengstorf and Kortzfleisch, *Kirche und Synagoge I*, 473.
[12] Le Roi, *Die evangelische Christenheit I*, 201.
[13] Le Roi, *Die evangelische Christenheit I*, 201.
[14] Le Roi, *Die evangelische Christenheit I*, 202.
[15] Le Roi, *Die evangelische Christenheit I*, 215–46.
[16] Le Roi, *Die evangelische Christenheit I*, 206–7.
[17] Le Roi, *Die evangelische Christenheit I*, 207.

be practiced towards the Hebrew nation. Although the broad masses did not accept Spener's message, it made him happy just to know that the Jews of Frankfurt were treated better as a result of his preaching.[18] Le Roi sums up Spener's life and work by commenting that he lacked the right combination of Luther's courage and energy in conjunction with his Christian nobleness.[19] Had this right combination been the case, writes Le Roi, perhaps the course of events for mission efforts among the Jews and for the statues of Jews in Germany would have been better.[20]

August Hermann Francke was known in his lectures at the University of Halle and in his sermons as a philo-Semite. Jews respected him and read his writings. Johann Caspar Schade of Berlin, another Pietist, was highly esteemed by the Jews and was deeply mourned by them at his death. At the beginning of the eighteenth century, Christian Götze, a preacher in Lockwitz near Dresden, chided Christian ministers for only mentioning Jews in an invective manner in sermons, forgetting all the great promises given to them in the Hebrew Scriptures. Christians, he believed, were obligated to be winsome towards the Jews. Christian Gerber, another preacher in Lockwitz from 1690 to 1731, is remembered for saying:

> There are many thousands of Christians living who their entire lives not once have had the thought of saying a single prayer for the poor Jews, even though the Lord Jesus Christ while on the cross prayed for them.[21]

In 1707, the mayor of Essen, Theodor M. Beckmann, called for a meeting with the rabbis so it could be determined if the time of the conversion and salvation of the Jews was imminent. In 1718, Dr. Johann Georg Pritius published a text written by a certain J.L. von B. entitled *Ohnmaßgeblicher Vorschlag von Beförderung des Heils der Juden [Non-Authoritative Suggestion for Promoting the Salvation of the Jews.]*[22] Without a doubt, this text is one of the most excellent testimonies of sympathetic stance of Pietism towards Jews. The faults of Jews and Christians as well are discussed, but a clear call to action is sounded for all Protestant Germany to become active in a campaign among the Jews. The thrust of the work would be carried out by special preachers and

---

[18] Le Roi, *Die evangelische Christenheit I*, 214.
[19] Le Roi, *Die evangelische Christenheit I*, 214.
[20] Le Roi, *Die evangelische Christenheit I*, 215.
[21] Le Roi, *Die evangelische Christenheit I*, 216.
[22] Le Roi, *Die evangelische Christenheit I*, 217.

by using materials written in Yiddish and Hebrew. Yet a dark cloud to be seen in the bright sides of Pietism's friendly relations with Jews was Sigismund Hosmann and his text *Das schwer zu bekehrende Juden-Hertz [The Hard-to-Convert Jewish Heart]* (1699 and 1701).

Abundant evidence exists for interest in the Jews as well as Talmudic and rabbinic literature. Between 1700 and 1750, a flurry of publications appeared, mainly dissertations and university publications. The authors and titles are too numerous to mention, but one author that cannot go unmentioned is Johann Philipp Storr. He worked in Heilbronn, had much contact with rabbis and other Jews and was a careful student of rabbinic literature. His book *Anima Judaismi jugalata [The Soul of Judaism Summarized]* (1721) has to be considered one of the most thorough attempts to use both the Old Testament and the New Testament, as well as rabbinic literature, in proving that Jesus of Nazareth was the true Messiah. Some writers, for example, Michael Heineccius and Johann Gottlieb Biedermann, lamented how the Jews had been brought to total despair by so many pseudo-messiahs and had lost the inner dimension of religion because of the Talmud's influence. A Rostock minister, M.J.B. Niehenk, preached in 1717 that he had given up all hope of the conversion of the Jews.[23] In 1728, Anton van der Hardt wrote exhaustively and critically of the sophistry employed by the rabbis in their interpretations of the Law and the Prophets.[24] For a period of time in 1720s and 1730s Johann Georg Walch occupied himself with the reasons why Jews in their theology saw no need for the forgiveness of sins. Later in this period, he emphasized the duty Christians had to work towards the conversion of Jews in their midst, learning how to do it mostly from Johann Heinrich Callenberg in Halle.[25] More on Callenberg and his work will follow.

Another admirable example from the circles of Pietism was Gottfried Olearius. In his text *Jesus der wahre Messias* [Jesus the true Messiah] (1714), he went beyond mediocrity in proving from the New Testament that Jesus is the true Messiah. His method was to let Jews express their most meaningful objections against Jesus, and then he answered with witnesses from the New Testament texts. Furthermore, he quoted extensively from Jewish sources.

One of the most knowledgeable men with regard to the entire corpus of Jewish literature was Christian Schöttgen.[26] His writings span

---

[23] Le Roi, *Die evangelische Christenheit I*, 223–4.
[24] Le Roi, *Die evangelische Christenheit I*, 225.
[25] Le Roi, *Die evangelische Christenheit I*, 226.
[26] Le Roi, *Die evangelische Christenheit I*, 228–9.

from 1719 to 1750: *Erklärung von Wörtern aus dem Jüdischen* (1719); *Jüdisches Zeugnis von der Wahrheit des allbereits gekommenen Messias* (1726); *Jüdisches Zeugnis von den Leibern der Heiligen, die mit dem Messias auferstanden sind* (1736); a weekly journal *Der Rabbiner* (1742); *Jesus der wahre Messias aus der alten und rein jüdischen Theologie darstellt* (1748). According to Le Roi, no one before Schöttgen ever treated the Jewish teachings on the Messiah so thoroughly.

Reviewing this brief glance at some of the names and events associated with Jewish missions, we close this section by emphasizing the following points: (1) For Protestant Orthodoxy, missions among the Jews meant simply that secular rulers compelled Jews and Muslims in their territories to hear Christian preaching; (2) The period of 'philo-Semitism' took its cue probably from early Luther, not late Luther; (3) The role of Pietism's Philipp Jakob Spener was quite decisive for 'philo-Semitism;' (4) The idea of the 'fullness of times', as Johannes Molther described it in 1601, no doubt influenced Pietism's stance; (5) Pietists made an effort to use warm and friendly language to bring the Christian message to Jews; (6) Limiting factors for Pietism's ultimate influence were its extreme subjectivism and possibly Spener's lack of courage and energy; (7) Although their names and works have long since faded into oblivion, the following philo-Semites deserve credit for promoting missions among Jews: Christian Gerber, Christian Götze, Gottfried Olearius, Johann Georg Pritius, Johann Caspar Schade, Christian Schöttgen and Johann Georg Walch.

Johann Heinrich Callenberg

As mentioned above, in this section we will take a closer look at Callenberg and his work. However, before outlining the life and work of Johann Heinrich Callenberg, it is appropriate to recall some important figures and events which set the stage for his work. Three highly influential men regarding the Jewish question prior to Callenberg were Johann Christoph Wagenseil (1633–1705), Philipp Jakob Spener (1635–1705) and August Hermann Francke (1663–1727). In 1681, Wagenseil published his monumental book *Tela Ignea Satanae* [Fiery Dart of Satan] in which he – sharply at odds with the Orthodox position – pleaded for understanding towards the Jewish question and for hope of their conversion.[27] In the foreword, he addressed princes, authorities,

---

[27] Rengstorf and Kortzfleisch, *Kirche und Synagoge II*, 89–90.

theologians and all of Christianity to urge them to show more tolerance based on genuine, gentle, patient, understanding love, not on violent, short-sighted love that seeks only conversion. These men were entering new territory in their thinking. Spener's teacher, Johann Konrad Dannhauer (1603–66), however, along with others from the Lutheran Orthodoxy, were heirs of a tradition started by the late Luther that all hopes of Jewish conversion were to be abandoned.[28]

As mentioned above, during this time, Pietism emerged as a viable aspect of Protestant Christianity. Interestingly, though, Pietism survived without much reference to the Old Testament.[29] It is a striking fact, however, that one of Pietism's strongest leaders, August Hermann Francke of Halle, was, by training, an Old Testament scholar and orientalist.[30] The Old Testament and New Testament, as Wagenseil had emphasized, represented a continuum and belonged together. They are of one and the same character.[31] Spener, influenced by Pietism's mystical spiritualism, emphasized the importance of the mystery of holiness when trying to bring the message of Jesus to the Jews.[32] The influence of Wagenseil and Spener was strong on Esdras Edzardi (1629–1708), a man mentioned above who spent fifty-one years devoted to Jewish missions in Hamburg. It is to this city that Francke journeyed and came under Edzardi's influence. Edzardi had been taught in the very first Insitutum Judaicum, founded by Spener in 1650 in Straßburg.[33] In Halle, Francke founded the Collegium Orientale, the intention of which was to work towards conversion of the Jews. This 'spirit of Halle' inspired the founding of two other institutes – The Royal Institute for Proselytes founded in Darmstadt by Johann Philipp Fresenius (1705–61) and the Institutum Judaicum founded also in the city of Halle by Callenberg. The latter existed from 1728 to 1792. Viewing the purpose of the institute merely as a means of helping Jews transition into German society, one author's opinion is that the Enlightenment made the institute superfluous.[34]

The life of Johann Heinrich Callenberg spans from 12 January 1694 to 16 July 1760, being born in the village of Molschleben as the son of

---

[28] Rengstorf and Kortzfleisch, *Kirche und Synagoge II*, 89.

[29] Rengstorf and Kortzfleisch, *Kirche und Synagoge II*, 100.

[30] Rengstorf and Kortzfleisch, *Kirche und Synagoge II*, 100–101.

[31] Rengstorf and Kortzfleisch, *Kirche und Synagoge II*, 98.

[32] Rengstorf and Kortzfleisch, *Kirche und Synagoge II*, 100.

[33] Rengstorf and Kortzfleisch, *Kirche und Synagoge II*, 103.

[34] Martin Schmidt in Rengstorf and Kortzfleisch, *Kirche und Synagoge II*, 104.

a farmer.[35] In handwritten letters on repository in the library of the orphanage in the city of Halle, Callenberg himself states that he was reared by 'modest but honest parents in all chastity and discipline'. Callenberg became fatherless at an early age. A local preacher took an interest in him and saw to it that the young Callenberg would attend a preparatory school in the city of Gotha. The school's widely respected director, Pastor Vockerodt, took him under his wing in a splendid manner. The Pietism of Spener and Francke had earlier had a strong influence on Vockerodt. This strong influence was directly transferred to Callenberg at an early age and would remain quite decisive for the remainder of his life. In 1715, at the age of 21, Callenberg entered the University of Halle and enthusiastically became a protégé of August Hermann Francke. While residing at the university, Callenberg made the acquaintance of a scholar named Salomon Negri. Originally from Damascus, Negri was broadly experienced as a translator and received an offer from Francke to become a professor of oriental languages. Negri was able to help Callenberg work his way through doubts about his faith, having himself experienced similar doubts while working and teaching among free thinkers in France and Italy. Ultimately, however, it was the sermons of Francke that had decisive influence on Callenberg and his religious thinking.

The idea of Christian missions fascinated him and occupied him most intensely during his greatest doubts. Initially he thought of missions among the Muslims and devoted himself to a study of Arabic, Turkish and Farsi under Professor Negri. Under the influence of Pietism, he avoided any form of exuberance in his Christian life and views on missions. He called his fellow missionaries 'itinerant co-workers'. He had a strong distaste for whatever smacked of appearances. He believed nothing compared to the inner peace that comes through faith in Jesus Christ; thus, he had a deep sense of obligation towards people who did not know this peace. The salvation of non-believers was a burden of the heart for him. At one point, he interested himself in preparing and distributing missionary literature among the Muslims of Russia. Originally a student of philosophy, he changed his study major to theology. His scholarly accomplishments and zeal for the kingdom of God attracted the attention of Francke who

---

[35] Le Roi, *Die evangelische Christenheit I*, 247–54. A work no doubt of great pertinence to this topic, Christoph Rymatzki's *Hallischer Pietismus und Judenmission. Johann Heinrich Callenbergs Institutum Judaicum und dessen Freundeskreis, 1728–1736* (Tübingen: Max Niemeyer, 2003), came to this writer's attention shortly before submitting the text for publication.

then desired to have him for a faculty position at the University of Halle. Thanks to the influence of King Friedrich Wilhelm I, in 1727 Callenberg was hired as professor of philosophy. By 1739, he was full professor of theology. Moser's *Lexikon* of 1740 states:

> Callenberg lectures on the history of scholarship in general and of every discipline in particular, on recent Jewish literature, on Arabic, inasmuch as a piece in the Koran is explained after a preceding explanation of the grammatical theories, on Syriac, on the rights of Christians under the Muslims, on metaphysics, especially on its application in theology, on rabbinics, and on Yiddish, and he keeps ascetic hours.[36]

Beginning in 1735, Callenberg lectured on the topic: 'How one can be helpful in converting Jews.' In some years, as many as 100 students attended this lecture.

Callenberg's academic career reaped praise as well as criticism. The praise was mainly for his knowledge of languages and rabbinics. The criticism was mainly for his lack of originality and lack of writing skills. According to Le Roi,[37] scholarship made no advances through Callenberg. The published texts we have examined are far removed from *belles lettres*. He is not numbered among outstanding German scholars. In the area of missions, however, his contributions were considerable. Callenberg was one of the most consummate Pietists who ever lived and taught. As Le Roi observes,[38] he was one of the most pious teachers a German university ever had. It was his Pietism that made him what he was – his love for men's souls, his diligence in work, his meaning for church history. 'It is through his Pietism that he truly became the father of evangelical Jewish missions', says Le Roi.[39] Were it not for him the question of Jewish missions would not have become what it became. All of this is inextricably tied with the so-called 'Jewish question' in German history.

Because of the limitations of time and space, it is possible to give only selected examples of Callenberg's work. He concentrated his efforts mainly on teaching at the University of Halle, on publishing materials to be distributed to the Jewish population and on training and sending out itinerant teachers or co-workers as he called them. A typical example of his publishing activity was the appearance, in 1729,

---

[36] Quoted in Le Roi, *Die evangelische Christenheit I*, 251.
[37] Le Roi, *Die evangelische Christenheit I*, 251–2.
[38] Le Roi, *Die evangelische Christenheit I*, 253.
[39] Le Roi, *Die evangelische Christenheit I*, 253.

of a tract entitled *Sendschreiben an die europäische Judenschaft* ['Message to European Jewry']. In this tract, the centuries-old accusation that the Jews used the blood of Christians is refuted. However, an attempt is made to point out real guilt and how forgiveness of sins comes only through the Messiah. The tracts published in Halle found wide circulation among the Jewish population and played an important role in the founding of the Institutum Judaicum.

As mentioned above, Callenberg thought of missions initially in terms of teaching Christianity to the Muslims. Thus, it is no surprise when he requested support to propagate Christian teaching not only among Jews, but also among the Muslims.[40] The resulting generous support suggests that Callenberg's request struck a resonant chord among eighteenth-century Protestant Germans. A powerful stimulus for Callenberg to continue his work in Halle was the view of a prelate named Hochstetter from Württemberg; Hochstetter, in a conversation with A.H. Francke, expressed the view that the evangelical church should try to expunge the criticism by Catholics that they were not doing enough for the conversion of the nations. Furthermore, he believed the Protestants should be doing a better job of showing love to the Jews. By way of Francke, these views reached Callenberg. After receiving the generous donations of money, he was convinced that a serious initiative should begin to bring the Christian message to the Jews.

Among the other printing projects foreseen by Callenberg were translations of the Gospel of Luke as well as the Acts of the Apostles, of course translated into Yiddish. Eventually plans were made to translate the Gospel of Luke into Hebrew. One converted Jew, Fromann (medical student and typesetter), was asked to help in this task. Students at the University of Halle paid attention to Callenberg's efforts and a good number were motivated to begin learning Yiddish with the intentions of serving as missionaries among the Jews. Callenberg was eager to see these future servants of the church carry his work into wider circles. Normally working as a professor of philosophy and theology, Callenberg began in 1729 teaching a course in missions and Yiddish. Further courses were added, for example, rabbinic writings, conditions among the Jews and how one should seek to win Jews for the truth of the gospel. Such projects and activities were nothing short of phenomenal in view of the past centuries of Christian history. Just fifty years prior, these activities would have been rare if not inconceivable!

---

[40] Le Roi, *Die evangelische Christenheit I*, 262.

Callenberg recognized that he needed a definite plan of action to create mission literature.[41] High priority would be a New Testament edition with partly short and partly exhaustive explanatory notes, some of which were specifically to refute Jewish objections to the Christian message as well as to prove the unity of the Hebrew Scriptures and the New Testament Scriptures. Furthermore, a brief church history text would be prepared to oppose Jewish distortions and misrepresentations of the Christian church. Finally, a text would present information about the various Christian churches – seen in the light of New Testament teaching – in order to counteract the objections to the rather splintered scene of Christendom and hopefully to encourage membership in a particular church.

Callenberg's ambitious publication and distribution endeavours appeared to be crowned with blessings for, as far away as Vienna, as well as in Hungary and Poland, one itinerant co-worker was using Callenberg's literature. Callenberg avoided the terms 'missions' and 'missionary' in connection with his work and had no intentions that the itinerant teachers should make this activity their life's work. He apparently wanted them to spend only a few years in this work and then move on to other duties as theologians and pastors. His strategy was to remain flexible with regard to commitments and obligations to the young men in the event the financial sources dried up.

As Le Roi comments,[42] these overly cautious characteristics of Callenberg's reflect how firmly rooted he was in Pietism's posture of anxiety. In evangelical circles, Callenberg is blamed for not having more faith and seeing the success of his institute as a sign of God's blessing and proceeding on with further expansion. Le Roi believes the missions could have taken on greater expansion if Callenberg had been less modest. The historical irony is that, had it not been for Pietism, the mission activity among the Jews would have never begun. Yet Pietism was, at the same time, the hindering barrier to further expansion. The young itinerant co-workers were expected, in addition to their rather Spartan lifestyle of denial and relinquishment, to write up reports of their journeys and conversations.

In one Jewish community after another, the rabbis placed a ban on the itinerant teachers from Callenberg's institute to prohibit them from entering Jewish lodgings or conversing with Jews. In spite of this, the opposite of what the rabbis desired occurred: a sizeable number

---

[41] Le Roi, *Die evangelische Christenheit I*, 266.
[42] Le Roi, *Die evangelische Christenheit I*, 271.

engaged in friendly conversations with the co-workers. Categories could be found, Callenberg writes, to describe the Jewish population. The stubborn ones persisted in the prohibitions and railed against accepting the books and listening to the co-workers. Thoughtful people, however, were insightful and realized that the books were effective. According to Callenberg, more and more rabbis actually began to foresee and fear the coming judgements on their people. One rabbi said: 'Wherever you people go forth to admonish Israel to repent, you are doing good and will receive eternal life for it; God will certainly reward you.'[43] In some instances, after a sermon was heard the ban was lifted.[44]

Throughout the more than 4,000 pages of text examined for this study, there runs the common thread that the co-workers sought humane, loving interactions with all Jews they encountered in their travels. Deborah Hertz, in her recent study, also validates our findings, stating that 'Pietists were enthusiastic to do good, and they did a great deal of it, administering orphanages, workhouses, and a wide variety of schools.'[45]

---

[43] Johann Heinrich Callenberg, *Relation von einer weitern Bemühung, Jesum Christum als den Heyland des menschlichen Geschlechts dem jüdischen Volck bekannt zu machen* (Halle: Buchdruckerey des jüdischen Instituti, 1738–45), *Erstes – Einund-zwanzigstes Stück* [Vols. 1–21], (Halle: Orientalische Buchdruckerey des Jüdischen und Muhammedanischen Instituti, 1745–51), *Zweiundzwanzigstes – Dreißigstes Stück* [Vols. 22–30]. Hereafter cited as CR with volume and page numbers.

[44] CR, Vol. XXV, Vorrede.

[45] See Deborah Hertz, *How Jews Became Germans. The History of Conversion and Assimilation in Berlin* (New Haven: Yale University Press, 2007), 31. We call attention to other remarks by Hertz pertaining to the Pietists, Callenberg and the work of Callenberg's Institute: 'Across Germany, pietist activists struggling against the Lutheran establishment became more interested in Hebrew and Judaism and more sympathetic to Jewish suffering.' (26) 'A far more serious challenge for the rabbis across Germany were the pietist missionaries, who were becoming ever more focused on Jewish conversion in these decades. Pietists resembled the messianic Jews insofar as they craved a more emotional faith and deeper communitarian experiences . . . Some of the pietist missionaries took Judaism very seriously and felt themselves to be sympathetic to the trials of the poor Jews . . . To be sure, the goal of the pietist missionaries was to make more Jews into Christians. But still, it is important that they thought they were showing respect for individual Jews.' (31) 'The pietist missionaries were innovative in how they tried to improve life circumstances after baptism . . . It was in Halle, a university town in Prussia, where pietists created a haven for converts . . . Moreover pietists were ready to take on various social welfare projects which would stimulate productivity and alleviate acute distress.' (32) 'Callenberg proposed the creation of residential communities for converts . . . The twenty traveling missionaries who worked for the Institute

To restate briefly the findings of this study, we conclude with the following points: (1) With regard to the question of Jewish missions, Callenberg was strongly influenced by Wagenseil, Spener, Francke and Edzardi; (2) Callenberg was heir of such Pietistic qualities as inner peace, a burden to share this inner peace with non-believers and a strong distaste for whatever smacked of mere appearances; (3) apparently Callenberg's plan to teach the Jews about the Christian faith became a reality when he commenced his publishing enterprise with the publication of Johann Müller's tract '*Licht am Abend*' in Yiddish; (4) the next development in his enterprise was to give formal training to young men (itinerant co-workers, as Callenberg called them) who would be sent out to Jewish communities; (5) the vast records of the co-workers' activities (thirty-four volumes) are admittedly not *belles lettres*, but they do disclose much detailed information about their daily routines and their conversations with the Jews; and (6) whereas not every encounter or conversation was friendly or led to immediate conversion, we believe we have presented convincing evidence that there were numerous congenial, memorable encounters between Christians and Jews. This, undoubtedly, is a great credit to the Pietist movement.

---

during the peak decades during the 1730s and 1740s all spoke Yiddish and knew their Jewish theology, both necessary to engage Jews in dangerous conversations.' (33) 'The rabbis did have cause for concern, because the innovative techniques employed by Callenberg's staff could be quite effective in attracting curious Jews . . . One reason for their success in attracting Jewish interest was that Callenberg's traveling missionaries paid close attention to the details of daily life.' (34) 'Just how successful the missionaries were in increasing baptisms is alas not known . . . some even call the phenomenon a 'plague of conversions' . . . In the fifty years between 1700 and 1750, scholars suggest that "several hundred" Jews became Protestants.' (35) This author is thankful for how the views and findings of Hertz corroborate in some respects the findings of this study.

7

Urgent Issues in Jewish Evangelism Around the Year 1900

Kai Kjær-Hansen

Translated from Danish into English by Birger Petterson

With the publication of papers from the Berlin 2008 conference, the World Evangelical Alliance can mark a 200-year anniversary, namely the foundation of the first Jewish mission society in modern history, The London Society for the Promotion of Christianity Amongst the Jews, popularly referred to as The London Jews Society (LJS), which was founded on 15 February 1809.[1]

In this essay, I confine myself to a few glimpses of urgent issues in Jewish evangelism in Europe in the last third of the nineteenth century. These glimpses may throw light on issues like direct and indirect Jewish mission and how we Christians should relate to the Jesus-believing Jews (Messianic Jews)[2] *of our time* and their relationship to the law and national customs. If these were burning issues in the period leading up to 1900, they are not less so today, which can be seen by the on-going discussion among Messianic Jews and others involved in Jewish evangelism.

---

[1] For the first 100 years, see W.T. Gidney, *The History of the London Society for Promoting Christianity Amongst the Jews. From 1809 to 1908* (London: London Society for Promoting of Christianity amongst the Jews, 1908).

[2] I am using the terminology of that time and refer to Jesus-believing Jews as Hebrew Christians, in German Judenchristen. The term 'Messianic Jews' began to be used in some groups about 1900.

Jewish Mission in Europe About 1900

After the formation of the London Jews Society in 1809, a large number of other Jewish mission societies came into existence in nineteenth-century Europe.[3] Louis Meyer, the Chicago Hebrew Mission and the Jewish mission's statistician about 1900, lists a total of forty-seven societies in Europe (including Russia) as well as thirteen auxiliaries about 1906.[4] For the year 1911, Meyer lists sixty-eight societies, as well as twenty-four auxiliaries in Europe and 137 centres.[5]

From the end of the nineteenth century, International Jewish Missionary Conferences were held regularly where networking among the various societies took place, and urgent issues in Jewish evangelism were treated.[6]

Concerning Jewish people's receptiveness to the gospel in the nineteenth century and in the first third of the twentieth century, large numbers are mentioned. Based on other scholars' investigations, Mitchell Glaser concludes:

> Therefore, the number of Jews who became Christians during the first third of the 20th century may have been upwards of 230,000 – far more than the 224,000 Jews during the 19th century mentioned by Rev. J.F. de le Roi for the entire 20th century [read: 19th century].[7]

There is no reason to query the claim that a large number of Jews did go over to Christianity in the period, but it is difficult to say how many did so for pragmatic, political or social reasons. The same applies to the

---

[3] To this, and to the history of Jewish mission in the nineteenth century in general, see what is still considered the standard work, J.F.A. de le Roi, *Geschichte der evangelischen Judenmission seit Entstehung des neueren Judentums* (2 vols.; 2d ed.; Leipzig: J.C. Hinrichs'sche Buchhandlung, 1899). The latest treatment of the history of Jewish mission in the first half of the twentieth century is by Mitchell L. Glaser, *A Survey of Missions to the Jews in Continental Europe, 1900–1950* (Ann Arbor, Mich.: UMI Dissertation Services, 1999).

[4] Louis Meyer, 'Protestant Missions to Jews', in *Jahrbuch der evangelischen Judenmission*/Yearbook of the Evangelical Missions among the Jews (ed. Herman L. Strack; Leipzig: J.C. Hinrichs'sche Buchhandlung, 1906), 93–123.

[5] Louis Meyer, 'Directory of Protestant Missionary Societies', in *Jahrbuch der evangelischen Judenmission/Yearbook of the Evangelical Missions among the Jews* (ed. Hermann L. Strack; Leipzig: J.C. Hinrichs'sche Buchhandlung, 1913), 86–96.

[6] A brief historical survey of the first of these conferences is given by Herman L. Strack in *Jahrbuch* (ed. Strack; 1906), 5–10.

[7] Glaser, *Survey of Missions to the Jews*, 409.

question of how many of them later returned to Judaism, but it seems to be a significant number. When a check is made of the mission societies' registers of baptisms performed, it becomes clear, however, that only a small percentage of these conversions and baptisms took place within the framework of the missions.

During the nineteenth century, clergymen would sometimes carry out Jewish mission alongside their regular activities. The work of the Jewish missions was normally based at a centre, though there were also 'wandering missionaries', such as the well-known Joseph Wolff, who travelled widely.[8] Sometimes the missionaries also made journeys from the centres. At the 'station', there was often a library and a reading room where not only mission literature, but also daily newspapers, were available. They published a number of pamphlets and books; especially popular were biographies of Jews who had come to faith in Jesus. In 1837, The London Jews Society published the *Book of Common Prayer* in Hebrew – followed by, in 1838, a new translation of the New Testament in Hebrew. In 1877, Professor Franz Delitzsch's translation of the New Testament in Hebrew appeared.

People were invited to Bible studies and meetings at the centres. The missionaries could be seen in the Jewish streets and market squares, in restaurants and on trains where they distributed Bibles and New Testaments in different languages and tried to come into contact with Jews. They tried to prove from the Scriptures that Jesus was the promised Messiah. In time, chapels were sometimes built. Schools were set up and, depending on circumstances and resources, so were medical clinics, etc. Diaconal work and humanitarian relief in connection with pogroms and disasters were also part of the work.

In some locations, the missions set up so-called proselyte homes where converted or seeking Jews could stay, be trained in a workshop and, not least, receive Christian instruction. The objective in all this was, of course, that Jews came to faith, were baptized and incorporated in the Christian church. Some of the proselytes became involved in the mission's service. Others needed help to get away from the environment where they were converted since they had lost their livelihood because of opposition from their Jewish background. The Jewish community regarded the convert as an apostate; sometimes the family even declared such a person dead and announced it publicly as such.

---

[8] See e.g. Hugh Evan Hopkins, *Sublime Vagabond. The Life of Joseph Wolff – Missionary Extraordinary* (Worthing, UK: Churchman Publishing, 1984). About Wolff's three visits to Jerusalem as a Bible man, in 1822, 1823 and 1829, see my articles in *Mishkan* 49 (2006):42–58; 54 (2008): 64–79 and 58 (2009): 60–72

Missionary candidates, be they Jewish or non-Jewish, often received their training at seminaries where the instruction included a thorough knowledge of the Talmud and rabbinical writings, so the candidates could be well equipped to present the gospel in a Jewish environment.

Towards the end of the nineteenth century, four important Hebrew Christians came into focus.[9] In chronological order, they were Yechiel Lichtenstein or Herschensohn (ca. 1830–1912), Joseph Rabinowitz (1837–99), Chajim Jedidjah (Christian Theophilus) Pollak known as Lucky (1854–1916) and Isaac Lichtenstein (1825–1908) – all four of Eastern European origin.[10]

Let us now put the clock back to 1872 and look at a description of an evangelistic outreach in Poland.

The Dworkowicz Team in the Late Summer of 1872

Yechiel Lichtenstein, one of the above-mentioned important Hebrew Christians, was in the summer of 1872 attached to the work which the Jewish believer Paul Dworkowicz had begun in Warsaw in 1870. Dworkowicz decided to make a missionary journey in the late summer of 1872 and visited ten major towns. Dworkowicz was one of the missionaries who wrote a travelogue which gives us an insight into this journey.[11]

After visiting two towns, the outreach team, consisting of Dworkowicz, Koschade (referred to as 'colporteur') and Lichtenstein, ministered in Lublin from 28 August to 12 September 1872. And what a colourful description Dworkowicz gives!

A careful record was kept of statistics. Ten towns were visited during the seven-week missionary journey – Lichtenstein was with them approximately half of the time; they sold or distributed 239 complete Bibles, 366 New Testaments, 3,772 parts of Holy Scripture and 1,248 tracts; a total of 5,625 portions of Holy Scriptures and tracts in seven languages, namely Hebrew, Polish, Russian, German, French, Yiddish and Slavic.[12]

---

[9] Apart from Rabinowitz, only biographical information relevant for the main issues will be given for the other three.

[10] We are still waiting for a survey of similarities and differences between these four important Hebrew Christians.

[11] Paul Dworkowicz, 'Aus dem Reisejournal des Pastor Dworkowicz', *Saat auf Hoffnung* (1873): 152–9.

[12] Dworkowicz, 'Aus dem Reisejournal', 152.

Non-Jews also were approached. The primary objective of the mission-ary journey was to reach Jews with the gospel, but they also took the opportunity to meet non-Jews and distribute Bibles, for example, to Roman Catholics. This met with opposition from Catholic quarters but there was support from some Protestant ministers and others.

Strategy and division of labour. The members of the team knew their own strengths and weaknesses and divided the tasks among them-selves accordingly. Dworkowicz wrote the following about the out-reach in Lublin and the strategy for reaching the Jews with the gospel:

> Koschade went from house to house and presented the Word of God to Russians, Poles and Germans; Lichtenstein went to see Chasidim, Kabbalists and Talmudists in order to dispute with them, and I chose the educated, enlightened and learned Jews in order to proclaim the gospel to them. We also wrote public notices in Hebrew and had them put up in all the synagogues. We did this in all towns. Soon the Jews started coming to us in great numbers, some to buy our books, others to dispute with us, and others again to berate us.[13]

A few glimpses of their activities. On 5 September, some Jews asked the team to give a *derascha* [sermon] the following Saturday. This took place on 7 September. A poster was put up on the house where they stayed. On it was written, in Hebrew, the sentence from Matthew 3:2: 'Repent, for the kingdom of Heaven is near!' The poster also announced the theme of the meeting: Sin and redemption, Messiah and righteousness – together with the texts: Isaiah 53, Daniel 9 and Zechariah 12. Almost 150 people from all walks of life showed up for the meeting, which started at 3 p.m. First, Dworkowicz preached; he opened his sermon in the name of Abraham, Isaac and Jacob; it lasted forty-five minutes and there were no interruptions from the audience. Next, Lichtenstein preached in the Jewish-German tongue – also for forty-five minutes and without inter-ruptions. After this, most of those assembled left the room, only Chasidim, scholars and zealots stayed behind and debated with them for two hours. During this discussion, Professor Pruetz, a man of the church, served as scholarly authority. At the conclusion of the meeting, some tracts were handed out, and they were thankfully received.[14]

On 9 September, Lichtenstein was having a meal in a restaurant, but people came in from the street and asked him to proclaim the Word of

---

[13] Dworkowicz, 'Aus dem Reisejournal', 153.
[14] Dworkowicz, 'Aus dem Reisejournal', 156.

God to them. He then preached about the crucified Jesus. Because of their activities, the team were banned from all synagogues. The Catholic priests also banned them from their churches.

On 11 September, a large crowd of Jews gathered outside the house where the missionaries were staying. Because of a ban imposed on the missionaries by the rabbis, the crowd dared not enter the house. 'They remained in the street outside our windows and demanded that we preach to them through the window. We obliged them by fulfilling their legitimate request', wrote Dworkowicz and continued: 'So Mr Lichtenstein stood in front of one window, and I in front of another, and we preached the gospel of the revealed Messiah to the assembled people.'[15]

It is worth noticing that the Dworkowicz team operated on the assumption that Jews were different and, therefore, needed to be approached with the gospel in different ways. This they were able to do because they worked as a team making use of different methods and resources, but this was far from always the case. The direct mission method practised by the team would be met with severe criticism almost twenty years later (see below). In the meantime, Joseph Rabinowitz had appeared on the stage.

Joseph Rabinowitz and his Congregation in Kishinev

The story of Joseph Rabinowitz is a fascinating one.[16] He was born in Russia in 1837 and raised under the influence of Chasidism. In his youth, he had turned to Enlightenment Judaism and become a well-known Haskala Jew who published articles in the Jewish journals in Russia and made a living as a solicitor. In the 1870s, he became active in the Zionist groups in Russia and began to wonder whether an immigration of Russian Jews to Palestine might solve the Jewish question.

In 1882, he went to Palestine to look into the possibility of a Jewish settlement. During this trip, his Zionist expectations were frustrated and he came to believe in Jesus on the Mount of Olives. Returning to his native town, Kishinev, in south western Russia, he established a Jewish Messianic congregation, *Bnei Israel, Bnei Brit Hadasha*, Israelites

---

[15] Dworkowicz, 'Aus dem Reisejournal', 157–8.

[16] In order to avoid a multitude of notes with long titles, I refer, where possible, to my own book on Rabinowitz: Kai Kjær-Hansen, *Joseph Rabinowitz and the Messianic Movement* (Edinburgh/Grand Rapids: Handsel Press/Eerdmans, 1995).

of the New Covenant, and became its leader. He held services almost every Sabbath and on Christian and Jewish holidays and feasts until he died in 1899 at the age of 62 and was buried in the graveyard of the Israelites of the New Covenant. In accordance with his own wish, his tombstone bears the inscription: 'An Israelite who believed in Jehovah and His Anointed One, Jesus of Nazareth, King of the Jews. Joseph Ben David Rabinowitz.'

Rabinowitz's ideas and his work are still worth noting, as are Jewish as well as Christian reactions to him. He launched a development which has deeply influenced the messianic movement of Jesus-believing Jews. With a few exceptions, the general view before Rabinowitz was that a Jew who converted to Christianity ceased to be a Jew. Rabinowitz vigorously challenged this view, protesting against the idea that it was legalism if a Jesus-believing Jew wanted to retain national Jewish customs. The lasting importance of Rabinowitz's work is that he stubbornly maintained that his faith in Jesus had not turned him into an ex-Jew, that his Jewish identity had not been 'drowned' in baptism and that a Jesus-believing Jew has freedom to live in a Jewish manner.

Rabinowitz made the question of Jesus a Jewish matter and, thereby, provoked the Jewish world. He complicated the situation for the Jews who had converted to Christianity in order to get rid of their Jewish identity, and he insisted to Gentile Christians that it was not a sin for Jewish believers to continue to be Jews after their conversion.

Rabinowitz's Adherence to Jewish Customs

In March 1884, a conference was held in Kishinev. It was the first official meeting between Rabinowitz and representatives from the Jewish missions; these included the British Society for the Propagation of the Gospel among the Jews and W. Faber, who represented Professor Franz Delitzsch and the German Central Agency. Some of the Gentile Christians present voiced their misgivings about Rabinowitz 'smuggling the law in through the back door'.

According to Rabinowitz, he and others similarly disposed wanted to observe Jewish customs inherited from the fathers, in so far as these did not clash with the spirit of Christianity. From a *religious* point of view, he and his adherents believed that the law had been completely fulfilled by the Messiah. But from a *patriotic* point of view, they considered themselves under obligation to observe the law, in so far as nationality and circumstances made it possible.

This gave rise to a debate about circumcision and the Sabbath. The Gentile Christians were worried that Rabinowitz might want to observe these commandments – not just for national, but also for religious, reasons. Therefore, they asked Rabinowitz if he believed that a Hebrew Christian who did not circumcise his child committed a sin. Rabinowitz answered, 'He does not commit a sin, but he alienates himself from his own Jewish people.' He gave a similar answer to the question about whether a Hebrew Christian who did not observe the Sabbath committed a sin.[17]

For Rabinowitz, circumcision was a sacred sign given to Abraham and the Jewish people. Rabinowitz was convinced that it was wrong for Gentiles to be circumcised – and he quoted Galatians 5:2.

He also believed that the Sabbath had been given to Israel as an eternal commandment. The Israelites of the New Covenant should, Rabinowitz believed, keep this commandment. However, if they did not keep it, they did not commit a sin. Moreover, he believed them to be totally free concerning the laws conditional on the possession of the land of Israel, on the temple service, on the instalment of the authorities, on the hot climate and on fighting an idol-worship that no longer existed.

Therefore, Rabinowitz had no scruples, for example, about turning on the samovar and lighting a cigarette on a Sabbath – much to the surprise of Pastor A. Venetianer, a Hungarian Hebrew Christian visiting him in Kishinev in 1887.

Networking in Connection With Rabinowitz's Baptism

The circumstances surrounding Rabinowitz's baptism provide a fine example of networking among the leaders of the missionary societies. They had very different views on baptism but they accepted a solution for the benefit of Rabinowitz and his cause although none of them were one hundred per cent satisfied. There is another noteworthy matter: Rabinowitz himself participated in the efforts to find a solution.

Rabinowitz was baptized in Berlin in 1885 and under quite extraordinary circumstances, one has to admit. He was baptized in the Bohemian-Lutheran Church by the Congregationalist (Methodist) Pastor and Professor C.M. Mead from Andover, Massachusetts, in the presence of a few invited people. He was baptized on the confession of

---

[17] Kjær-Hansen, *Joseph Rabinowitz*, 54–6.

a creed that he himself had written in Hebrew, having first testified to his belief in the Apostles' Creed. But still he wanted his own creed in seven points for his own congregation.

In that way, and this is the important point, Rabinowitz was baptized into the universal church of Christ without becoming a member of a particular denomination and without losing his Jewish identity. Delitzsch recognized this and defended Rabinowitz when he was later attacked for the method of his baptism.[18]

For Rabinowitz, it was important that his baptism became *publicly* known; for him it was not a private matter. Later, he criticized another contemporary Jesus-believer, Isaac Lichtenstein, for not being baptized. They met in 1891, in Budapest, where the last member of Rabinowitz's family, his wife, was baptized. After her baptism, Rabinowitz wired back to their children: '*Mama gerettet*' (Mum saved) which, better than any words, tells us something about Rabinowitz's view of baptism. Isaac Lichtenstein never took the decisive step of being baptized. In a letter, published in German, Rabinowitz writes: 'If Rabbi Lichtenstein verily loves his people Israel . . . let him be baptized. By being baptized, he will set a good example for others.'[19]

Although Rabinowitz himself was baptized, he never got permission to baptize others or to administer the sacraments. The authorities would only allow him to function as a preacher. So when the term 'Rabinowitz's congregation' is used, it should always be borne in mind that he was never given permission to establish a church proper. It goes without saying that a church proper cannot exist without baptism and Holy Communion. In 1887, it looked as if this situation could be remedied when the above-mentioned A. Venetianer baptized some members of his congregation in Rohrbach. However the authorities put a stop to such baptisms – possibly due to behind the scenes protests by Pastor Rudolf Faltin or others from the Lutheran church in Kishinev. Without baptism or Holy Communion, it is no wonder that Rabinowitz's movement crumbled after his death.

Franz Delitzsch, Gustaf Dalman and Hermann L. Strack all defended Rabinowitz when he came under attack. Pastor Faltin in Kishinev and others found Judaistic elements in his theology and accused him of Ebionitism. From the very beginning, Delitzsch was electrified at what went on in Kishinev. He translated and published Rabinowitz's writings. Regarding Rabinowitz's circumcision, the Sabbath and

---

[18] Kjær-Hansen, *Joseph Rabinowitz*, 75–90.
[19] Kjær-Hansen, *Joseph Rabinowitz*, 174–5.

special Jewish feasts, things Rabinowitz was most determined not to abandon, Delitzsch cherished the hope that Rabinowitz, with his Pauline attitude, would reach the same conclusion as the Apostle Paul had and abandon this view. Delitzsch stated that Israel's national distinctiveness must be maintained, and would be maintained, without circumcision and with Sunday instead of the Sabbath.[20] But when, for example, Faltin maintained that a Hebrew Christian congregation must be built within the evangelical church in Russia, Delitzsch asked: 'Lutheran or Reformed?' Delitzsch continued to argue in a way which shows that he took Rabinowitz and those like-minded seriously and saw the problem: as they wished to retain the Sabbath and circumcision, how could a Lutheran or Reformed church government officially legalize this retention![21]

But Delitzsch's disapproval was not so strong that he could not rejoice in Rabinowitz's work. He knew that Rabinowitz's doctrine of justification was in agreement with the Bible and the Reformation Fathers; this was the crucial point for Delitzsch. In this connection, it must also be mentioned that, at an early stage, Rabinowitz had made Romans 10:4 one of his key verses: 'The Messiah is the end of the law.' This was evident in his sermons; it was also evident because this was the text inscribed on the Torah school on his house of prayer (at least in the period 1885-1890, after which he acquired a new building, the Somerville Memorial Hall). This Torah scroll bore this very inscription in Hebrew: 'The Messiah is the end of the law.'

In Rabinowitz, we thus have a Hebrew Christian leader who was a member of the universal church without belonging to a denomination; his baptism was publicly known; he wanted to retain Jewish customs in order not to alienate himself from his people; he forms a congregation; he did not criticize others' mission methods; he was not particularly enterprising regarding evangelistic outreach (not due to a programme or a mission strategy but to his personality). In his last years, however, he had plans for railway evangelization: to have a railway coach built and travel in it round Russia; He would then run the coach into a siding at stations, and hold meetings and distribute New Testaments at places where the gospel would not otherwise be preached to Jews. The project was never realized, but it shows that Rabinowitz wanted to carry out direct mission.[22]

---

[20] Kjær-Hansen, *Joseph Rabinowitz*, 113, 203.

[21] Kjær-Hansen, *Joseph Rabinowitz*, 139.

[22] Kjær-Hansen, *Joseph Rabinowitz*, 198–9.

Another example of Rabinowitz's direct mission methods was: facing the street, on the side wall of Somerville Memorial Hall in Kishinev, where Rabinowitz held services from 1891, were written the words from Acts 2:36 in gilt Hebrew and Russian letters: 'Therefore let all the house of Israel know assuredly, that God hath made the same Jesus, whom ye have crucified, both Lord and Christ.'[23] It could hardly have been a more direct way of saying that Jews needed Jesus for salvation.

For Delitzsch, it was also important that Rabinowitz's movement remain independent, so that it would not get into the clutches of a single mission society. According to his plan, the movement would, in time, become financially independent of money from abroad. This never happened.

Rabinowitz was also struck by the criticism that came from the so-called Leipzig programme from about 1890, with which we will now deal briefly.

The Leipzig Programme's Criticism of the Mission Practice

From about 1890, the Jewish mission societies were fiercely attacked and criticized for their mission practice. The criticism came mainly from people who were, or had been, attached to the Institutum Judaicum in Leipzig. These people were pious and wanted the best for Israel as to salvation. While the spokesmen for the criticism were Gentiles such as Johannes Müller and August Wiegand, it was a Hebrew Christian, Chajim Jedidjah (Christian Theophilus) Pollak, better known as Lucky who fuelled the criticism. It is no exaggeration to say that Lucky spent more time missionizing among Gentiles than among his own dearly-loved Jewish people.

Lucky had come to faith while studying in Berlin in the mid-1870s. He was in the USA for some years during the 1880s. In 1889, he returned to Europe, where he immediately took up his mission work – among the candidates educated at the Institutum Judaicum in Leipzig.

Lucky loved Jesus and his people, I said. But few, if any, have fought against Jewish mission like Lucky did. He became the principal architect behind a new mission strategy, later known as the Leipzig programme. He befriended people who had been at the Institutum Judaicum in Leipzig and spent much time with them.

---

[23] Kjær-Hansen, *Joseph Rabinowitz*, 144–5.

The way I read the sources, Lucky had indeed been baptized – even three times. Be that as it may, Lucky did not advertise his baptism, as for example Rabinowitz did. For Lucky, baptism was a private matter. In this way, he avoided being considered a *Meschummad*, an apostate, and could be buried in a Jewish graveyard when he died in 1916.

The Leipzig Programme

The Leipzig programme was a mission strategy that confronted the traditional organized Jewish mission work which was quick to offer interested Jews baptism, education in a proselyte home and sometimes money so they could travel to Western Europe. In its most radical form, the Leipzig programme maintained that no one of Jewish descent should be a paid missionary to the Jews. The use of paid Jewish missionaries was, it was said, counterproductive when witnessing to Jews. The traditional mission was criticized for de-nationalizing Jews who came to faith in Jesus. In Western Europe, there was no need for special missionaries to the Jews or for Jewish mission or a special training for people to reach Jewish people with the gospel. This was for the churches to do.

Talmud Jews were the primary target, and the majority of those lived in Eastern Europe. So the missionary candidates should first of all be trained to help them to meet the East European Orthodox Jews. But not even in Eastern Europe should they engage in direct mission. The first task of a missionary to the Jews was to work for the formation of living, evangelical Christian congregations – in contrast to the Roman Catholic and Greek/Russian Orthodox churches; this would generate interest among Jews. The vision was to fight anti-Semitism and to call forth love for Israel in these Gentile Christian congregations. In other words: a missionary to the Jews should work from such a Diaspora mission, associate with, for example, congregations in the German colonies and make them ardent and zealous for the cause of Israel. The motivating factor was the salvation of all Israel at some time in the future. The few Jews who accepted the gospel were seen as a prerequisite for this future.

Even if a discussion about these things might be justified, the Leipzig programme was often presented in an unreasonably polemical tone. About the mission carried out until then, Johannes Müller, mission secretary for the Leipzig-based Jewish mission, The German Central Agency, stated that it was not a question about a few mistakes but about a wrong principle. The earlier mission was, Müller claimed, characterized by proselytizing (*Proselytenmacherei*) and was of an anti-Semitic nature. The mission's proselytes were scum (*Ausschuss*) and deserved the Jewish term of abuse, *Meschummadim*, for apostates they were, they had abandoned their people, their past, present and future. The earlier mission was only directed at individuals, not the Jewish people as a nation. It was among Eastern European Jews who had retained a Jewish faith that the gospel had a future.[24]

This is not the place to arbitrate between the conflicting parties in which several individuals, for example, Professor Gustaf Dalman and G.M. Löwen, the Berlin Society's Jewish missionary, were very critical of the so-called new method.[25] Each had a legitimate concern. This debate was carried out by means of a long series of publications over a period of time. This literary feud showed that something important was at stake, theologically and missiologically, but it also showed how difficult it was for the different groups to speak together, make concessions and avoid generalizations on the basis of isolated cases of, for example, proselytes' and Jewish missionaries' moral flaws.[26] Even though history did show examples of the establishment of living, evangelical Diaspora congregations, modelled on the Leipzig programme, which attracted Jews, this indirect mission did not give the desired results. The accusation against the direct mission for its lack of results rebounded upon those who argued for indirect mission like a boomerang – perhaps even with double force.

Naturally no one involved in Jewish mission at that time could have anything against living Christian congregations where they tried to create love for the Jewish people. All involved in Jewish mission at that time looked forward to the time when Israel *as a people*, sometime in the future, would come to faith in Jesus. A crucial question for *opponents* of

---

[24] Cf. e.g. Johannes Müller's articles in *Saat auf Hoffnung* (1890): 156–68; (1891): 7–12 and (1891): 65–77.

[25] See e.g. G. Dalman 'Falsche Wege', published anonymously in *Nathanael* (1891): 161–81 and W.G. Löwen, 'Zur Abwehr wider eine neue Verunglimpfung der Judenmission', *Nathanael* (1893), 33–50. Both articles have references to contributions to the ongoing debate.

[26] The Swedish Israel Mission had a situation in the late 1880s when the wife of the proselyte home's leader ran away with a proselyte; after some time she returned to her husband, who then left his post. In 1900, the Jewish missionary Paulus Wolff was found to have submitted a report about his work in Krakow which was published; it appeared to be an exact translated copy of a section from 'The British Workman', May 1873; he resigned but was re-employed for service a few years later. Cf. Lars Edvardsson, *Kyrka och Judendom* (Lund: CWK Gleerup, 1976), 56–7.

the Leipzig programme was whether it was enough here and now to *prepare* oneself for that time; they did not think it was. Some of the Leipzig programme's people seem to have been so intent on that future that they failed their responsibility to meet the Jews of their own time, in a direct manner, with the gospel. With some right, the *opponents* of the Leipzig programme could ask its advocates if it was more important for *them* that Jews who came to believe in Jesus retained the connection with Judaism than that they somehow identified with the Christian church through baptism.

To sum up regarding the Leipzig programme: struggle against all mission hypocrisy, no direct Jewish mission, no paid Jewish missionaries and, for Jesus-believing Jews, no national breach with their Jewishness. The issue of how Jews who came to faith in Jesus should relate to the Christian church remained unresolved.

Lucky won quite a few Germans and some Danes, Norwegians and others who had been at the Institutum Judaicum over to his side. It should, however, be mentioned that not all advocates of the Leipzig programme were as pronounced in their views and mission practice as Lucky was. For those who were born Jewish, who were then paid missionaries to the Jews and who worked energetically and faithfully in order to reach other Jews with the gospel in a 'direct' way, Lucky was not, to say the least, popular.

Löwen, who despite some tensions between himself and Lucky, kept a friendly, lifelong correspondence with him, summed up his opinion of Lucky in the following words:

> Lucky's exaggerated love of his Jewish people destroyed, unfortunately, what he had laboriously achieved. He led the souls to Christ and then drove them back into the synagogue, the same synagogue where they daily recite Moses Maimonides' confession which consciously defame Christ as an idol.[27]

Urgent Issues Today

The urgent issues in Jewish evangelism about 1900, briefly described here, continue to be urgent issues in Jewish evangelism today – more than one hundred years later.

---

[27] G.M. Löwen, 'Christian Theophilus Lucky', *Nathanael* (1917), 16. Did Lucky in his last years regret his struggle against the Jewish missions? This is an issue I hope to be able to deal with in a forthcoming issue of *Mishkan*.

A few groups in the messianic movement today want, for example, to distance themselves from the Christian church and Gentile Christian missionaries; they seem to believe that Jesus-believing Jews are *obliged* to observe the law, they are critical of direct mission and are, in some cases, willing to open the door a crack for the view that Jews who have not accepted the gospel of Jesus are nevertheless included in his salvation.[28]

In 2007, Tuvya Zaretsky, president of the Lausanne Consultation on Jewish Evangelism (LCJE), commented on published statements about evangelism by a few writers associated with the American messianic congregational movement with the following words:

> 'Some statements reflected a potential negative influence regarding the uniqueness of Christ for salvation and the necessity of a direct, vocal witness to the gospel of Jesus Christ among the Jewish people.' This was said in connection with the publication of the resolution An Appeal for Unity, drawn up by LCJE North America, which joyfully acknowledged that the existence of messianic congregation is a visible and identifiable expression of Jewish faith in the Messiah. But a certain concern was also expressed that some within the messianic movement were not properly emphasizing active Jewish outreach.[29]

In this essay I have not been able to – nor have I wanted to – hide the fact that, of the four important Hebrew Christians around the year 1900, Joseph Rabinowitz was, in my opinion, the one who still is most relevant for Jesus-believing Jews today. With reference to the freedom given by the gospel, Jesus-believing Jews can go on living as Jews and yet obey the command to make the name of Jesus known among other Jews. Jesus-believing Jews have a different 'dress code' from the Christian church, but through baptism, made publicly known, they express the fundamental unity with the Christian church. This unity also entitles them to criticize this church publicly and point out its sins, past and present; just as some of us feel *obligated* to keep alive the memory of the church's infamous deeds against the Jewish people.

---

[28] See *Mishkan* 53 (2007) with excerpts from papers from the Borough Park Symposium, New York, 8–10 October 2007. Similar themes and discussions are treated in the journal *Kesher* 22 (2008), published by the Union of Jewish Messianic Congregations. See also other papers from the Berlin 2008 conference in this volume.

[29] Tuvya Zaretsky, 'Explanation for "An Appeal for Unity"', *LCJE Bulletin* 88 (2007): 10. The Appeal is printed on pages 10–11.

Like everybody else, Rabinowitz was, naturally, conditioned by his own time, as were the other people of the mission, Delitzsch, Dalman and Strack included. It is a shame that the discussion in our time is often conducted without much knowledge of and familiarity with the discussion that took place in Germany around the year 1900.

But all other things being equal, I urge that not one person or one group within the messianic movement today, even if they believe that Jewish believers in Jesus are *obligated* to observe the law or should strive to live within the synagogue, will be allowed to decide Christians' attitude to the question about the fundamental liberty that the gospel gives to *all* and Jesus-believing Jews *first*. Messianic Jews and Christians have to go on struggling with the complicated New Testament passages. In spite of all our differences, there is only one church, one baptism, one body of the Messiah, one way to be saved. We belong together!

When I have argued that Jesus-believing Jews have freedom to observe Jewish customs, this question suggests itself: Have I played down the danger of legalism? I do not think so. I am fully conscious of the danger. But a concession is in order here. It is true that legalism is a danger to Jewish believers in Jesus, but it is important to add that Christians, also evangelicals, are not exempt from this danger. Over the years evangelicals and other Christians have made a number of by-laws which take the form of legalism, something we still have to be wary of.

So, in this matter, Messianic Jews and Christians are facing the same problem.

Last word: Rabinowitz on 'Joseph's Misfortune'

And with this I conclude, but not without letting Joseph Rabinowitz have the last word – as a reminder to us all of what is basically at stake.[30]

> The misfortune of my people has always been on my heart. I have also tried various remedies to relieve it, but all has been in vain.
>
> When a doctor comes to a patient, he first has to question the patient closely before he can prescribe a remedy for the disease. He feels the

---

[30] Rabinowitz's story *Joseph's Misfortune* is found in slightly variant versions and can be traced back to 1884–85. Cf. Kjær-Hansen, *Joseph Rabinowitz*, 235.

pulse, presses here and there, asking all the time, Does it hurt here? Is there pressure there? Have you pain here? But not until the doctor touches the tender spot, does a really clear answer come from the patient. The pain squeezes the words from him, Don't press so hard, it hurts!

That was my experience when I concerned myself with my people's sufferings. I have in vain pressed various places. As I was not striking the tender spot, there was hardly any answer.

If I said, The Talmud and all the rabbinical extraneous matter do not come, as is claimed, from Sinai, but they are human matters full of wisdom and unwisdom, then these words made little impression upon my people.

If I said, Nor does the Tanakh (the Old Testament) contain anything other than human words, unproven stories, and unbelievable miracles, then all the time I remained the respected Rabinowitz; that did not cause my people any pain either.

My people remained calm when I placed Moses on an equal footing with the conjurors of our day; it did not hurt them when I called the same Moses an impostor. Indeed, I might even deny God without my people uttering a single sound of pain.

But when I returned from the Holy Land with the glad news: Jesus is our brother, then I struck the tender spot. A scream of pain could be heard and resounded from all sides, Do not press, do not touch that, it hurts!

Well, it does hurt: But you must know, my people, that that is indeed your illness; you lack nothing but your brother Jesus. Your illness consists precisely in your not having him. Receive him and you will be healed of all your sufferings.

8

'No Exit' for the Jews: Germany's Romantic Nationalism and the Modern Reality of Anti-Semitism

Mike McDuffee

In his history of the twentieth century, *The World Revolution of Westernization*, Theodore H. von Laue interprets the global state of integration at present to be based upon Western expansion:

> For the first time in all human experience the world of revolution of Westernization brought together, in inescapably intimate and virtually instant interaction, all the peoples of the world, regardless of their prior cultural evolution or their capacity – or incapacity – for peaceful coexistence.[1]

This European-led world, enamoured with imperialism and driven by industry, was forged in the nineteenth century. It suffered the seizures of world war twice in the twentieth. As a consequence of these developments, accelerated by Europe's repeated civil wars, the peoples of the nations and the Jewish people have been 'thrust into a common harness, against their will, by a small minority commonly called 'The West' – the peoples of Western Europe and their descendants in North America.' However it might be challenged, and whether overturned or not, Laue rightly points out: 'the human condition in the present and

---

[1] Theodore H. von Laue, *The World Revolution of Westernization* (New York, Oxford: OUP, 1987), 3.

the future can only be understood within the framework of the Westernized world.'[2]

This global inheritance means we have together entered upon that phase of history which Eugen Rosenstock-Huessy, from his planetary perspective, described as a condition of 'worldwide mutual permeation where everybody knows and hears of everybody else, where the earth is so small that words fly like lightning and men fly like words.'[3] Our modern era has soldered together the hard-wiring of intransitive humanity. The social reality in which we live and move and become who we are works like a circuit board of communication and exchange that has integrated us into its single route of connections.

What historian Geoffrey Barraclough noted twenty-five years ago about this modern world is even truer today. The essential nature of modern integration is that, in an unprecedented way, 'no people however small and remote,' can 'contract out'[4] from its promises, benefits, threats or its negative effects. The dilemma for Jews living in the modern age is that, since its having been ushered in with the nineteenth century, the 'Jewish question', so-called, remains: 'Where shall they live? Who shall tolerate them as their neighbour?' In the world in which Jewish men, women, families and communities cannot opt out, they face the existential irony that those who harbour a modern hatred for them desire of them the one thing they cannot do. In the very age when the ideas of anti-Semitism have concocted a stigma most persistent, virulent and of an immutable nature, those who believe these vile things wish that Jews would simply go away – and there is nowhere for them to go.

The contemporary historical approach to understanding the past seeks to figure out where we are, by examining from a worldwide perspective, the path we have travelled to arrive here.[5] At the present, as a living part of where we all find ourselves, is the Jewish state of Israel. This political body is not just a piece of real estate located on a Middle Eastern map. Israel consummates the Zionist dream for a Jewish homeland and, as one critical advocate for this cause put it, Zionism embodies 'the ultimate expression of Jewish freedom'. This fact is as much an

---

[2] von Laue, *World Revolution*, 3.

[3] Eugen Rosenstock-Huessy, *Out of Revolution, Autobiography of Western Man* (Norwich, Vt.: Argo Books, 1969), 24.

[4] Geoffrey Barraclough, *An Introduction to Contemporary History* (Harmondsworth, UK: Penguin, 1967), 42.

[5] Barraclough, *Contemporary History*, 9–42.

[6] Steven T. Katz, *Historicism, the Holocaust, and Zionism* (New York/London: New York University Press, 1992), 290.

existential reality as it is a cause of great controversy. It ignites passions which continue to fuel a series of tragic conflicts. Nevertheless, the Jewish state of Israel can no more be undone than it can be ignored. It belongs to and is part of the Jewish place in the modern world *as it actually is for really existing Jews*. It is an essential part of their modern life, regardless of what any particular non-Jewish bloc of opinion thinks of this or judges whether it should be or not.

Founding of the Jewish State

The founding of the modern Jewish state is an event that happened within the 'transition from a European to a global pattern of international politics.'[7] Intrinsic to this transition was the rabid, secular form of anti-Semitism of the late nineteenth century, which was made up of a concoction of components including racial biology, social Darwinism and condemnation of a fictitious international Jewish financial and political conspiracy. This modern manifestation of Jewish hatred found its most radical, thorough and consistent outworking as official state policy in the *Final Solution* perpetrated by Nazi Germany under Adolf Hitler. Hitler's anti-Semitism, 'the central motivating force of his political mission',[8] prompted the methodical denial of the civil standing of Jewish citizens, followed by their systematic deportation to concentration camps; after 1941, it culminated in the implementation of a plan that sought to achieve the total destruction of the Jews.

The exposing of these horrendous events after the defeat of Nazi Germany, and the struggle to come to terms with them, helps us to understand and respect as an inviolable conclusion that: 'Zionism is the momentous Jewish response to modernity.'[9] Hitler's unleashing of his twelve years of terror, during which he oversaw the deliberate effort to exterminate European Jewry, transformed Zionism into more than a movement of mere political aspirations. In the face of the murderous reality of the Holocaust, Zionism meant 'life not death; dignity rather than despoliation; an open future brimming with possibilities rather than a funeral end to all hope and to all meaning.'[10] More than a national liberation movement, Zionism's successful establishment of

---

[7] Barraclough, *Contemporary History*, 25.
[8] Eberhard Jäckel, *Hitler's World View* (trans. Herbert Arnold; Cambridge, Mass./London, UK, 1981), 53.
[9] Katz, *Historicism, the Holocaust, and Zionism*, 289.
[10] Katz, *Historicism, the Holocaust, and Zionism*, 290.

the Jewish state of Israel summarizes the efforts of its adherents in their attempts to guarantee the life of future Jewish generations.

> On the collective, the national level, it meant that the sepulcher that Hitler had planned for the Jewish people would yet remain empty; that they would survive to continue their struggle with seemingly recalcitrant reality in order to bring out of it a perfected creation.[11]

The defeat of Nazi Germany, and the ensuing bringing to light of the brutal horrors of the Holocaust, provided the historical ellipsis in which the Jewish state of Israel was founded. Anti-Zionism rejects the modern Jewish state of Israel, bracketing it off from the community of nations as problematic. Some even refuse outright to recognize it as a legitimate modern nation-state at all, demanding that it cease to exist. This disallowance would demand future Jewish generations to go again into exile, forcing Jewish men, women, children, families and communities to overcome their plight of alienation and anxiety elsewhere and somehow else in Diaspora, without their own sovereign state, lawful government or autonomous territory.

The backdrop to the hatred of the Jews prevalent today, continued as anti-Zionism, is the set of choices men and women made, gave voice to and subsidized in their efforts at creating and cultivating modern, secular anti-Semitic attitudes against Jews in nineteenth- and twentieth-century Europe, especially in Germany. Anti-Semitism in the late nineteenth century threatened to roll back the endowments of full civil rights for European Jews, which the ideas of the Enlightenment had made possible. Particularly in Germany, from both the left and the right, the place of political affinity and safety for the Jews became increasingly fragile. Jews could not freely and openly affirm or advance their traditions of worship, personal identity and communal life with any hope of being fully integrated into a larger, viable political constituency within a post-Christian, secular state.

Tradition of Liberalism

The tradition of liberalism, which emphasized the value, rights and freedoms of the individual, would have offered such political participation. Its ideological ordering of state and society to promote the

---

[11] Katz, *Historicism, the Holocaust, and Zionism*, 290.

well-being of the individual, regardless of nationality or race would have assured Jewish citizens open mobility and unhindered participation in German society. In Imperial Germany, however, liberals did not prevail in advancing their cause. They never succeeded in overcoming the combined political power of conservative and socialist interests. With the decline of liberalism in Germany in the second half of the nineteenth century, the alliances it could have forged among different confessional groups, including politically active Jewish citizens, lost authority.

In the wake of this weak tradition of liberalism, Jewish men, women, children, families and communities were forced to make difficult choices. They could enter the modern world by denying their own sense of identity to embrace the secularized anonymity that socialist theory imposed upon them, or they could stand condemned in the eyes of national conservative forces, which struggled to preserve notions of a traditional Christian state in opposition to the modern process of secularization perceived as a spiritual crisis. Therefore, for the Jews of Central Europe, there was no exit from the traditional world of the eighteenth century untainted by the stigma of prejudicial condemnation. In the words of Sartre: 'l'enfer, c'est les autres.' Jews became politically trapped between the crisis of conservatism and the vision of socialism.

This is particularly the case within the context of German cultural developments. The German intellectual world of literature and university lecture produced a story that described and, through the description, helped generate and nurture a new kind of collective life that it bestowed upon the German people. These ideas literally gave Germans a conserving, culturally based understanding of their group identity. Although not intrinsically anti-Semitic, this collective sense of cultural identity working as a group process contributed to the German people's acquiescing to the rule of Hitler, under which, 'Hitler's will was not merely defined as law; it was felt as law.'[12] Only here under Hitler did the 'Jewish question' lead men and women to design and to implement the horrible answer of the *final solution*. A political explanation for why this happened points out that the liberal road to modern nation-state building, though always a viable option, ultimately was blocked in Germany owing to the refusal of the German people to come to terms with the military defeat of World War I,

---

[12] Rudolph Binion, *Past Impersonal: Group Process in Human History* (DeKalb: Northern Illinois University Press, 2005), 47.

followed by the failure of the Weimar Republic to resist the extremist attacks of national socialism.

An important reason for the failure of liberalism in Germany ought to be attributed to the German people's embracing a sense of romantic nationalism that compensated for their sense of shame and their fear of weakness. This cultural sense of belonging, being part of one *Volk* with its own feelings of vitality, language, history and character is a unique German contribution to the ideas of the Enlightenment. The historicist understanding of culture shaped modern German mentality, allowing the German people to retain a collective sense of the sacred, while transferring this experience over to what was understood to be a distinctively German sensibility of the heart internalized as an effect of the German people's exclusive cultural consciousness. This idea of being German offered a sense of cohesion and harmony throughout the nineteenth century and became especially potent as an antidote for 'the shock and pain felt by Germans collectively after their 1918 defeat'.[13] Hitler's successful manipulation of this traumatic corporate feeling to his political advantage gave him the opportunity to situate his anti-Semitic agenda within this wounded sense of German cultural nationalism.

Modern anti-Semitism of late nineteenth century combined the idea of German superiority asserted as a fact based upon the pseudo-scientific principles of racial biology with critiques of financial internationalism. Jews were accused of being carriers of culturally decadent solvencies such as cosmopolitanism and egoism. At the same time, they were accused of following out a sinister conspiracy to dominate the world. By internalizing these ideas, Hitler made himself a true believer of them. He further radicalized them and used them to serve the racist ideology that explained and gave rationale for his efforts to eliminate the Jews of Europe. Hitler's 'new universalist-missionary'[14] anti-Semitic zeal condemned Jews in absolute terms.

The Christian Heritage

This disposition, and even the potential for producing such a policy aimed at murdering all Jews, is rooted in the older anti-Judaism conceived and cultivated by Christian pastors and teachers. Specifically,

---

[13] Binion, *Past Impersonal*, 46.
[14] Eberhard Jäckel, *Hitler's World View*, 53.

the total destruction of Jewry is grounded in the charge of deicide, which early Christian church leaders levelled against all Jews. Reaching back to the fourth century, this peculiarly Christian charge against the Jews stigmatized them as having committed an act that epitomizes evil, an evil than which none greater could be conceived. Having committed such a sin subjected them corporately to eternal destruction, an existential category *sui generis*.

The church took charge of the Jewish person who converted to Christianity to be his or her guardian. Upon being baptized by the church, the individual Jew was no longer a Jew but a Christian. Baptized Jews were absolved and, thus, removed from the contemptible group that continued to be possessed of its cosmic evil. Those who refused to convert were relegated to the status of a sober reminder, serving as condemned witnesses to the supremacy of Christian truth, tolerated like Cain to bear a sign of their own evil. This earlier form of anti-Judaism removed the individual Jew from the Jewish group's evil. Hitler's German form of modern anti-Semitism would require removal of the Jewish group from the German people.

The Reformation era, with the resulting confessional fissure it left upon Germany, did not overcome the Christian tradition of anti-Jewish sentiment. If anything, through the writings of Martin Luther, the stereotype of the Jew as the evil other was more deeply entrenched. This was the case because, throughout the nineteenth century, German proponents of modernity portrayed Luther as a 'hero in the history of freedom',[15] who helped give life and shape to German nationalism. As a German nationalist figure, Luther was more than just the founder of the Protestant Reformation. He was a champion of the German spirit and a genius of German language and literature.

The decision to condemn all Jews for all generations and to make this a crucial part of the church's teaching that elevated the standing of the church before God at their expense incurs the history of Christianity with guilt *sui generis*. Neither the category of condemnation conceived, nor the ensuing guilt stemming from the wanting and imagining of such a category, can be undone. These beliefs can only be rejected and repented of by way of admitting their historical reality and, further, by determining to assume responsibility for resisting their effects wherever they continue.

---

[15] Thomas Nipperday, *Nachdenken über die deutsche Geschichte* (Munich: Verlag C.H. Beck, 1986), 31–2.

Christianity not only produced the social-psychologically unique capacity for stigmatizing the Jews, but it also initiated the modern process of secularization which, in turn, created the alternative collective loyalties into which this unique hostility could be grafted. Western Christianity served as 'the religion for departing from religion'.[16] Sometime around 1700, the West underwent a 'silent revolution',[17] marked by a 'reform of prophecy'[18] that changed how people read the Bible. The educated elite in Europe became increasingly more sceptical of the legitimacy of biblical prophecies. Miracles, divine revelation and divinity itself too were questioned. God's providence became interchangeable with natural law, which, because it could be scientifically grasped and applied as technology, became less feared as a dangerous mystery. Demystification of the natural world laid down the groundwork for the secularization of European culture in the nineteenth century. Religion no longer dictated social hierarchy or social unity. As modern society began to develop, 'religious institutions and religious explanations of events were slowly being displaced from the center of life to its periphery.'[19]

People increasingly placed their confidence in scientific advancement, technological development and social improvement. Confidence increased that these changes could be gained through human initiatives rationally conceived and organized. The optimistic viewpoint of the Enlightenment encouraged the study of history for finding 'meaning and justification for life'.[20] In the minds of those who made up the ranks of higher culture and, increasingly as part of the ordinary walk of daily life, fewer were concerned with discerning the will and ways of God.

The 'radical originality' of this modern western lifestyle is its normative personhood, a 'post-theological individuality'[21] that lives in a 'society subject to itself as a society structured outside of religion'.[22] This secularized modernity oversees all functions of society, which

---

[16] Marcel Gauchet, *The Disenchantment of the World* (trans. Oscar Burge; Princeton: Princeton University Press, 1997), 101.

[17] William Monter, *Ritual, Myth and Magic in Early Modern Europe* (Athens, Ohio: Ohio University Press, 1983), 117.

[18] Charles van Doren, *A History of Knowledge* (New York: Ballantine, 1991), 205.

[19] Peter Gay, *The Enlightenment: An Interpretation, the Rise of Modern Paganism* (New York: Vintage Books of Random House, 1966), 338.

[20] Stephen Kern, *The Culture of Time and Space, 1880–1918* (Cambridge: Harvard University Press, 1983), 60.

[21] Gauchet, *The Disenchantment of the World*, 3.

[22] Gauchet, *The Disenchantment of the World*, 172.

operate together as if God, if not impotent, was at the very least irrelevant. Within the modern world of science and technology, the idea of God, if not dismissed as an obstruction to progress, could best be tolerated as a compatible, yet dispensable, factor of contingency. Because the modern world was meliorable, 'evil was always technically surmountable according to the perfectibility and the progress which realized the human sphere's ontological self-sufficiency in infinite time.'[23]

Considering these two factors together – secularization and, with it, Christianity's anti-Judaism replaced by modern anti-Semitism – makes visible the terrible plight of the Jewish people in the modern world. Within the integrated condition of modern society from which none can opt out, the culpability of the Jews as the bearers of categorical evil carried over from Christian tradition becomes a constant onus, susceptible to resolutions that must be worked out in the secular arena, first without the existence of the Jewish state of Israel and now with it. The desire to expel or disperse Jews under such circumstances has as its modern logic the open-ended propensity to become increasingly more expansive, tending towards a universal scope until reaching the ultimate boundary of eradication. Modernity, as it has really been thus far, seeks to reach what is taken to be a part of its systematic state of entropy, of rest: to be alleviated entirely of any Jewish presence.

Romantic Nationalism

These ideas of modernity and anti-Semitism were disseminated among German men and women who were affected by a distinctive interpretation of German identity; these ideas had their grounding in the eighteenth-century concept of romantic nationalism. This cultural sense of group identity did not offer a form of social integration that depended upon traditional Christian ideas about social practices, nor was it sanctioned by an established relationship between church and state. This sense of social cohesion captured the loyalty of German mentality in the nineteenth century when 'there did not exist a truly secularized culture.'[24] This lack of a clear 'border-line between religious and national identity'[25] demarcates the religious *sonderweg* peculiar to

---

[23] Gauchet, *The Disenchantment of the World*, 168.
[24] Gabriel Motzkin, 'Säkularisierung, Bürgertum und Intellecktuelle in Frankreich und Deutschland wärend des 19. Jahrhunderts', in *Bügertum im 19. Jahrhundert*, vol. 3 (ed. Jurgen Kocka; Munich: DTV, 1988), 151.
[25] Motzkin, 'Säkularisierung, Bürgertum und Intellecktuelle', 157.

Germany's path to modernization. Commitment to Christianity and the social significance of the church indeed did decline in Germany. Rather than forsaking them outright, people transferred their religious consciousness over to national affections. Because this sense of nationalism was of a cultural character, it collared political participation across the entire spectrum of competing ideologies.

The significance of Christianity declined insofar as providing affections and explanations for the purpose of life or for issuing life-guiding values. While this was happening, secular realities were increasingly awarded an emotional sense of the sacred. 'Love, family, labor or art gained a religious quality in the nineteenth century (theater and museum became temples), this hallowing of the secular especially happened to political movements.'[26] As the sanctioning sentiment for this process, 'romantic nationalism assumed to a great extent both the function and style of religion.'[27]

Germans infused a nationalist attitude with religious affection probably because this feeling of belonging served as the primary emotional compensation for the territorial fragmentation, which defined Germany from the Thirty Years War of the seventeenth century until unification in 1871. It also bridged the confessional divide between Catholics and Protestants that marked the exceptional make-up of Germany in comparison to other European nations since the Reformation. Within this unique context of a religiously charged sense of German nationalism during the nineteenth century, Jews were permitted greater access to professional, public and intellectual life than in other parts of the continent, even as anti-Semitic agitation increased.

Finally, too, the Marxist-socialist movement was most successful in organizing labour support in Germany. The rapid growth of the Socialist Party of Germany with its heightened hostility towards organized Christianity, the religion of Judaism and its Marxist philosophy promoting a secular, materialist and atheistic point of view among members of the working class was part of the uniquely modern German experience with its religiously imbued sense of nationalism.

German sociologist M. Rainer Lepsius coined the term 'socio-moral milieu' to define these competing constellations of semi-secular, religiously charged allegiances. Lepsius understood milieus to be 'social units' that were stabilized 'through the coincidence of several structural dimensions' to include 'religion, regional tradition, economic position,

---

[26] Nipperday, *Nachdenken über die deutsche Geschichte*, 120.
[27] Nipperday, *Nachdenken über die deutsche Geschichte*, 120.

cultural orientation [and] the class composition of the intermediate groups.'[28] Lepsius identified four milieus, which remained decisive for political organization in Germany up until 1933: Catholic, the Conservative-Protestant, the Protestant bourgeois and the socialist. Each of these worked as a 'socio-culture object' on different parts of the German population. Prior to World War I, 'the segregation of political blocks led to a lack of democratization.'[29] In the period of the Weimar Republic, 'these milieus lost their unifying force', producing an 'orientation vacuum', which 'provided a chance for the National Socialists (NSDAP) to gain votes'.[30]

German Enlightenment

Romantic nationalism remained the one sentiment that functioned as the social cement uniting all Germans, even while they were divided among these contending political blocks. This distinctive social cohesion based upon a cultural disposition rather than political organization or ideology was first conceived and discussed in the period of the German Enlightenment in the eighteenth century. It grew in strength as a reaction to the French Revolution's turn to a reign of terror after 1793. Its popularity increased with Napoleonic militarism, occupation and exploitation. The flames of fear were fanned further by the threat of a French imperial victory, which would impose a European-wide rule of uniformity and secure foreign hegemony over Germany. Excited with anti-French feelings in a combative setting, this cultural sense of identity took on an additional nativist layer of resentment against the ideas of the Enlightenment in general. German resistance and its war of liberation against Napoleon included hostility towards all things French, including the universal rights of humanity.

Suspicion over the Enlightenment's advocacy of secular rights for the autonomous individual based upon the organon of reason to promote happiness and utility merged with the increasing popularity of romantic nationalism. The sense of German exceptionality this outlook offered provided a new paradigm for collective identity that proved itself

---

[28] Rainer M. Lepsius, *Demokratie in Deutschland, Soziologish-historische Konstellationsanalysen* (Göttingen: Vandenhoeck & Ruprecht, 1993), 38.

[29] Ingvill Constanze Mochmann, *Lifestyles, social milieus and voting behaviour in Germany* (2002). Online: http://geb.uni-giessen.de/geb/volltexte/2003/1278/pdf/MochmannIngvillC-2003-10-10.pdf. Accessed 2 Oct. 2009.

[30] Mochmann, *Lifestyles, social milieus*.

amiable to endorsing racist notions of national supremacy. Racist ideas would not be applied to the Jews in Germany until the second half of the nineteenth century.[31] Nonetheless, the capacity to be attracted to such ideas is intimately related to the pervasive influence of romantic nationalism. This is not a question of collective guilt, but rather a condition of collective empathy and affinity that gave words to fit the feelings generated as part of the group process of being German.

Leading writers of the German Enlightenment expressed sentiments of European supremacy as part of their advocacy for the reality of universal standards of beauty. Critical thought in the field of aesthetics spilled over into the subject of philosophical anthropology, which examined human physiology and psychology. Through his 1764 work on the history of art, author Johann Winckelmann (1717–68) greatly influenced public taste throughout the nineteenth century and not just in Germany.[32] He judged the Greek idea of the beautiful to be a perfect ideal-type for all times and cultures. Winckelmann further concluded a people's appearance made visible their character. For him, the Greek expression of beauty 'symbolized the perfect human form within which a true soul would be bound to reside.'[33] As one of the founders of modern anthropology, Johann Friedrich Blumenbach (1754–1840) ordered his classification of human races based upon a similar aesthetic judgement. The most appealing appearance of the greatest beauty he judged to be so 'because it approximated the "divine" works of Greek art'.[34] As the leading German philosopher of the Enlightenment, Immanuel Kant (1724–1804) too understood race to be an attribute maintained in a people as a constant quality, which he defined as 'an unchanging substance and the foundation of all physical appearance and human development, including intelligence.'[35]

J.G. Herder and the *Volkgeist*

The ideas of the German philosopher and theologian Johann Gottfried Herder (1744–1803) presented the alternative to this universal

[31] George L. Mosse, *Toward the Final Solution, A History of European Racism* (Madison: University of Wisconsin Press, 1985), 14.

[32] Jacques Barzun, *From Dawn to Decadence, 1500 to the Present* (New York: HarperCollins, 2000), 417.

[33] Barzun, *From Dawn to Decadence*, 11.

[34] Barzun, *From Dawn to Decadence*, 21.

[35] Barzun, *From Dawn to Decadence*, 31.

approach. He first gave voice to the view that cultural consciousness is the collective medium of a people. Herder gave life to the idea of cultural unity as a people's vital character, rather than church membership or political order. His 'discovery of a new historical consciousness'[36] helped the Enlightenment in Germany to become a dual undertaking, making it as much a study in the history of culture as an agenda based upon the abstract, universal use of reason. He was most responsible for introducing to the academy and the public the life orientation of romantic nationalism. This sense of collective consciousness worked as the crucial element of German mentality, providing the constant of German identity in cultural terms, rather than in terms of traditional religious affiliation or in terms of allegiance to any particular political ideology. This unique sense of being German would hold throughout the nineteenth century, World War I, the Weimar Republic and the reign of Hitler.

As the architect of this new sense of identity, Herder is 'the father of the related notions of nationalism, historicism and the *Volkgeist*.'[37] He is 'the outstanding representative of a new German philosophy of history that ran counter to the French current of linear, rationalist progression.'[38] He was instrumental in changing 'the traditional historical perspective and the universe of historical discourse in a revolutionary manner.'[39] He imbued the German enlightenment with a secularized sense of pietistic enthusiasm. His reaction against the French reasserted the value of matters of the heart, from which, he claimed, originated all the great issues of life. These ways of the heart were experienced through feeling, through instinctive inclinations and impulses. The roots of these drives and desires derived nourishment from religious feelings fundamental to human experience. His *Ideas on the Philosophy of History of Mankind* (1784–91) 'became the Bible of nationalism and nationalist history',[40] not only for Germany, but also for Eastern Europe.

Herder set aside the traditional Christian teaching about divine providence, which claimed the will of God worked through the instrument

---

[36] Frank E. Manuel, 'Editor's Introduction', in Johann Gottfried von Herder's *Reflections on the Philosophy of the History of Mankind* (ed. Frank E. Manuel; Chicago/London: University of Chicago Press, 1968), xxii.

[37] Isaiah Berlin, *Three Critics of the Enlightenment* (ed. Henry Hardy; Princeton/Oxford: Princeton University Press, 2000), 168.

[38] Manuel, 'Editor's Introduction', xiii–xiv.

[39] Manuel, 'Editor's Introduction', 14.

[40] Frank E. Manuel, *Shapes of Philosophical History* (Stanford: Stanford University Press, 1965), 83.

of political authorities. He replaced the state as God's vessel for advancing history with his notion of organic culture. According to Herder, religious sentiment was the means by which humanity manifested its highest form. Far from being superfluous or something scientific progress supersedes, it was the most sublime flowering of the human heart. Apart from universal abstract reason, Herder celebrated a superior, affective kind of knowledge that was directly derived from the experience of life. This wider and more deeply satisfying body of knowledge joined like-hearted together in ways that reason could not fathom alone. These feelings of belonging arose from indigenous religious feelings peculiar to each particular entity of genius Nature embodied in men of every tribe and tongue. Each unique people possessed a matching place in which they enjoyed their ideal environment and climate. All the peoples of the world together made up humanity, which 'manifested itself quintessentially not in the state and the organization of power but in music, literature, art, and science, in that order of importance.'[41]

As a philosopher of history, Herder looked on each cultural group as a unique creation of God. God alone grasped the ways of change through time. Often God used cultural fermentation, the stirring up of the passions as a creative process. Men could not expect that the instrument of reason was sufficient to understand or deny this mysterious work of divine providence, never mind master it. Each person had the privilege of experiencing the cultural revelation of vital genius into which he or she was born. Those particularly gifted could express this genius through the revelation of the people's language, music and art. Everyone, however, as a member of a given particular flowering of humanity's glory, possessed its linguistic lifeblood and was rooted in its religious sense of affinity and orientation.

According to Herder: 'every nation is one people, having its own national form' and its own 'original national character'.[42] Climate had an effect upon national character but could not destroy it. Behind climate and original genius worked the invisible power of creative Nature, 'who never thinks inactively'.[43] Herder confessed he did not know what this vital power is. He is quite clear, however, that it 'is not the faculty of reason', and that the principle of this vital power is innate, organical, genetic: 'it is the basis of my natural powers, the internal genius of my

[41] Manuel, 'Editor's Introduction', xxi.
[42] Johann Gottfried von Herder, *Reflections on the Philosophy of the History of Mankind* (trans. Frank E. Manuel; Chicago/London: University of Chicago Press, 1968), 7.
[44] von Herder, *Reflections*, 21.

being.'[44] Each people or *Volk* possessed a national soul, a *Volkseele*, which revealed its character in both the generational life of the nation, as well as in each member of the nation. The cultural soul of a people was as precious in the eyes of divine providence as the individual soul was held to be in the eyes of the God of traditional Christianity. This *volkish* essence was carried through each people's language, history and folklore. Each person had the privilege of enjoying the unique experience of the cultural revelation in which he or she was born.

Herder's thinking placed great emphasis upon the feeling of belonging to a group. 'For Herder, to be a member of a group is to think and act in a certain way, in the light of particular goals, values, pictures of the world: and to think and act so is to belong to a group.'[45] Herder rejected any accent of the individual ego; for him the value of the individual is connected with his or her group membership. Integration of individuals into the group, and the group-given voice, the beauty and style made available by its intellectuals and artists create the cohesive harmony of the culture to which one belongs. Experiencing this harmony is what makes the individual feel *wohl*: healthy, happy and well.

Although Herder believed physiognomy to be 'the expositor of the living *nature* of man, the interpreter of his genius rendered visible',[46] he was not a cultural chauvinist. Since each *Volk* enjoyed an equal standing with all others, he believed it would be a crime before humanity and a religious evil in the presence of God to obliterate the original genius of a people through invasion, conquest and occupation. This applied to the Jews as well; they too deserved residence in their rightful place and climate, which would guarantee them reaching their fullest maturity so they too could make their contribution for bringing to perfection the harmonious growth of humanity. Herder, however, faulted Jews for being an intransigent people. They persisted in maintaining their distinct character, which was praiseworthy, but they did so at the expense of other peoples. Herder admired the antiquity of the Jews. He acknowledged that their 'written annals of their actions . . . distinguishes them in an eminent manner'[47] He believed, however, that 'the misconception and abuse of these writings have been detrimental to the human mind in various respects; and the more as they have operated upon it under the claim of being divine.'[48]

---

[44] von Herder, *Reflections*, 22.
[45] Isaiah Berlin, *Three Critics*, 220.
[46] von Herder, *Reflections*, 25–6.
[47] von Herder, *Reflections*, 134–5.
[48] von Herder, *Reflections*, 141.

Herder defined Jews as a 'widely diffused republic of cunning usurers' that, in his estimation, 'unquestionably restrained many nations of Europe for a long time from exercising their own industry.'[49] He commended them for their 'warlike courage', complimenting them as a people who 'have always borne themselves up under the severest oppression from other nations.'[50] Herder, nonetheless, claimed the Jews 'were a people spoiled in their education, because they never arrived at a maturity of political cultivation on their own soil and consequently not to any true sentiment of liberty and honour.'[51] Rather than fulfil the unique destiny providence offered them, the Jews preferred to depend upon the vitality of other peoples to make their place in this world. 'The people of God, whose country was once given them by Heaven itself, have been for thousands of years, nay almost from their beginning, parasitical plants on the trunks of other nations.'[52]

The Jews in Diaspora were sufficient proof for the perpetual character flaw that kept them from living in the land that providence provided them, the land that was best suited for the well-being of their national soul and spirit. Instead of doing their allotted share for the well-being of all humanity, they remained 'a race of cunning brokers, almost throughout the whole World; who, in spite of all oppression, have never been inspired with an ardent passion for their own honour, for a habitation, for a country, of their own.'[53]

The Modern Reality

Herder's impact upon German life and culture does not stem from these ambiguous, less than commendable, judgements he passes upon the Jewish people. Of far greater importance were his ideas about group identity and social solidarity, which he taught were expressed through a people's religious feelings, language, customs and history. These distinctive qualities radiated from a people's indigenous vitality and, in turn, gave shape to the mentality of their national character. His thinking crystallized and realized the German notion of romantic nationalism. His thought first gave shape to German identity as an organic collective *persona* that persisted apart from the machinery of

---

[49] von Herder, *Reflections*, 142.
[50] von Herder, *Reflections*, 143.
[51] von Herder, *Reflections*, 143–4.
[52] von Herder, *Reflections*, 144.
[53] von Herder, *Reflections*, 144.

the state. Regardless of political affiliation, each individual lived this vital sense of corporate originality and creativity by expressing or celebrating being part of the organic whole.

Herder's thought was instrumental in designing the one vehicle of cultural consciousness that transported all Germans through their travails on the road to modernization. Throughout the nineteenth century, through restoration, revolution, reaction, unification, industrialization and imperialism, the cultural undercarriage of romantic nationalism remained the one German constant. This rubric continued to cultivate religious-like feelings garnered through group participation in a semi-secular social environment. This cultural sense of belonging nurtured the belief that a sense of harmony was essential for both a healthy individual and a healthy society. The state of things both psychologically as well as socially were right when they felt right, when their arrangement was intuited as pleasing. It created the essential sense of German identity to which anti-Semitism was an unnecessary attachment. Germans came to believe that their organic collective nature was the basis of their national identity.

This sense of being German and belonging to Germany was grounded in cultural consciousness rather than bound by a set of liberal, constitutional ideas. This made the German people particularly susceptible to Hitler's propaganda that promoted anti-Semitism as part of his campaign to overcome the trauma of humility suffered as defeat on the battlefield of World War I. This dishonour, he claimed, was caused by the betrayal of productive, creative and heroic Jewish sweethearts, friends, neighbours, colleagues, comrades, residents and citizens, who nonetheless were never Germans at all.

9

Messianic Jewish Reflections on the Holocaust and Jewish Evangelism[1]

Michael L. Brown

In the early 1990s, I did a lot of reading on the Holocaust, some of it historical, some of it anecdotal. Not surprisingly, the anecdotal literature had a more profound effect on me, as the accounts of almost unimaginable suffering were far more moving than bare statistics and historical facts.[2] I still remember being totally overwhelmed some nights after hours of reading to the point of falling asleep shaking and crying. And then, in the midst of the tears, an awful thought would hit me: 'Are they forever lost? It is horrific enough that these Jewish people died such cruel, prolonged, agonizing deaths, but are they now separated from God for eternity? Are they now in a worse hell than the Holocaust?'

At that point, my mind and emotions would short circuit and I simply had to dismiss the question and try to find refuge in a good night's sleep. Yes, the thought of a fate worse than the Holocaust – and an endless one at that – was too disturbing even to contemplate, especially for

---

[1] Since this paper has been prepared with the WEA consultation in mind, including the concomitant time constraints, I have kept footnote references to a minimum. The emphasis of this paper as well reflects pragmatic more than academic concerns.

[2] Among those many books, two in particular stand out in my memory: Martin Gilbert's *The Holocaust: The Jewish Tragedy* (London: Collins, 1986) and the Albert H. Friedlander collection, *Out of the Whirlwind: A Reader of Holocaust Literature* (New York: Shocken, 1976).

people whose fate at the hands of the Nazis seemed totally undeserved. Succinctly stated, if Jewish guilt could not justify the Holocaust, how could it justify hell?

Jewish Suffering, the Holocaust and Hell

To put this into focus, consider the words of Alexander Donat, who survived both the Warsaw Ghetto and the concentration camps:

> What had we done to deserve this hurricane of evil, this avalanche of cruelty? Why had all the gates of Hell opened and spewed forth on us the furies of human vileness? What crimes had we committed for which this might have been calamitous punishment? Where, in what code of morals, human or divine, is there a crime so appalling that innocent women and children must expiate it with their lives in martyrdoms no Torquemada ever dreamed of?[3]

What kind of Torquemada-like God, then, would be so cruel and demented as to fashion an eternal hell for Jews who simply did not believe in Jesus?

Indeed, simply implying that Jewish guilt brought on the Holocaust – let alone hell – has seemed more than obscene to many. As expressed in the bold and now classic formulation of Rabbi Irving Greenberg:

> [S]ummon up the principle that no statement should be made that could not be made in the presence of the burning children. On this rock, the traditionalist argument [viz., that the Holocaust was a divine judgment] breaks. Tell the children in the pits they are burning for their sins. An honest man – better, a decent man – would spit at such a God rather than accept this rationale if it were true. If this justification is loyalty, then surely treason is the honourable choice. If this were the only choice, then surely God would prefer atheism.[4]

---

[3] Cited in Barry Leventhal, 'Theological Perspectives on the Holocaust', *Mishkan* 6/7 (1987): 16.

[4] 'Cloud of Smoke, Pillar or Fire: Judaism, Christianity, and Modernity after the Holocaust,' in *Auschwitz: Beginning of a New Era?* (New York: Ktav, 1976), 34, cited in Leventhal, ibid., 28-9. For my own approach to the Holocaust in terms of Jewish apologetics, see Michael L. Brown, *Answering Jewish Objections to Jesus: Vol. 1, General and Historical Objections* (Grand Rapids: Baker, 2000), 177–96, where these quotes from Donat and Greenberg are also referenced. Cf. Irving Greenberg, *For the Sake of Heaven and Earth: The New Encounter Between Judaism and Christianity* (Philadelphia: JPS, 2004).

In reality, however, as acute as the question of hell is for many believers, the Holocaust does not really affect this question, since divine punishment in the world to come is a question in its own right. That is to say, if a person enjoyed a long, healthy life in this world but died of old age as an unbeliever, is the question of divine punishment any less acute than if that person died of cancer at the age of forty or, for that matter, died horribly in the Holocaust? Does the difference of a few years or the nature of one's death make the reality of hell any more or less bearable?[5]

Moreover, there is no doubt that many of the Jews who died in the Holocaust had not lived observant Jewish lives and would gladly have renounced their Jewishness, along with the God of Israel, if that would have saved them. How then can martyrdom be conferred on them (as is done in much contemporary Jewish thought) if they really did not die in *Kiddush HaShem* (sanctification of the Lord's name)?[6] Thus, the fact that their tragic fate was to die in the Holocaust does not address the question of their own relationship with God or their own sin, unless one argues that they suffered enough in this world to pay for their sins, a distinctly non-Christian viewpoint.[7]

---

[5] One could potentially cite Abraham's words to the rich man in Hades in Luke 16:25 as standing against my point here ('Child, remember that you in your lifetime received your good things, and Lazarus in like manner bad things; but now he is comforted here, and you are in anguish.'), but that would be to misuse a statement in the midst of a story (or, more probably, parable) for the purpose of elucidating doctrine. If there is a corollary doctrine in the New Testament to the 'bad life now, good life later' concept, it is that if we suffer with and for the Lord in this world, we will experience his glory and reign with him in the world to come (see, e.g. Matt. 5:10–12; Rom. 8:17; 2 Tim. 2:12a; 1 Pet. 4:12–13; Rev. 2:10a). For rabbinic parallels to the story of Dives and Lazarus, cf. *y. Sanh.* 6:9, 23c; *y. Hag.* 2:2, 77d; *Ruth Rab.* 3.3.

[6] As explained by David Novak, *Talking with Christians: Musings of a Jewish Theologian* (Grand Rapids: Eerdmans, 2005), 152: 'So I would say that any Jew who was murdered in Auschwitz, who at the moment of death accepted being a Jew, one of the elect of God, and was able to die with the affirmation of the uniqueness of God and the uniqueness of Israel His people asserted by the shema on his or her lips, such a person is definitely a martyr.' He continues, however: 'And since we refuse to believe that any Jew in his or her heart of hearts would not be grateful to God for the election, despite our humanly unbearable suffering in this world, when we Jews mourn the dead of the Holocaust, we refer to all of them, religious or irreligious or even antireligious in life, as qedoshim, as "saints."'

[7] For the concepts of death as an atonement, in particular, the atoning power of the death of the righteous, which is richly attested in rabbinic literature, see Michael L. Brown, *Answering Jewish Objections to Jesus: Vol. 2, Theological Objections* (Grand Rapids: Baker, 2000), 153–67.

To be sure, the very concrete, hellish nature of the Holocaust brought the more abstract concept of hell into sharper focus, since Jewish people, automatically consigned to hell by so many professing Christians, were suffering in so many ghastly ways. Not surprisingly, this generated sympathy and compassion from the same Christians who seemed completely unbothered by the presumed, eternally lost state of these very same people. The Holocaust, then, was a reality check for many Christians, forcing them to re-evaluate their beliefs in divine punishment.

Corporate Christian Shame

Yet the question of hell is not the primary concern that has arisen in terms of Christian evangelism of the Jewish people in light of the Holocaust. Rather, it is the issue of corporate Christian shame over the history of church anti-Semitism that paved the way for the Holocaust. As stated famously by Eliezer Berkovitz, the Nazis, although anti-Christian themselves, were the children of Christians – at the least, of Christians in name.[8]

Thus, Michael Wyschogrod noted: 'even without the Holocaust, it is not unlikely that Christian scholarship would have been forced to deal more seriously with the Jewish roots of Christianity', continuing, however, with these telling lines:

> But this was not to be. The Holocaust occurred, and instead of an organic development prompted by scholarly and theological considerations, a world historical evil event of unprecedented proportions intervened and cast Jewish-Christian relations, and many other things, in an entirely new light. The Christian side in the dialogue found itself burdened with a heavy guilt. While Nazism was hardly a Christian phenomenon, there was widespread agreement that two thousand years of the Christian teaching of contempt prepared the ground for the 'final solution.' Christianity was forced to face up to the implications of its

---

[8] The significance has not been missed by atheistic, anti-Christian diatribes; see, e.g. Sam Harris, *The End of Faith: Religion, Terror, and the Future of Reason* (New York: Norton, 2004), 79: 'The Holocaust is relevant here because it is generally considered to have been an entirely secular phenomenon. It was not. The anti-Semitism that built the crematoria brick by brick – and that still thrives today – comes to us by way of Christian theology. Knowingly or not, the Nazis were agents of religion.'

teaching which were taken to insane extremes by the Nazis but which also built on Christian foundations.[9]

By what right, then, can Christians today, in particular European, Gentile Christians, urge Jewish people to believe in Jesus? This view was recently expressed by Willem J.J. Glashouwer in his widely translated and sensitively written book, *Why Israel*, a book in which he explicitly expresses his faith in God's sovereign ability to reveal Jesus to Jewish people. That being said, he states:

> We can leave it [namely, Jewish evangelism] to the Lord, and to our messianic Jewish brothers and sisters who, like Paul, feel an urge to speak to their Jewish brothers and sisters. We Gentiles (and we are Gentiles, no matter how full of faith we may be!) stand at a distance, often with the heavy load of church history hanging around our necks . . .
>
> But if we were to evangelize the Jews, their response would be similar to what we would have expected from the Dutch had Germans returned to Holland after the Second World [War] to tell the Dutch that they needed to be converted. We would expect the Dutch to say: 'Get out! Go back to your own country. Get your own house in order first!' We Christians fail to recognize how much guilt is on our heads. Some Jews even argue that Jesus cannot be the Messiah because there is so much Jewish blood on the hands of his followers, the Christians. He must be some kind of false god, lusting after Jewish blood.[10]

So then, according to Glashouwer, if there is to be evangelism of the Jews, it must be left to the Lord's sovereign hand and to Messianic Jews.

A German Christian Expression of Guilt

Understandably, the Holocaust brought with it a tremendous sense of guilt for many European Christians, most notably in Germany and, for

---

[9] Michael Wyschogrod, *Abraham's Promise: Judaism and Jewish-Christian Relations*, ed. and with an introduction by R. Kendall Soulen (Grand Rapids: Eerdmans, 2004), 149–50.

[10] Willem J.J. Glashouwer, *Why Israel?* (trans. Mineke Spencer; 2d ed.; Nijkerk, The Netherlands: Christians for Israel International, 2005), 141–2. For some very strong Jewish statements that back up Glashouwer's last two sentences, see Michael L. Brown, *Our Hands Are Stained with Blood* (Shippensburg, Penn.: Destiny Image, 1992), 88–91.

some, that guilt remains even to this day. Basilea Schlink expressed this with real pathos barely a decade after the Holocaust, and because of the passion of her expression, which reflects both her nearness to the *Shoah* and her love for Jesus and his people Israel, I will quote her at length:[11]

Can we Germans really continue to walk under the open sky of our fatherland, in daytime in the sunshine and at night beneath the stars, enjoying it all without feelings of shame? Must we not remember that not long ago, under that same sky, in the midst of our people, gigantic flames ascended from the burning bodies of millions of people day and night? Were not these flames like a cry of desperation and a raised finger of accusation? (38)

We Germans were Satan's henchmen. In the midst of our people this hell was created. After reading the reports of those who survived it, we can only confess that never before in the whole span of history has a civilized nation been guilty of a crime such as has been committed here in Germany, a Christian country, a land of culture . . . Within a few years, millions of people were murdered, gassed, burnt alive or tortured to death in every conceivable way. Who can still eat his fill at a nicely laid table without visualizing the emaciated forms of the thousands of victims in the extermination camps? (39–40)

We are personally to blame. We all have to admit that if we, the entire Christian community, had stood up as one man and if, after the burning of the synagogues [on Krystallnacht], we had gone out on the streets and voiced our disapproval, rung the church bells, and somehow boycotted the actions of the S.S., the Devil's vassals would probably not have been at such liberty to pursue their evil schemes. But we lacked the ardor of love – love that is never passive, love that cannot bear it when its fellowmen are in misery, particularly when they are subjected to such appalling treatment and tortured to death. Indeed, if we had loved God, we would not have endured seeing those houses of God set ablaze; and holy, divine wrath would have filled our souls . . . Oh, that we as Germans and as Christians would stand aghast and cry out ever anew, 'What have we done!' At every further evidence of our guilt may we repeat the cry (42–3).

Oh, how can we now look upon German children playing happily and not think of the many, many thousands of children who screamed in

---

[11] Israel, *My Chosen People: A German Confession before God and the Jews* (Eng. trans., Old Tappan, N.J.: Chosen, 1987; originally published in German in 1958).

anguish and terror when they were burnt alive or when they, either with or without their parents, choked to death in the gas chambers! May we not close our eyes but face up to what we have done, for these are the plain facts, and innocent blood cries for retribution: 'If any one slays with the sword, with the sword must he be slain' (Revelation 13:10). Thus says Holy Scripture (44).

Is it reasonable, then, that we can expect Jews to believe in Jesus after the Holocaust?

> How are the Jews to believe in Jesus? Have not we ourselves blind-folded them? They cannot see Jesus because of our conduct. They cannot believe in Him, because in our lives we have not presented to them the image of Jesus; rather we have shown them the image of mer-cilessness. 'Your deeds in Germany talk so loud that I cannot hear your words,' a Jew of our times comments. Our words about Jesus must cut Jews to the heart, considering the cruelties we have perpetrated against them in the name of this Jesus from the time of the Crusades up to the present day. And not only that. How many acts of love have we neg-lected to do? Thus we share in the horrible guilt of our people in mur-dering six million Jews. This guilt still hovers over us like a cloud (36–7).

Beyond Guilt to a 'Radical Reconstruction' of the Faith

For some Christians, the Holocaust even called for the 'radical recon-struction' of their faith. As explained by Alice Eckhardt:

> Even more than my focus on Israel, it was the *Shoah* that compelled me to question and rethink fundamental issues of faith . . . It led me in 1974 to write an extensive article focusing on the ways a number of Jewish and Christian thinkers have been rethinking their faith in the response to the *Shoah*. I saw 'a church in vast apostasy . . . still linked to a supersessionist theology that bears the genocidal germ . . . and] without credibility because of its failure to understand Auschwitz.' I saw the Jewish people as having 'experienced resur-rection in history through the rebirth of the State of Israel and a new vitality in its various Diaspora communities.' At the same time I saw 'a Christianity that continues to insist that the world's redemption has already occurred' [and] 'that by and large maintains a

triumphalism which strives for a religious genocide [of Jews] through conversion.'[12]

This 'radical reconstruction', then, was aided and abetted by a fresh appreciation for Judaism, the result of a recognition of the power of a Jewish faith that could survive a Holocaust and then rebuild after it, as well as the result of first-hand contact with Jewish scholars and leaders, opening up a new world to many Christian theologians and ministers. The result was a repudiation of supersessionism that was so comprehensive that it expressly affirmed dual covenant theology.

Thus, the first point in 'A Statement by the Christian Scholars Group on Christian-Jewish Relations' affirms:

> God's covenant with the Jewish people endures forever. For centuries Christians claimed that their covenant with God replaced or superseded the Jewish covenant. We renounce this claim. We believe that God does not revoke divine promises. We affirm that God is in covenant with both Jews and Christians. Tragically, the entrenched theology of supersessionism continues to influence Christian faith, worship, and practice, even though it has been repudiated by many Christian denominations and many Christians no longer accept it. Our recognition of the abiding validity of Judaism has implications for all aspects of Christian life.[13]

---

[12] Alice L. Eckhardt, 'Growing into a Daring, Questioning Faith,' in *Faith Transformed: Christian Encounters with Jews and Judaism* (ed. John C. Merkle; Collegeville, Minn.: Liturgical Press, 2003), 25, with reference to her article 'The Holocaust: Christian and Jewish Responses,' *Journal of the American Academy of Religion* (September 1974): 454, reprinted in Naomi W. Cohen, ed., *Essential Papers in Jewish-Christian Relations in the United States* (New York: New York University Press, 1990), 210–11.

[13] In Merkle, ed., *Faith Transformed*, 203. Note that this claim of 'the abiding validity of Judaism' closely resembles the language of Messianic Jewish scholar Mark Kinzer who states: 'Our thesis – the legitimacy, value, and importance of rabbinic Judaism – remains intact. That thesis is crucial. If rabbinic Judaism is not valid, then no Judaism is valid.' See Mark S. Kinzer, *Postmissionary Messianic Judaism: Redefining Christian Engagement with the Jewish People* (Grand Rapids: Brazos, 2005), 260; I have taken strong issue with this statement, most particularly in my paper, 'Is a Postmissionary, Truly Messianic Judaism Possible?', esp. 6–7, delivered at the LCJE North American conference, San Antonio, 18 April 2007. For the online version of this paper, see http://www.realmessiah.com/postMissionary.htm. It should be noted that Dr. Kinzer explained to me privately in October 2007 that I misunderstood his references to 'rabbinic Judaism' when I took him to mean Orthodox or traditional Judaism. Rather, he was referring to all forms of 'Judaism', from ultra-Orthodox to Reconstructionist.

This, then, is the crux of the matter and the ultimate question that must be addressed: Can followers of Jesus hold to 'the abiding validity of Judaism' – meaning, quite specifically, that the Jewish people have a fully legitimate, spiritually complete religion *without Jesus* – while at the same remaining true to the teachings of the New Testament? Has the Holocaust truly forced such a wholesale reconsideration of the Jewish people and the gospel?

The Muting of Jewish Evangelism in Post-Holocaust Christianity

Before answering these questions, let me summarize briefly the principal reasons why some Christians feel that they can (or should) no longer share their faith with Jewish people in the post-*Shoah* era:

1. An embarrassment over, and even reconsideration of, the subject of hell, since very few Christians think that Jews deserved the inhuman horrors of the Holocaust, forcing them to ask: 'How then do Jewish people who reject Jesus deserve an eternal hell?' It is one thing to talk about an abstract, future, invisible realm; it is another thing to look at concrete, present, visible suffering. The reality of the latter forces us to re-evaluate our beliefs about the former.
2. A sense of shame and inferiority that basically says: 'Can I really say that my Christianity is superior to your Judaism? It was my professedly Christian forbears who opened up the floodgates of Nazism and your Judaism that sustained you through it. What do I have to offer you?' Related to this was the re-evaluation of Judaism as an entirely valid, complete faith in and of itself.
3. An openness to dual covenant theology, since many theologians recognized that it was supersessionism that led to 'Christian' anti-Semitism and, therefore, only the complete and total repudiation of supersessionism would be righteous in God's sight.
4. A sense that Christian outreach to Jews was a form of spiritual genocide, a charge echoed by counter-missionaries today who exclaim: 'Hitler wanted our bodies. You want our souls.'[14]

---

[14] Expressed another way, and used as a signature in all of the counter-missionary postings of Dr. Uri Yosef (one of the main contributors to the Messiah Truth website): 'WHOSOEVER DESTROYS A SINGLE SOUL OF ISRAEL, SCRIPTURE IMPUTES [GUILT] TO HIM AS THOUGH HE HAD DESTROYED A COMPLETE WORLD; AND WHOSOEVER PRESERVES A SINGLE SOUL OF ISRAEL,

In his article 'Jesus the Pacifist', Professor John Howard Yoder encapsulated some of these sentiments:

> In its scale and style, the Nazi genocidal project surpassed in qualitative impact the many other pogroms and massacres of Jewish memory. It has provoked a round of theological debate such as had not been experienced since the beginning of the age of assimilation.
>
> Only a few thinkers believe that the old answer, namely that the suffering of God's people is 'for our sins', can be stretched to fit this new level of tragedy . . .
>
> Even if Christianity as the ideology of oppressive Christendom had not been behind 'the Holocaust', Christianity as conversational partner in the battle for the minds of the children of Western Jews has become less interesting.[15]

The Holocaust has not Altered the Foundations of the Faith

How then should we respond? The answer is shockingly simple: The Holocaust, despite its monstrous evil, has actually changed nothing. Either the New Testament message that Jesus came to fulfil what was written in Moses and the Prophets is true or it is not (see e.g. Matt. 5:17; Luke 24:25–7, 44–5; John 1:45; Acts 3:18–26; Rom. 16:25–7). Either Yeshua is the Messiah of Israel and, therefore, the Saviour of the world or he is not (see e.g. Matt. 1:21; 28:18–20; Luke 1:31–3, 68–79; 2:29–32; 24:46–7; Acts 4:12 [spoken to the Sanhedrin]; Rom. 10:9–13 [in the midst of Paul's discussion of Israel]; 11:25–32). Either there is a place of judgement known as hell or there is not (see e.g. Dan. 12:2; Mark 9:42–9; Rev. 20:11–15). Either Jewish people, in some very real sense, 'need Jesus' or they do not, the law being unable to save (see e.g. Acts 13:38–48; 28:16–28; Rom. 3:9–31).

What *has* been shaken is the confidence in 'Christendom' (a term used by some in distinction from the real Christian faith) – and that

---

(SCRIPTURE ASCRIBES [MERIT] TO HIM AS THOUGH HE HAD PRESERVED A COMPLETE WORLD. (Babylonian Talmud, Tractate Sanhedrin, 37a)' (emphasis in the original; see, e.g. http://messiahtruth.yuku.com/reply/33199/t/ Re-Xtian-self-criticism-.html#reply-33199). He adds to this a final comment: 'The fruits of our effort: The battle against spiritual terrorism is being won, one soul at a time!!!' (Emphasis original).

[15] John Howard Yoder, *The Jewish–Christian Schism Revisited* (eds. Michael G. Cartwright and Peter Ochs; Grand Rapids: Eerdmans, 2003), 87.

confidence needed to be shaken. All too often the professing church has fallen terribly short of God's standards, and this has been true on both the Catholic and Protestant sides of the fence. It was altogether necessary, then, that post-Holocaust Christians asked themselves searching questions, wrestling with the Jewish blood that was on 'Christian' hands through the centuries, wrestling with the anti-Semitism that helped prepare the way for the slaughter of the six million, wrestling with the toxic words of Luther's *Concerning the Jews and their Lies* (among other Luther writings) that were resurrected by Hitler and his henchman, wrestling with the demonization of the Jews by some of the Church Fathers, and ultimately wrestling with the decisive question, namely, was the New Testament itself the source of this poisonous stream? For some, the answer to that last question has been 'Yes', hence the writing of many books by authors professing fealty to the Christian faith but devoted to identifying and repudiating the 'anti-Semitism of the New Testament'.[16]

In all candour, however, it must be asked: If the New Testament is, in fact, the source of 'Christian' anti-Semitism, how then can its message be trusted? If some of the authors of our foundational documents had already taken a stance displeasing to God – in those very documents – how could we possibly call their writings 'the Word of God'? More pointedly still: If the primary thesis of the New Testament was untrue – namely, that God's promises to Israel were now realized in and through Yeshua – what remains of 'Christianity'?

A Letter from a Rabbi

Frankly, these are the kinds of questions that many of us faced as Jewish believers from our first days in the Lord, questions about what happened to our non-believing (and deceased) loved ones, questions about the Crusades and Inquisitions (which would have been asked even without a Holocaust), questions about the veracity of the New Testament, not least regarding its alleged anti-Semitism (or anti-Judaism). As a brand new believer in Jesus, freshly delivered from an abusive, drug-filled lifestyle and barely seventeen years old, I was given a copy of Malcolm Hay's book *Europe and the Jews* by the local

---

[16] For a representative sampling, see the works cited in Brown, *Answering Jewish Objections to Jesus*, vol. 1, 240–41, n. 169.

Conservative Jewish rabbi.[17] Included in the book was this handwritten note, which I still have:

> Dear Mike:
> I'm lending you this book so that as you read its pages you can share in the thousands of years of agony your people have undergone for the sake of the Almighty G-d of Israel and His absolute unity. Perhaps it will touch a note in your heart which will help you realize what your destiny on earth is to be. As you read it please keep three verses in mind:
>
> '. . . the LORD GOD will wipe tears away from all faces, and He will remove the reproach of His people from all the earth; for the LORD has spoken.' (Isaiah 25:8)
>
> 'And the LORD will be King over all the earth; in that day the LORD will be the only one, and His name the only one.' (Zech 14:9)
>
> and finally, together with millions of your martyred brethren, 'Hear O Israel, the LORD is our God, the LORD is one' (Deut 6:4).
>
> I pray our G-d give you the inner strength to face the truth no matter what the consequences.[18]

These challenges have been with me since early 1972.

Just this month (July 2008, as I write) I was speaking to a dear friend who is an ultra-Orthodox rabbi, Yisroel C. Blumenthal, a learned, devoted man with whom I try to interact once a week by phone for up to an hour at a time. I asked him how connected the Holocaust and Christianity are perceived to be in his circles. He replied at once: 'Totally', explaining to me that these religious Jews do not know that there is a difference between those who merely profess Christianity and true Christians, and that the only kind of Christianity they know

---

[17] Malcolm V. Hay, *Europe and the Jews: The Pressure of Christendom on the People of Israel for 1900 Years* (Boston: Beacon Press, 1960); Hay's book has been published under other titles, including *The Foot of Pride* (with the same subtitle; 1950) and *The Roots of Christian Anti-Semitism* (1984).

[18] All the verses were written in Hebrew, which I did not understand at that point, so I had to reference them in English. Quite understandably, the letter remains moving to me to this day. Of personal significance to me, this same rabbi, William Berman, formerly an instructor of Bible at Jewish Theological Seminary, penned an endorsement for my work *Our Hands Are Stained with Blood: The Tragic Story of the 'Church' and the Jewish People*, stating: 'Though strongly disagreeing with the book theologically, I was deeply moved as I read it. I pray that Dr. Brown's message penetrates the souls of Christians everywhere. If his words are absorbed "like showers on young grass, like droplets on the grass," glory will indeed be given to God (Deut 32:2–3).'

is the anti-Semitic brand. He then recounted to me the story of a Slovakian Jew who helped rescue Jews from the Nazis – and, according to Rabbi Blumenthal's source, was opposed in his efforts by a Vatican emissary – and who wrote that the pope was glad that, at last, one of his disciples succeeded.

This conversation simply underscored what many Messianic Jews have known all their lives: 'Christianity' has often been a massive stumbling block to our people, obscuring the face of Jesus-Yeshua and making it much more difficult for *klal yisra'el* to recognize their Redeemer. As the great nineteenth-century Old Testament scholar Franz Delitzsch observed:

> The Church still owes the Jews the actual proof of Christianity's truth. Is it surprising that the Jewish people are such an insensitive and barren field for the Gospel? The Church itself has drenched it in blood and then heaped stones upon it.[19]

With the Holocaust and its perceived connection with Christianity, a massive boulder was heaped upon this blood-drenched field, but this again was nothing new. It was simply a more extreme act – unspeakably more extreme – but not of an entirely different 'kind'. After all, hadn't Raul Hilberg long ago presented his damning charts, comparing the restrictive, discriminatory, anti-Semitic actions of the Nazis with the earlier, restrictive, discriminatory, anti-Semitic actions of the church, with the exception of extermination, but including herding Jews into ghettos and forcing them to wear the yellow star?[20]

What I am saying is that the Holocaust forced the church at large – in particular, the European church – to wrestle with the very issues that Jewish believers wrestled with before the Holocaust, issues that they would still be forced to wrestle with today even without a Holocaust. The horrors of the Holocaust, to be sure, brought those issues into sharper focus for Jewish believers too, but in our perception, the Holocaust is not something that the Nazis did 'to them' but 'to us'. Our people – including believers in Jesus – were slaughtered by the Nazis, and our people – including believers in Jesus – were sometimes persecuted by the church. This brings a very different perspective to the questions in hand.

---

[19] Cited in Brown, *Our Hands Are Stained with Blood*, 92.
[20] Raul Hilberg, *The Destruction of the European Jews* (3d ed., New Haven: Yale University Press, 2003); it was first published in 1967.

It is Good to be Troubled by the Question of Hell

To return to the issue of hell, I personally do not see how anyone can believe in the doctrine of future punishment without considerable anguish of heart, without relating, at least on some level, to Paul's words in Romans 9:1–5 that he had 'great sorrow and unceasing anguish' because of Israel's 'cut-off' estate; without understanding, at least in part, the prophetic anguish expressed by Jeremiah, who wished that his head were a fountain of tears because of his slain people (Jer. 9:1; Heb. 8:23),[21] without feeling, at least to some degree, the same pain that Yeshua felt when he wept over Jerusalem (Luke 19:41–4; see also Matt. 23:37–9). If we cannot glibly talk about the Holocaust – God forbid! – how can we glibly talk about hell? How can we make this a mere test of doctrinal correctness without experiencing a broken heart for the lost? To the extent, then, that the Holocaust has forced people to rethink their beliefs in future punishment, all the better, as long as this is done with sincerity before the Lord and with total dependence on the Scriptures.[22]

To be sure, it is not our part to stand at this distance and offer authoritative pronouncements about the final state of those who died in the Holocaust, and the truest answer remains: 'You and I are not their judge. God is their Judge, and the Judge of the all the earth will do what is right.' Nonetheless, as I have emphasized, the horrors of the

---

[21] There is a lively scholarly discussion as to when and where the Lord and Jeremiah alternate as speakers in 8:21 – 9:3[2] or whether there is one speaker throughout (the Lord or Jeremiah). Although Jeremiah 9:1 is best put on the prophet's lips, there is clearly a fluidity between the divine and human speakers, making it unclear, so to say, when God ends and the prophet begins (and vice versa). See Michael L. Brown, 'Jeremiah', in *The Expositor's Bible Commentary, Revised Edition* (ed. Tremper Longman III and David E. Garland; Grand Rapids: Zondervan, 2009); cf. further Kazoh Kitamori, *Theology of the Pain of God* (Eng. trans.; Richmond: John Knox, 1965).

[22] Some of the more important, recent treatments of the question of eternal punishment include: William Crockett, ed., *Four Views on Hell* (Grand Rapids: Zondervan, 1992); Jonathan L. Kvanvig, *The Problem of Hell* (New York/Oxford: OUP, 1993); Ajith Fernando, *Crucial Questions about Hell* (Wheaton, Ill.: Crossway, 1994); Robert A. Peterson, *Hell on Trial: The Case for Eternal Punishment* (Phillipsburg, N. J.: 1995); John W. Blanchard, *Whatever Happened to Hell* (Wheaton, Ill.: Crossways, 1995); David Powys, 'Hell': A Hard Look at a Hard Question: The Fate of the Unrighteous in New Testament Thought* (Paternoster Biblical and Theological Monographs; Carlisle: Paternoster, 1998); Christopher W. Morgan and Robert A. Peterson, eds., *Hell Under Fire: Modern Scholarship Reinvents Eternal Punishment* (Grand Rapids: Zondervan, 2004).

Holocaust force us to preach about the kingdom of God and eternal reward and punishment with much greater sobriety, as is fitting for such extraordinarily weighty topics. Indeed, Paul's words to the Corinthians, written in a similar life and death context, immediately come to mind: 'Who is sufficient for these things?' (2 Cor. 2:14–16 [NRSV]). For Jewish believers, the question of the 'fate of the Jews' has never been a mere theological abstraction, and so we are glad when the question becomes more acute for the church at large. Join us as we wrestle through these painful issues together.

How Should We Respond?

How should we respond to the anti-Semitic words and concepts and deeds that have blemished church history and helped prepare the way for the Holocaust? In the same conversation with Rabbi Blumenthal, mentioned above, he told me that in his yeshiva library (the world famous, Lakewood Yeshiva), there is a Hebrew book that discusses different world religions and then explains why they are not true. He explained, however, that the section on Christianity was quite short, since all it had to do was recount church history through traditional Jewish eyes. It was disqualified at once.

What then is the right Christian response to this? Is it renunciation of the Christian faith, embracing of dual covenant theology or, at the least, refraining from evangelizing Jews? God forbid. Rather, the aberrant must be renounced in the name of the real and the counterfeit must be exposed in the light of the true. The bankrupt Christianity that produced Crusades and Inquisitions and made Jews into devils does not negate the glory of the faith that has transformed countless millions of lives, the faith that has sought to emulate the way of the Master, the faith that has sacrificed and served rather than slandered and slaughtered, the faith of the Corrie Ten-Booms and others who risked – and sometimes lost – their own lives to save Jewish lives. We must not let shame over past sins blind our eyes today.

Here too Messianic Jews can add a useful perspective since it is commonplace in our witness to our people to *begin* with a repudiation of 'Christian' anti-Semitism, assuring them that this is not a real reflection of Jesus and the New Testament. And if we do not start with the subject, we are confident that it will soon be raised, at least by traditional Jews and/or Jews who know their history. Even on the level of public debates with rabbis, I have often started with a recapitulation and renunciation of Christendom's sins against the Jews, knowing that this spectre of the past will raise its ugly head quickly if I do not address it first.

We must also be convinced through careful study that the New Testament is not, in fact, the source of anti-Semitism, a task that has become much easier in recent decades with the wide-scale philo-Semitism that exists in so many parts of the evangelical church, most notably in America.[23] Yet it is those very Christians who tend to take the words of the New Testament most seriously, reminding us that it is only when the church cuts itself off from its biblical foundations and severs its Jewish roots that it becomes anti-Semitic.[24]

Our message then, to the Jewish people, is simple: 'I deeply regret what so-called Christians have done in Jesus' name, and I do not for a second deny the ugliness of it. And as a follower of Jesus today, I apologize for what these hypocritical Christians have done. [This is especially effective when it is a Gentile Christian doing the apologizing.] Allow me to introduce you to the real Jesus, and let me demonstrate to you first hand what a real Christian is.' All of us in Jewish ministry have heard wonderful testimonies from our Gentile Christian friends who have used this very approach with sincerity and conviction.

An Appreciation of Judaism is Healthy

Finally, what should be said of the fresh appreciation of Judaism that has arisen in many Christian circles since the Holocaust? In many ways, that too can be a good and healthy thing. For example, Christians have often had a skewed view of Judaism, and this new, more positive assessment is much closer to the truth. Truth is good and Christians can learn much from Jewish traditions and the observant Jewish lifestyle. Also, it is only to the extent that we realize that the Jewish people, in particular religious Jews, are 'so near and yet so far' that we can fully appreciate the tragedy of their lostness and the pain of their missing the Messiah, thereby entering into their

---

[23] For a lively account, see Zev Chafets, *A Match Made in Heaven: American Jews, Christian Zionists, and One Man's Exploration of the Weird and Wonderful Judeo-Evangelical Alliance* (San Francisco: Harper Perennial, 2008).

[24] For insights on the theological consequences of supersessionism, see Ronald E. Diprose, *Israel and The Church: The Origins and Effects of Replacement Theology* (Carlisle: Authentic Media; 2004). This represents an abridgement of the Italian original, which, the author informed me, contains far more indicting material.

corporate longing for redemption through our prayers and sacrificial acts.[25]

Yet once more, the Messianic Jewish perspective is helpful, since some of us came from observant backgrounds, and others, who came from secular backgrounds, have helped lead observant Jews to Jesus, and together we lift our voices to say: 'Judaism without Yeshua is not enough, even in its most committed, devoted, spiritual forms.[26] Our people need our Messiah, and we either preach what the Scriptures teach, namely the Good News that he has already come, died and rose for our sins, or we throw out the Book.'

To reiterate what should be self-evident to all, the gospel was birthed in Jewish soil; it is the story of the Jewish Redeemer; all its main characters are Jews, from Miriam the young virgin to devout Simeon waiting for the consolation of Israel, and from old Zechariah and Elizabeth to New Testament authors named Jacob and Judah. And the Messiah's death and resurrection was first proclaimed to Jews alone, by Jews, and it was Jews alone who made up the first thousands and thousands of disciples. Need I even supply Scripture references for these everyday facts? Either the account is true and Jesus is the promised Messiah without whom there is no salvation for our people and for the world, or we admit that he or his followers were mistaken. There simply is no middle ground.

A Closing Appeal

The bottom line is that, outside of Jews living in Israel, most Jewish people will come to faith through the witness of Gentile Christians, in particular, their Gentile Christian friends, co-workers and neighbours, and therefore I implore you, as one saved through these very means: Please do not withhold the water of life from my thirsty people (John 7:37; Rev. 22:17). Please do not deprive them of the words of eternal life (John 6:68). Please do not discourage them from finding for themselves the one who is the truth and the life (John 11:24–5; 14:6). Do you not want them to live for ever in the presence of our God?

---

[25] See Brown, *Our Hands Are Stained with Blood*, 107–15 (this is the chapter entitled, 'So Near and Yet So Far'), for relevant reflections.

[26] Many Jewish believers today who came out of very strict, traditional backgrounds have also testified that while there was beauty in their traditions, there was also much bondage, at least for them.

It is my hope and prayer that the memory of the Holocaust will provoke each of you to a more compassionate, fervent and effective outreach to the lost sheep of the house of Israel. Now is *not* the time to deny God's mercy to them.

10

Two Covenant Theology and its Implications for Jewish Missions

Henri Blocher

The negative stance towards 'missions to the Jews' one encounters in contemporary Christendom most commonly finds its *theological* justification in the so-called 'two covenant' (or dual covenant) scheme. In a nutshell, non-Christian Jews are said to be related to God under the terms of their own covenant, still the channel of divine blessing to them, and Christians who belong to *another* covenant are not to interfere and seek for a change in the Jews' religious allegiance.

This viewpoint has been predominant in ecumenical circles at least since the Faith and Order Bristol conference (1967), though, at the time, the preferred language was that of the two parts of the one people of God, neither of which (Israel and the church) may claim to be more obedient to God than the other. The conviction that Israel's covenant has not been revoked and provides, in the present era, a way of faith and life approved by God, distinct from the Christian one, gained momentum and found expression in many documents, such as the documents collected in the World Council of Churches publication (Geneva, 1988) *The Theology of the Churches and the Jewish People: Statements by the World Council of Churches and its member churches*, with a commentary by representative theologians Allan Brickway, Paul van Buren, Rolf Rendtorff and Simon Schoon.[1] It may entail the rejection of

---

[1] I reviewed the book in my 'L'Œcuménisme et les juifs,' *Fac-Réflexion* 13 (July 1989): 25–31.

the very phrases 'old' and 'new' covenants or testaments (p. 158).[2] At the end of the same year, a Consultation held at Sigtuna, Sweden spelled it out: 'We see not one covenant displacing another, but two communities of faith, each called in existence by God, each holding its respective gifts from God, and each accountable to God.'[3]

In Germany, the review *Kirche und Israel* constantly promoted it.[4] Even Wolfhart Pannenberg was led (under Rolf Rendtorff's influence?) to recant his 1964 'judgment that for Christians the cross of Jesus means the end of Judaism as a religion' – he now sees 'the essence of Jewish faith in the same way as the proclamation of Jesus, i.e. in terms of faith in the God of Israel';[5] however, his position remains moderate and nuanced, including a positive use of 'mission to the Jews'.[6] The harder form has spread far and wide: one can cite a splinter group from the Southern Baptist Convention, 'The Alliance of Baptists', who typically 'espouses Dual Covenant Theology' and denounces attempts to convert Jews instead of acknowledging 'the efficacy of the Jewish faith'.[7] Fairly recently, Colin Chapman could complain that 'anyone who cannot accept a two-covenant . . . theology is automatically labelled as holding Replacement

---

[2] Jacques Ellul, *Un Chrétien pour Israël* (Monaco: Ed. du Rocher, 1986), 18 n.1, refuses to say 'Old' and 'New' Testament: only First and Second.

[3] 'The Churches and the Jewish People: Towards a New Understanding', as published in the *International Bulletin of Missionary Research* 13/4 (October 1989): 154 n.8.

[4] Eckhard Schnabel's magisterial synthesis, from which I am drawing much help, offers a reply to the main spokesmen for this theology in the said review, 'Die Gemeinde des Neuen Bundes in Kontinuität und Diskontinuität zur Gemeinde des Alten Bundes' in *Israel in Geschichte und Gegenwart. Beiträge zur Geschichte Israels und zum jüdisch-christlichen Dialog*, TVG (ed. Gerhard Maier; Wuppertal/Giessen & Basel: Brockhaus/Brunnen, 1996), 147–213.

[5] *Systematic Theology II* (trans. Geoffrey W. Bromiley; Edinburgh/Grand Rapids: T&T Clark/Eerdmans, 1994), 342 n.54; he refers to Rendtorff on the next page.

[6] *Systematic Theology III* (trans. Geoffrey W. Bromiley; Edinburgh/Grand Rapids: T&T Clark/Eerdmans, 1998), 474: 'all Christians in conversations with Jews have to confess their belief in Jesus as the Christ of Israel and to bear witness to this belief in the conversations. This is the inalienable core of the Christian mission to Jews', and he used again the phrase on the next page. Contrary to common dual covenant theologians, 'the apostle', for Pannenberg, 'was not advocating a "special path" for Israel on the way to eschatological salvation, a path that would bypass Jesus Christ and his gospel' (472); he believes – not far, it seems from Franz Mussner's interpretation (n.102) – that Paul in Romans 11 ('In distinction from what the Gospels say' and 'in contrast to his initial judgment in 1 Thess. 2:15–16') teaches that Israel will be brought into the *new* covenant by the *parousia*, 'for Israel [the] renewal of the old covenant relationship with its God' (472f.).

[7] According to the account by Jim R. Sibley, 'On the Record': Official Statements of Southern Baptists Regarding the Jewish People', *Mishkan* 36 (2002): 58.

Theology. Since it is so widely regarded as being "a bad thing", it seems to have become a convenient way to "give the dog a bad name".[8]

On the Roman Catholic side, the well-publicized statement in *Nostra Aetate* (§ 4), hailed as a turning point in the church's attitude towards the Jews, remained cautious: while it only quoted *positive* phrases to define the present status of Israelites, it did include the clause 'Although the Church is the new people of God' (*Licet autem Ecclesia sit novus populus Dei*); indeed, as Denise Judant shrewdly observes, one should also take into account *Lumen Gentium* which did not muffle the missionary imperative, Jews not excepted (I,5), affirmed the church as the *unus Populus Dei* (II,13) to which the people of Israel is 'ordained' (*ordinantur*, II,16), the old covenant being recognized as preparatory and prefigurative (II,9: *in praeparationem et figuram . . . foederis illius novi et perfecti*). Denise Judant even argues that *Lumen Gentium*, a 'Dogmatic Constitution', carries a greater weight of authority than the 'Declaration' of *Nostra Aetate*.[9]

Soon afterwards, however, the two covenant scheme emerged. Denise Judant analyzes an 'orientation note' from the French Episcopal Committee for Relations with Judaism (April 1973) which recommended a new way of looking upon the Jewish people 'also in the order of faith', which affirmed that 'the first Covenant was not made obsolete (*caduque*) by the New one' and that the Jewish people today have their 'own peculiar mission' in God's design. Cardinal Jean Daniélou protested that such statements amounted to 'changing the faith'.[10] Though he did so with an exquisite choice of words, Pope John Paul II often suggested the kind of symmetry or parallelism that goes with Two Covenant Theology; when addressing the Jewish community in Vienne, he declared:

> Peace [Shalom] comprises the offer and the possibility of forgiveness and mercy, the outstanding qualities of our God, the God of the Covenant. You *experience* and celebrate *in faith* this certainty, when you annually keep the great Day of Reparation, the Yom Kippur, as a feast day. We Christians contemplate this mystery in the heart of Christ.[11]

---

[8] 'God's Covenant – God's Land,' in *The God of Covenant: Biblical, Theological and Contemporary Perspectives* (eds. Jamie A. Grant and Alistair I. Wilson; Leicester: Apollos [IVP], 2005), 242.

[9] Denise Judant, *Jalons pour une théologie chrétienne d'Israël* (Paris: Ed. du Cèdre, 1975), 20.

[10] Judant, *Jalons*, 28–9 (26–31 relevant).

[11] On 24 June 1988, as quoted by Peter Hocken, 'Catholic Statements on the Church, the Jewish People and Mission to the Jews', *Mishkan* 36 (2002): 72 (italics mine).

In a lecture given at the Israel Museum, Jerusalem, on 21 November 2001, Cardinal Walter Kasper stated: 'Now we are aware of God's unrevoked covenant with His people and the permanent and *actual salvific significance* of the Jewish religion for its believers.'[12] Cardinal Joseph Ratzinger – as he was known at the time – adopted a stricter view, excluding 'recognition of Judaism as an integrally valid way of salvation'.[13] However, in an article in *l'Osservatore Romano* (dated 29 December 2000), he spoke of the faith in the one God and added: 'Our gratitude, therefore, must be extended to our Jewish brothers and sisters who despite the hardships of their own history, have held on to faith in this God right up to the present';[14] Judaism is 'not another religion to us, but the foundation of our own faith' and 'since we are both awaiting the final redemption, let us pray that the paths we follow may converge.'[15] Though he kept clear of the dual covenant scheme, the identification of present day Judaism with Old Testament religion (the foundation of our own faith) by the future pope did reflect some influence of the new vision the scheme informs.

The aim of this paper is not once more to expound the said theology. It wishes first of all to dispel ambiguities and other obscurities, and so both to clarify and sharpen issues. The attempt will be made in the perspective of evangelical theology, the canonical Scriptures of the Old and New Testament being the final court of appeal and supreme 'judge of controversies', approached in the hermeneutical confidence that the role of presuppositions and context in interpretation does not *preclude* ascertaining the one, objective, meaning of the Word – still the goal towards which theologians may reasonably tend and strive.

---

[12] Quoted by David Neuhaus, 'Kehilla, Church and Jewish People', *Mishkan* 36 (2002): 83 (italics mine).

[13] Peter Hocken, 77, referring (76) to the Cardinal's collection of essays *Many Religions, One Covenant* (San Francisco: Ignatius Press, 1999).

[14] 'New Vision of the Relationship Between the Church and the Jews', English translation in *Origins* 30:35 (15 February 2001): 565.

[15] 'New Vision', 566. 'Final redemption' is vague enough to be true to fact; when Jewish hope in the Messiah still to come at the end of the age and Christian hope in the Messiah already come but also coming again, are set in parallel fashion (e.g. the *Catechism of the Catholic Church*, § 840), this betrays some ignorance of the reduced part the expectation of a personal Messiah plays across contemporary Judaism. Denise Judant, already, had made the point, *Jalons*, 120 n.2.

Focusing on the Heart of Debate

The wording may convey the wrong impression: the key and controversial issue raised by Two Covenant Theology is *not* that of the number of divine covenants, or whether we should speak of one or two. Most scholars, across a wide spectrum of opinions, will grant that the biblical data are flexible enough to legitimize various forms of expression. Paul R. Williamson announces that his discussion of covenants 'assumes a total of nine', some 'renewals' not included, but that he will delineate them 'under the following convenient headings: Noahic, Abrahamic, Mosaic, priestly, Davidic and new.'[16] Reformed theologians who emphasize the unity of the covenant of grace still speak of several 'administrations', a word which could be considered as a candidate for translating *diathēkē* (not so far from 'disposition' that some, like Yves Congar, preferred). Conversely, those who contrast 'Old' and 'New' do not deny continuities within the one over-arching purpose of God.

Advocates of the new theology of Israel and critics of Christian missions to Jews have not seldom started with a strong one covenant emphasis.[17] This is the case of Paul van Buren who, only in the 1990s, 'modified his strict single-covenant view and moved towards a double-covenant understanding of Israel and the church.'[18] At the risk of over-simplification, I would sketch the development as follows: at a *first* stage, in order to unseat Gentile boasting in the church (Rom. 11:18), to cast out all thought of 'replacement' and forms of 'supersessionism', the emphasis fell on Israel's possession of all the (one) covenant privileges, by birthright and never to be withdrawn and, on the secondary status, in the one Olive-Tree, of 'engrafted' Gentile Christians; in that light, the latter's proselytism among Jews looked unbecoming, to say the least. At a *second* stage, however, the sentiment

---

[16] 'Covenant', in *New Dictionary of Biblical Theology* (eds. T. Desmond Alexander and Brian S. Rosner, Leicester: IVP, 2000), 419b–429b; 421b.

[17] Denis Müller estimates that a 'majority of protestant theologians (Jürgen Moltmann, Bertold Klappert, Peter von den Osten-Sacken, Paul van Buren) . . . uphold the thesis of one covenant, thus underlining the fundamental continuity between Judaism and Christianity', in *Encyclopédie du protestantisme* (ed. Pierre Gisel; Geneva/Paris: Labor & Fides/Cerf, 1995), 803a; the statement has not been modified in the second, revised, edition (Geneva/Paris: Labor & Fides/Presses Universitaires de France 'Quadrige', 2006), 701a, though I would not adopt it unchanged.

[18] Krista Rosenlund Larsen Bellows, 'Paul van Buren – A Single-Covenant Theologian', *Mishkan* 36 (2002): 113, cf. 122 n.6 (whole art.: 113–22).

has prevailed that the same unrevoked possession of covenantal privileges is definitely different from the Christian covenant in Jesus Christ – thus eliminating the difficulty of explaining how believing and not-believing in Jesus as Lord could be joined in the same covenant.[19]

Factors in the development may have been: a growing realization of the core differences between Christianity and Judaism, and indeed Old Testament religion (especially as depicted by ordinary critics); Jewish dissatisfaction with a scheme drawn up by Christians, Gentiles who 'generously' decide about Jewish identity; the encouragement drawn from the work of such a powerful and generous Jewish thinker as Franz Rosenzweig (to some degree, also Martin Buber); a general climate favourable to *pluralism* in the name of tolerance, so that the idea of parallel and equally acceptable ways (ultimately converging) may also be applied to other 'faiths'.

If the issue is not the number of covenants, neither is it whether one acknowledges or denies a *peculiar* note attaching to Jews who reject the claims of Jesus. Even those who deny any special future to Israelites 'according to the flesh' still must make room for their 'natural' connection with the Olive-Tree and their being loved 'because of (their) fathers'.[20] Many who resist the ecumenical Two Covenant Theology go much further: they hope for a future massive conversion of Israel; not a few see a positive meaning in the creation of the State of Israel; some degree of Zionism is even compatible with their basic theological option.

Conversely Dual Covenant theologians cannot deny that the peculiar status conferred by the Mosaic covenant has been affected by what happened at the beginning of the Christian era: they cannot claim that rabbinic Judaism is simply identical with the faith of the Tanakh; they cannot ignore the import of the loss of the temple; if they profess the Christian faith, even a pale residue, how could they fancy that the rejection of Jesus be of no consequence whatsoever for the status of Israelites in covenant with God, the Father of Jesus? The issue, therefore, is how

---

[19] This difficulty was felt at the first stage, mainly as the contradiction between the theological solidarity of Israel and the church and their concrete mutual estrangement. It was interpreted as a deep, essential, wound of the church, which cannot be the people of God without Israel. F. Lovsky, *Antisémitisme et mystère d'Israël* (Paris: Albin Michel, 1955), 525–30, concludes that the 'Jewish question' is the 'Christian question'; he sees all the divisions in the body of Christ as stemming from the first-century 'schism' between the church and Israel (511).

[20] Even Denise Judant, *Jalons*, writes that they are called 'in a most particular fashion' (83, cf. 100) and loved with a 'particular love' (110).

to define what is 'peculiar' in the situation of non-Christian Jews – since all must allow for some peculiarity.

The outcome may be the easiest criterion to handle. The new theology of Israel, now usually a Two Covenant one, yields as its conclusion that mission to the Jews, Christian proselytism among them, is improper. One could define this theology as such an interpretation of the old and new covenants (biblical names) and the relationships between them, that enough of the Old remains in force in the present era: (a) to provide a way of acceptance with God and final salvation for those who are called 'Jews', while they fail to believe in Jesus as Christ and Lord; and (b) to cast an unfavourable light on endeavours by disciples of Jesus to change the 'Jews' stance towards him. The condemnation of proselytism usually accompanies the commendation of 'dialogue', through which 'mutual enrichment' takes place, and of 'cooperation' in a spirit which, owing to an extension of the original sense, may be labelled 'ecumenical'.

To locate the heart of debate, I should add a brief comment on a somewhat paradoxical convergence between Two Covenant Theology and an important evangelical school whose sympathies do not lie near ecumenical (WCC) dialogues. Dispensationalism has been characterized by a clean separation between the Lord's covenant with Israel and the one, unforeseen by Old Testament prophecy, in which Christian believers are saved during the 'parenthesis'[21] of the church dispensation. Dispensationalism has proved a fertile ground for a Christian form of Zionism, with sizable political consequences.[22] Some dispensationalists – in my experience, very few – show themselves reluctant to support missions to the Jews.[23]

I will bypass, in the present communication, the *dispensationalist* Two Covenant Theology.[24] I consider the negative consequence for gospel witness as a fringe phenomenon. For dispensationalist orthodoxy,

---

[21] Lewis S. Chafer even preferred 'intercalation' (*Systematic Theology* [Dallas: Dallas Seminary Press, 1947–8], IV,41; VI,81.

[22] This obviously distresses C. Chapman, 'God's Covenant – God's Land', in *The God of Covenant* (eds. Grant and Wilson), 234ff.

[23] One that I encountered was Dr Wim Malgo (1922–92), founder of Midnight Call ministries and publisher of a magazine of the same name.

[24] I dealt with dispensationalism as a doctrinal and hermeneutical system (though not with its specific eschatology) in my *La Doctrine du péché et de la rédemption*, coll. Didaskalia (Cléon-d'Andran/Vaux-sur-Seine: Excelsis/Edifac, 2000), 105–16, and, on the specific issue of the postponement of the kingdom, in *Evil and the Cross* (trans. David G. Preston; repr. Vancouver: Regent College Publishing, 2003), 111–13.

there is no difference between Jew and Greek as long as our parenthetical dispensation endures: whatever hopes may be entertained as to a future 'national' conversion of Israel in other times and under other conditions, a Jewish individual can only be saved *now* through faith in Jesus Christ, whereby he or she joins the church; the promises for Israel (consubstantial with covenant) are 'in abeyance', and the situation of two parallel ways and covenants, both in force at the same time, is avoided. Furthermore, dispensationalism has undergone considerable changes in the last decades and 'Progressive Dispensationalism', while it remains part of the family, has come much nearer to other evangelical options.[25] All these reasons warrant concentration on other issues.

Drawing a Firm Biblical Framework

In order not to miss the wood for the trees, we must remind ourselves of basic scriptural teachings: a general overview cannot enter into detailed argument and, inevitably, depends on my own sense of sufficient certainty!

The first feature is so obvious and massive, that one could easily overlook its presence. The realities proclaimed in the gospel and unfolded in apostolic *didachē* represent the *fulfilment* of everything that had been said and done before. This is more than continuity, it is *fruition*. The prophetic hymns in the 'infancy' chapters announce that God is about to intervene as he has given his word to Abraham and his seed (Luke 1:55); he now remembers 'his holy covenant' and his oath in favour of Abraham (Luke 1:72f.). Jesus starts preaching 'The time has come' (Mark 1:15), a theme which will become, with Paul, that of the *plērōma tou chronou* or *tōn kairōn* (Gal. 4:4; Eph. 1:10); Jesus stresses

---

[25] Rodney J. Decker, in a very helpful overview, *Contemporary Dispensational Theology* (Kansas City: Calvary Theological Seminary, 1992), leaving aside hyperdispensationalism, distinguishes classic (Scofield and Chafer), sometimes called traditional or scholastic, *modified* (Ryrie) and *progressive* (Craig Blaising, Darrell Bock, Robert Saucy) forms. He observes, 17 n.44, that Charles Ryrie, in 1953, emphatically defended 'the two covenants position' but had moved to one covenant teaching in 1975–6. Progressive dispensationalists go further and concede a partial fulfilment of Old Testament prophecies in the church; they insist, however, that the promises must *also* be fulfilled in a strictly literal fashion. On this trend, I am chiefly indebted to Robert L. Saucy, *Progressive Dispensationalism: The Interface Between Dispensational and Non-Dispensational Theology* (Grand Rapids: Zondervan, 1993), Vern S. Poythress, *Understanding Dispensationalists* (Grand Rapids: Zondervan, 1987) and the conversation in *Grace Theological Journal* 10 (1989): 125–82.

that his disciples are given to see what prophets, righteous people, kings, longed to behold and could not (Matt. 13:16f.; Luke 10:23f.). The *words* are fulfilled, as the things that were foretold, more or less literally, now happen (countless references!). The *events* and *institutions* are fulfilled as the reality they foreshadowed and 'pictured' in advance has now arrived (according to the type/antitype correspondence, e.g. 1 Cor. 10:1ff.), and whatever grace they carried in some measure now flows down from heaven. All the writings of the previous covenantal history of Israel were written for those who believe in Jesus (Rom. 15:4; 1 Cor. 10:11).

Such New Testament convictions do not represent the *projection* on older material of meanings that were not intrinsically there: I would argue that they match the very movement that drives the faith of Abraham, Moses and the prophets. 'The Old Testament', David Seccombe aptly summarizes, 'strains forward to a greater king than David, a greater revelation than Moses', a better priesthood than Aaron's, a more effective atonement than the temple's, a better covenant than Sinai and a mission to embrace all the nations of the earth.'[26] Many formal features warrant the recognition of this forward-looking character of the Old Testament:[27] truly, the New Testament is 'latent' in the Old and the faithful in Israel were those who 'in advance had set their hopes on Christ' (Eph. 1:12: *tous proēlpikotas en tō Christō*). The witness, from both sides, is overwhelming.

Yet the reader soon encounters statements of difference, discontinuity, some of them in strong terms indeed. The theme of fulfilment, already, implies some difference with what preceded, as the fruit may be contrasted with the flower, bud or seed. But apostolic language goes much further than that. Types, including the Sabbath ordinance and food regulations, can be described as 'shadows' in comparison with

---

[26] 'The Story of Jesus and the missionary strategy of Paul', in *The Gospel to the Nations: Perspectives on Paul's Mission, In honour of Peter T. O'Brien* (eds. Peter Bolt and Mark Thompson; Leicester: Apollos [IVP], 2000), 115.

[27] The place of promises, with express reference to the future (the days are coming, *bĕʾaḥarît hayyāmîm*, etc.) is one of these features (which Jürgen Moltmann exploited to great effect in his earlier work). I point to several of them in *La Doctrine du Christ*, 29–32; one of them is the ambiguity – I believe, studied ambiguity – affecting the working of the ritual system, with the prophetic attacks on ritualism, on the one hand, and in the law itself the restriction of atonement to sins of 'error', on the other. Who will dare say that there is no element of highhanded rebellion (*bĕyād rāmâ*) in his/her sins? Where, then, is atonement to be found? The ambiguity was enough to generate deep anguish in scrupulous souls and to thrust the believer's hope beyond Old Testament dispositions.

the substantial reality (*sōma*) enjoyed by Christians (Col. 2:16f.). These are no longer under the law, but under grace; they benefit from the ministry not of the letter (written on the stone tablets of the Decalogue), which *kills*, but of the Spirit who alone grants eternal life; salvation is not by works of law (as defined by Lev. 18:5) but by faith in God who reckons as righteous the *ungodly*; Moses, who towered above everyone else according to the older disposition (Num. 12:7f.; Deut. 34:10), was the divine instrument for the gift of the law, but grace and truth, the very glory of the Lord (Exod. 33:18; 34:6), came through Jesus Christ (John 1:17); the earlier commandment is abrogated (*athetēsis ginetai*) because it was weak and useless (Heb. 7:18). Other samples could be added to the list.

One is not so surprised that Marcion chose *Antitheseis* as his title and one need not be a Marcionite to observe many antitheses in the New Testament. Here also, the Old Testament promise, although less distinctly (since it announces the New in terms borrowed from the Old), converges: the newness of the work God is about to perform is such that the people will no longer remember the former events (Isa. 65:17) and nobody, for instance, will care any longer about the Ark of the Covenant (Jer. 3:16). Discontinuity, it seems!

If such, in broad strokes, is the biblical balance of continuity and discontinuity, what can one say more precisely on the people and the covenant – these two belong inseparably together?[28] How are continuity and discontinuity, fulfilment and novelty in this regard, combined?[29]

As already quoted, the *Benedictus*, on the threshold of the Gospel, sings the good news in terms of God remembering 'his holy covenant'. The form of the eucharistic words of Jesus, according to Matthew and

---

[28] Most scholars will grant this close association (though the word *bĕrît* may be used for a treaty that binds individuals) which is obvious in the so-called 'covenant formula' (on which, see for instance David L. Baker, 'Covenant: An Old Testament Study', in *God of Covenant* [Grant and Wilson, eds.], 22f.): I will be your God and you will be my people. Kim Huat Tan, 'Community, Kingdom and Cross: Jesus' View of Covenant', ibid., 124, writes: 'The first thing to note is that the concept of a covenant inexorably demands the attendant concept of a community. The covenant is, above all, relational. Those in covenant relationship with Yahweh are regarded as his people.' Similarly, W. Pannenberg, *Systematic Theology III*, 465: 'The concept of a covenant finds a correlate in that of the people of God with which the covenant is concluded and which is constituted by the covenant.'

[29] I have offered my revision of 'covenant theology' in *Always Reforming: Explorations in Systematic Theology* (ed. Andrew T. B. McGowan; Leicester: Apollos [IVP], 2006), 240–70.

Mark 'This is my blood of *the* covenant' suggesting the unity of the various covenants made with the fathers, illustrates the conviction of continuity. Hence, the community that shares in the fellowship of that blood, while 'sociologically' it appears as one 'sect' (*hairesis*) among the several 'sects' of first-century Judaism (Acts 24:14), considers itself as the true covenant people, heir to the covenant promises and the beneficiary of the long hoped-for 'redemption of Israel'.

This claim and self-understanding lends itself to comparison with those of the Qumran community,[30] whose members also thought of themselves as the 'children of light' and as the *rabbîm* for whom the Servant of Isaiah 52 – 53 was to secure atonement and justification; the assurance of the 'Jesus party' has his resurrection (as eyewitnesses could testify) as a sure ground, and the Qumran analogy breaks down at this point.

Hence, the disciples who acknowledged in the risen Jesus the Messiah of Israel, Redeemer and Lord, called their gathering *ekklēsia*, the LXX rendering for the *qāhāl*, the 'assembly' of Israel (cf. Acts 7:38); they were in their age, the age of fulfilment, the *qĕhal* YHWH. The same claim was made in several other words with a practical equivalence of meaning. The members of the church, believers in Jesus as the Christ, are the true seed of Abraham (Gal. 3:7, 29). They constitute the true 'circumcision' (Phil. 3:3). Since they have undergone the circumcision inwardly, the 'circumcision of Christ', they rightly own the title 'Jews' (Col. 2:11; Rom. 2:28f.). The peace-blessing rests upon them as the 'Israel of God' (Gal. 6:16).[31]

Characteristic images tell the same story: the Olive-Tree is Israel and is the church (Rom. 11); the true Vine, a frequent symbol of Israel, is Christ and those who are 'in him', that is, again, the Christian church (John 15); the church is the Bride of prophecy, the Bride of the Lamb who is the Lord and, if one is not ready to speak of divine bigamy, she is no other than YHWH's wife, Israel! The church is also the eschatological temple, which Jesus Christ is to build, in accordance with Jewish tradition, on the Rock (Matt. 16:13–20; Eph. 2:20–22; 1 Pet.

---

[30] Pannenberg, *Systematic Theology III*, 464, draws such a comparison.

[31] Strong considerations rule out that Paul should have in view only those circumcised in the flesh among Christians: the preceding verse has just affirmed that the difference between circumcision and uncircumcision counts for *nothing*! If he rebuilds in v. 16 what he has destroyed in v. 15, he constitutes himself a transgressor. The *kai* is epexegetical; it explains why the blessing of Pss 125:5 and 128:6 accrues to Christians, who walk by the 'canon' of spiritual new creation: they are the 'Israel of God', a name which contrasts with 'Israel after the flesh' in 1 Cor. 10:18.

2:5–6).[32] Following the last passage referred to, Peter confers to the Christian community the threefold title that defined Israel's privilege as God's covenant people in Exodus 19:5–6 (1 Pet. 2:9). How could he comment more forcefully on the title 'Israel of God'?

The presence of many Gentiles, and after a few decades a majority of Gentiles, in the church and among the addressees of the discourse we have just heard does not contradict its claims: Gentile believers in Jesus Christ have been grafted into the Olive-Tree (Rom. 11), they have been granted a co-citizenship with the 'saints' (Eph. 2:19); they do not modify the theological identity of the Lord's Bride. To borrow Pius XI's phrase, they have become spiritually 'Semites' – if one takes 'Semite' as equivalent of 'Israelite'.

Yet the novelty in the age of fulfilment is not limited to an extension of membership. Important changes affect covenant and people. The form of Jesus' eucharistic words as preserved by Paul and Luke indicates that, in his blood, the *new* covenant is established. The phrase, of course, comes from Jeremiah's prophecy, which stresses that the new covenant will *not* be like the covenant with the fathers (Jer. 31:32). Andrew G. Shead warns about 'the increasing tendency to read the new covenant passage in a way that minimizes or denies any substantive difference between it and the Mosaic covenant, a tendency shown especially by German-speaking and American scholars involved in Christian-Jewish dialogue';[33] his own study redresses the balance. E. Schnabel draws, from his analysis of the New Testament evidence, the conclusion that 'discontinuity overshadows continuity'.[34] The epistle to the Hebrews uses strong language: speaking of a new covenant that 'has made the first one obsolete' (8:13, New International Version for *pepalaiōken*) and the Old that is soon to disappear; the first covenant incurs blame (8:7), a 'reformation' was needed (*diorthōsis*, 9:10); the contrast between the two covenants is as strong as possible (12:18–24; 'new covenant' appears in v. 24). Paul can speak of the 'end' of the law, so essential a component of the older disposition (Rom. 10:4; cf. 2 Cor.

---

[32] E. Schnabel, 'Die Gemeinde', 197f, insists: 'This is also important because, according to Jewish tradition, the Rock of Mount Zion upon which the temple was built, the *'eben wĕtiyyâ*, constitutes the centre of the world. It binds together Heaven and Hades.' On the temple motif, with a wealth of information on the Jewish background, see Greg K. Beale, *The Temple and the Church's Mission: A Biblical Theology of the Dwelling Place of God* (New Studies in Biblical Theology 17; Downers Grove: Apollos [IVP], 2004).

[33] 'The New Covenant and Pauline Hermeneutics', in *The Gospel to the Nations* (eds. Bolt and Thompson), 34.

[34] Schnabel, 'Die Gemeinde', 209.

3:13 on the end of what was losing its efficacy, *katargoumenon*, the law-giver's ministry of Moses). The Old Testament religion of Israel involved enslavement to the 'cosmic elements' as pagan religion did (Gal. 4:9f.).[35] The true circumcision is no circumcision made-with-hands as was required on pain of death by God's holy covenant stipulation.

The whole sacrificial system is done away with (Heb. 10:9: he abolishes, *anairei*, the first disposition), when the once for all atoning sacrifice is offered. The new temple is spiritual, made of living stones; worshipping there 'in spirit and truth' means no longer to be bound to particular places, whether Jerusalem or Mount Gerizim. If the church receives Israel's title 'holy nation', it *must* be with a new, transpositive, sense, since Israel was a nation literally, among other nations, whereas the new community is made up of citizens of many nations, who remain such while participating in a kingdom which 'is not of this world'. E. Schnabel shows that the New Testament interprets consistently the covenant promises in a 'spiritual' manner.[36] As to the Israel of God, he speaks of a change in the people's 'identity'; there is now 'a new criterion for membership: the new people is a people in which someone does not belong automatically by right of birth, but a people which brings fruit (a theme introduced and prepared in Matt. 3:8–10; 7:15–23; 8:11–12; 12:29–32; 21:28–31).'[37] The fruit is, obviously, faith in Jesus. Correlative of the experiential bond of knowledge *each person* is to enjoy with the Lord (Jer. 31:34; cf. John 6:45, 1 John 2:20),[38] there are

---

[35] For the Gentile Christian readers of Paul, submitting to the Judaizers' demands that they observe the Torah calendar would be falling back to the kind of slavery they experienced as pagans; one cannot retort that Torah ritual observance has only *become* slavery after Christ has come, for Paul affirms of himself and fellow Jews 'when they were infants' (i.e. before the time set by the Father, therefore before Christ), in v. 3: they were enslaved under the cosmic elements.

[36] Schnabel, 'Die Gemeinde', 179f., 184f., 196, 203.

[37] Schnabel, 'Die Gemeinde', 183. Cf. 185: John 1 shows that 'natural descent – including Abrahamic descent! – is irrelevant for acceptance as a child of God when the Logos comes into the world'; 201; 'The identification mark . . . is no longer circumcision, but faith in Jesus Christ'; 210: 'belonging to God's people only depends on faith in the crucified and risen Messiah'.

[38] It is noteworthy that Pannenberg, *Systematic Theology III*, 27, acknowledges: 'It was typical of Jesus' proclamation of the imminent coming of God's reign that he addressed it directly to individuals . . . To this fact which characterizes the message and work of Jesus there corresponds in the context of the life of the Christian church the *immediacy of individual believers to Jesus Christ* notwithstanding the fact that their faith is mediated by the church's proclamation and its administration of the sacraments' (my italics; cf. 122ff. on this immediacy and the role of the church).

no longer any specialized priests to mediate between God and the worshippers – the whole people is a 'royal priesthood' (1 Pet. 2:9; Rev. 5:10 shows that 'royal' implies reigning with Christ). The new features of the *qāhāl* of the Lord, now of the Lord *Jesus*, give it a new face indeed, even a unique face in the field of human religions.

In that deeply altered situation, how does the New Testament view 'Israel after the flesh' (*kata sarka*) or, maybe more exactly, the nation Israel?[39] A distinction must be made between 'Israel' and the 'Israelites', and then among these. As Scot Hafemann beautifully elucidates,[40] Paul solves the difficulty of the apparent failure of God's promises to Israel by distinguishing between the elect community as such and individuals, not all elect: 'Not all who are descended from Israel are Israel' (Rom. 9:5); if he can say that God has not rejected his people he chose beforehand (*proegnō*, using the volitional sense of *yāda'*) it is because there are individual Israelites like himself who believe in Jesus Christ and form the 'remnant' (Rom. 11:1–6). For other individuals, he uses the phrase 'the rest of them', *hoi loipoi* (Rom. 11:7) and avoids for them *laos*, 'people' with a tinge of honour, as Denise Judant observes.[41]

The status of the 'remnant' Jews like Paul, who were born Jews and confess Jesus as Lord, is clear: all titles belong to them fully, unproblematically. They inherit all the promises. They constitute the first and foundational component of the Christian *ekklēsia* – thousands, a 'multitude' (*plēthos*), including former Pharisees and priests, at the early stage (Acts 2:41; 4:4, 32; 5:14; 6:7; 15:5; 21:20) – and their presence makes it beyond dispute that the Christian community is the 'Israel of God', the Olive-Tree growing on. This theological truth remains valid, though it has been historically obfuscated. It would remain valid theologically (answering 'Israel' as a theological notion) even if there were only a handful of them, but this should not be granted: 'If all the Jews who have embraced Christianity', Gustav Dalman wrote, 'had remained a distinct people instead of being among whom they dwelt,

---

[39] Though the mode is original, Israel in the first century AD can fairly be called a 'nation' in the ordinary sense; things become much more complex later, with very few remaining in the land and some massive additions of proselytes – like the kingdom of the Khazars – assimilation and *haskala* in modern times and the foundation of the State of Israel, where a significant minority of the 'Jews' of the world are citizens.

[40] Scot Hafemann, 'The Salvation of Israel in Romans 11:25–32: A Response to Krister Stendahl', *Ex Auditu* 4 (1998): 38–58; I am using a copy of the manuscript, then with the printer, which Professor Hafemann gave me at the time; the pages are numbered 13–33 (31–3 endnotes). On the point I am making 19f., 23f.

[41] Judant, *Jalons*, 18, 69.

their descendants would now be counted in millions.'[42] The 'remnant' is the true Israel (already in the Old Testament) and continues under the name 'church'.

The 'rest of them', individuals of Jewish descent who do not believe in Jesus, 'have been hardened' (Rom. 11:7), they fall under God's 'severe' judgement (v. 22), they are the object of the divine *apobolē*, a word which strictly means 'rejection' (v. 15), the context showing it should be seen as temporary.[43] As Isaiah had foretold, they stumble on the Rock and Chosen Cornerstone, 'which is also what they were destined for' (1 Pet. 2:8). Wrath has overtaken them at last (1 Thess. 2:16). In Smyrna, they are not truly Jews and their synagogue is a synagogue of Satan (Rev. 2:9); the same is true in Philadelphia, but some of them, the Christian Philadelphians are told, will come to Christ and acknowledge that the church inherits the promises made to Jerusalem in Isaiah 45, 49, 60 (Rev. 3:9).

In the imagery of Romans 11, they are *cut-off* branches of the Olive-Tree; this, I suggest, corresponds to the branches of the Vine which the divine Gardener cuts off if they bear no fruit – to a fate of burning (John 15). Paul highlights God's ability to graft them back: if they turn from unbelief to faith (clearly in Jesus as Messiah and Lord). Interpreters are divided on the way Paul envisioned the divine working: one by one, through successive generations, as long as resounds the 'Today' of grace; or, in addition, through a massive conversion at the end of our dispensation, a kind of symmetrical counterpart to the first-century *apobolē*? This is not the place to settle the issue. I will just mention an original argument Scot Hafemann offers in favour of the latter reading: since God's answer to Elijah (1 Kgs. 19:18), which Paul quotes in Romans 11:4, replies to the prophet's complaint: 'I am left alone!' and reveals a multitude of elect (7,000 is an impressive number, though it cannot be interpreted of the totality of Israel, as Karl Barth boldly tried), the conversion of Paul and his fellow Jews in his time may be taken as the promise of the future conversion of a *plērōma*. 'The point is the promise to Elijah and to the remnant of Paul's day that their experience points forward to the salvation of a greater number.'[44] A stimulating suggestion!

---

[42] As quoted by Donald Robinson, 'Not Boasting Over the Natural Branches: Gentile Circumspection in the Divine Economy' in *The Gospel to the Nations* (eds. Bolt and Thompson), 171.

[43] F. Lovsky, *Antisémitisme*, 492, struggles with the text; he affirms that Rom. 11:15 makes its point by reducing it to the absurd: hardly convincing!

[44] Hafemann, 'The Salvation of Israel', 24.

To what extent may we say of Israel as a 'nation' *kata sarka* what we say of hardened Israelite individuals? As already noted, Paul avoids using *laos*; yet, in his main discussion of the topic, he does not refrain from speaking of 'Israel' when he thinks of 'the rest of them'. Israel has not reached the law of righteousness (Rom. 9:31); Israel is rebuked for unbelief (Rom. 10:21); Israel did not obtain what it was seeking (Rom. 11:7) and has been partially hardened (v. 25). Israelite unbelief begins in the earthly ministry of Jesus: Pilate tells Jesus that his 'nation' (*ethnos*) and the high priests have delivered the prisoner (John 19:35); the parable of the 'wicked tenants' seems first to target the leaders who take care of the vineyard, but the judgement is that the kingdom of God will be given to (another) *ethnos* (Matt. 21:43) – which suggests that the tenants also represent the people, while the vineyard stands for the set of privileges, the divine presence, etc., that form the contents of the 'kingdom'.[45] Jesus frequently inveighs against the unbelieving *genea*. It is 'Jerusalem' that was blind at the time of divine visitation (Luke 19:41–4). Paul's daring interpretation equates the literal (earthly) Jerusalem with Hagar – and her with Sinai – and with her son Ishmael, while Isaiah 54 belongs to the Christian church (Gal. 4:24–31).

Such elements intimate that the broken branches are not mere individuals, but that a collective dimension warrants calling them 'Israel', at least in New Testament times.[46] Reference to 'majority' is probably insufficient to account for the collective dimension: most Jews, as Jules Isaac protested, had not heard about Jesus at the time of his passion, and the fickle crowd which hailed him on Palm Sunday was so easily manipulated into vociferous 'Crucify! Crucify!' The emphasis should fall on the choice of the elite, of the official leaders. Though despicable in their own persons, the high priests were still invested with the dignity of their office (John 11:51; Acts 23:5)[47] and, thus, able to steer the 'nation' into their tragic choices.

---

[45] It is interesting to note that F. Lovsky, *Antisémitisme*, 489, who insists that there is no change in the vineyard = Israel, fails even to mention v. 43.

[46] The forty years between Jesus' death and the destruction of the temple, which was the central institution of the old regime, the 'generation' between the Cross-Easter-Pentecost complex of events and the end of the Jewish 'world' that typifies the end of world, Matt. 24:3, may be considered a transition period.

[47] This stance contrasts with the rigorous separatism of the Essenes or Qumran people; it is difficult to deny that the latter were right under the canons of strict legal logic. But if one recognizes that the Old Testament system was a preparatory and *typological* economy, involving pedagogical adaptations to a stiff-necked people (e.g. Matt. 19:8) and a temporary submission to the 'cosmic elements', one can understand the flexibility of the New Testament.

Is the collective dimension to play a role in the 'grafting back' operation? If one expects a future massive conversion, it is rather easy to fit
in the perspective (the meaning of 'all Israel' in Rom. 11:26 is too hotly
disputed a point to settle the issue). Anything beyond? E. Schnabel's
thorough examination finds no pronounced evidence in the New
Testament that a national, probably political, restoration was thought
to be in store for 'Israel'.[48] The oft-quoted question in Acts 1:6 ('Lord, is
this the time when you will restore the kingdom to Israel?' [NRSV]) can
be read in various ways. If one does not consider (as many do) that
Jesus' answer is intended to discourage the disciples' misguided
expectations, it is by no means established that the 'kingdom' restored
to Israel (*apokathistaneis tō Israēl*) means an earthly political regime.
Jesus' teaching, according to v. 3, had centred on the *kingdom of God*,
which many would think of in terms of political independence; but
according to Matthew 21:43, the kingdom would be taken from apostate Israel and given to a nation bearing corresponding fruit (faith and
obedience), which is clearly the church, the nation of faith. Thus, we
may understand the 'kingdom' of Acts 1:6 as referring to the spiritual
privilege of being God's people in full acceptance, i.e. the kingdom of
God as defined by Romans 14:17.

Restitution would signify conversion. Assessing the import of Old
Testament promises heavily depends on one's hermeneutical presup-
positions, especially on the role their apparent understanding in the
New Testament is to play.[49]

One thing should be agreed upon: no one can ever hope to be saved
eternally, to receive eternal life, who rejects the faith of Jesus Christ.
Whoever refuses to believe (*apeithōn*) in the Son shall not see life: on
the contrary, the wrath of God rests on him (John 3:36) – John certainly intends this for his fellow Jews first; whoever does not believe
God's testimony about his Son makes him a liar, he does not have life
(1 John 5:9–12). This was already the case in the Old Testament. Even
the dispensationalist master Charles C. Ryrie wrote: 'The *basis* of salvation in every age is the death of Christ; the *requirement* for salvation
in every age is faith; the *object* of faith in every age is God', though he
added: 'the *content* of faith changes in the various dispensations.'[50]

[48] Schnabel, 'Die Gemeinde', 174 ('Hope of a restoration of the political independence
    of Israel plays no role in the preaching of Jesus'); 177; 184 ('Jesus, apparently,
    expected no earthly-literal fulfilment of the national promises for Israel'); 196 (mis-
    sion into the whole world takes the place of the 'land'); 203; 207; 211.
[49] Cf. the remark by Schnabel, 207.
[50] Charles C. Ryrie, *Dispensationalism Today* (Chicago: Moody Press, 1965), 123.

While I would not subscribe to the fourth proposition, the ambiguity it introduces is not enough to invalidate the strong confession in the first three. The teaching of Scripture as a whole on human sinfulness and guilt, God's holiness and justice, and the provision of atonement leave no other possibility.

Tackling Delicate Issues Regarding Non-Christian Jews

Moving in a firm framework of biblical truth gives us a chance to untie some subtle knots regarding non-Christian Jews today (who would be 'non-Jews' by the standards of Revelation 2:9; 3:9; Romans 2:28). Since we basically enquired so far about New Testament data, a further and still preliminary remark is needed: contemporary, and even historical, Judaism should not be confused with Second Temple Judaism, much less Old Testament religion. Judaism was born, through the work and debates of several generations, of the victory of one party over the others (basically the Pharisaic party) in the radically changed situation created by the ruin of the temple.[51] As a historical phenomenon, it is contemporary with early Christianity, a rival interpretation of the Law and the Prophets. They are heterozygous twins, like Jacob and Esau, as Alan Segal perceives.[52] To some extent, the Mishnah is the counterpart of the New Testament. If we treat Judaism as the legitimate heir of Moses, David and the Prophets, we *ipso facto* surrender the original Christian claim.

Are Jews still 'God's People'?

Indications, I must admit, point both ways. Paul, as was seen, avoids labelling non-Christian Israelites *laos*, as he remembers, maybe, Hosea's judgement prophecy: *lō' 'ammî*, for you are not my people (Hos. 1:9).[53] But he calls them 'Israel' and the import seems to be the

---

[51] I was struck, in modern accounts of Judaism such as I. Epstein's, by the minimal attention paid to the sacrificial system.

[52] Alan Segal, *Rebecca's Children: Judaism and Christianity in the Roman World* (Cambridge: Harvard University Press, 1986), according to Harvey Cox, *Many Mansions: A Christian's Encounter with Other Faiths* (Boston: Beacon Press, 1988), 105.

[53] Paul quotes from the following verse, the announcement of the reversal of grace, not-my-people become my-people and applies it to the Gentiles grafted into the church (Rom. 9:25f.; also 1 Pet. 2:10). Some readers are embarrassed by this use, since Hosea seems to have in mind Israelites (*kata sarka!*), first condemned and

same. He questions their right to be called Jews (Rom. 2:28), but frequently calls them by that name. The same duality obtains in the tense dialogue between Jesus and the 'Jews' in John 8: Jesus grants that they are Abraham's descendants (v. 37), then denies it (v. 39) and charges them with having the devil for their father (v. 44). As 'sons of the kingdom', they are cast out in darkness (Matt. 8:12): do they lose their title or retain it? The logic of Romans 9:3–5 implies that they are 'anathema' and 'cut-off' (hence the apostle's unceasing grief, v. 2), and yet to them still belong[54] the filial status, the glory, the covenants, everything which goes with being the people of God. Of the *broken* branches of the Olive-Tree, he says that they are still beloved for the sake of their fathers, since God's gifts of grace and calling are not revoked (Rom. 11:28f.), and he stresses a specific *holiness* that still pertains to them (v. 16). Karl Barth's eloquence is here on target:

> This is certain: This people as such is the holy people of God, the people with which God has dealt in his grace and in his wrath, in whose midst he has blessed and exercised judgement, enlightened and hardened, accepted and rejected. In one way or another (*so oder so*) he has accepted it and never ceased to do so, and he will accept it and never cease to do so. They are all in one sense sanctified through him, sanctified by nature (*von Natur*) as the ancestors and relatives of the only Holy One in Israel, as no Gentile is by nature, not even the best among the Gentiles, and not even the Gentile Christians, also the best among them, despite their belonging to the church: despite the fact and in the fact that they are also sanctified by the Holy One of Israel and have become Israel.[55]

---

then restored by pure mercy. Yet, the logic is unimpeachable: if Israelite sinners are no longer the people of God, there is no difference remaining with sinners from other nations, and, therefore, the promise of grace cannot distinguish between them: it must also avail for *gôyîm*.

54 The present tense seems to be required by the logic of the passage, and its use in the first clause: they are (*eisin*) Israelites.

55 *Kirchliche Dogmatik II/2* (Zollikon-Zurich: Evangelischer Verlag, 1946), 315f. My translation (since I had no access to the English translation). It is striking that Jacques Ellul, *Un Chrétien*, 78, quotes from this page (from the French translation) omitting all the references to judgement and rejection. There is no echo of Barth's statement (p. 316) that 'on the left hand side, it is Israel sanctified only by God's wrath'. However, Ellul's universalism is ultimately faithful to Barth's more dialectical progress.

I suggest that, despite *lō' 'ammî*, non-Christian Jews may be called the people of God as those who continue in some way[56] that part of the people constituted before Christ who refused to recognize him when he came, and yet retained enough of their older prerogatives still to bear the name 'Israel'. The proper way to account for the paradoxical formulations of Scripture is to acknowledge the contradiction in the reality itself: these Jews are, in God's sight, living contradictions; as they refuse to believe the word of their God and turn their back on him, they deny their very identity; their 'truth' or 'essence' is being the people of God, and they live alienated lives, their 'existence' is that of enemies, with suicidal consequences for themselves.

Is the Mosaic covenant still in force for Jews?

The question is interested in the objective truth of the matter, *coram Deo*, for it is obvious enough that it is subjectively so in the conviction, tradition and practice of many Jews – but are they *right* in God's eyes? The strong language of the epistle to the Hebrews would seem to settle the issue: disappearance (*aphanismos*, 8:13), abrogation (*athetēsis*, 7:18) and many other statements we have already reviewed. The frequent occurrence of the phrase 'for ever' (*lĕ'ōlām*) in Old Testament texts is no objection: because of its indefinite meaning (it may mean 'as long as the overlord does not decide a change'); because of conditional clauses associated; above all because the Old Testament is fulfilled, rather than made null and void, in the New (circumcision and Sabbath, though abrogated as 'fleshly ordinances' are fulfilled in their antitypes).[57] Paul's polemics against the Judaizers testify that Old Testament stipulations that are not taken up 'in Christ' are obsolete, no

---

[56] The qualifier *quodammodo* is frequently used in theology: sometimes as an easy way out of difficulty (a cheap facility), yet sometimes it is indispensable. Since the Jewish identity is a complex and even elusive reality (with genealogical, cultural, religious components and, maybe, a dose of free identification) the criteria for its continuation are hard to pinpoint.

[57] Herman Witsius, *The Economy of the Covenants Between God and Man comprehending a complete Body of Divinity* (trans. William Crookshank; London: T. Tegg and Son, 1837), II, 387 [Bk. IV, ch. 4 § 17] argues that *katalusai* in Matt. 5:17 does not mean 'abrogate' but 'destroy', and writes: 'That abrogation of ceremonies, which we say was made by Christ, is their glorious consummation and accomplishment, all their signification being fulfilled; not an ignominious destruction, which our Lord justly disclaims.' He distinguishes, 402f., eight stages in the process of abrogation, from the death of Christ (veil rent) to the destruction of Jerusalem and the temple [§ 54].

longer binding, on Christians;[58] there is no hint that they would keep their force and carry divine authority for those outside of Christ, although the opposite is not expressed in explicit terms. The emphasis falls on the change of the times, for all: true and acceptable worship, from the 'hour' of Christ's mission, is *no longer* offered in the form that bound it to specific places, to Jerusalem, as the old covenant stipulated it (John 4:21).

Yet other elements warn about possible complexity. While Jeremiah 31:32 charges the Israelites with *breaking* the covenant (hence God will establish a new one), the Lord has solemnly declared that he would never do so himself (Lev. 26:44) – not in simple leniency, for he *will* punish with dreadful blows rebellions and betrayals (v. 14–39). We keep in mind that God does not revoke his gifts and calling (Rom. 11:29). Is the import of these texts exhausted with the thought that the covenant is confirmed and fulfilled as the new covenant (so God did not break it) and re-entrance (being grafted back) is offered to the cut-off branches? One helpful insight may be that covenant *sanctions* proceed from the covenant itself and manifest its force: being 'cut off from one's people' is the supreme sanction for covenant-breakers. Being cut off from the Israel of God, non-Christian Jews may be considered covenant-breakers under old covenant sanctions (Jesus tells his unbelieving hearers that they are indicted *by Moses*, John 5:45). These sanctions may apply as a residual consequence of an arrangement belonging to a previous stage of God's historical design. This is the case for the creational covenant, the arrangement made with Adam (whose re-publication was one component of the Mosaic covenant),[59] which, though superseded by the new creation in Christ, still entails that 'all die in Adam'.

If the old covenant is still in force for non-Christian Jews 'residually', as its sanctions apply, are there also some *positive* elements one could discern in the residuum? I venture to advance a cautious 'yes'. When undergoing the punishment of exile, the Israelites were invited

---

[58] In Phil. 3:2f., legal circumcision is no longer *peritomē*, but only *katatomē*, incision with a pejorative note.

[59] I have developed this view elsewhere. Geerhardus Vos, for instance, could write in *Redemptive History and Biblical Interpretation. The Shorter Writings of Geerhardus Vos* (ed. Richard B. Gaffin; Phillipsburg: Presbyterian and Reformed, 1980), 255: 'the older theologians did not always clearly distinguish between the covenant of works and the Sinaitic covenant. At Sinai it was not the "bare" law that was given, but a reflection of the covenant of works received, as it were, in the interests of the covenant of grace continued at Sinai.' Hence Paul's use of Lev. 18:5.

to contribute to the *šālôm* of the pagan city and empire, and so to improve their own condition (Jer. 29:7); something similar may be ascribed to the world dispersion of non-Christian Jews, some benefits attached to the form of the sanction. The honour and special holiness of Abrahamic descent *kata sarka* cannot be separated from what remains of old covenant status. Punishment itself is a form of recognition on the part of God: it pays respect to responsibility (and this is why it is infinitely more loving than indifference).[60] Following this insight, the extraordinary *permanence* of a Jewish identity, still marked by Mosaic traits, is an impressive sign. It will look even more positive if one accepts the perspective of a future massive conversion of Israel *kata sarka*.

Does what is 'left over' from the old covenant include possibilities of salvation?

Once it is granted that the old covenant (as such) still generates some effects among non-Christian Jews, and not entirely negative, the question arises whether salvation (life eternal) could possibly be one of them. Undoubtedly, under the old covenant, many were saved (the 7,000 remnant!): they were not saved if they relied superstitiously on the intrinsic efficacy of rites and sacrifices, they were not saved if they relied on their *own* righteousness (Rom. 10:3), they were saved by virtue of Jesus Christ's atonement which alone does away with human sin (Rom. 3:25f.; Heb. 9:15; 10:4), they were saved through faith in the God of grace, that is the God of Jesus Christ. Some may have received a deep insight into the form of the then future saving grace, as Abraham did, who 'saw' Christ's day (John 8:56) – how precisely, we are not told; it is reasonable to imagine that most such believers exercised a little-informed faith: prompted, indeed, by the revealed teachings and promises, but yet vague and frail, as through the fog of ignorance and inadequate representations. Is it allowable to make room for similar exercises of faith *after Christ* among officially non-Christian Jews?

The New Testament does not consider this possibility. If animal sacrifices had provided atonement – this only in a typical way and towards cleansing of the 'flesh' (Heb. 9:13) – even this does not avail

---

[60] I elsewhere pursued this thought by means of an interpretation of a remark by George Steiner: There is something more terrible than to fall into the hands of a living God: to fall into the hands of a *dead* God.

any more: 'no sacrifice for sins is left' in Judaism (Heb. 10:26). There seem to be only two categories among the people of Israel: on the one hand, those believers who had set their hope in advance on Christ and were waiting for the consolation of Israel – they hailed the longed-for Saviour when they saw him, together with the other elect who came to a similar faith at this time; and on the other, the unbelievers. The former are the fruit-bearing branches of the Vine (who undergo pruning with the change from old to new covenant); the latter, the cut-off branches.

The complications of the human heart, however, and those further complications which a painful history has produced through bloody centuries, make it permissible to conjecture a situation in which a Jew would be gripped in his/her heart by the gospel as already revealed in the Tanakh and be led to trust, 'through the fog', in the God of grace, the God of Jesus Christ – and yet, because of ignorance, because of misinformation, that person would not know or recognize that this God is the God of Jesus Christ. Normally, such a person would overcome this ignorance when presented with the clear and explicit truth of Jesus Christ. But do things always work 'normally', even when grace is at work? I introduce this admittedly speculative possibility, which is parallel to one of the positions held among evangelical theologians (since the reformer Zanchi in the sixteenth century) on the fate of 'those who have not heard' among all humankind,[61] in order not to encroach on the sovereign freedom of God's grace. It envisions a salvation that happens, by God's grace, in spite of the religion that goes by the name of Judaism: in spite of its dominant pattern, basis stance and claim to provide a way to life with God. Rightly understood, it will not dampen but deepen the zeal of Christian missions to the Jews.

Should gospel witness to the Jews take on a special form?

If non-Christian Jews bear specific marks and find themselves in a particular situation, the principle of missiological adaptation quite obviously applies – in the service of the true gospel, not watering down the Word of God (2 Cor. 2:17). Paul himself, at the risk of being misunderstood and the target of slander, made himself like a Jew under the law to win as many as he could (1 Cor. 9:20). While making room for a variety of missionary callings and personal leadings of the

---

[61] I develop it in my 'Le christianisme face aux religions: une seule voie de salut?' in Louis Schweitzer, ed., *Conviction et dialogue. Le dialogue interreligieux* (Cléon-d'Andran: Excelsis, 2000), 156–70.

Lord, two recommendations will be the object of a ready consensus. A special *sensitivity* is required that will avoid all appearance of Gentile 'boasting' and remember the wounds of hurtful memories; words, such as 'conversion', which cannot be heard in their true sense in most Jewish contexts, should be replaced by less objectionable equivalents. The message, as the sermons in Acts exemplify, can properly emphasize the *fulfilment* of the older promises, if possible using admissions here and there, that revered teachers of the Jewish tradition were led to make.

I dare add two thoughts less common. Efforts could aim at *dis-joining* components of Jewish identity, especially culture and historical memory on the one hand and religion on the other; against the spurious claim of a clear-cut identity, one strategy could highlight the diversity and the antagonism within contemporary Judaism, for instance, the fierce condemnation of Zionism by at least some *harēdîm*.

The other reflection is attached to Paul's hope that Gentile Christians might arouse his brothers *kata sarka* to jealousy or envy (Rom. 10:19; 11:11, 14). In the original context, Deuteronomy 32:21 is a word of judgement, and the object of envy is worldly victory by barbarians. Paul is able to transpose this to the new covenant at a spiritual level, and envy becomes the motive of emulation. How could *we* arouse the Jews around us to sound noble envy? I suggest that a fuller and more rigorous knowledge of the Tanakh is often an efficient element of witness; Franz Delitzsch deserved the title of 'the Christian rabbi' and I believe he did arouse a few to jealousy.

Exemplifying the fear of the Lord and its beauty, the sense of the Lord's reality, could be a most relevant witness, as the contrast is so telling between the canonical Word and what leading thinkers of Judaism commonly write. Levinas can preach 'loving the Torah more than God' and claim: 'His majesty does not provoke fear and trembling, but fills us with higher thoughts';[62] God fades behind the ethical imperative. And then again the theme of fulfilment: our being fulfilled Christians would bring out the truth of the fulfilment *in Christ* of the most precious gifts of the old covenant so conspicuously lost in Judaism: atonement for sin, God's residence in the midst of his people.

If fulfilled Christians can arouse Jews to jealousy or envy, it is because there cannot be an ultimate separation – 'Is God the God of Jews only?' (Rom. 3:29). The mystery of Israel is that of being chosen as

---

[62] A text published (in English translation) by Frans Josef van Beeck, *Loving the Torah More Than God? Towards a Catholic Appreciation of Judaism* (Chicago: Loyola University Press, 1989), quotations 40.

the representative humanity, in grace and in judgement, in sin and salvation, and in mission. Whatever may be said of Israel may be extended to all humankind: God's original children and the objects of his tender love, ungrateful and stiff-necked, living contradictions as they exist contrary to their true being, the family in which Christ was born, who is God above all, eternally blessed! They are ones who must convert and, thereby, find fulfilment, in Jesus the Jew, in Jesus the Man!

God *will* bring this solidarity and unity to light – and presently uses Christian missions to the Jews to further this ultimate purpose of his.

11

Implicit Universalism in Some Christian Zionism and Messianic Judaism

Richard Harvey

Introduction

In their taxonomy of universalism in the introduction to *Universal Salvation: The Current Debate*, Robin Parry and Chris Partridge propose three main types of universalism, divided up into several subtypes.[1] 'Multiracial universalism' sees the universal relevance of the gospel to all nations but makes no judgement about their eternal state. 'Arminian universalism' states that while God desires to save all and offers salvation to all, the exercise of human free will may prevent God from achieving his purposes of universal salvation. The third type of universalism, 'Strong universalism', is the focus of the typology and includes a 'family of quite different views' rather than a single intellectual position. This view states that not only does God desire all to be saved, but that he will achieve his purpose. Those who hold this position operate within a Christian theological perspective but may be pluralists (Hick) operating from unorthodox Christian beliefs, or those within orthodoxy on other issues who justify their position from Scripture, reason and tradition.

The type of universalism that is implicit within the theology of some Christian Zionism (CZ) and Messianic Judaism (MJ) does not easily fit any of the above categories. It could best be labelled as an *Israel-focused*

---

[1] Robin A. Parry, Christopher Partridge, *Universal Salvation? The Current Debate* (Carlisle: Paternoster, 2004), 4.

universalism or an *Israelocentric eschatological soteriology.* The emphasis of such groups is on the special purposes, nature, privileges and guarantee of salvation that is extended to Israel (the Jewish people) on the grounds of their ongoing election. The issue of universalism arises not as the question of 'what about the eternal fate of the unbeliever?' or even 'what of the faithful believer in another religion?' but rather 'what of the fate of Israel – those past, present and future Jewish people who may either choose not to, or not be given the opportunity to, acknowledge their Messiah?' It is possible to be *exclusivist* in one's position on the salvation of those of the nations who do not believe in Christ whilst being *inclusivist* about the Jewish people because of their special role in the purposes of God.[2] On the basis of such a limitation, we will proceed to discuss some examples of CZ and MJ which argue for the salvation of Israel without acceptance of Christ.

Christian Zionism

Definition

For the purposes of this paper, a general definition of Christian Zionism is used. CZ is the teaching that promotes political support for the Zionist project and the State of Israel based on particular readings of Scripture.[3]

---

[2] The pluralist, inclusivist and exclusivist terminology of such discussions do not readily fit here and will not be used in this presentation, except to flag the difficulty in applying them. Cf Christopher Wright, *Thinking Clearly about the Uniqueness of Jesus* (Tunbridge: Monarch, 1995). I am grateful to Robin Parry for his suggestion that the discussion in MJ and CZ circles is to be associated with types of inclusivism.

[3] The hermeneutical systems of dispensational premillennialism (classical, modified and revised), historic premillennialism and covenantal amillennialism have all contributed to forms of Christian Zionism. John Wilkinson gives a more dispensationalist understanding, which would rule out Pawson's position and approach in *For the Sake of Zion* (Carlisle: Paternoster, 2007), 4: 'Christian Zionism is an umbrella term under which many Christians who support Israel have congregated. However, although there is broad agreement among those who acknowledge God's prophetic purposes for Israel, and who point to 1948 as the fulfilment of prophecy, there is considerable disagreement relating to the interpretation of those scriptures which speak of the rapture of the church, the identity and role of the Antichrist, the Great Tribulation, and the Second Coming. I believe that Christian Zionism, properly defined, incorporates the following key elements:

> Christian Zionism . . . is a movement among Gentile believers in the
> Jewish Messiah to advocate and support the Jewish return to their own
> land, convinced that they still have a God-given right to be there and,
> indeed, that he would bring and has brought them home again, thus
> keeping his promises recorded in the scriptures.[4]

In most of its forms, and for most of its history, Christian Zionists have
been unashamedly evangelistic and have combined their political support for the Zionist project and the State of Israel with a strong evangelistic agenda which has not excluded the Jewish people. Indeed,
William E. Blackstone and Arno Gaebelein were earnest supporters of
Jewish missions.[5] The London Society for the Promotion of Christianity
amongst the Jews (CMJ) combined an evangelistic priority with a sub-
sidiary concern for the restoration of the Jewish people to the land.[6]
Historic premillennial and amillennial orientations that motivated
other evangelistic mission agencies did not rule out support for the
political programme of Zionism or a Christian version of the same.

---

1. A clear, biblical distinction between Israel and the Church.
2. The any moment, pre-tribulation Rapture of the Church.
3. The return of the Jews to the Land.
4. The rebuilding of the Temple.
5. The rise of the Antichrist.
6. A seven-year period known as the Great Tribulation.
7. The national salvation of the Jews.
8. The return of Christ to Jerusalem.
9. The thousand-year reign of Christ on earth.

In presenting this working definition, I have no wish to alienate any Christian
friend of Israel. However, such a definition is necessary in order to dispel confusion, correct misunderstanding, and provide a sound, biblical foundation on which
to base that "friendship" and support. Consequently, I will, on occasion, quote
from those who would not subscribe to my definition, but whose contributions I
consider to be of value.'

[4] David Pawson, *Defending Christian Zionism* (Bristol: Terra Nova, 2008), 10. Whilst
some limit CZ to a dispensationalist hermeneutic and eschatology (Sizer, who
turns all who support Israel for theological reasons into dispensationalists whether
they admit it or not), others such as Walter Riggans have used terms such as
'Biblical Zionism' to avoid to narrow a linkage of any one particular eschatology or
hermeneutic to a concern for the Jewish people and their national aspirations. See
also Dan Cohn-Sherbok, *The Politics of Apocalypse: The History and Influence of
Christian Zionism* (Oxford: Oneworld, 2006) for a general survey of CZ teaching.

[5] David Rausch, *Zionism within Early American Fundamentalism, 1878–1918: A
Convergence of Two Traditions* (Texts and Studies in Religion; New York: Edwin
Mellen, 1979).

[6] Kelvin Crombie, *For the Love of Zion* (rev. ed.; Bristol: Terra Nova, 2008).

However, there have always been exceptions. It is in the nature of prophetic teachings to develop a wide diversity of interpretation, and on matters of eschatology the church and the missions community are often divided. In recent years, CZ groups such as the *Christian Embassy in Jerusalem* and *Operation Exobus* have given clear and well-publicized undertakings not to be involved in evangelistic activities, in order to be permitted to function with the blessing of Israeli governmental agencies in assisting Jewish people making *aliyah* and in providing welfare to new immigrants and the poor.[7] Such undertakings could be understood as 'implicit universalism', as the refusal to share the good news of the Messiah could be taken as an acknowledgment that, in the light of hastening the end times through providing physical and political support for the Zionist project, the task of direct evangelism could be left to others or was not considered necessary. But it would be dangerous to extrapolate from such a stance without clear evidence and teaching from such CZ practitioners that such were their views.[8]

It is with those caveats that we come to examine CZ teaching which can be interpreted as 'implicit universalism'.

John Hagee

John Hagee pastors a non-denominational church of 19,000 in San Antonio, Texas and is founder of Christians United for Israel (CUFI). The purpose of CUFI is to 'stand in support of Israel and the Jewish people, thus fulfilling Isaiah 62:1.'[9] According to Hagee's website:

---

[7] Baruch Maoz, 'The Christian Embassy in Jerusalem', in *Mishkan* 1990: 1–6, esp. 2–3: 'It is readily acknowledged that not all evangelical bodies must be involved in evangelism . . . There would be no difficulty if the Embassy issued a statement to the effect that, while it believed in the necessity of evangelism per se, it did not itself engage in such activity. But the Embassy's repeated hedging on this issue gives credence to the growing conviction of some that the Embassy believes political and economic support in the name of Christ are all that is needed, and that evangelism is, at best, peripheral.' See also John Ross, 'Beyond Zionism: Evangelical Responsibility towards Israel', in *Mishkan* 1/1990: 8–27, esp. 16. I have been unable to locate a statement from the Christian Embassy on its policy on the need for evangelism.

[8] It has not been possible to identify other clear statements of universalism in CZ teaching in the course of this research. Rich Robinson also sees Hagee as the exception among CZ teachers, rather than the rule: 'I do think Hagee stands out by his explicit remarks.' (July 2, e-mail to author).

[9] Online: http://www.jhm.org. Accessed April 2008.

The mission of John Hagee Ministries is to aggressively fulfill the commission that Jesus Christ gave to his followers to go into the world and make disciples of all people. Our purpose is to bring the lost to Jesus Christ and to build up and encourage those who are already believers. We pledge to our viewers and supporters to take The Gospel to all the World and to all Generations.[10]

However, there are contradictory reports as to Hagee's position on Jewish evangelism. The *Jerusalem Post* reported of John Hagee and Jerry Falwell:[11]

An evangelical pastor [Hagee] and an Orthodox rabbi, both from Texas, have apparently persuaded leading Baptist preacher Jerry Falwell that Jews can get to heaven without being converted to Christianity.[12]

Hagee was also reported in the *Houston Chronicle* as believing that the Jewish people already have a covenant and relationship to God without needing to come to the cross:

---

[10] G. Richard Fisher, 'The Other Gospel of John Hagee: Christian Zionism and Ethnic Salvation'. Online: http://www.pfo.org/jonhagee.htm.

[11] Ilan Chaim, 'Falwell: Jews can get to heaven', *Jerusalem Post*, 1 March 2006. Online: http://www.jpost.com/servlet/Satellite?cid=1139395509016&pagename=JPost%2 FJPArticle%2FShowFull. Accessed 18 July 2008.

[12] Jerry Falwell issued a prompt denial of the report: 'Earlier today, reports began circulating across the globe that I have recently stated that Jews can go to heaven without being converted to Jesus Christ. This is categorically untrue. These false reports originated from a March 1 *Jerusalem Post* front page column which said: "An evangelical pastor and an Orthodox rabbi, both from Texas, have apparently persuaded leading Baptist preacher Jerry Falwell that Jews can get to heaven without being converted to Christianity. Televangelist John Hagee and Rabbi Aryeh Scheinberg, whose Cornerstone Church and Rodfei Sholom congregations are based in San Antonio, told the *Jerusalem Post* that Falwell had adopted Hagee's innovative belief in what Christians refer to as 'dual covenant' theology. This creed, which runs counter to mainstream evangelism, maintains that the Jewish people have a special relationship to God through the revelation at Sinai and therefore do not need 'to go through Christ or the Cross' to get to heaven." While I am a strong supporter of the State of Israel and dearly love the Jewish people and believe them to be the chosen people of God, I continue to stand on the foundational biblical principle that all people – Baptists, Methodists, Pentecostals, Jews, Muslims, etc. – must believe in the Lord Jesus Christ in order to enter heaven.' (reported by Albert Mohler, http://www.albertmohler.com/blog_read.php?id=532. Accessed 18 July 2008).

I believe that every Jewish person who lives in the light of the Torah, which is the word of God, has a relationship with God and will come to redemption.[13]

The *Houston Chronicle* article further reported:

John Hagee, fundamentalist pastor from San Antonio and friend of Israel, is truly a strange fish . . . The man has a mission. He's out to attack anti-Semitism. He also believes that Jews can come to God without going through Jesus Christ.[14]

The Houston newspaper then quoted Hagee's own shocking words: 'I'm not trying to convert the Jewish people to the Christian faith' and further revealed:

In fact, trying to convert Jews is a 'waste of time,' he said. 'The Jewish person who has his roots in Judaism is not going to convert to Christianity. There is no form of Christian evangelism that has failed so miserably as evangelizing the Jewish people. They (already) have a faith structure.' Everyone else, whether Buddhist or Baha'i, needs to believe in Jesus, he says. But not Jews. Jews already have a covenant with God that has never been replaced by Christianity, he says.[15]

According to Hagee, Paul abandoned the idea of Jews knowing Christ when he went to the Gentiles. The Christian Research Institute has also reported on this highly unorthodox view held by Hagee:

Information about Hagee from other sources reveals he seriously differs with the vast majority of dispensational teachers because he believes that Jewish people do not need to be saved, since they are under a different covenant.[16]

Hagee goes further in his recent book 'In Defense of Israel'. Jesus never claimed to be the Messiah of Israel, so the Jewish people never had the option of either accepting or rejecting him.

---

[13] 'San Antonio fundamentalist battles anti-Semitism', *Houston Chronicle* (30 April 1988): sec. 6, 1.

[14] 'San Antonio fundamentalist battles', 1

[15] 'San Antonio fundamentalist battles', 1

[16] 'San Antonio fundamentalist battles', 1

Most evangelicals believe the Jews rejected Jesus as Messiah and there-fore qualify of God's eternal judgement . . . Is this statement about the Jewish people biblically true? No![17]

Hagee contrasts Jesus with Moses, who was 'God's messiah' for that generation:

The Jews were accustomed to their leaders demonstrating their call from God with supernatural signs. When God called Moses from the backside of the desert to go into Egypt and lead millions of Hebrew slaves out of bondage, God gave Moses four signs to convince the children of Israel that he was their *messiah*.[18]

God did not authorize and Jesus did not perform signs which would confirm any messianic claims he might but did not make:

If God intended for Jesus to be the Messiah of Israel, why didn't he authorize Jesus to use supernatural signs to prove he was God's Messiah, just as Moses had done? . . . Jesus refused to give a sign. He only compared himself to the prophet Jonah, who carried the message of repentance from God to the Gentiles at Nineveh.[19]

Therefore, it was Jesus himself who kept his messiahship secret and impossible to accept as such:

Why did he constantly command those who were excited about his supernatural abilities to 'tell no one'? The Jews were not rejecting Jesus as Messiah; it was Jesus who was refusing to be the Messiah to the Jews.[20]

At the Last Supper, whilst inaugurating communion for the nations, he refused messianic acclamation:

In refusing to drink the [fourth Passover] cup, Jesus rejected to the last detail the role of Messiah in word or deed. The Jews did not reject Jesus as Messiah; it was Jesus who rejected the Jewish desire for him to be the Messiah.[21]

---

[17] John Hagee, *In Defense of Israel: The Bible's Mandate for Supporting the Jewish State* (Strang: Frontline, Lake Mary, 2007), 132.

[18] Hagee, *In Defense of Israel*, 136.

[19] Hagee, *In Defense of Israel*, 138.

[20] Hagee, *In Defense of Israel*, 140.

[21] Hagee, *In Defense of Israel*, 143.

After the Emmaus road appearance:

> He instantly disappeared. He refused to be their Messiah, choosing instead to be the Savior of the world.[22]
>
> Even after his resurrection and his repeated denials that he would not be the Messiah, his disciples were still hanging on to the last thread of hope that he would now smash Rome (Acts 1:6). They wanted him to be their Messiah, but he flatly refused.[23]

There is a curious inverted anti-Judaism here. In order for Jesus to fulfil his true calling as Saviour of the Gentiles, he must reject the misplaced hopes of Israel for the Messiah. He is a docetic Christ, denuded of his Jewish flesh and his identity as the true representative of his people Israel. But, therefore, his people have no inherent connection with his saving role and cannot be judged by Christian claims to have rejected Jesus or to, in any way, forfeit salvation.

Hagee's argument, based on such inaccurate readings of Scripture, reaches its conclusion:

> Five main points must now be made that are crucial to understanding that the Jews did not reject Jesus as Messiah.
>
> 1. Jesus had to live to be the Messiah [as a conquering, reigning Messiah]
> 2. If it was God's will for Jesus to die from the beginning
> 3. If it was Jesus' intention to be obedient unto death
> 4. If there is not one verse of Scripture in the New Testament that said Jesus came to be the Messiah
> 5. And if Jesus refused by his words and actions to claim to be the Messiah to the Jews, then *how can the Jews be blamed for rejecting what was never offered*? [emphasis his].[24]

Hagee has taken Wrede's 'Messianic Secret' too far in order to construct a portrayal of Jesus' messiahship relevant only to the nations, thus excusing Israel of unbelief. If God's stated purpose was not to send the Messiah to Israel but only to the nations, Israel is released from the responsibilities of repentance, faith and acceptance of her Messiah. And thus all Israel *has* been saved!

---

[22] Hagee, *In Defense of Israel*, 143.

[23] Hagee, *In Defense of Israel*, 141.

[24] Hagee, *In Defense of Israel*, 135–6.

Hagee's position is an extreme one, as shown by the criticism levelled at him within his own organization by James Hutchens, a regional director for Christians United for Israel:

> I come to you today with a heavy burden and a request for prayer.
>
> I also serve as a regional director for Christians United for Israel, whose national director is John Hagee. The stated purpose of CUFI is to support Israel in matters related to Israel. There is no doctrinal statement that all members of CUFI have to agree on. However a doctrinal issue has arisen.
>
> In some statements that Pastor Hagee has made in chapter 10 of his book *In Defense of Israel* have caused considerable concern and controversy among pro-Israel supporters. These are statements that I personally cannot agree with.
>
> Let me explain – originally Pastor Hagee asserted that the Jews did not reject Jesus as Messiah because Jesus never presented himself as a Messiah to them.
>
> He also suggested that Jesus never did the signs and miracles as Moses did that would have confirmed his messiahship to the Jews. He then concludes that Jews cannot be blamed for not accepting Jesus, or what Jesus offered, namely, that he was the Messiah. These are assertions that simply cannot be supported from the scripture. I understand he has rewritten chapter 10 of his book, and has attempted to draw distinction between Jesus as the suffering Messiah, and Jesus as a reigning Messiah. Unfortunately, I do not believe the scriptures make these distinctions. On the contrary, when Jesus asked Peter 'who do you say that I am?' Peter answered, 'You are the Christ, that is the Messiah, son of the living God' (Matthew 16:16).
>
> Peter further affirms his declaration in his sermon on the day of Pentecost when he said 'Therefore let all Israel be assured of this, that God has made this Jesus whom you crucified both Lord and Christ, that is his Messiah. That's Acts 2:36, plus John 20:30–31. Whilst there are serious errors in these assertions of Pastor Hagee, assertions that I cannot agree with, I do know the heart of John Hagee, and I highly respect and esteem him. I know that he loves Israel and the Jewish people. That's why I am requesting special prayer, that this crowd of confusion and controversy, this error regarding the Messiah be lifted from Pastor Hagee and from CUFI, that we might not be hindered from our stated purpose, which is to support Israel in matters related to biblical issues.[25]

---

[25] Transcript of YouTube Video (http://www.youtube.com/watch?v=jHL0ROjEl9o). Accessed 12 May 2008. After Hutchens confronted Hagee, CUFI removed him as

In the light of such criticisms, Hagee appears to have modified his position. A recent e-mail from his organization states:

> The Jews are God's chosen people, BUT THEY ARE NOT SAVED UNLESS THEY BELIEVE AND ACCEPT JESUS AS THEIR LORD AND SAVIOR . . . The same need for the Jews to receive Christ as Savior exists as the need for the gentiles. Pastor [Hagee] believes that witnessing Jesus to the Jewish people ONE ON ONE is the most effective way instead of targeting them as a group or nation. Keep in mind that God has 'blinded the eyes' of the Jews and hardened their hearts for having denied Christ.[26]

The anti-Judaism of such a response from a member of Hagee's organization does little to confirm that Hagee has changed his official position from that expressed in the first edition of *In Defense of Israel*. But Hagee has recently issued a statement on his website regarding the interpretation of *In Defense of Israel*:

> It has come to my attention that my choice of language and some of the interpretation being given that language in Chapter Ten has caused some confusion and actually led some readers to question whether I believe that Jesus is the Messiah. If people are reaching such a conclusion, then I have clearly failed to communicate my views as well as I should have.
>
> I have decided to release a new edition of *In Defense of Israel* with an expanded Chapter Ten. The new version will make the same point as the prior one, but using language which cannot mislead anyone about my bedrock belief that Jesus was and is Lord, Savior and Messiah.
>
> Over the centuries, Christians have been quick to condemn the Jews for failing to recognize Jesus as Messiah. This approach led to Replacement Theology and the viewpoint of some that God has rejected and broken covenant with the Jewish people. These ideas, in turn, opened the door to a vicious Christian anti-Semitism that led to the Crusades, the Inquisition and countless pogroms.
>
> I tried to challenge this view by highlighting a distinction that has been long recognized in Christian theology between the role Jesus

---

Mid-Atlantic regional director. He was offered a co-director position for the District of Columbia, but he has now disassociated himself from CUFI completely (http://barthsnotes.wordpress.com/2008/07/13/cufi-director-ditched-over-hagees-missionary-position. Accessed May 2008).

[26] E-mail correspondence of 28 February 2007, from Edward Martinez of John Hagee Ministries, reported by Horowitz, ibid.

played in His first coming, and the role He will play in his second coming. Jesus came the first time as the suffering Messiah, as exemplified by His persecution, rejection and crucifixion. Jesus will come back as the reigning Messiah, who will rule the world from His throne in Jerusalem as King of Kings and Lord of Lords . . .

In the expanded Chapter Ten, I will make the same point with language that does not hide my own perspective on the matter. The primary change will involve how I use the word 'Messiah.' In the expanded version, I will clarify the clear distinction between the 'Suffering Messiah,' the Lamb of God and the 'Reigning Messiah,' the Lion of the Tribe of Judah!

I am deeply grieved for any confusion my writing may have caused the body of Christ. It was never intended. I trust this letter and the expanded edition of *In Defense of Israel* will clarify what I believe. I also hope that we can return our focus to what I had anticipated to highlight all along, the fact that we Christians must shift from condemning the Jews for what they missed to thanking them for what they gave.[27]

Hagee's statement shows some reversal of his position, but is clearly unsatisfactory. To confuse the two roles of the Messiah, of Suffering Servant and Conquering King, with the need to keep Israel from believing in Jesus as Messiah so that the nations could receive the gospel, is an inadequate understanding of the ministry and message of Jesus. And one is left wondering whether such a reversal will be made known at the level of interaction with Jewish leaders. As Ellen W. Horowitz notes:

The differing accounts seem to be indicative of Pastor Hagee's own evolving theology and flip-flopping on this issue. He is personally on public record for opposing organized and targeted proselytizing campaigns directed at the Jewish people, but at the same time he enthusiastically endorses efforts to spread the gospel in Israel.[28]

---

[27] 'A Special Message from Pastor John Hagee Regarding His Book In Defense of Israel', (http://www.jhm.org/ME2/Sites/dirmod.asp?sid=&type=gen&mod=Core+Pages&gid=F9D83613EC574E6D8A2530B583FE9B95. Accessed 18 July 2008).

[28] Ellen Horowitz, 'The Other Side of CUFI (Part 1)'; http://shiloh-musings .blogspot.com/2008/07/other-side-of-cufi-part-1.html. Accessed 18 July 2008. Cf. 'Hagee and Falwell deny endorsing 'dual covenant', *Jerusalem Post* (2 March 2006) and *Jerusalem Post* (1 March 2006) 'Falwell, Jews can get to Heaven.'

Michael Brown, a Messianic Jew, is also unconvinced by Hagee's retraction:

> Since the publication of the book, Pastor Hagee issued some clarifying remarks, but the clarifications only complicate the issues and fail to renounce and remove the error.[29]

Messianic Judaism

Paul Lieberman, Executive Director of the International Messianic Jewish Alliance, sees a connection between the universalism of Hagee's Christian Zionism and that found in some Messianic Jewish streams:

> Dr. John Hagee and Stuart Dauermann may not have set out to be in agreement. After all, Rev. Hagee opposes Messianic Judaism, while Messianic Rabbi Dauermann embraces it. Yet, on the crucial matter of Jewish salvation, they both are deceived and in opposition to the plain words of Yeshua.
> '. . . no man cometh unto the Father, but by me'. (John 14:6)
> Let there be no mistake. Our love for Jewish people cannot cause us to compromise. Ultimately, is it really caring if we flinch from telling people the one truth that can solve their dying problem? Our Lord submitted to physical extinction of his earthly flesh so that we would live. Being inoffensive to traditional Jews in this way blocks Heaven's reward. It isn't really caring at all.[30]

As we turn to Messianic Judaism, we recognize several streams of theological reflection within the movement.[31] The issue of soteriology has become a key concern, and a recent issue of *Kesher* reports on two messianic theological consultations which discussed the issue, the Borough Park Symposium (October 2007) and the Theological Forum on Soteriology (March 2008) hosted by the Union of Messianic Jewish Congregations (UMJC).[32]

---

[29] Michael L. Brown, 'Is There Serious Error In The New Book, *In Defense of Israel?*' (private publication, 2008).

[30] Paul Lieberman, 'Dual Covenant', in *International Messianic Jewish Alliance Magazine*, no. 145 (Rancho Mirage, Calif., 2007).

[31] Cf. Richard Harvey, *Mapping Messianic Jewish Theology: a Constructive Approach* (Milton Keynes, Paternoster, 2009), notes eight theological streams.

[32] *Kesher: A Journal of Messianic Judaism*, Issue 22, Spring/Summer 2008 (Albuquerque, New Mexico). Online: www.kesherjounal.com.

Several of the participants spoke of the essential need for salvation through personal repentance and faith in the Messiah Yeshua (Jesus). David Sedaca responds to both John Hagee's and Mark Kinzer's views:

> These two events – the Borough Park Symposium and John Hagee's book – have indeed made the topic of soteriology and the Jewish people very relevant, especially for Messianic Jews who have believed that Jesus is the Messiah and have made his Great Commission their *raison d'être* for their missionary endeavours.[33]

He states clearly:

> There are only two possibilities to the dilemma of salvation and the Jewish people; if we stand firm with the principles of salvation as expressed in the scriptures, we then have to consider Jesus as the Messiah as the provider (*soter*) of salvation. Conversely, if we deviate from biblical principles and replace them with man-made systems, albeit they seem reasonable, we may be at risk of having devised a way for salvation that puts in peril our eternal life. Although present day Judaism denies the need for individual and personal salvation, it acknowledges the need for forgiveness, atonement and repentance. I make mine the words of the Apostle Peter, when addressing the people of Israel after their rejection of Jesus of Nazareth as Messiah; he declares *'Salvation is found in no one else, for there is no other name under heaven given to men by which we must be saved.'* I have chosen to put my hope in Jesus the Messiah.[34]

But not all hold Sedaca's unqualified assertion of Acts 4:12 or his assumed distinction between what is 'biblical' and what is 'man-made'. We will consider three more speculative proposals from Daniel Juster, Stuart Dauermann and Mark Kinzer.

Daniel Juster's Narrow, Wider Hope

Daniel Juster, President of Tikkun Ministries and former President of the UMJC, summarizes the Narrow Hope (NH) views of classical evangelicalism and dispensationalism, wherein 'the Jewish people are as lost as any other people. The election of the Jewish nation does not

---

[33] David Sedaca, 'Salvation and the People of Israel: Harmonising a Soteriological Dilemma', in *Kesher* (2008): 129–36; 132.

[34] Sedaca, 'Salvation and the People of Israel', 136.

imply their personal salvation which is only attained by the confession of Yeshua and experiencing being born again.'[35]

Conversely, the Wider Hope (WH) perspective believes in a broader application of the sacrifice of Yeshua, leading some to universalism, which holds that all human beings will ultimately be saved. Not all WH exponents are universalists, as many believe that 'some will have a positive eternal destiny, and others will not.' It may be possible to receive the benefits of the atonement of Christ through other means than an 'explicit response to the message of the Good News.' Jewish people might, according to this view, be 'rightly responding to God and the revelation of God in the Hebrew Bible' without personal faith in Jesus.

Juster is cautious about this and proposes his own 'Narrow Wider Hope' (NWH), that there are 'ways to respond to God other than by explicit response to the Good News and Confession of Yeshua.'[36] However, because Scripture teaches that 'people *do not generally respond positively* to these sources of revelation and truth', the NWH proponent believes that 'it is not wise to put much hope in this possibility.' Our responsibility and obligation to present the gospel does not change, and the NWH proponent holds that 'it is generally true that people are destined for a positive everlasting destiny only by their explicitly embracing Yeshua.'[37]

Whilst it is possible for Jewish people to be included within the salvation that is in Christ by 'rightly responding to the true revelation of God that is contained in Judaism' and there is 'more revelation within Judaism than in any other religion or culture', such a possibility should not be presumed.

Juster then critiques the weaknesses he sees of both Narrow and Wider Hope exponents and advocates his own 'Narrow Wider' hope (NWH) option. Narrow Hope views are supported by various Scriptures[38] and Francis Schaeffer, a 'moderate Calvinist who asserts both election and human responsibility for a response to God',[39] proposes this view. But while Juster can find no logical objection to Schaeffer, 'there may be reasons of the heart to resist such a stark position.' Juster is unwilling to affirm that Judaism should be seen as a 'deficient culture' because of the 'failure of our ancestors to embrace the testimony of the Apostles to ancient Israel'.

---

[35] Daniel C. Juster, 'The Narrow Wider Hope', in *Kesher* (2008), 14.
[36] Juster, 'The Narrow Wider Hope', 18.
[37] Juster, 'The Narrow Wider Hope', 19.
[38] John 1:12, 3:16, 8:24, 14:12, Acts 4:12, Rom. 3:22–3, 6:23, 10:9–10.
[39] Juster, 'The Narrow Wider Hope', 23.

Juster is unhappy with WH positions also. He discusses the accusation of universalism levelled at Karl Barth by Cornelius Van Til.[40] Juster is not convinced by Van Til's criticism. Barth holds in tension the paradox of the universal hope of salvation for all, while also arguing for the 'embrace of the gospel' as the necessary way of salvation. Barth 'never resolves the paradox' and this has special relevance to the election of Israel in Romans 11, which fits 'the same pattern of his [Barth's] Wider Hope affirmation.'[41] Juster's comments on Barth have significance, for although he is reluctant to follow what he sees as Barth's universalist tendencies, he has begun to explore Barth's doctrine of the church and Israel, in a way that may prove fruitful to Messianic Jewish theology in the future.

For Juster, the weakness of both NH and WH views is the 'failure to recognize that we live with mystery'.[42] C.S. Lewis reflected that 'God has not explicitly told us or made himself clear concerning those who have not had the opportunity to embrace the Good News.' Whilst unwilling, like Barth, to 'embrace contradictory paradox', Juster wishes to avoid the extremes of both NH and WH views. He refers to John Wesley, who combines the motivation to proclaim the good news 'born of a passionate love and desire to minimize the number who would be lost' while, at the same time, 'not precluding the possibility of people turning to God through the revelation of Yeshua in nature, culture and conscience.'[43] Wesley's notion of prevenient grace, according to Juster, leaves room for mystery and uncertainty about those who cannot be categorized into two groups, of 'saved' and 'lost', but may be able to embrace Yeshua after they die. This NWH position, according to Juster, is espoused by evangelicals such as Kenneth Kantzer and Billy Graham, as well as others such as Jacques Maritain, C.S. Lewis and Douglas Harink.[44]

Juster considers the implications of the NWH view for Jewish evangelism. Whilst WH views have never been sufficient to motivate for evangelism, the NWH, according to Juster, is able to motivate effectively:

---

[40] Juster, 'The Narrow Wider Hope', 26, citing Cornelius Van Til, *Karl Barth and Evangelicalism* (Nutley, N.J., Presbyterian and Reformed Publishing, 1964).
[41] Juster, 'The Narrow Wider Hope', 26.
[42] Juster, 'The Narrow Wider Hope', 32.
[43] Juster, 'The Narrow Wider Hope', 33.
[44] Juster, 'The Narrow Wider Hope', 31.

Only the motivation of compassion to see that people are not lost to eternal death has proven sufficient throughout history. *Only this produces the requisite intercession and anointing of the Spirit to be effective.*[45]

Juster concludes with two key affirmations. First, we are to 'act on the basis of the general "lost-ness" of people, both Jew and Gentile.'[46] We cannot be at rest or have confidence in the eternal destiny of anyone until they have embraced Yeshua. But this is held in tension with the second affirmation:

> We are also to hold open the possibility of a wider mercy or hope . . . This hope should be held in a way that does not blunt our zeal to see people embrace Yeshua. At the same time, this hope enables us to give a more powerful theodicy arguing for the justice of God in the face of evil . . . Indeed, many who claim to hold to no Wider Hope view show that this is not so when they are asked concerning their departed loving grandmothers. Somehow they hope that there was some transaction whereby they were received into heaven.[47]

Juster, thus, cautions that the 'holding of our Wider Hope views will eventually produce a decrease in the numbers in our messianic Jewish movement'.[48] But he is reluctant to espouse the NH position. Reflecting current uncertainty in evangelicalism as a whole, he reflects a 'Wider, Narrow Hope' position. As a leading Messianic Jewish thinker, his reliance on the terms of the debate within the classical and evangelical theological traditions demonstrates that the issue is one where the messianic movement has yet to come to its own clear view. The positions of Stuart Dauermann and Mark Kinzer that follow depart more radically from the evangelical tradition.

Stuart Dauermann's gospel in times of transition

Stuart Dauermann calls for a 'new paradigm' for the gospel in the light of changing contexts.[49] He is motivated by a concern for his people and a sense of frustration with the prevailing paradigms he sees in Jewish

---

[45] Juster, 'The Narrow Wider Hope', 36.
[46] Juster, 'The Narrow Wider Hope', 39.
[47] Juster, 'The Narrow Wider Hope', 40.
[48] Juster, 'The Narrow Wider Hope', 36.
[49] Stuart Dauermann, 'What is the Gospel we should be commending in these times of transition?', in *Kesher* (2008): 42–78.

mission circles which automatically consign Jewish people who do not believe in Jesus to hell. Unhappy with both Narrow and Wider Hope perspectives, he attempts to recast the biblical metanarrative of salvation history into one which includes the election of Israel as a corporate community, where emphasis is given to salvation in communal as well as individual aspects.

In the light of five eschatological signs of changing times, God's agenda has 'begun to shift from a focus on the ingathering of the fullness of the Gentiles to the ingathering of the fullness of Israel.'[50] Therefore, the old paradigms need changing, one of which is the 'Bad-News Gospel' which fails to see that the gospel is, in fact, 'good news' for Israel:

> Many will recoil from this aspect of our text [Luke 2:8–11] due to reflexively regarding the Jewish people as fundamentally spiritually lost, eternal losers, and the coming of Christ as not being good news for *the* Jewish people, but at best, good news only for *some* Jews who are exceptions to the rule.[51]

Dauermann uses an anecdotal, autobiographical style to explain his reaction against this approach:

> In 2002, I attended the meeting of the ETS at the Opryland Hotel in Nashville, Tennessee. Riding from the airport to the hotel, a missionary to the Jews whom I hardly knew, without any foreplay whatsoever, badgered me with one question: 'Do you believe that a Jew who does not believe in Jesus goes to hell?' Aside from being put off by his abrasive approach, I was mystified as to why, of all questions he might have selected, he chose *this* one test of my orthodoxy? Why this pre-occupation with the population of perdition?[52]

To Dauermann, the 'find-heaven-avoid-hell' approach is missing from the apostolic *kerygma* of the eighteen sermons in the book of Acts as either a motivation for the messenger or the hearer. He notes how

---

[50] Dauermann, 'What is the Gospel', 44. The five signs are the founding of the modern State of Israel; the liberation of Jerusalem; the regathering of the Jews to Israel from the land of the north; the repentance-renewal of the Jewish people evidenced by the rise of the Messianic Jewish movement; and a new concern for Messianic Jewish covenant faithfulness.

[51] Dauermann, 'What is the Gospel', 48.

[52] Dauermann, 'What is the Gospel', 60.

'current vehemence' surrounding the issue leads some to see his 'calling to ease off on this approach is nothing less than an attack on the mission to the Jewish people, through disassembling its engine.'[53]

Dauermann's approach does not call for the disassembling of the engine of Jewish mission, but rather the addition of shock-absorbers and silencers to make the engine run, as he sees it, more effectively. He wants to proclaim a gospel that is truly 'good news':

> Our people will rightly continue to find an individualistic message of soul salvation which fails to highlight God's continued commitment and consummating purposes for the community of Israel to be stale, irrelevant and foreign – far less and far other than God's invitation to participate in the anticipated vindication and blessing of the seed of Jacob. We must repent and return to this perspective.[54]

But Dauermann is reluctant to propose an alternative soteriology, preferring to state a studied agnosticism:

> I argue not *for* the wider hope as *against* the wider ego. It has been decades since I have heard anyone in our circles, speaking on a theological or missiological issue, say, 'I do not know.[55]

Dauermann quotes approvingly the caveat of Lesslie Newbiggin on the question of final destinies:

> I confess that I am astounded at the arrogance of theologians who seem to think that we are authorized, in our capacity as Christians, to inform the rest of the world about who is to be vindicated and who is to be condemned at the last judgment . . . I find this way of thinking among Christians astonishing in view of the emphatic warnings of Jesus against these kinds of judgments which claim to pre-empt the final judgment of God.[56]

Dauermann does not explicitly state a universalist position. But he is clearly reacting, at an emotional level, to the charged language of some exclusivist positions as applied to the Jewish people. Without

---

[53] Dauermann, 'What is the Gospel', 61.

[54] Dauermann, 'What is the Gospel', 56.

[55] Dauermann, 'What is the Gospel', 70.

[56] Lesslie Newbiggin, *The Gospel in a Pluralist Society* (Grand Rapids: Eerdmans, 1989), 177–8 in Dauermann 2008:71.

proposing a coherent alternative, he raises the significance of doubts, questions and 'mystery' to the point at which they discredit, for him, the viability of any soteriological statement about the final destiny of those Jewish people who do not believe in Yeshua. Rather than label him an 'implicit universalist', it would be more charitable to see him as a 'determined agnostic', as he makes no statement to the effect that his unbelieving grandmother will be in heaven, as much as he would like to hope for that. Rather, he suggests that we are asking the wrong question or looking for answers that cannot be given.

Mark Kinzer's 'Final Destinies'

Mark Kinzer's paper 'Final Destinies' is limited to a discussion of what the New Testament writings have to say about the topic. Kinzer realizes this is a severe restriction to impose, as there are major areas of theological discussion that also need consideration:

> Relevant theological issues include the meaning and significance of God's attributes of mercy and justice and the relationship between them: the divinity of Yeshua and his mediatorial role in creation, revelation and redemption; the validity of the traditional doctrine of 'original sin', and its implications for a free human response to God's gracious initiative; the implications of the paradigmatic cases of infant mortality and those with severe mental limitations; and the nature of Israel's enduring covenant and the ecclesiological bond between the Jewish people and the Christian church.[57]

Kinzer is well aware of these larger issues. While his survey of biblical materials leads him to the conclusion that the New Testament writers, particularly Peter and James, see moral living circumscribed by Torah-observance as a key constituent in the determination of final destinies, he makes certain theological assumptions about the significance of such statements within an overall theological framework, which is not supplied in that particular article. We will, therefore, examine Kinzer's approach to soteriology by supplementing material from his larger work *Postmissionary Messianic Judaism* where it impinges on soteriological issues.

---

[57] Mark S. Kinzer, 'Final Destinies: Qualifications for Receiving an Eschatological Inheritance', in *Kesher* 22 (Spring/Summer 2008): 87–119; 88 n. 4.

The hidden Messiah of Postmissionary Messianic Judaism

Mark Kinzer's *Postmissionary Messianic Judaism (PMJ)* proposes that Jesus the Messiah is hidden in the midst of the Jewish people, already present with them. Kinzer proposes a 'bilateral ecclesiology' made up of two distinct, but united, communal entities:

> (1) The community of Jewish Yeshua-believers, maintaining their participation in the wider Jewish community and their faithful observance of traditional Jewish practice, and
> (2) The community of Gentile Yeshua-believers, free from Jewish Torah-observance yet bound to Israel through union with Israel's Messiah, and through union with the Jewish ekklesia.[58]

Kinzer's stress on the inherent 'twofold nature' of the *ekklesia* preserves 'in communal form the distinction between Jew and Gentile while removing the mistrust and hostility that turned the distinction into a wall'. Kinzer argues that a bilateral ecclesiology is required if the Gentile *ekklesia* is to claim rightfully a share in Israel's inheritance without compromising Israel's integrity or Yeshua's centrality.

In chapter six of *PMJ*, Kinzer turns to the Jewish people's apparent 'no' to its own Messiah. Kinzer argues that Paul sees this rejection as 'in part providential, an act of divine hardening effected for the sake of the Gentiles'. Paul, according to Kinzer, even implies that this hardening involves Israel's mysterious participation in the suffering and death of the Messiah:

> In the light of Christian anti-Semitism and supersessionism, the Church's message of the Gospel comes to the Jewish people accompanied by the demand to renounce Jewish identity, and thereby violate the ancestral covenant. From this point onward the apparent Jewish 'no' to Yeshua expresses Israel's passionate 'yes' to God – a 'yes' which eventually leads many Jews on the way of martyrdom. Jews thus found themselves imitating Yeshua through denying Jesus! If the Church's actual rejection of Israel did not nullify her standing nor invalidate her spiritual riches, how much more should this be the case with Israel's apparent rejection of Yeshua![59]

---

[58] Mark S. Kinzer, *Postmissionary Messianic Judaism: Redefining Christian Engagement with the Jewish People* (Grand Rapids: Brazos/Baker, 2005), 23–4.

[59] Mark Kinzer, 'An Introduction to *Postmissionary Messianic Judaism*' (private publication, 2004), 5.

The Jewish people's apparent 'no' to Jesus does not rule them out of God's salvation purposes, any more than the church's *actual* 'no' to the election of Israel. Both are within the one people of God, although there is a schism between them. The New Testament 'affirms the validity of what we would today call Judaism'.[60]

Kinzer recognizes that the presence of Yeshua is necessary in order to affirm Judaism:

> Those who embrace the faith taught by the disciples will be justifiably reluctant to acknowledge the legitimacy of a religion from which Yeshua, the incarnate Word, is absent.[61]

Judaism's validity cannot be demonstrated if Jewish people have a way to God that 'bypasses Yeshua'. However, Kinzer argues that, in some mysterious and hidden way, 'Yeshua abides in the midst of the Jewish people and its religious tradition, despite that tradition's apparent refusal to accept his claims.'[62] This divinely willed 'disharmony between the order of knowing and the order of being' means that Yeshua is present with his people without being recognized. The *ontic* is to be distinguished from the *noetic*, what exists from what is known. The New Testament affirms that Yeshua is the representative and individual embodiment of the entire people of Israel, even if Israel does not recognize Yeshua and repudiates his claims. Even this rejection testifies to his status as the despised and rejected servant. Echoing Karl Barth's doctrine of the church in relation to Israel, Israel's 'no' is answered by the church's 'yes' to Jesus, and in Jesus himself both 'yes' and 'no' are brought together, just as Jesus is both divine and human, accepted and rejected.

Both church and Israel are 'bound indissolubly to the person of the Messiah', one in belief, the other in unbelief. Therefore, 'Israel's no *to* Yeshua can be properly viewed as a form of participation *in* Yeshua!'[63]

> If the obedience of Yeshua that led him to death on the cross is rightly interpreted as the perfect embodiment and realization of Israel's covenant fidelity, then Jewish rejection of the church's message in the second century and afterward can rightly be seen as a hidden participation in the obedience of Israel's Messiah.[64]

---

[60] Kinzer, *Postmissionary Messianic Judaism*, 215.
[61] Kinzer, *Postmissionary Messianic Judaism*, 217.
[62] Kinzer, *Postmissionary Messianic Judaism*, 217
[63] Kinzer, *Postmissionary Messianic Judaism*, 223.
[64] Kinzer, *Postmissionary Messianic Judaism*, 225.

This sounds decidedly paradoxical. How are we to understand and respond to it? Kinzer's argument draws from earlier thinkers like Lev Gillet, the friend of Paul Levertoff:

> His entire notion of 'communion in the Messiah' presumes that faithful Jews and faithful Christians can have communion together in the one Messiah. In fact, he seems to hold that the Messiah is also hidden for Christians to the extent that they fail to understand or acknowledge the ongoing significance of the Jewish people in the divine purpose.[65]

Gillet views the Jewish people as a *'corpus mysticum* – a mystical body, like the church'.[66] The suffering of the Jewish people is to be understood in the light of Isaiah 53, as both 'prophetic and redemptive', but Gillet does not, according to Kinzer, lose 'his christological bearings'. Gillet's aim is to build a 'bridge theology' that links the mystical body of Christ with that of the mystical body of Israel.

> The *corpus mysticum Christi* is not a metaphor; it is an organic and invisible reality. But the theology of the Body of Christ should be linked with a theology of the mystical body of Israel. This is one of the deepest and most beautiful tasks of a 'bridge theology' between Judaism and Christianity.[68]

Gillet aims to heal the schism between Israel and the church, showing that both Christian and Jew are united in the Messiah:

> The idea of our membership in Israel has an immediate application in all the modern questions concerning Jewry. If we seriously admit the mystical bond which ties us, as Christians, to the community of Israel, if we feel ourselves true Israelites, our whole outlook may be modified, and our lives of practical action as well.[69]

However, Gillet's argument relies on 'the mystery of the [future] restoration of Israel, who are still, in Paul's words, experiencing "Blindness in part".'[70] The Messiah is hidden from them, because of the

---

[65] E-mail from Mark Kinzer to author, 8 June 2007.
[66] Kinzer, *Postmissionary Messianic Judaism*, 280.
[67] Kinzer, *Postmissionary Messianic Judaism*, 281.
[68] Lev Gillet, *Communion in the Messiah* (London: Lutterworth, 1942), 215.
[69] Gillet, *Communion in the Messiah*, 215.
[70] Gillet, *Communion in the Messiah*, 215.

blindness of unbelief. Whilst he is hidden within his people, he is also hidden from them by their partial hardening.

Kinzer's concept of the 'hidden Messiah' derives not from the anonymous Christianity of the Roman Catholic theologian Karl Rahner, but from Karl Barth and Franz Rosenzweig, and later Jewish-Christian relations thinkers such as Paul van Buren. Kinzer also refers to Edith Stein, the Jewish philosopher who became a Carmelite nun, who saw the sufferings of the Jewish people as 'participating in the sufferings of their unrecognized Messiah'.[71] Thomas Torrance lends support to this christological understanding of the suffering of Israel as participation in the suffering of the Messiah, albeit unconsciously:

> Certainly, the fearful holocaust of six million Jews in the concentration camps of Europe, in which Israel seems to have been made a burnt-offering laden with the guilt of humanity, has begun to open Christian eyes to a new appreciation of the vicarious role of Israel in the mediation of God's reconciling purpose in the dark underground of conflicting forces within the human race. Now we see Israel, however, not just as the scapegoat, thrust out of sight into the despised ghettos of the nations, bearing in diaspora the reproach of the Messiah, but Israel drawn into the very heart and centre of Calvary as never before since the crucifixion of Jesus.[72]

Kinzer echoes Catholic theologian Bruce Marshall in arguing that the Jewishness of Jesus implies his continuing membership of and participation in the Jewish people. God's incarnate presence in Yeshua thus 'resembles God's presence among Yeshua's flesh-and-blood brothers and sisters'.[73] According to Marshall, the doctrine of the incarnation of God in Christ is analogous to the doctrine of God indwelling Carnal Israel, as articulated by Michael Wyschogrod, the Jewish thinker, in his book *Carnal Israel*:[74]

> The Christian doctrine of the incarnation is an intensification, not a repudiation, of traditional Jewish teaching about the dwelling of the divine presence in the midst of Israel.[75]

---

[71] Kinzer, *Postmissionary Messianic Judaism*, 227.
[72] Thomas Torrance, *The Mediation of Christ* (Colorado Springs: Helmers and Howard, 1992), 38–9, in Kinzer, *Postmissionary Messianic Judaism*, 227.
[73] Kinzer, *Postmissionary Messianic Judaism*, 231.
[74] Michael Wyschogrod, *The Body of Faith: God and the People Israel* (2d ed.; Northvale: Jason Aronson, 1996).
[75] Marshall, Bruce, *Trinity and Truth* (Cambridge: CUP, 2000), 178, in Kinzer, *Postmissionary Messianic Judaism*, 231.

If God is 'present in Israel, Yeshua is also present there' and, according to Robert Jenson, the 'church is the body of Christ only in association with the Jewish people':

> Can there be a present body of the risen Jew, Jesus of Nazareth, in which the lineage of Abraham and Sarah so vanishes into a congregation of gentiles as it does in the church? My final – and perhaps most radical – suggestion to Christian theology . . . is that . . . the embodiment of the risen Christ is whole only in the form of the church *and* an identifiable community of Abraham and Sarah's descendants. The church and the synagogue are together and only together the present availability to the world of the risen Jesus Christ.[76]

Kinzer is covering much new ground here, painting in broad brushstrokes an ecclesiology developed by post-liberal Christian theologians in dialogue with contemporary Jewish thinkers. Much of the discussion draws from Karl Barth's christological doctrine of the election of the one 'community of God' as church and Israel, and the doctrine runs the same risks of universalism on the one hand and a continuing supersessionism on the other. Whilst Karl Barth withdrew from participation in Rosenzweig's 'Patmos group' because of its perceived Gnosticism, there is also a danger of Gnosticism in this doctrine of the hidden Messiah incarnate in his people Israel.[77] Kinzer relies on a 'divinely willed disharmony between the *ontic* and the *noetic*, following Bruce Marshall:

> For most Jews, Paul seems to say, there is at this point a divinely willed disharmony between the order of knowing and the order of being which will only be overcome at the end of time.[78]

But if the mystery of God's dwelling in Christ is known to the church, it cannot be equally true that Israel can know that the opposite is the case and that Jesus is not the risen Messiah. Whilst Christians recognize a continuing election of Israel (the Jewish people) and, thus, a continuing commitment of Jesus *to* his people, they will be reluctant to admit that this commitment in itself is salvific, or that the hidden presence of the Messiah *with* his people is the means by which he is

---

[76] Jenson, 2003:13, in Kinzer, *Postmissionary Messianic Judaism*, 232.

[77] Mark R. Lindsay, *Barth, Israel and Jesus: Karl Barth's Theology of Israel* (Aldershot: Ashgate, 2007), 28.

[78] Kinzer 2007:1.

revealed to them. The hidden Messiah of *PMJ* owes more to a Christian re-orientation of perspective on Jesus and the election of Israel than on a Jewish recognition of a hidden Messiah. The hidden Messiah of *PMJ* is more a Christian re-evaluation of the presence of Christ within the Jewish people than a Jewish recognition of the messianic claims of Jesus. As such, it cannot be an acceptable statement of eternal destinies and gives no guarantee of salvation.

Conclusion

A venerable Jewish anecdote describes a man hired by his *shtetl* to sit on the outskirts of town and alert his village should he see the Messiah coming. When asked why he had accepted such a monotonous form of employment, the watchman would invariably reply: 'The pay is not so good, but it's a lifetime job.' Judaism considers waiting for the Redeemer a lifetime job, and Jewish people are obligated not only to believe in the coming of the Messiah but also to yearn for his coming.[79] But waiting and yearning are not enough. Neither is the belief that it is only necessary to announce his coming to one group, the nations, and not others, Israel. Nor can we say that not knowing is better than knowing and rejecting, or that the failure of the watchman diminishes the responsibility of the hearers. The last thing we should say is that there is no need for a Messiah, because his work has already been done. The good news of the Messiah's coming should be announced with all the urgency we can muster.

Jewish evangelism exists to put the watchman out of business by announcing that the Messiah is here and we are called to be his disciples. It may still be a lifetime job (unless he returns first), but the job has changed from being a watchman to being a herald of good news. To make the announcement of the Messiah's coming in a half-hearted way, or to imply that he has come for some, but others can wait until he comes again, would be a gross failure to fulfil the job description and divine commission.

The dangers of universalism, in either its stronger or weaker forms, must not cloud our judgement over the urgency of the imperative to preach the gospel to all nations. This not only includes but, in the light of Romans 1:16, suggests as a historic and missiological priority for

---

[79] Meir Soloveitchik, 'Redemption and the Power of Man', *Azure* 16 (Winter 2004). Online: http://www.azure.org.il/magazine/magazine.asp?id=172.

evangelism to the Jewish people. Whilst the survey above has shown some universalist tendencies within Christian Zionism and the messianic movement, our responsibility is to proclaim the Messiah until he returns and no other hope of salvation can be given except through faith in his redeeming work.

12

Replacement Theology with Implications for Messianic Jewish Relations

Darrell L. Bock

Reaching out to Jews with the gospel has been with us ever since Jesus Christ came to earth to accomplish the mission the God of Israel sent him to perform. Jesus is Jewish (Luke 1 – 2). His mission with the Twelve and those who followed him was to the cities and towns of Israel (Matt. 10). After the resurrection, Peter, James and Paul all went to Jews and even into synagogues to share the good news that God calls us to covenantal reform and faithfulness through his Messiah who offers forgiveness of sins (Acts, especially 13:13–43). This is what John the Baptist preached and what Jesus affirmed when he partook in John's baptism (Matt. 3:13–17; Luke 3:15–21). Jesus and Peter proclaimed that God would send the Spirit to God's people to give them the needed enablement. God was providing this gift to enable them to share about a renewed and restored relationship with God (Luke 24:44–9; Acts 1:4–5; 2:14–41). The gospel is for people of every nation, to exclude the Jewish people would be to exclude those to whom the gospel came first and represents a form of religious discrimination the gospel came to avoid (Matt. 28:18–20; Rom. 1:16–17).

Replacement Theology is an approach to the New Testament that argues that the church has replaced Israel as the people of God, so that Israel (and by implication the Jews) are no longer a participant in the covenant commitments God made to Abraham and to his seed long ago (Gen. 12:1–3). Abraham's seed is now any Jew or Gentile who responds to Jesus. This new mixed community, who are beneficiaries of the work of Jesus Christ, are the heirs of the covenant promises (Gal. 3:1 – 4:7). Israel's unbelief is the cause of her lost position (Luke 13:6–9; 19:41–4). Most often this theology is connected to forms of amillennialism or some expressions of premillennialism or to postmillennialism. Its roots are often associated with Reformed theology or with covenant theology.

Historically, the Messianic Jewish movement and Christians concerned to take the gospel to Jewish people have had important questions about Replacement Theology. Did God make promises years ago to Abraham and his physical seed that God now has stepped away from by substituting new beneficiaries? Does the inclusion of more people mean the exclusion of those to whom the promise was originally given? Was the promise only made to the single seed of Abraham (Jesus) or was it to the Jewish people as Genesis and Exodus argue? Does Jewish rejection in any single period disqualify Jews for all time? What do these questions suggest about God's promises, faithfulness and the truthfulness of His Word as well as his commitment to Jews and to us? These questions have led many to reflect on what the implications of Replacement Theology are for Jewish evangelism.

This essay will try to clarify biblically and missiologically the kinds of replacement theologies that exist and assess these views for their implications for outreach to the Jewish people. Three questions dominate: (1) Are there kinds of Replacement Theology? (2) On what basis do some build such a view and how should it be assessed? (3) What implications exist for Messianic Jewish movements? We shall tackle these questions one at a time.

Kinds of Replacement Theology

One of the issues that can bring confusion to this discussion is that there are different kinds of Replacement Theology. People often do not note these differences in discussing the topic. The options do make a difference in theological implications as we shall see.

My choice to speak specifically of 'replacement' theology is a reflection of the North American scene, where one often uses this terminology to dismiss a point of view from the conversation rather than engaging it. Such labelling as a rhetorical move is also made in Europe. However, this is often made with a lack of awareness that (1) there are kinds of replacement views (so my categories are designed to ask what is the ultimate outcome for Jews for the replacement in view); and

(2) a lack of clarity about how the term 'Israel' is being used with reference to Jews (Is the term national or ethnic?). Both ambiguities need attention if we are to be clear about the role of Israel in the Bible.

Others speak of supersessionism and various kinds of supersessionist models to get at the same set of issues. This is another excellent way to raise these issues and think about them. Two recent supersessionist models exist.

One comes from Gabriel Fackre in his *Ecumenical Faith in Evangelical Perspective*.[1] His list of options about Israel includes: (1) Retributive Replacement (God has judged Israel permanently and replaced it with the church); (2) Non-retributive Replacement (God has replaced Israel with Christ but says nothing explicit about Israel's future); (3) Modified Replacement (only Jesus saves, but there is a right of Jews to be protected from injustice and to live culturally as Jews); (4) Messianic Replacement (conversion to Christ for Jews, but with complete retaining of Jewish custom); (5) Christological Election (Israel has an eternal election, a view tied to Karl Barth). One could challenge whether all but his retributive category is really supersessionist, since they all leave room for a potential future for Israel at the end. Fackre's point in using the word supersessionist is that the church *now* has the central role in God's programme, not Israel.

Fackre goes on to name various antisupersessionist views. They are (1) dispensationalism, which retains a hope for the majority of Israel in the future; (2) the *One People* view of Marcus Barth, where Israel is God's representative people of God who have no need to be converted and deserve a political state that itself should be rooted in peace and righteousness; (3) the paradoxical view, which says the covenant with Israel is still in full force, but that the church is still called to call all to Jesus; (4) the eschatological view, where Jews will meet Jesus in the end and be saved; (5) the Dual Covenant view, where Israel is saved through her covenant and the nations are saved through the new covenant; (6) the Midrashic view, rooted in the work of Paul van Buren, argues that all Scripture must be subject to the portrait of God as revealed in Israel, making all statements about Jesus' deity, the Trinity and salvation through faith inappropriately supersessionist; (7) the moral pluralism view, where one accepts that certain religious views are true for some but not others; and (8) the cultural-linguistic view, where all such statements are simply seen as linguistic constructs, not communicating a reality.

---

[1] Gabriel Fackre, *Ecumenical Faith in Evangelical Perspective* (Grand Rapids: Eerdmans, 1993), 147–67.

To my eyes, most of these antisupersession models reject the centrality and truthfulness of Scripture in religious discourse because most of these models have to deny the meaning of several biblical texts to be accepted. This problem applies especially to the last three views in Fackre notes.

Another discussion comes from R. Kendall Soulen in *The God of Israel and Christian Theology*.[2] This entire work challenges supersessionism and notes its beginnings in Justin Martyr and Irenaeus in the second century. For Soulen, a key point is whether the church can allow Jewish people to come to Christ and maintain their Jewish identity, something the positions of Justin Martyr and Irenaeus lost and lack. He speaks of (1) economic supercessionism, where the value of the previous era was completely overcome in the new economy. A part of this economic way of reading Scripture also affirms (2) a punitive supercessionism, where Israel lost her place because of her rejection of Jesus as Messiah. Finally, there is (3) a structural supersessionism, which argues that the canon is structured in such a way that the Hebrew Scripture is irrelevant for understanding God's purposes. Here is where Soulen sees the major problem because it is the structural reading of Scripture that leads to the other expressions of supersessionism. Soulen's book challenges such models by claiming supersessionism rejects a key place for the God of Israel in all of Scripture and in God's own purposes. Soulen's options ultimately belong together and are three ways of looking at supersession or Replacement Theology.

I choose to refer to replacement taxonomy. It focuses on how the fate of Israel, either as a nation or as people, is *ultimately* seen. In other words, Israel can be 'replaced for now' at the centre of God's programme without being permanently replaced. There are two key ambiguities of terminology that plague our discussion in this area. First, Replacement Theology is often a poor and inaccurate term to apply in discussion about the fate of Jews, for reasons the taxonomy below makes evident. Some views of the church replacing Israel still see a future either for Jews or for the nation of Israel, so the term replacement is used in a less than absolute temporal sense. Second, the phrase 'future for Israel' is ambiguous because it is not clear whether we mean (1) ethnic Jews, or (2) Israel as a nation. Without clarity about which exact form of replacement is meant and how one sees the ultimate future for Israel, we can talk past one another or, even worse, mislead

---

[2] R. Kendall Soulen, *The God of Israel and Christian Theology* (Minneapolis: Fortress, 1996).

people about what a position holds. Thus, we distinguish between three types of Replacement Theology, of which only the first is absolute when it comes to the people of Israel in the future.

Some versions are unequivocal that Israel, either as a people or a nation, has no future as God's chosen people. We might call this *complete replacement*. The church has utterly and totally replaced Israel as God's covenant people. Israel has no special future in God's programme. The Jewish people are like anybody else. Older historic forms of Replacement Theology fall here, starting with the second-century *Epistle of Barnabas* and Justin Martyr. Martin Luther held to such a view.

However, other approaches in Replacement Theology argue that, although the church has replaced Israel in God's programme, such a replacement does not preclude a role for a majority of Jews in the future to respond to Jesus. This option might be more reticent about a future for Israel as a nation. This is a *partial replacement* view. This option holds that the church is the focus of the kingdom on earth, but God is still committed to his covenantal promises to Israel. In this view, it is sometimes argued that heavenly blessing or the blessing of the new heaven and earth is the goal in such a programme. The eschatological work of Anthony Hoekema fits here.[3] In such cases, the argument is that, although the church has replaced Israel as the covenant recipients through Jesus, God will keep his word to the Jewish people by restoring them to faith in Jesus as Messiah in the end, but the end is still part of an amillennial hope. Some 'replacement' theologians read Romans 9 – 11 this way. Some have even apologized for how these chapters have been read in the past in a way that excludes hope for Jewish people.

For example, C.E.B. Cranfield in his famous commentary on Romans in the ICC series says, in commenting on Barrett's view, that there is an election 'of a new Israel in Christ to take the place of the old.' He continues: 'And I confess with shame to having also myself used in print on more than one occasion this language of replacement of Israel by the church.'[4] In his own exposition, he warns against 'the ugly and unscriptural notion that God has cast off His people Israel and simply replaced it by the Christian church. These three chapters [Rom. 9 – 11] emphatically forbid us to speak of the Church as having once and for all taken the place of the Jewish people.'[5] In other words, although the

---

[3] Anthony Hoekema, *The Bible and the Future* (Grand Rapids: Eerdmans, 1989).

[4] C.E.B. Cranfield, *Romans*, vol. 2, (ICC; Edinburgh; T & T Clark, 1975), 448, n. 2.

[5] C.E.B. Cranfield, *Romans*, vol. 2, 448.

church is the current locus of blessing for God's people, its presence does not represent a final judgement on the role of Israel or the Jewish people either now or in the future, since Jews can come to the Messiah now (Messianic Jews) and one day God will act to restore the bulk of the people as a whole.

A third kind of replacement view can be called the *temporary replacement (current replacement but future eschatological inclusion)* view. This approach argues that the church is now the focus of God's work in the world, but there will be a day in the future when ethnic Israel, with whom God continues to have a covenant relationship, becomes the focus of God's work. This is the approach of some who hold to various forms of historic premillennialism, a view most often associated with George Ladd.[6] People in this approach are less than clear if (1) the nation of Israel has a future; (2) whether Jews are incorporated into the church in the future; or (3) whether God turns back to Israel as he completes promises for them as he sets up the millennium. Regardless of these details, the view argues that Jews will again respond to the gospel.

In noting this distinction of views as it is related to Replacement Theology, I have not even included those Christians who speak of two completely distinct plans of God, one for Israel and one for the church, and so have no room at all for any replacement of Israel at any time in God's programme (also known as classical and/or revised dispensationalism). This dispensational view does not hold to Replacement Theology at all. Still other dispensationalists hold that the church functions as 'new Israel' today, but not at the expense of hope for ethnic Jews or the nation of Israel in the future (progressive dispensationalism).[7] Others who hold to a progressive dispensational view avoid any equative language between Israel and the church. None of these dispensational views question that God will keep his promises with the original national recipients of the promise.

These distinctions mean that when one speaks of Replacement Theology as a view incompatible with a future of Israel or for Jews, the only form that totally fits are those who give no place in the future of

---

[6] George E. Ladd, *The Presence of the Future* (Grand Rapids: Eerdmans, 1974).

[7] For an up-to-date comparison of the various types of dispensationalism, see Herbert W. Bateman, ed., *Three Central Issues in Contemporary Dispensationalism: A Comparison of Traditional and Progressive Views* (Grand Rapids: Kregel, 1999). This approach to Scripture is often poorly described and summarized, especially in European contexts where the interaction is usually very out-of-date or focuses only on more popularizing presentations.

God's programme to Israel or to the Jewish people (i.e. the complete replacement view). The concern is that such a reading appears to ignore Paul's key point about the future of the people of Israel in Romans 9 – 11, as well as the point about God being a God of the patriarchs who keeps his promises (Acts 3:13–26). In addition, although other replacement views do not deny doing evangelism to the Jewish people, there is a sense and a momentum to this view in all its forms that does not anticipate much in terms of response, except perhaps at the end. As a result, the practical effect is that Jewish evangelism becomes a less than vibrant concern.

Another way to say this is: because of their rejection of Jesus, the Jewish people no longer have any covenantal uniqueness or significance, which therefore makes Jewish evangelism simply another type of evangelism. There is no greater significance to Jewish evangelism than any other kind because Israel has been 'replaced'. In fact, for some, the nation as a whole stands permanently under divine rejection for having engaged in covenantal unfaithfulness. So the saving of Jewish individuals becomes a kind of gracious exception to the rule. One need only look at church history to see how some Replacement Theology has very easily slipped into a kind of anti-Semitism. One need only read how Martin Luther spoke of the Jews to see how easy it is to turn theologically in this direction. The seeds reflected there are something the world still sees all too often, even experiencing a mammoth and inhumane lack of concern for Jewish people in the last century.

If I were to turn it around, I would state the case of Jewish evangelism this way. If the Jewish people still have some type of covenantal uniqueness, then Jewish evangelism is both the same and yet somewhat different, from evangelizing other types of people. It is a reconnection with the roots and original promises of the faith, made in faithfulness to the Jews and resting on God's commitment and character. It is clear from the Bible that Jews originally were the corporate chosen seed of Abraham, since part of the point of Genesis and Exodus is to demonstrate this idea and tell the story of how the promise to Abraham resulted in a blessed nation called to honour God. If one day God is going to restore the Jewish people to his purposes through the national Jewish acceptance of Christ (see Rom. 11:25 ff.), then the Jewish acceptance of Jesus and restoration to covenantal favour makes evangelizing Jewish people significant.

First, it provides for a remnant that reaches back to the original promise. Second, it represents the gracious commitment of God to fulfil his promise. Third, it provides genuine evidence of the famous reconciliation between Jews and Gentiles that runs through the New Testament (Eph. 3:1–13; Gal. 3:29). Such outreach is no more important than reaching other people for Jesus, but it does represent a connection to our Christian roots and the founding of Christianity that shows God's ultimate commitment to faithfulness, grace and his promises. Here we see realized the eschatological promise of Zechariah 12:10:

> I will pour out on the kingship of David and the population of Jerusalem a spirit of grace and supplication so that they will look to me, the one they have pierced. They will lament for him as one laments for an only son, and there will be a bitter cry for him like the bitter cry for a firstborn [NET].

Such a view also reflects the spirit of Romans 11:12, 15, 25–7 [NET]:

> v. 12: Now if their transgression means riches for the world and their defeat means riches for the Gentiles, how much more will their full restoration bring?
> v. 15: For if their rejection is the reconciliation of the world, what will their acceptance be but life from the dead?
> vv. 25–27: For I do not want you to be ignorant of this mystery, brothers and sisters, so that you may not be conceited: A partial hardening has happened to Israel until the full number of the Gentiles has come in. And so all Israel will be saved, as it is written: "The Deliverer will come out of Zion; he will remove ungodliness from Jacob. And this is my covenant with them, when I take away their sins."

These texts seem to suggest such a commitment to Israel (or at least to the Jewish people) by God.

Basis and Assessment of Various Views

It is important to ask why so many Christians disagree about Israel and her future. There is an attempt to make a biblical argument for replacement. It rests on at least three ideas: (1) Christ is the real recipient of the promise; (2) disobedience led to Israel losing her role; and (3) the church, rooted in Jesus' selection of the Twelve, is now the recipient of the blessings of promise.

Key passages in this discussion are: (a) Jesus seen as the *singular and ultimate* seed of Abraham into whom both Jew and Gentile are incorporated (Galatians 3:1 – 4:7); (b) the parable of the wicked tenants, where the vineyard picturing promise to Israel is given to another (Mark 12:1–12 = Matt. 21:33–46 = Luke 20:9–19); (c) texts where the nation is judged for disobedience;[8] and (d) passages where the church is now seen as the structure through which God works (Eph. 2:11–22), described in ways that show she takes up the task Israel once possessed (1 Peter 2:4–10; John 2:18–22; 4:20–24; Matt. 19:28 = Luke 22:30–31).

The points made in the above passages are obvious, but the question is whether the implication drawn from these ideas means the ultimate exclusion or replacement of Israel in God's programme. Does fulfilment through the Messiah of Israel's promise and Gentile inclusion, even in a new structure called the church, require the nullification of hope for Israel as a *corporate* people or even as a nation? The most emphatic of replacement theologians would say yes. But others, both replacement theologians and others, would say no. Here is why.

(1) The method of evangelism as seen in Acts shows that going to the synagogue and preaching Jesus as the fulfilment of expectation from the Hebrew Scriptures was undertaken by those Jesus commissioned. The two keys texts here are Acts 3:13–26 and 13:16–41. In both cases, it is the exposition of the promise to the nation that is either invoked or traced. In Acts 3, there is an explicit appeal to the Jewish audience as natural recipients of the message about the Christ rooted in the corporate and national reading of the seed of Abraham (vv. 25–6). In Acts 13, the pivot is the promise to David (vv. 33–4). If there had been a clear understanding of replacement, would Luke have recorded this to his church in the sixties to eighties when Acts was probably written? Why not speak more directly of a completely distinct structure if that is what was created?

(2) Luke-Acts also seems to affirm a restoration of kingdom blessing to Israel. Nothing in what Jesus said to the disciples in the forty days after his resurrection precluded them from asking if now Jesus would be restoring the kingdom to Israel in Acts 1:6. More than that, nothing in Jesus' answer says they had asked a wrong question. His reply simply said that they were not to know the times and seasons the Father had fixed for such an act. This reading seems confirmed when we go to Acts 3:21 where Peter says that heaven holds Jesus 'until the times of the restoration of all the things about which God has spoken by the

---

[8] Such texts include Jesus' prediction of destruction of the temple in the Olivet Discourse and Jesus' warnings that Israel is judged for covenantal disobedience (Luke 13:6–9, 33–5; 19:41–4).

mouth of his holy prophets' [NKJV]. The understanding of this text is that the rest of the programme has been revealed in the writings of the Prophets. In other words, to understand what God is still going to do, just read your Hebrew Scriptures. Those texts of the Hebrew Scriptures affirm a role for Israel as a people and nation.

(3) When Jesus says the times of the Gentiles are fulfilled as he describes Jerusalem under the feet of Gentiles in Luke 21:24, this likely implies that there is a time to come when Jews will again have a role in the sacred city. In fact, Jesus' own prediction of woe in Luke 13:34–5 suggests the same thing, since Israel's house is said to be desolate *until* she says: 'Blessed is he who comes in the name of the Lord.' This temporal limitation suggests that covenantal unfaithfulness will not be permanent in Israel.

(4) Romans 9 – 11 make no sense unless it is about ethnic Jews at the least. Everything about these chapters is precipitated by the pain Paul feels because Jews en masse are not currently responding to the gospel (Rom. 9:1–5). It is the people of Paul's own flesh that he despairs over in these chapters and nothing he says in these passages suggests that his concern for them has been redirected as the result of any judgement. When he contemplates the possibility that God can, and will, graft the original recipients back into the promise, it is the Jewish people Paul has in mind (Rom. 11:25–31). Even a covenant theologian such as John Murray held to such a hope for Israel.

(5) This same pattern is reiterated in what Paul says in Romans 1:16–17 ('to the Jew first'), as well as in his own missionary method in Acts, where his first contact was always with Jewish people preaching the hope of Israel.

(6) All of the passages mentioned above were penned in the era of the church, when her identity as an entity becoming distinct from Israel was well in process. If Jesus had proclaimed a judgement excluding Jews from evangelism because of the church's existence, then none of the above historically noted activities really make sense.

These considerations exclude a Replacement Theology that argues that, because God has brought blessing into the church, Israel is permanently excluded from God's plan. It also argues against a view that says that all we need be concerned about is individual evangelism to everyone, including Jews. In sum, God's promise is trustworthy. He is quite capable of bringing Israel into covenantal faithfulness, obedience and incorporation into her Messiah one day, as the texts noted above are most naturally read in this way.

Implications for Messianic Faith

The implications of these New Testament patterns we see include:

(1) The need to preach still to people of every nation (including Jewish people for whom God has a special concern). This can be done in the hope that, one day, what is currently a minority response will grow into something more significant. This message should be presented in terms like that of the earliest generation of Jesus followers. The promises to Israel point to what God did, and does, through Jesus. The resurrection is the divine vindication of Jesus who sits at God's right hand and mediates his blessings of salvation in restoring our broken relationship to God, whether we are Gentile or Jewish (Rom. 1 – 3).

The rationale for such an outreach comes from the Great Commission, the practice of the apostles and, most importantly, from Jesus himself. Appreciating such a theological emphasis represents the ground for response to issues like a dual covenant or a covenant of a hidden Christ. If these two other models are right, then the early church had no need to take a gospel to Jews and Jesus had no right to challenge the theology of his people in his time. However, the problem of these other models is that the thrust of Jesus' ministry was to call Israel to renewed covenantal faithfulness and embrace of the Promised One God had sent. The example of Jesus is not only that he represents Israel and offers forgiveness to her, but that he also gives a severe critique of Israel's spiritual need as one speaking from inside Judaism. This fact is very relevant for the church's own conversation with Israel and Jews today. The claim of the church was, and has been, that Jesus was, and is, Israel's Messiah. Jesus showed how to engage Torah in a way God desires.

(2) The range of practice with regard to Jewish customs we see in the first-century church is still possible for us today. Those with sensitivities to Jews and a desire to reach out to them may well take on a series of Jewish practices over which Paul said we should not fight (1 Cor. 9:19–23; Rom. 14 – 15). Such sensitivity motivated a solution like that of the Jerusalem Council, where concern for the Jewish audience led to requests to believers to be sensitive to Jews (Acts 15). Only when such practices got in the way of Jew-Gentile believer fellowship or an understanding of salvation through Christ alone did Paul challenge practices that led to an undue separation between the groups (Gal. 2:1–10).

A justification for this kind of flexibility in practice is that, although the church exists as the bearer of revelation today through Jesus, a hope exists for Israel and Jews extending into the future. The church is

'Jew and Gentile' in Christ. This new entity Jesus formed is seen as existing in a manner that honours their past and present ethnic orientation. Part of the beauty of reconciliation is that God has brought together distinct peoples into one new entity, but this unity need not mean that each ethnicity loses some of the distinctiveness that makes that entity distinct.

We are one, but that does not mean we must be completely the same. If God still has a covenantal relationship with the Jewish people and Israel that will be realized in the future and has not been completely replaced by the church, then it is permitted and even natural for Jewish people to retain their national distinctiveness within the body of Christ. This means that Jews are Jews in every age. If Jews believe in Jesus, then they not only can remain Jews from a theological perspective, but also serve as an identifiable part of that community Christ has reconciled corporately in the body. They may act as Jews from a practical vantage point. *Therefore, Messianic Jews can live as Jews, but they also need to affirm their oneness with Messiah's body as a whole. To be so distinct that oneness is not evident is to deny the reconciliation the gospel stresses as a key goal standing at the core of Jesus' work.* Of course, this variety of practice can be enacted in many different ways.

One common implication of Replacement Theology is that, since the church has replaced Israel once and for all and the church is made up of Jew and Gentile, Jews should worship and engage in religious practice like all other Christians. But is this conclusion necessary in the case of messianic believers? For example, if a replacement theologian does not believe there is any ongoing covenantal uniqueness to Israel and the Jewish people, then such a theology will not see any need for Jewish people to live as Jews. Yet if Jews do not live as Jews, at least in some cases, then the testimony of these Jewish believers who are part of the present-day remnant could well be impaired.

In addition, all of us may need to reflect on this question. Are we called to embrace an ecclesiology that only sees oneness? Is there not a place to appreciate an appropriate kind of diversity in the body that ultimately testifies to a reconciled oneness in the midst of that diversity? Is this not what is testified to in the permitted diversity of practice between Jewish Christians in Jerusalem and other Christians in the early church? Is this not why Paul allows room for various practices in Romans 14 – 15? Is this not what motivated the kind of advice given to Gentile churches in proximity to Jewish communities at the Jerusalem Council in Acts 15?

(3) To affirm a future for Israel also has eschatological implications for the church. If some believe that there will be an end time revival of the Jewish people at some level in association with Christ's second coming, then Jewish evangelism is not simply one type of evangelism among many. At least from the Pauline of view of things, Jewish evangelism today has eschatological significance, by pointing to the future consummation in a special way. Romans 9 – 11 keeps Jewish evangelism a Christian theological concern. Jewish evangelism today points to God's programme tomorrow. This might not change the specific way in which the church evangelizes the Jewish people, but it lends credence to the notion that Jewish evangelism has a special theological significance.

Jewish evangelism grows out of a natural love, affinity and appreciation for the ongoing role of the Jewish people in God's plan. Believers should express their hope for, concern to and share the gospel with their Jewish neighbour. An appreciation of Israel's future produces a greater momentum for Jewish evangelism because it is rooted in an appreciation for God's ongoing commitment to the original recipients of the promise.

In sum, we have argued that Replacement Theology can risk minimizing a need to reach out to the Jewish people. It also risks becoming a denial of the Great Commission and the model for mission that the early church itself undertook. It may well understate the eschatological significance of keeping connected to the historical, national Jewish roots of the Christian faith. It may also underestimate the power of a church testimony that possesses diversity even as it expresses its oneness of faith in Jesus the Messiah. The call of those who follow Jesus is to take the gospel to every nation, Jew and Gentile, because every human being has the same need for restoration before God. In going to the Jews, the church reaffirms its commitment to God's promises made originally to Jews and testifies to an appreciation of the church's own roots, since Jesus came as Israel's Messiah and called that nation to faithfulness. When Jesus died for all those who needed salvation, he died with Jews also very much in mind.

13

Karl Barth, Mark Kinzer and the Jewish People, with Implications for Jewish Evangelism

Eckhard J. Schnabel

The negative stance towards missionary outreach to the Jewish people has many causes. Karl Barth's views have been, and continue to be, influential among Christian theologians. Most recently, Mark Kinzer has suggested a 'postmissionary' messianic Judaism which represents a construction of Jewish and Jewish-Christian identity that takes up some of Barth's ideas. The following essay first analyzes the basic outlines of Barth's 'theology of Israel' before evaluating Kinzer's procedures and proposals.

Karl Barth and the Election of the Jewish People

Karl Barth's theology of Israel has received much attention. This is not so much due to the place that this question occupies in Barth's theological work. Rather, the attention to this question arises from the significance of the Jewish-Christian dialogue particularly since the 1960s.

Karl Barth has been accused of having been indifferent to the plight of the Jewish people during the Nazi period. This is incorrect. Eberhard Busch argues that Barth played a crucial role in establishing the theological basis for the insistence that the church had to stand in solidarity with the Jewish people and that the church had to resist Hitler's anti-Semitic agenda.[1] Mark Lindsay rejects the assumption that Barth was indifferent to the Jewish plight and suggests that his resistance was at least as comprehensive as Dietrich Bonhoeffer's.[2] Manuel Goldmann asserts that Barth's structural and material proximity to the anti-Jewish Christian tradition is prevented from developing momentum in terms of a fuller anti-Jewish position on account of his christological focus.[3]

A criticism that has more justification is the observation that Barth's theological language at times betrays 'an ignorance of the Judaism of his day'.[4] Katherine Sonderegger thinks that Barth had only a superficial knowledge of contemporary Jewish thought, revealing 'in his own magisterial way the Christian obsession with Judaism, marked, as all obsessions are, by the controlling ambivalence of deep hostility and deep, unshakeable attachment.'[5] Karl Barth has been accused even by sympathetic interpreters such as Friedrich-Wilhelm Marquardt that Jewish self-understanding is either missing entirely or treated as a *quantité négligeable.*[6] Manuel Goldmann agrees that Barth did not really engage in a real dialogue with the Jewish tradition.[7]

Some critics go further. Michael Wyschogrod observes that 'reading Barth, one would gain the impression that there is nothing but

---

[1] Eberhard Busch, 'Karl Barth und die Juden 1933/34. Auch ein Beitrag zu einem umstrittenen Aspekt der "Theologischen Erklärung" von Barmen', *Judaica* 3 (1984): 158–75; Eberhard Busch, *Unter dem Bogen des einen Bundes. Karl Barth und die Juden 1933–1945* (Neukirchen-Vluyn: Neukirchener Verlag, 1996).

[2] Mark R. Lindsay, *Covenanted Solidarity: The Theological Basis of Karl Barth's Opposition to Nazi Antisemitism and the Holocaust* (Issues in Systematic Theology 9; New York: Lang, 2001).

[3] Manuel Goldmann, *'Die grosse ökumenische Frage'. Zur Strukturverschiedenheit christlicher und jüdischer Tradition mit ihrer Relevanz für die Begegnung der Kirche mit Israel* (Neukirchener Beiträge zur Systematischen Theologie 22; Neukirchen-Vluyn: Neukirchener, 1997), 107–8. He speaks of a 'christologische Domestizierung des theologischen Antijudaismus' in Barth's theology of Israel (108). Goldmann does not discuss CD IV/3.2 §72.4.

[4] Mark R. Lindsay, *Barth, Israel, and Jesus: Karl Barth's Theology of Israel* (Barth Studies; Aldershot/Burlington: Ashgate, 2007), 17.

[5] Katherine Sonderegger, *That Jesus Christ was Born a Jew: Karl Barth's 'Doctrine of Israel'* (University Park: Pennsylvania State University Press, 1992), 3.

[6] Friedrich-Wilhelm Marquardt, *Die Entdeckung des Judentums für die christliche Theologien Israel im Denken Karl Barths* (Abhandlungen zum christlich-jüdischen Dialog 1; Munich: Kaiser, 1967), 296; cf. Bertold Klappert, *Israel und die Kirche. Erwägungen zur Israellehre Karl Barths* (Theologische Existenz heute 207; Munich: Kaiser, 1980), 27.

[7] Goldmann, *Ökumenische Frage*, 110–24.

faithfulness on God's part and unfaithfulness on Israel's.'[8] Even though Wyschogrod is generally sympathetic to Barth, he argues that Barth suffers from 'the traditional anti-semitism of European Christendom . . . and the anti-semitism of Christian theology.'[9] Alan Davies accuses Barth of 'religious totalitarianism in which Jews are not permitted to know anything concerning their own identity except what they are taught at the gates of the church.'[10] Theodor Adorno goes a step further and accuses Barth of anti-Judaism.[11] Such an accusation, however, is indicative of a thorough misunderstanding of the Israel passages in Barth's *Church Dogmatics*. This is not the place to provide a full exposition of Barth's view of Israel and of the Jewish people. I want to focus on the following four points.

Barth's christological focus and the existence of Israel

Karl Barth insists that the mission and the existence of Israel have a christological structure – the prophetic, priestly and royal mission of the people of Israel is identical with the will and work of God, which has been carried out and revealed in Jesus Christ. The emphasis of this christological context has serious consequences for his understanding of 'the rejection of Israel'. Barth asserts with regard to Israel *post Christum* that the 'Old Testament Gestalt' of the community has no theological right to exist:

---

[8] Michael Wyschogrod, *Abraham's Promise: Judaism and Jewish-Christian Relations* (ed. R.K. Soulen; Radical Traditions; Grand Rapids: Eerdmans, 2004), 223; Michael Wyschogrod, 'Why Was and Is the Theology of Karl Barth of Interest to a Jewish Theologian?', in *Footnotes to a Theology: The Karl Barth Colloquium of 1972* (ed. M. Rumscheidt; Waterloo: Corporation for the Publication of Academic Studies in Religion in Canada, 1974), 95–111; 109.

[9] Wyschogrod, 'Theology of Karl Barth', 107. Cf. Lindsay, *Barth, Israel, and Jesus*, 24–5. One should note that Wyschogrod believes that 'it is not for gentiles to see the sins of Israel. It is not for gentiles to call Israel to its mission, to feel morally superior to it and to play the prophet's role towards it. It is for gentiles to love this people if need be blindly, staunchly, not impartially but partially and to trust the instincts of this people whom God has chosen as his own' (Wyschogrod, *Abraham's Promise*, 224).

[10] Alan T. Davies, *Anti-Semitism and the Christian Mind* (New York: Herder and Herder, 1969), 120; cf. Stephen R. Haynes, *Prospects for Post-Holocaust Theology* (American Academy of Religion Academy Series 77; Atlanta: Scholars, 1991), 80.

[11] Theodor W. Adorno and Max Horkheimer, 'Elemente des Antijudaismus. Grenzen der Aufklärung', in *Dialektik der Aufklärung* (Gesammelte Schriften 3; Frankfurt: Suhrkamp, 1981), 192–235; 203.

In view of the act of Judas there can be no further doubt about the rejection of this people and the seriousness of the typical rejection of all these individuals within it. For it was delivered up to the Gentiles for death the very One in whom it is elect. This Judas must die, as he did die; and this Jerusalem must be destroyed.[12]

This, and similar statements of Barth, need to be understood in the context of his christological conviction according to which both rejection and election are real only in Jesus Christ: he is the hope of those who have been rejected as well, which means that both the rejected and the elect stand in indissoluble solidarity.[13] It can be argued that Barth's understanding of the fulfilment of God's saving will in Jesus Christ 'ends in the historical removal of important elements of Israel's history, and even the people of Israel itself.'[14]

The church and Israel: Barth's model of integration

Barth relates Israel and the church largely in terms of the 'ecclesiological model of integration' which is dependent upon the substitution model and the illustration model in his interpretation of Romans 9 – 11 in the *Church Dogmatics*.[15] Barth wants to avoid a traditional supersessionist understanding of the relationship between the church and Israel.[16] This is evident in his conviction:

Jesus Christ is the crucified Messiah of Israel. As such He is the authentic witness of the judgment that God takes upon Himself by choosing fellowship with man . . . Jesus Christ is the risen Lord of the Church. As

---

12 CD II/2 §34, 505.
13 Goldmann, *Ökumenische Frage*, 79.
14 Haynes, *Post-Holocaust Theology*, 82, with reference to Marquardt, *Entdeckung des Judentums*, 246. Marquardt formulates more cautiously than Haynes assumes, when he states that 'die historische Ablösung so wichtiger Einzelheiten innerhalb der Geschichte Israels, wie sie Propheten, Priester und Könige sind, *kann nur zu leicht* als historische Ablösung des Volkes Israel selbst verstanden werden' (emphasis mine).
15 Klappert, *Israel und die Kirche*, 3852; cf. Marquardt, *Entdeckung des Judentums*, 1278; Goldmann, *Ökumenische Frage*, 85–6. Klappert describes five models which eliminate the distinctive particularity of Israel – substitution, integration, typology, illustration, subsumption – and three models which preserve the distinctive particularity of Israel – complementarity, representation, christological-eschatological participation (ibid. 14–25).
16 Klappert, *Israel und die Kirche*, 34.

such He is the authentic witness of the mercy in which God in choosing man for fellowship with Himself turns towards him His own glory . . . But precisely as the risen Lord of the church He is also the revealed Messiah of Israel which by His self-giving God establishes as the scene of His judgment, but also as hearer of his promise, as the form of His community determined for a gracious passing.[17]

Barth's christological focus eliminates the lasting significance of Israel's particularity and asserts an integration of Israel into the church. Bertold Klappert argues that, in terms of the premises of Barth's theology in which the particular has priority over the universal, it would have been more consistent not to integrate Israel into the church but the church into Israel's history of promise, with Israel retaining its dignity and its form as having been confirmed by Jesus Christ. Klappert calls this the 'christological model of participation' which he finds in Barth, albeit not applied in a consistent manner.[18]

There seems to be a serious tension at the centre of Barth's doctrine of Israel.[19] He is convinced, on the one hand, that the calling and election of the church depend completely and permanently on the calling and election of Israel, whose covenant was fulfilled in Jesus Christ (christological dependence). He is convinced, on the other hand, that the essence and the future of 'the synagogue' are tied to the church which is its end and goal (ecclesiological integration).

The witness of the church to Israel

Richard Harries and Mark Lindsay interpret Barth's position in CD IV/3.2 §72.4 in terms of a rejection of a Christian mission to the Jewish people. They argue that, since the crucial issue is the credibility of the Christian church, Barth's concern is 'not any attempt to convert individual Jews'.[20]

In the context of the mission of the church to the nations, Barth asserts that the Jewish people take on a 'highly singular' aspect.[21] The

---

[17] CD II/2 §34, 198.
[18] Klappert, *Israel und die Kirche*, 32–4, with reference to KD IV/1, 182; Goldmann, *Ökumenische Frage*, 86 refers further to KD II/2, 307, 328; IV/3, 1005.
[19] Klappert, *Israel und die Kirche*, 38–52; cf. Haynes, *Post-Holocaust Theology*, 84, and the discussion in Goldmann, *Ökumenische Frage*, 57–109.
[20] Richard Harries, *After the Evil: Christianity and Judaism in the Shadow of the Holocaust* (Oxford: OUP, 2003), 135, approvingly quoted by Lindsay, *Barth, Israel, and Jesus*, 105.
[21] CD IV/3.2, 876; cf. KD IV/3.2, 1005 ('ein schlechthin singuläres' Zeugnis).

Christian community can seek to 'convert' Jews only in the most qualified sense, because, unlike all other nations, Israel has already heard 'the awakening call of God'. Thus, Barth states:

> [I]n relation to the Synagogue there can be no real question of 'mission' or of bringing the Gospel. It is thus unfortunate to speak of Jewish missions. The Jew who is conscious of his Judaism and takes it seriously can only think that he is misunderstood and insulted when he hears this term. And the community has to see that materially he is right.[22]

Barth makes two points. First, the Jewish people are not beholden to false gods. The God whom the church must proclaim to the nations:

> was the God of Israel before the community itself ever came forth from his people, and to this day He can only be the God of Israel . . . The Gentile Christian community of every age and land is a guest in the house of Israel. It assumes the election and calling of Israel. It lives in fellowship with the King of Israel. How, then, can we try to hold missions to Israel? It is not the Swiss or the German or the Indian or the Japanese awakened to faith in Jesus Christ, but the Jew, even the unbelieving Jew, so miraculously preserved, as we must say, through the many calamities of his history, who as such is the natural historical monument to the love and faithfulness of God, who in concrete form is the epitome of the man freely chosen and blessed by God, who as a living commentary on the Old Testament is the only convincing proof of God outside the Bible. What have we to teach him that he does not already know, that we have not rather to learn from him?[23]

Second, the Jewish people have rejected Jesus the Messiah and, thus, denied Israel's election and calling. Barth argues:

> [M]eantime the Synagogue became and was and still is the organisation of a group of men which hastens towards a future that is empty now that He has come who should come, which is still without consolation, which clings to a Word of God that is still unfulfilled. Necessarily, therefore, the Jew who is uniquely blessed offers the picture of an existence which, characterized by the rejection of its Messiah and therefore of its salvation and mission, is dreadfully empty of grace and blessing.[24]

---

[22] CD IV/3.2, §72, 877.
[23] CD IV/3.2, §72, 877.
[24] CD IV/3.2, §72, 877.

Barth asserts that 'we certainly can and should hold talks with the Jews for the purpose of information', but then questions whether this will be useful:

> But how can the Gospel help as proclaimed from men to men when already it has been repudiated, not just accidentally or incidentally, but in principle, a priori and therefore with no prospect of revision from the human standpoint? And in the long run what is the use of conversations? If the Jew is to go back on the rejection of his Messiah and become a disciple, is there not needed a radical change in which he comes to know the salvation of the whole world which is offered to him first as a Jew and in which he thus comes to read quite differently his own Holy Book? Is there not needed the direct intervention of God Himself as in the case of the most obstinate of all Jews, Paul himself? Can there ever be a true conversion of the true Jews, therefore, except as a highly extraordinary event? Can we ever expect a gathering of Israel around the Lord who died and rose again for this whole people of Israel except, as Paul clearly thought in Rom. 11. 15, 25f., in and with the end of all things and as the eschatological solution of this greatest of all puzzles?[25]

This argument fails to answer the question why the Jews' rejection of the gospel of Jesus Christ *in the past* should preclude the possibility of acceptance of the gospel in the future. Why should there be 'no prospect of revision'? Why should Jews not come to faith in Jesus Christ in the present or in the future? Paul never gave up hope that his preaching among the Jewish people would convince some of the truth of the gospel.

Barth argues that the only responsibility of the church is the passive witness of the life of the Christian community:

> Does this mean that the Christian community has no responsibility to discharge its ministry of witness to the Jews ? Not at all! What it does mean is that there can be only one way to fulfill it. To use the expression of Paul in Rom. 11:11, 14, it must make the Synagogue jealous (πασαζηλωαι). By its whole existence as the community of the King of the Jews manifested to it as the Saviour of the world, it must set before it the fact of the event of the consolation of the fulfilled Word of God, confronting it with the monument of the free election, calling and grace of God which have not been despised but gratefully accepted and grasped. It must make dear and

---

[25] CD IV/3.2, §72, 878.

desirable and illuminating to it Him whom it has rejected. It must be able to set Him clearly before it as the Messiah already come. It must call it by joining with it as His people, and therefore with Him. No particular function can be this call, but only the life of the community as a whole authentically lived before the Jews.[26]

Barth accuses the church of having failed in this task, as the church has not been a convincing witness. This is indeed a valid and important point. The reality of the life of Christians and of Christian churches throughout history has not been attractive for Jews. But Paul does not say in Romans 11:11–14 that the life of the church is the *only* witness to the Jewish people. His own missionary activity demonstrates that he is convinced that the Jewish people need to be won over to faith in Jesus the Messiah by people like him who are 'ambassadors for the Messiah' appealing to people who do not yet believe to be reconciled to God through Jesus Christ (2 Cor. 5:11–21).

Salvation and humanity

Barth's view of the Jewish people cannot be separated from his view of people with different faiths in general. This is not the place to describe Barth's view of religions.[27] Suffice it to say that, in CD IV/2, Barth argues that, since God assumed the humanity of all human beings in the incarnation of Jesus the Son of God, the whole of humanity exists in Jesus: 'In Jesus Christ it is not merely one man but the *humanum* of all men, which is posited and exalted as such to unity with God.'[28]

God's covenant of grace is not an afterthought, but the reason of salvation. And this means that redemption and reconciliation are universal. Thus, there is no sphere in creation, which is a fallen creation, which is alien to the Creator.[29] Barth, thus, says in the summary of his study on Christ and Adam in Romans 5:

---

[26] CD IV/3.2, §72, 878.

[27] Paul F. Knitter, *No Other Name? A Critical Survey of Christian Attitudes Toward the World Religions* (Maryknoll: Orbis, 1985), 23–31; Peter Harrison, 'Karl Barth and the Non-Christian Religions', *Journal of Ecumenical Studies* 23 (1986): 207–24; Veli-Matti Kärkkäinen, *Trinity and Religious Pluralism: The Doctrine of the Trinity in Christian Theology of Religions* (Aldershot/Burlington: Ashgate, 2004), 13–27; Veli-Matti Kärkkäinen, 'Karl Barth and the Theology of Religions', in *Karl Barth and Evangelical Theology: Convergences and Divergences* (ed. S.W. Chung; Bletchley/Grand Rapids: Paternoster/Baker, 2006), 236–57.

[28] CD IV/2, 49.

[29] Kärkkäinen, 'Karl Barth and the Theology of Religions', 251.

What is said here applies generally and universally, and not merely to one limited group of men. Here 'religious' presuppositions are not once hinted at. The fact of Christ is here presented as something that dominates and includes all men. The nature of Christ objectively conditions human nature and the work of Christ makes an objective difference to the life and destiny of all men. Through Christ grace overflows upon them, bringing them pardon and justification and opening before them a prospect of life with God. In short, 'grace rules,' as it is put in v. 21. And all that is in exact correspondence to what happens to human nature in its objective relationship to Adam. There sin rules, in exactly the same way, and all men become sinners and unrighteous in Adam, and as such must die. The question about what is the special mark of the *Christian* is just not raised at all. What we are told is what it means for man as such that his objective relationship to Adam is subordinate to and dependent upon and included in his objective relationship to Christ . . . What is said in vv. 1–11 is not just 'religious' truth that only applies to specially talented, specially qualified, or specially guided men; it is truth for *all* men, whether they know it or not, as surely as they are all Adam's children and heirs. The assurance of Christians, as it is described in vv. 1–11, has as its basis the fact that the Christian sphere is not limited to the 'religious' sphere. What is *Christian* is secretly but fundamentally identical with what is *universally human*.[30]

If all human beings are included in the election of Jesus Christ and if indeed in Jesus Christ all human beings are condemned as sinners, it follows that there is no condemnation left. Since not all human beings are living as elected, it is the task of the church as the elect community to proclaim that such a person 'belongs eternally to Jesus Christ and therefore is not rejected, but elected by God in Jesus Christ . . . that the rejection which he deserves on account of his perverse choice is borne and canceled by Jesus Christ; and that he is appointed to eternal life with God on the basis of the righteous, divine decision.'[31]

Veli-Matti Kärkkäinen interprets Barth to assert that 'the triune God has bound himself to humankind in an everlasting covenant. This binds humankind into a solidarity rather than into an arrogant "sheep" and "goats" divide.'[32] Responding to these conclusions of Barth, the

---

[30] Cf. Karl Barth, *Christ and Adam: Man and Humanity in Romans 5* (trans. T.A. Smail; New York: Harper, 1956), 88, 89.

[31] CD II/2, 306.

[32] Kärkkäinen, 'Karl Barth and the Theology of Religions', 252.

Zurich systematic theologian Emil Brunner raised the following questions:

> What does this statement, 'that Jesus is the only really rejected person,' mean for the situation of Man? Evidently this, that there is no such thing as being 'lost,' that there is no possibility of condemnation, and, thus, that there is no final Divine Judgment . . . The decision has been made in Jesus Christ – for all men. Whether they know it or not, believe it or not, is not so important. The main point is that they are saved. They are like people who seem to be perishing in a stormy sea. But in reality they are not in a sea where one can drown, but in shallow water, where it is impossible to drown. Only they do not know it. Hence the transition from unbelief to faith is not the transition from 'being-lost' to 'being-saved.' *This* turning-point does not exist, since it is no longer possible to be lost.[33]

Barth makes sin irrelevant when he places Christ 'above' and 'before' Adam who is 'below' and 'second' since Christ 'reveals the true nature of man', claiming that

> man's nature in Adam is not, as is usually assumed, his true and original nature; it is only truly human at all in so far as it reflects and corresponds to essential human nature as it is found in Christ . . . And so Paul makes no arbitrary assertion, and he is not deceiving himself when he presupposes this unity as simply given even in Adam. He does so because he has found it given first and primarily in Christ. Christ is not only God's Son; He is also a man who is not a sinner like Adam and all of us. He is true man in an absolute sense, and it is in His humanity that we have to recognize true human nature in the condition and character in which it was willed and created by God.[34]

Barth ignores the fact that, for Paul, sin is indeed the power which negates God and his will. And he thus does not see that for Paul, the 'excess' of God's grace consists in its power to abrogate universal sin.[35]

---

[33] Emil Brunner, *Dogmatics. Vol. I: The Christian Doctrine of God* (trans. O. Wyon; Philadelphia: Westminster, 1950), 348, 351, interacting with Barth's doctrine of election in CD II/2.

[34] Karl Barth, *Christ and Adam*, 90, 93–4.

[35] For a critique of Barth's interpretation of Rom. 5:12–21 cf. Ernst Käsemann, *An die Römer* (4. Auflage; HNT 8a; Tübingen: Mohr-Siebeck, 1980), 133–4; Ulrich Wilckens, *Der Brief an die Römer* (EKK 6/1–3; Neukirchen-Vluyn/Einsiedeln: Neukirchener

Veli-Matti Kärkkäinen concludes that Barth's Christology 'makes him first an "anonymous universalist" and later, when the implications are spelled out by Barth himself, a "reluctant universalist".'[36]

In the context of Barth's understanding of God's revelation in Jesus Christ, any active missionary outreach to people of other faiths – whether Jewish, Islamic, Hindu, Buddhist or otherwise – loses the urgency, the clarity and the directness which we see in the ministry of Jesus and the apostles.

Mark Kinzer and Postmissionary Messianic Judaism

In his book *Postmissionary Messianic Judaism: Redefining Christian Engagement with the Jewish People*,[37] Mark Kinzer seeks to clarify what faith in Jesus by messianic Jews means for their relationship to the church. He argues for a particular form of Messianic Judaism which he calls 'postmissionary'. This is defined as follows: First, postmissionary Messianic Judaism calls upon Jews who believe in Jesus as the Messiah 'to live an observant Jewish life as an act of covenant fidelity rather than missionary expediency' (13). Second, it thus embraces the Jewish people and its religious traditions 'and discovers God and Messiah in the midst of Israel' (14). Third, it 'serves the (Gentile) Christian church by linking it to the physical descendants of Abraham, Isaac, and Jacob, thereby confirming its identity as a multinational extension of the people of Israel' (15). Kinzer believes that this approach allows the Gentile

---

Verlag/Benzinger, 1978–82), 1:335–6; James D.G. Dunn, *Romans* (WBC 38; Dallas: Word, 1988), 1:277; Joseph A. Fitzmyer, *Romans: A New Translation with Introduction and Commentary* (AB 33; New York: Doubleday, 1993), 407–8; sympathetic is C.E.B. Cranfield, *The Epistle to the Romans* (ICC; Edinburgh: T & T Clark, 1975–9), 1:294–5.

[36] Kärkkäinen, *Trinity and Religious Pluralism*, 25.

[37] Mark Kinzer, *Postmissionary Messianic Judaism: Redefining Christian Engagement with the Jewish People* (Grand Rapids: Brazos, 2005). Page numbers in the text refer to Kinzer's book. The following discussion is adapted from Eckhard J. Schnabel, 'The Identity and the Mission of Believers in Jesus Messiah', *Mishkan* 48 (2006): 28–53. Cf. Eckhard J. Schnabel, 'Die Gemeinde des Neuen Bundes in Kontinuität und Diskontinuität zur Gemeinde des Alten Bundes', in *Israel in Geschichte und Gegenwart. Beiträge zur Geschichte Israels und zum jüdisch-christlichen Dialog* (ed. G. Maier; Wuppertal: Brockhaus, 1996), 147–213. For dialogue between myself and Kinzer, see Eckhard J. Schnabel, 'The Identity and the Mission of Believers in Jesus Messiah', *Mishkan* 48 (2006):28–53 and Kinzer, 'Response to Mishkan Reviewers of My Book', *Mishkan* 48 (2006):54–65, especially 60–5 where Kinzer deals with my criticism.

church to participate in Israel's riches without displacing Israel, while 'in the process' providing a second home for Messianic Jews, 'a home away from home' (15).

Confessing Christians will wholeheartedly agree with many of Kinzer's assertions. He rejects the suggestion that the Holocaust and the rebirth of the State of Israel have revelatory significance because 'this way of looking at history and revelation fails to acknowledge the unique position of the central revelatory events recounted in the biblical narrative' (41). He recognizes that the Holocaust was not caused by Christians or in the name of the Christian church but by the Nazis whose 'hatred of Jews was linked to their hatred of all forms of traditional Christianity' (45). His emphasis on the Jewishness of Jesus and on the foundational significance of Israel and of the synagogues for the early church, while not new, is an important reminder for Gentile Christians. The following dialogue with Kinzer focuses on his hermeneutical approach and on his views concerning the Jewish people, the significance of Jesus the Messiah and the church.

Kinzer's hermeneutical approach

While Kinzer recognizes that his exegetical arguments for his description of postmissionary messianic Judaism 'have their limits' since 'other reasonable interpretations exist', he posits that his proposal should be accepted on account of 'several non-textual factors' (27). Kinzer follows Charles Cosgrove who argues that the historical-grammatical approach to biblical interpretation can rule out certain readings of the text, and who also argues that the 'irreducible ambiguity' of the text results in the fact that it is never possible to 'enthrone' one particular reading as the definitive 'meaning originally intended by the author'.[38]

Kinzer suggests that three non-textual factors must be brought into play, factors that 'will dispose us to go in certain directions' (30) in the process of interpretation. 1. The Jewish nature of the New Testament texts. 2. The possibility that 'the divine intention for the text may transcend the limited understanding of those who composed and edited it', which is particularly the case in contexts in which 'practical or functional criteria' are equally important for determining theological truth

---

[38] Charles H. Cosgrove, *Elusive Israel: The Puzzle of Election in Romans* (Louisville: Westminster John Knox, 1997), xi–xii. See Kinzer, *Postmissionary Messianic Judaism*, 27–9.

as 'abstract and theoretical criteria' (33). 3. The relevance of God's actions in postbiblical history, in particular the loss of a visible Jewish presence in the *ekklesia*, the survival and flourishing of the Jewish people and Judaism, the emergence of violent anti-Judaism in the Christian tradition, the Holocaust, the return of the Jewish people to the land of Israel and the emergence of the Messianic Jewish movement.

Kinzer's second and third non-textual factors are especially problematic. The second factor opens the way for prejudiced and subjective interpretations that the interpreter may freely impose on a text whose proposition or implication he finds unacceptable, allowing the claim that it is possible to understand the author better than he understood himself. Kinzer's third factor is equally subjective. If, for example, the interpretation of Romans 9 – 11 is controlled by the 'non-textual' perspective of the history of Christian anti-Semitism, or by the influence of 'the traditional Christian supersessionist theology of Israel and the church' (36), the results of exegetical investigation are fixed before the exegete allows Paul to say what he wants to say. If past history in which Christians persecuted Jews 'for ostensibly Christian reasons' has an inherent theological significance (44) which helps decide exegetical ambiguities, the exegetical results are again predetermined. This is especially true if the question of the theological significance of Jews persecuting Christians – examples from the first century and from the twentieth century are not difficult to find – is left unexplored. As all anti-Jewish interpretations which blame Jesus' death on all Jews (of all times) must be rejected as historically incorrect and as ethically sordid, interpretations which are biased against all Gentile Christians of all times must be rejected as equally prejudiced.

As regards the insistence that theological truth can be discovered by employing 'practical or functional criteria', as Jewish theologians do (33–5), the question must be raised whether the locus of truth is indeed in the biblical text as God's revelation or whether truth is decisively found in the consciousness of the interpreter and in his values and praxis. Kinzer accepts the Jewish rabbinic premise that the written Torah is insufficient and that it requires a living tradition of interpretation and application (236). He argues that authority is vested not in the biblical text alone but 'in the people of Israel as a whole' (242). If there are indeed all kinds of truth – abstract and practical, theological and functional, biblical and historical, Scriptural and national – and if it is the modern interpreter who decides which 'truth' to favour, then there is no truth. Marc-Alain Ouaknin readily admits this when he asserts that the aim of this approach is to silence the voice of the Bible, 'to erase [its] mastery'.[39] Kevin Vanhoozer is correct when he asserts that 'truth is lost when there are no facts, only historically located interpretations.'[40]

Kinzer's 'Pauline syllogism'

Kinzer acknowledges with regard to Galatians 2:11–14 that 'it has usually been assumed that Peter was eating non-kosher food with the Gentile Yeshua-believers in Antioch' (83). He is determined, however, to 'avoid such a conclusion' (84). He wants to preserve the validity of 'the Pauline syllogism' which he has constructed from three passages (72–3). The 'major premise' is derived from 1 Corinthians 7:17–20: 'All those who are circumcised should remain circumcised.' The 'minor premise' is Galatians 5:3: 'All who are circumcised are obligated to observe the Torah.' The 'necessary conclusion' is derived from Galatians 5:11: 'All those who are born as Jews are obligated to live as Jews.' Kinzer argues that Galatians 2:12 does not specify *what* Peter eats, that the people from James criticize Peter not for eating non-kosher food but for eating with Gentile Yeshua-believers and that the phrase 'live like a Gentile' is the language of the critics of Paul and Peter which Paul uses in order to shame Peter into recognizing that his behaviour sent the wrong message that Gentile believers must convert to Judaism (83–5).

Kinzer misses the plain meaning of the text. The meaning of the phrase 'eat with the Gentiles' in Galatians 2:12 is to be established, first, by the context of Paul's reminder to Peter, 'you, although you are a Jew, live like a Gentile and not like a Jew' (Gal. 2:14 [NET]) and, second, by the fact that the law did not prohibit eating in the company of Gentiles – it prohibited eating certain food that the Gentiles were eating. When Peter shared meals with Gentile Christians, he did not observe the food laws of the Torah.[41] The suggestion of James Dunn, whom Kinzer follows, that Peter's 'living like a Gentile' only meant that he practised

---

[39] Marc-Alain Ouaknin, *Le livre brulé. Philosophie du Talmud* (repr. 1986; Paris: Seuil/Lieu commun, 1993), 16; cf. Henri Blocher, 'The Willowbank Declaration and Its Present-Day Relevance – Some Reflections after 12 Years', *Mishkan* 36 (2002): 100–115; 114.

[40] Kevin J. Vanhoozer, 'Lost in Interpretation? Truth, Scripture, and Hermeneutics', *JETS* 48 (2005): 89–114; 91.

[41] Cf. J. Louis Martyn, *Galatians* (AB 33A; New York: Doubleday, 1997), 232, 235; Richard N. Longenecker, *Galatians* (WBC 31; Dallas: Word, 1990), 73, 78.

the Jewish dietary laws, albeit in a less strict manner than the men from James expected him to do,[42] is hardly convincing. Ben Witherington cogently argues that

> if the problem had merely been an insufficient attention to the food law details, the solution would surely have been not 'withdrawal' from table fellowship with Gentiles but more restrictions on or more rigor in the already accepted practice of basically following Jewish dietary laws. Withdrawal is what the men from James precipitated on charges of living like a Gentile. This charge surely meant being non-observant of Kosher requirements.[43]

Kinzer's 'Pauline syllogism' breaks down as his minor premise is wrong. Galatians 5:3 ('Once again I testify to every man who lets himself be circumcised that he is obliged to obey the entire law' [NRSV]) does not stipulate for Jewish Christians that they are obligated to observe the Torah. Rather, it is a warning to Gentile Christians that once they are circumcised they cannot pick and choose which commandments of the law they want to obey.[44]

Kinzer's interpretation of Galatians 5:11 ('But my friends, why am I still being persecuted if I am still preaching circumcision? In that case the offense of the cross has been removed' [NRSV]) does not hold up to exegetical scrutiny: the text does not say, by any stretch of the imagination, that 'Paul urged Jewish Yeshua-believers to live as faithful Jews' and be circumcised (73). Kinzer cites James Dunn when it suits him[45] but fails to interact with Dunn's exegesis when it runs counter to his own viewpoint.[46]

---

[42] James D.G. Dunn, *A Commentary on the Epistle to the Galatians* (BNTC; London: Black, 1993), 127–8.

[43] Ben Witherington, *Grace in Galatia. A Commentary on Paul's Letter to the Galatians* (Edinburgh/Grand Rapids: T. & T. Clark/Eerdmans, 1998), 153 n. 199.

[44] Cf. James D.G. Dunn, *The Theology of Paul's Letter to the Galatians* (New Testament Theology; Cambridge: CUP, 1993), 99: 'to accept circumcision . . . would involve adopting the whole Jewish way of life.'

[45] Kinzer cites Dunn, *Galatians*, 279: 'Paul was accused by the other missionaries of being inconsistent: that although he preached a circumcision-free gospel to the Galatians, he continued to "preach circumcision" among Jews.'

[46] Dunn, *Galatians*, 279 actually formulates the sentence which Kinzer cites as a question, representing the sixth interpretive option for Galatians 5:11a; he does regard this as the most plausible explanation, but points out that the formulation '*preach circumcision*' may be the Jewish Christian traditionalists' elaboration of Paul's position (280). Dunn correctly points out that Paul 'does not stop to discuss or explain his policy regarding circumcision (of Jews like Timothy), or his larger principle of accommodation' (279).

The identity of believers in Jesus the Messiah

Kinzer argues that postmissionary Messianic Judaism 'discovers God and Yeshua within the Jewish people and its tradition' and thus 'feels at home in the Jewish world' (15). He criticizes those Messianic Jews who find their 'primary home in the Christian church' while they 'feel away from home when among the Jewish people who do not accept Yeshua' (15). He posits that postmissionary Messianic Jews can, and should, feel 'at home' among the Jewish people because of 'Yeshua's mysterious presence throughout Jewish history' (16) and because 'Yeshua is still at home with those who are literally his family' (22). Since Israel's covenant endures, 'Yeshua remains the Messiah and Lord for both Jews and Gentiles' (16). This raises a crucial question: is the identity of believers in Jesus Messiah, at its core, controlled by faith in Jesus, the crucified and risen Messiah, or by one's ethnic identity and by the practice of the Jewish traditions?

When we read Paul's epistle to the Romans as an exposition of the identity of both Jews and of Gentiles who believe in Jesus, the authentic identity of the followers of Jesus is fundamentally tied to the *euangelion*, the good news of Jesus the Messiah and Lord in whom God reveals and actualizes his power 'for the salvation of everyone who believes: first for the Jew, then for the Gentile' (Rom. 1:16). In Romans 1:18 – 3:20, Paul establishes the truth that 'everyone' needs salvation because 'all, both Jews and Greeks, are under the power of sin' (3:9 [NRSV]). As regards the Jewish people, Paul argues in Romans 2 that neither the law nor circumcision lead to the righteousness that saves on the day of judgement, now that God provides saving righteousness through faith in Jesus Christ (Rom. 3:21–2).

This argument seems to contradict Kinzer's view that circumcision continues to have 'spiritual significance' for Jews (74). Kinzer does not discuss Romans 2:25–9, which is unfortunate because here it is not possible to argue that a statement such as 'circumcision is nothing' (1 Cor. 7:19) means, simply, that 'circumcision and Jewish identity do not elevate the Jew above the gentile before God' (74). Circumcision is 'nothing' since it does not provide Jewish people with a status that involves a right relationship with God, now that the Messiah has come, atoning for the sins of the people. Jews who obey the stipulations of the Torah cannot say that 'circumcision is nothing' unless circumcision no longer achieves what Jewish tradition expected it to achieve, viz., providing the descendants of Abraham with the covenant righteousness that is required for the status of being the people of God.

This is precisely the argument of Romans 4, a chapter on which Kinzer does not comment.[47] Paul asserts that it was Abraham's faith that was credited to him as righteousness before he was circumcised (Rom. 4:10–11a). He emphasizes that, in the present reality of the messianic era, Abraham has become 'the father of all who believe but have not been circumcised, in order that righteousness might be credited to them' (4:11b). When Gentiles believe in Jesus, the crucified and risen Son of God, they are children of Abraham. On the other hand, Abraham is the 'father of the circumcised' only if and when Jews 'also walk in the footsteps of the faith that our father Abraham had before he was circumcised', i.e. if they believe God's promise, specifically if they 'believe in him who raised Jesus our Lord from the dead, who was handed over to death for our trespasses and was raised for our justification' (4:24–5 [NRSV]).

The enumeration of Israel's historical and spiritual privileges in Romans 9:4–5 indeed reflects Paul's 'consciousness of Israel's continued dignity as God's chosen covenant partner', as Kinzer asserts (124). What Kinzer fails to see is that Paul has demonstrated in Romans 1 – 8 that the Jewish privileges of Romans 9:4–5, which summarize the basic categories of Jewish self-definition, have been transferred to Jesus the Messiah who is the 'representative' of God's people and that these privileges now apply to all those who are 'in Jesus the Messiah' (*en Iēsou Christō*), whether Jews or Gentiles.[48] All people who are believers in Jesus as Messiah and Saviour, whether they are Jews or Greeks, have sonship, glory, the covenants, the law, worship, God's promises and the patriarchs.[49]

For Paul, the identity of the fellowship of believers in Jesus is the 'church of God' (*ekklēsia tou theou* which consists of people 'who are sanctified in Christ Jesus, called to be saints' and who 'call on the name of our Lord Jesus Christ' (1 Cor. 1:2 [NRSV]). This *ekklesia* consists of both Jewish believers and Gentile believers. Most of the problems that Paul discusses in 1 Corinthians were caused by Gentile believers, while the presence of Jewish believers is attested by 1 Corinthians 16:15 and

---

[47] Kinzer also fails to address John 8:31–47 where Jesus asserts that love for the Son whom God has sent defines who are the 'children of Abraham', rather than mere ethnic descent from Abraham.

[48] Cf. N.T. Wright, *The Climax of the Covenant: Christ and the Law in Pauline Theology* (Philadelphia: Fortress, 1992), 237.

[49] Sonship: Rom. 8:14, 23; 9:25–6; Gal. 4:5; Eph. 1:5; glory: Rom. 3:23–4; 5:1; 8:17, 21; cf. 6:4.; the covenants: Rom. 4:16.; the law: Rom. 8:4; worship: Rom. 5:1–2; 12:1–2; God's promises: Rom. 4:16; 15:8; patriarchs: Rom. 4:16.

1:14.[50] In the Corinthian *ekklesia*, Jewish Christians and Gentile Christians worshipped together. The identity of both Jewish and Gentile Christians is bound up with 'the grace that has been given you in the Messiah Jesus' (1:4). Paul declares in 1:22–4:

> Jews demand signs and Greeks desire wisdom, but we proclaim Christ crucified, a stumbling block to Jews and foolishness to Gentiles, but to those who are the called, both Jews and Greeks, Christ the power of God and the wisdom of God [NRSV].

This emphatic statement confirms, on the one hand, that the *ekklesia* which consists of 'those who are called' (1:2) consists of 'both Jews and Greeks'. And it insists, on the other hand, that neither Jews nor Greeks possess the intellectual or spiritual capability of understanding God's revelation in the crucified Messiah and that it is alone the power of God that brings both Jews and Gentiles to faith in Jesus the Saviour (2:1–5). Thus, God is 'the source of your life in Christ Jesus, who became for us wisdom from God, and righteousness and sanctification and redemption' (1:30 [NRSV]). This means that outside a believing relationship to Jesus Messiah, there is no righteousness, no sanctification and no redemption. And this is true for both Gentiles and Jews.[51]

The significance of the cross

Kinzer is unclear on the question whether Jesus' death on the cross exclusively atones for sin. Had Kinzer placed Romans 9 – 11 in the context of Romans 1 – 5, he would not be able to say that Paul hints 'that Israel's temporary unbelief in Yeshua is itself, paradoxically, a participation in Yeshua's vicarious, redemptive suffering' (133). Nor would he be able to assume that, for Paul, the 'mystery' of Romans 11:25–9 'includes non-remnant Israel's present participation in the Messiah whom she does not yet consciously acknowledge' (136). Nor could he state that 'Israel, thus, has a rightful claim upon the Messiah' despite her unbelief (139).

---

[50] Stephanas and his family were 'the first converts in Achaia', and as Paul began his missionary work in the city of Corinth in the synagogue (Acts 18:4), this was a Jewish family. Crispus was the president of the Corinthian synagogue who had become a believer (Acts 18:8).

[51] Note that in 1 Cor. 1:20, Paul mentions both Jewish scribes and Greek-Roman philosophers as representatives of the wisdom of the world; cf. Stephen M. Pogoloff, *Logos and Sophia: The Rhetorical Situation of 1 Corinthians* (SBLDS 134; Atlanta: Scholars, 1992), 153–6.

In Romans 1:18 – 3:20, Paul argues emphatically that status does not provide an escape from the wrath of God – neither for the Gentiles who have been created in God's image (1:18–32), nor the Jews who have the law and circumcision (2:1–29). Despite the advantage which being Jewish conveys (3:1–2), Paul insists on the truth that God does not show favouritism (2:11). What counts in the last judgement is not status but obedience to the will of God. In view of the disobedience of the Gentiles to God's will and in view of Israel's rejection of Jesus Messiah, God insists 'that Jews and Gentiles alike are all under sin' (3:9).

The message that Paul preaches – both in synagogues before Jewish audiences and in market places before Gentile audiences – emphasizes that God's righteousness is now made known 'apart from law' (3:21), i.e. apart from the Torah and its stipulations which regulated the generation and the maintenance of righteousness and holiness. Righteousness and holiness come only 'through faith in Jesus Christ' (3:22). This reality applies 'to all who believe' (3:22) without any distinction between Gentiles and Jews, 'for all have sinned and fall short of the glory of God, and are justified freely by his grace through the redemption that came by Christ Jesus' (3:23–4). In Romans 4, Paul argues that it is not ethnic descent from Abraham which justifies before God, but faith in God's promise as faith in Jesus Christ. Peace with God, access to God's grace, the hope of sharing in God's glory, the presence of God's Spirit, salvation and reconciliation come only through the Lord Jesus Christ (Rom. 5:1–5). Paul's argument in Romans 9 – 11 is thoroughly misunderstood if it is taken to predicate salvation for Israel apart from faith in the crucified Messiah, a view which contradicts Romans 1 – 5.

In Kinzer's postmissionary Messianic Jewish theology, the cross is no longer central. The sub-heading in chapter 3, 'Israel, first and last' (137), suggests that, in Kinzer's theology, ethnic Israel occupies central place. Paul accuses the Jewish Christian teachers who want to impose circumcision and the dietary laws on the Gentile Christians in Galatia of preaching 'a different gospel' (Gal. 1:6–8). To imply that Jews do not need to believe in Jesus, the crucified and risen Messiah from Nazareth, in order to have a right relationship with God empties the cross of its effective reality.

Paul and the ritual stipulations of the Torah

Kinzer believes that Paul 'had a certain amount of halakhic flexibility' as a missionary but that he continued to observe basic Jewish practice such as eating kosher food and observing the Sabbath and the Jewish holidays (88). This suggestion cannot explain 1 Corinthians 9:21 [NRSV]: 'To those outside the law I became as one outside the law (though I am not free from God's law but am under Christ's law) so that I might win those outside the law.' If a Jewish Christian missionary seeks to win Gentiles for faith in Jesus Christ and insists on keeping the Jewish dietary laws and Sabbath observance, there are not many areas where he would actually 'become as one outside the law'. The halakhic flexibility that Kinzer seems to envisage (but does not specify) would be so minimal that it is difficult to see why Paul uses his 'flexible' behaviour as an argument to move Gentile believers in Corinth *not* to insist on their perceived rights.

Kinzer's view cannot explain Paul's reputation both in Judea and in Asia Minor. Luke relates that when Paul arrives in Jerusalem, James and the elders tell Paul:

> You see, brother, how many thousands of believers there are among the Jews, and they are all zealous for the law. They have been told about you that you teach all the Jews living among the Gentiles to forsake Moses, and that you tell them not to circumcise their children or observe the customs (Acts 21:20–21 [NRSV]).

Jews from Asia who recognize Paul in the temple shout:

> Fellow Israelites, help! This is the man who is teaching everyone everywhere against our people, our law, and this place; more than that, he has actually brought Greeks into the temple and has defiled this holy place (21:28 [NRSV]).

If Paul had told Jewish people who had come to believe in Jesus as the Messiah that they should continue to follow the ritual stipulations of the Torah, and if he personally had obeyed the dietary and Sabbath laws, this reputation would have no basis in reality. Statements such as Romans 14:3–4, 5–6, 14, 17 and Colossians 2:16–17 help explain his reputation as a travelling missionary, a reputation which was the cause for his arrest in Jerusalem. The reason why Paul kept coming back to the synagogues, despite being punished repeatedly with the forty lashes minus one (2 Cor. 11:24), was not the fact that 'Paul himself continued to be committed to Judaism and the Jewish community', as Kinzer suggests (164), but the fact that Paul continued to preach in synagogues the news that the crucified and risen Jesus is the Messiah.

The unity of the church

Kinzer's 'bilateral ecclesiology' abandons the unity of the local community of believers. It is disconcerting that Kinzer does not discuss 1 Corinthians 1 – 4, a foundational text for understanding the nature of the church. As the church in Corinth is composed of both Jewish and Gentile believers, Paul's insistence that divisions in the church contradict the gospel of the crucified and risen Messiah Jesus is a fundamental proposition. Paul does not tolerate believers who appeal for their identity to Peter or to Apollos or to himself. When Paul emphasizes the unity of the church in 1 Corinthians 12 in the context of a discussion of the gifts of the Holy Spirit, he presupposes that all believers in Jesus Christ meet together as one body in the local assembly of believers. If the gifts of God's Spirit cannot be allowed to create divisions, then different ethnic backgrounds cannot be allowed to be the basis for disunity either.

Kinzer's case for a 'bilateral ecclesiology' (160–5) is seriously flawed. He disputes what he acknowledges is the 'common view' that

> Paul considered a mixed community of Jews and Gentiles to be the ideal expression of the ekklesia in any given location, and sought to found such communities. In these groups, Jewish members would be permitted to maintain Jewish practice but only insofar as such practice did not conflict with unrestricted community relationships with their Gentile brothers and sisters (160–1).[52]

Kinzer's treatment of Romans 14 – 15 is problematic. He follows Mark Nanos who argues that the 'weak' are not Jewish Christians who insist on keeping the dietary laws, but non-Christian Jews.[53] Considering Paul's repeated use of the term 'brother' (14:10, 13, 15, 21), which is used by Paul to designate fellow Christians 130 times,[54] this interpreta-

---

[52] Kinzer refers to Alan F. Segal, *Paul the Convert: The Apostolate and Apostasy of Saul the Pharisee* (New Haven: Yale University Press, 1990), 265; E.P. Sanders, *Paul, the Law, and the Jewish People* (Philadelphia: Fortress, 1983), 177–8.

[53] Mark D. Nanos, *The Mystery of Romans: The Jewish Context of Paul's Letter* (Minneapolis: Fortress, 1996), 85–165.

[54] Cf. H. von Soden, 'αδελθος, in *Theological Dictionary of the New Testament* (eds. Gerhard Kittel and Gerhard Friedrich; Grand Rapids: Eerdmans, 1964–76), 1:145. The one exception is Rom. 9:3, where the context makes it unambiguously clear that Paul uses the term *adelphos* to refer to his Jewish compatriots.

tion is unconvincing.[55] Kinzer accuses scholars who refuse to adopt Nanos' interpretation (76) of being hostage to a certain view of 'Paul and Yeshua-faith in general'. Kinzer states that 'the reading of Romans 14 – 15 by Mark Nanos conforms to the Pauline syllogism' (76). This suggests that it is Kinzer who works with preconceived ideas of what Paul can and cannot say. What James Dunn says concerning the position of 'the more traditionalist Christian Jews' in Paul's time applies to Kinzer as well: 'The danger he clearly saw was that they were letting their own convictions shape their idea of God instead of vice versa.'[56]

Kinzer fails to understand Ephesians 2:14–16:

> For he is our peace; in his flesh he has made both groups into one and has broken down the dividing wall, that is, the hostility between us. He has abolished the law with its commandments and ordinances, that he might create in himself one new humanity in place of the two, thus making peace, and might reconcile both groups to God in one body through the cross, thus putting to death that hostility through it [NRSV].

Kinzer believes that Markus Barth has effectively challenged what he calls the 'traditional reading' of this passage, arguing that Barth shows that 'the *categories* of Jew and Gentile are not transcended but only the hostility between the two' (167). Kinzer has seriously misunderstood the thrust of Barth's interpretation[57] who interprets the 'law' that is abolished according to 2:15 as the law which 'has created and demonstrated a separation of the Jews from the Gentiles',[58] i.e. 'the formerly divisive effect of the law is terminated'. Barth asserts:

> [T]he law has lost its validity as a barrier between insiders and outsiders and as a sentence of death . . . The obnoxious use made of the law by self-righteous braggers of Jewish origin and by their imitators among the Gentiles is declared invalid by the same stroke.

---

[55] Note the arguments against Nanos' interpretation in Dunn, *Theology of Paul*, 684 with n. 59; Thomas R. Schreiner, *Romans* (BECNT 6; Grand Rapids: Baker, 1998), 707 n. 8, who further refers to 1 Cor. 8:11, 12, 13 for the term 'brothers' referring to the 'weak'.

[56] Dunn, *Theology of Paul*, 687.

[57] For Kinzer's interaction with Markus Barth, see 167–70. He extracts sentences from Barth's commentary that seem to support his view – statements that assert (correctly) the salvation-historical role of Israel – and omits statements that support the 'traditional' interpretation of Ephesians 2:14–16. Barth does not envision the kind of 'bilateral ecclesiology' that Kinzer argues for.

[58] Markus Barth, *Ephesians* (AB 34; New York: Doubleday, 1974), 1:290; the following quotations ibid. 306, 307.

Barth summarizes:

> [I]n Ephesians the community of Jews and Gentiles created by the
> Messiah is described as a temple, not a tent. Solidly founded and expect-
> ed to stand as long as the world exists, neither the saints nor God are
> transient guests in it. Because God will 'dwell' in his house, the saints are
> at home in the same house.[59]

And these 'saints' are the believers in the crucified and risen Messiah
Jesus, both Jewish believers and Gentile believers.

When Paul adds in Ephesians 2:18–19: 'for through him both of us
have access in one Spirit to the Father. So then you are no longer
strangers and aliens, but you are citizens with the saints and also members of the household of God' [NRSV], he clearly assumes a local assembly in which Gentile Christians, together with Jewish Christians,
worship the one true God on account of Jesus' death on the cross (2:16).
This holds true whether the letter was sent as a circular letter to a
group of churches or to a particular church; it would have been read to
a particular local congregation whose members would have related
Paul's teaching to their community in which Jewish believers and
Gentile believers worshipped together. There is no room here for an
apartheid of Jewish Christians with 'full membership' and Gentile
Christians with less than full membership. They are *together* members
of the household of God. Paul emphasizes, in Ephesians 4:3, the need
for unity within the Christian community, exhorting the believers to
make 'every effort to maintain the unity of the Spirit in the bond of
peace'.

There is no indication in the New Testament for the view that the
Jewish Christians met separately from Gentile Christians. Paul's statement in Romans 15:5–9 unambiguously argues for a local community
of believers in Jesus in which Jewish Christians and Gentile Christians
live together:

> May the God of steadfastness and encouragement grant you to live in
> harmony with one another, in accordance with Christ Jesus, so that
> together you may with one voice glorify the God and Father of our Lord
> Jesus Christ. Welcome one another, therefore, just as Christ has wel-
> comed you, for the glory of God. For I tell you that Christ has become a
> servant of the circumcised on behalf of the truth of God in order that he

---

[59] Markus Barth, *Ephesians*, 1:322.

might confirm the promises given to the patriarchs, and in order that the Gentiles might glorify God for his mercy [NRSV].

Jewish evangelism

Kinzer rejects missionary outreach of believers in Jesus the Messiah to the Jewish people. Kinzer's view of 'mission' is strange, to say the least. He suggests that 'postmissionary Messianic Judaism' has an 'inner mission' which consists of 'bearing witness to Yeshua's presence within the Jewish people' and an 'outer mission' which is directed to the Gentile church 'before whom it testifies to God's enduring love for the family chosen in the beginning to be God's covenant partner' (15). This 'inner mission' is understood by Kinzer in terms of the 'unveiling of the messianic mystery underlying Jewish historical existence and religious tradition' throughout Jewish history and not 'in a traditional missionary sense, as the conveying of a saving message – derived from an external source – that is discontinuous with the religious tradition of postbiblical Judaism' (301).

However, the 'traditional sense' of 'mission' which Kinzer rejects is the 'tradition' and praxis of Jesus and the apostles. For Kinzer, followers of Jesus are no longer 'fishers of people' (Mark 1:17) but fish who swim among the other fish. For Kinzer, Jewish Christians do not preach as Peter preached on Pentecost: 'Repent, and be baptized every one of you in the name of Jesus Messiah so that your sins may be forgiven; and you will receive the gift of the Holy Spirit' (Acts 2:38 [NRSV revised]). It seems that, for Kinzer, Jewish Christians do not even seek to lead Gentiles to saving faith in Jesus Messiah. Kinzer advises his readers *not* to do what Paul and the other (Jewish) apostles did as 'ambassadors' of Jesus Messiah – they were conscious of their calling that God presented through them an appeal to Jews and Gentiles alike, imploring them on behalf of Jesus Christ, 'Be reconciled to God', because they were convinced that 'God made him who had no sin to be sin for us, so that in him we might become the righteousness of God' (2 Cor. 5:20–21). Kinzer's 'postmissionary' believers do not go anywhere, they stay where they are; they do not preach the good news of the crucified and risen Jesus, the Messiah, Saviour and Lord, rather they share views of a mysterious presence in Jewish history; they do not call people to repentance, they dialogue; they do not make disciples, they are friendly associates. They are not ambassadors, they are home secretaries.

Kinzer's book is on ecclesiology, not on christology or on soteriology. However, New Testament ecclesiology without a consideration of Jesus' death on the cross and of his resurrection is meaningless. The last sentence of Kinzer's book is revealing: 'The church must come home to Israel, if it would again breathe freely and deeply.'[60] Jesus called Israel, the Jewish people of the first century, 'home' to God who forgives the sinner who returns from the pigsty with ritual impurity (Luke 15:11–32). Paul called both pagans and Jews 'home' to authentic faith in Jesus Messiah, Saviour and Lord. Kinzer's 'postmissionary Messianic Judaism' is neither missionary nor messianic.

---

[60] Kinzer, *Postmissionary Messianic Judaism*, 310.

14

Available Resources and Current Practices in Jewish Evangelism

Tuvya Zaretsky

Message and Methods

This chapter aims to increase knowledge of some practical resources and practices that are currently employed in Jewish evangelism. While it will provide only a brief survey, it will hopefully be a useful introduction to this field of ministry.

We begin with the message at the heart of Jewish evangelism. The gospel is that Messiah *Yeshua* (Jesus) died for our sins according to the Scriptures, that he was buried and then raised on the third day according to the Scriptures.[1] In this message alone is the power of God for salvation available to everyone who believes, to the Jewish people and also to the other nations.[2]

The process of Jewish mission work begins with making that message available to Jewish hearers by utilizing culturally appropriate means. Whatever the strategy now employed to broadcast the gospel, mission workers will typically follow through by making personal visits with Jewish hearers who are open to the message. They seek to engage enquirers' understanding, answer their objections and encourage them to progress beyond learned cultural and sociological barriers. Many will use the inductive Bible study method to discover spiritual truth. Old and New Testament Scriptures are essential to lead Jewish

---

[1] 1 Cor. 15:3–4.
[2] Rom. 1:16; Acts 4:12.

seekers towards finding faith in the Messiah. The discipleship process continues until the new Jewish believer in Jesus is rooted and growing in a local congregation of Christ followers.

The two sections of this chapter will survey some available resources and then practices that are currently employed in Jewish evangelism. The resource section features networking agencies and support services for missions and missionaries. The current practices in Jewish missions are grouped into direct outreach methods, some of the appropriate social structures for introducing the gospel and finally methods from Diaspora missiology. We begin with some of the available resources in support of efforts to reach Jewish people with the gospel of Christ.

Resources

We begin with a survey of some of the networking agencies for Jewish missions and missionaries. Four different types of support services follow. First, we list academic agencies that provide training for mission workers or pastors in Jewish evangelism. Second, we review available literature resources including published statements, journals, periodicals and a few online resources regarding the history of Jewish missions. Third, we list briefly publishers who provide resource materials for those engaged in Jewish evangelism. Last, we give a brief description of some media resources.

Mission networks

The Lausanne Consultation on Jewish Evangelism (LCJE)

The Lausanne Consultation on Jewish Evangelism (LCJE) exists for the purpose of networking Jewish evangelism. It is not an organization that does Jewish evangelism. It is a network of mission agencies, individual missionaries and interested people who come together to consider how they might more effectively reach Jewish people with the gospel of Jesus Christ.

The LCJE originated as a task force on 'reaching Jews' from a gathering in Pattaya, Thailand held in 1980 which was sponsored by the Lausanne Committee for World Evangelism (LCWE). Today the network membership comprises agencies, missiologists, mission workers and executives, scholars, authors, congregations and denominational representatives who are engaged in Jewish evangelism.

Membership in the Lausanne Consultation on Jewish Evangelism is by application online at www.lcje.net. Organizations may apply for *Society Membership*, of which there are now twenty-three, or individuals can register as *Individual Members*, of which there are about 100. Three requirements are necessary for acceptance:

- Agreement in principle with the Lausanne Covenant
- Agreement with the aims of the LCJE that are also listed on the website
- Payment of required membership dues

The Lausanne Consultation on Jewish Evangelism is the only global organization in existence today that brings people together for the purpose of networking Jewish evangelism. The stated functions are to:

- Share information and resources
- Study current trends in the field of Jewish evangelism
- Stimulate thinking on theological and missiological issues
- Strategize globally so more Jewish people may hear and consider the gospel of Jesus
- Organize consultations that are useful for those engaged in Jewish evangelism

An elected International Coordinating Committee (ICC) does the business of the network. The ICC is charged with planning and coordinating international conferences every three to four years. Conference papers are published and available on the LCJE website. The ninth international LCJE conference is planned for 2011. The ICC has also coordinated CEO conferences for affiliated LCJE mission leaders on three occasions, 2001, 2005 and 2009.

Area coordinators are elected every four years to represent seven regional LCJE networks. These volunteers provide periodic reports of activities within their networks for the international membership. Member agencies and area coordinators are listed on the LCJE network website.

LCWE strategic interest committees

The LCJE connects with the international Lausanne Committee on World Evangelism (LCWE) through the *Strategic Interest Committee on Jewish Evangelism*. It is one of several global issues that now fit within the scope of the Lausanne movement. The LCWE website at www.lausanne.org lists 'Jewish evangelism' as a live link among their eighteen global issues.

The International Messianic Jewish Alliance

The International Messianic Jewish Alliance (IMJA) is a fellowship of Jewish people who believe in Jesus. It is not a mission network, but its membership serves to connect many who are engaged in Jewish evangelism. The IMJA was originally founded in 1866 as the Hebrew Christian Alliance and Prayer Union of Great Britain. Forty years later, similar alliances were established among Jewish believers in other parts of the world. In 1925, the International Hebrew Christian Alliance was formed to network Jewish believers in Jesus around the world.

The purpose of the International Messianic Jewish Alliance is 'To care for the spiritual and material welfare of all Jewish believers and to maintain within the Jewish people a witness to Yeshua the Messiah.'[3] The International Messianic Jewish Alliance currently has offices in the United States.[4]

Other related networks

Other related networks engage in various blends of direct evangelism and social ministries to the Jewish people. Rich Robinson identified structures that can be sympathetic to Jewish mission agencies while not necessarily identified as evangelistic outreach ministries.[5] They include messianic congregational networks, voluntary associations, umbrella organizations, educational institutes and Philo-Semitic agencies.

Support services

Academic

The following is a sample of academic programmes that are providing practical preparation or degrees for vocational workers in the field of Jewish evangelism. It includes degree and non-degree programmes.

---

[3] Homepage www.imja.com.
[4] IMJA, 72–877 Dinah Shore Drive, Suite 103–141, Rancho Mirage, CA 92270; Phone (760) 837–0372; e-mail address pliberman@dc.rr.com.
[5] Rich Robinson (General Editor), Naomi Rose Rothstein (Contributing Editor), *The Messianic Movement: A Field Guide for Evangelical Christians* (San Francisco: Purple Pomegranate Productions, 2005), 21–85.

Master of Arts in Specialized Ministry – Jewish Ministry Track
Western Seminary offers the unique Master of Arts in Specialized
Ministry – Jewish Track. It is tailored for students who are currently
serving in or preparing for ministry in Jewish Missions. Courses are
offered on a modular format, allowing students to pursue the degree
while continuing in missionary service on the field. Half the courses
can be taken online through Western Seminary's *Center for Life Long
Learning.* The remainder are taken as a cluster of residential summer
intensives in Portland, Oregon.

The MA Specialization in Jewish Ministry is a partnership between
Western Seminary and the Jews for Jesus ministry. It was developed
from lessons gleaned from a previous MA Missiology programme at
another seminary. The degree requires sixty credit hours. Graduate cer-
tificates and a diploma in Jewish Ministry Specialization are also available. See http://www.westernseminary.edu/academicprograms/
pdx/masm_jewishministry.htm.

Jewish Studies
Moody Bible Institute in Chicago offers a Jewish Studies major under
the division of World Missions and Evangelism. This is the oldest programme in America preparing workers for the field of Jewish missions.
The Jewish Studies specialization is a minor in the Bachelor of Arts curriculum requiring 120 hours for graduation. See their website at
www.moody.edu.

The Pasche Institute of Jewish Studies is a ministry of Criswell
College in Dallas, Texas. A Bachelor of Arts in Biblical Studies with a
Jewish Studies minor along with a Master of Arts in Jewish Studies
(thirty-six hours) and a Master of Divinity degree with Jewish Studies
concentration. Information is available at http://pascheinstitute.org.

All Nations Christian College in the United Kingdom offers a mod-
ule on Jewish Studies. It offers practical training in Jewish witness. The
degree is a Bachelor in Biblical and Intercultural Studies –
Concentration on Jewish Studies. See their website at www.allna-
tions.ac.uk under the 'studying' tab.

Messianic Jewish Studies
The Kings College and Seminary offer Bachelor and Master level
degrees in Theology and Practical Theology with Concentration in
Messianic Jewish Studies. A graduate certificate and diploma are also
offered. The programme is a partnership between the Kings College
and Seminary associated with Church on the Way in Southern

California and Jewish Voice Ministry in Arizona. See their website at http://thekingsjewishvoice.org/index.html.

Talbot Seminary in Southern California offers a Master of Divinity degree, Emphasis in Messianic Jewish Studies in partnership with Chosen People Ministries at the Charles L. Feinberg Center in New York City. The degree programme requires ninety-eight units for graduation. It provides training for Jewish mission ministry and for messianic congregational leadership. See www.talbot.edu/academics/programs/mdiv/messianic_jewish.cfm. A pdf version of programme information and curriculum chart are available online.

Master of Divinity with Concentration in Messianic Judaism
Denver Seminary offers a Master of Divinity degree with concentration in Messianic Judaism. It is a partnership with messianic congregational leaders, Jeffrey Feinberg, Chaim Urbach and apologetics scholar Michael L. Brown. The ninety-eight units required for the MDiv with concentration in Messianic Judaism is appropriate for those who are going into messianic congregational leadership with attention to mission evangelism. See their website at www.denverseminary.edu/become-a-student/master-of-divinity-degree/mdiv-degree-with-a-concentration-in-messianic-judaism.

Non-Degree Programmes
The Caspari Center offers programmes and exists to support Jewish believers in Jesus through education and research. Training programmes are offered for pastors, scholars and church workers. It offers to raise awareness of Jewish believers in Jesus and to provide unique programming to encourage and support messianic congregations and community particularly in Israel.

Their scholars publish materials that educate the body of Christ internationally and strengthen the growing movement of Jewish believers in Jesus Christ. They sponsor a research team that is publishing the *History of Jewish Believers in Jesus*. Volume 1 was released in 2007 covering the early centuries corresponding to the first 500 years of church history. See their website at www.caspari.com.

The Institute of Diaspora Studies (IDS) was formed at Western Seminary in 2007 as a joint effort of researchers and practitioners seeking to understand and better minister to people of Diaspora. The mission of the programme is to investigate effective communication of the gospel among people of Diaspora through their own networks and to regions beyond. The IDS is sponsored through Western Seminary. No degree is currently being offered. Courses are provided through the Doctor of Missiology programme under the division of Intercultural Studies. Focus of the programme has initially been directed on Jewish, Chinese and Filipino people. See their website at www.westernseminary.edu/diaspora.

Literature

Published statements, journals, periodicals and newsletters are available to serve agencies and workers in the Jewish mission field. There are also resources for the study of Jewish mission history.

The Willowbank Declaration on the Christian Gospel and the Jewish People is a significant statement in the field of Jewish evangelism.[6] The Declaration was adopted in 1989 by all participants at the Consultation on the Gospel and the Jewish People held in Willowbank, Bermuda, as a task force meeting under the sponsorship of the World Evangelical Fellowship. Kenneth A. Meyers referred to it as a 'watershed document' expressing evangelical support of Jewish evangelism and current evangelical relations with the Jewish people.[7]

The Lausanne Consultation on Jewish Evangelism produces a quarterly *Bulletin*. It provides regional reports of network activities, book reviews, member-produced articles, media updates and theological papers. Subscriptions and past issues are available at www.lcje.net/bulletin.html.

The Lausanne Committee for World Evangelism has produced the series of *Lausanne Occasional Papers* (LOPs). The first of two specifically addressing the subject of Jewish evangelism was produced in 1980.[8] The most recent LOP was published in 2005 as a product of the Lausanne Forum in Pattaya, Thailand. It was a joint effort of Issue Group 31 on Jewish evangelism. Lausanne Occasional Paper No. 60, 'Jewish Evangelism: A Call to the Church' is available from the LCJE network in soft copy and PDF versions are freely available at www.lausanne.org/documents/2004forum/LOP60_IG31.pdf.

Mishkan is an international journal and a unique forum on the Christian gospel and the Jewish people. It is published twice yearly by the Pasche Institute of Jewish Studies in cooperation with Caspari

---

[6] The full text is available online at www.lcje.net/willowbank.html.

[7] Kenneth A. Myers, 'Adjusting Theology in the Shadow of Auschwitz' in *Christianity Today* (8 October 1990) in the 'CT Classic: Do Jews Really Need Jesus to be Saved' by Kenneth A. Myers, posted 1 August 2002 at www.christianitytoday.com/ ct/2002/augustweb-only/8-12-52.0.html.

[8] *No. 7 Thailand Report – Christian Witness to Jewish People*, LCWE, June 1980.

Center. Each issue thematically explores significant issues in the field of Jewish evangelism, Jewish–Christian relations and Messianic Jewish identity. The articles are written at a professional level, providing excellent research and lively dialogue around theory and practice. Back issues and subscriptions are online at www.mishkanstore.org/store.

Kesher: A Journal of Messianic Judaism is available as an online journal and in print form. It publishes two issues a year through The Union of Messianic Jewish Congregations (UMJC). The Spring/Summer 2008, Issue 22, was a double issue on soteriology. Information and subscriptions are available at www.kesherjournal.com.

The Messianic Times is an online and print periodical of information that serves the international messianic community. It provides a broad perspective on issues that are relevant to the international community of Jewish believers. It embraces the Jewish missions, highlights social services and provides an up-to-date list of messianic congregations and 'Churches, Fellowships and Organizations with a Love for Israel'. Both subscriptions and information are available online at http://messianictimes.com.

Jewish mission agencies typically publish one or more newsletters for believers and seekers. Most of the missions now host websites and a few also publish web-zines.

The Messianic Movement: A Field Guide for Evangelical Christians is a valuable resource with a self-explanatory name. The modern movement of Jewish believers in Jesus has developed some unique perspectives, its own terminology and nuanced understandings about Israel, the church and the remnant of Jewish believers in Jesus. Rich Robinson authored this helpful paperback that is available through Jews for Jesus.[9]

Jewish mission history resources are helpful collections for thinking about contemporary mission strategy and methods. One text and two online resources are worth noting. Jewish Israeli scholar and not a follower of Jesus, Yaakov Ariel, wrote *Evangelizing the Chosen People: Mission to the Jews in America, 1880–2000*.[10] His history is limited to the American scene, but it is a fine objective perspective of the forces that shaped the messianic movement in America.

---

[9] See store.jewsforjesus.org/ppp/product.php?prodid=843.
[10] Yaakov Ariel, *Evangelizing the Chosen People: Mission to the Jews in America, 1880–2000* (Chapel Hill: University of North Carolina Press. 2000), 367.

The Online Jewish Missions History Project is a collection of ninety documents that is a collaborative effort of members within the LCJE.[11] Scholars may initiate searches based on titles, authors, missionary subjects, organizations, creation dates, subjects and languages. Among the online resources are books, conference papers, encyclopaedia articles, newspaper articles and photographs. This free resource is found at www.lcje.net – click the 'History Project' button.

Worldcat.org is another online resource for Jewish history study. The site provides a powerful search engine for Jewish mission history. Go to www.worldcat.org, click on the 'Advanced Search' link and type in the 'Subject' line 'missions to Jews history'.

Publishers

Besides the larger publishing houses like Paternoster, Baker Book House and Kregel, three publishers in Israel and two in America specifically serve the messianic movement and mission societies.

Keren Ahvah Meshihit (KAM) is a non-profit society registered in the State of Israel.[12] It publishes and distributes literature for evangelism and spiritual edification including Bibles through *Yanetz Publishing Ltd.* KAM is staffed by Israeli citizens who produce and distribute over 170 titles supporting Jewish evangelism, discipleship and spiritual growth. It has also been republishing timeless works authored by Messianic Jews and Gentile Christian authors of the nineteenth and early twentieth centuries. Literature is published in Hebrew, English and Russian as is their website at www.kerenahvah.org. Click on 'Library' to find all the book titles available by subject in each of the published languages.

Ha-Gefen Publishing, also based in Israel, is an outgrowth of the church mission society known as Christian Witness to Israel (CWI). In the early twentieth century, CWI opened the Ha-Gefen Christian bookshop in Haifa as a gospel literature outreach centre, and from that came Ha-Gefen Publishing. Today, they publish material primarily in Hebrew for children and youth, commentaries, evangelism, discipleship, spiritual growth and formation. Books and CDs, videos and music are available in Hebrew, Russian and English. The newest Ha-Gefen materials are available on their home page and their catalogue provides a listing of all the titles and resources available online at www.ha-gefen.org.il/len/index.php?sid=613.

---

[11] Rich Robinson, 'Digital Jewish Mission History Project Moves to LJCE', *LCJE Bulletin* 74 (Nov. 2003).

[12] Hebrew: 'Messianic Brotherhood Fund'.

An added useful feature under 'Links' and then 'Resource Links' are connections to the *Digital Jewish Missions History Project*, mentioned earlier, and the *Library Messianica* that is described as a collection of historical messianic writings with gospel commentaries from a Jewish perspective. They also feature a link to the *Messianic Literary Corner*, a self-described 'Independent Messianic Jewish (Hebrew Christian) ministry offering grace oriented teaching, prophecy studies, biblically related science and archaeology topics, messianic poetry, Judaica and more'.

The Bible Society in Israel dates to the early nineteenth century. They currently operate from three locations – Jerusalem, Tel Aviv and Nazareth. Its roots are with the British and Foreign Bible Society (BFBS) and later jointly with the American Bible Society (ABS). It continues to serve the scriptural needs of missions, churches and congregations in Israel by translating, publishing and distributing the Bible throughout the land of Israel among Jewish and Arab peoples. They publish an online catalogue, accessible at www.biblesocietyinisrael.com.

Purple Pomegranate Productions (PPP) in the United States is a division of the Jews for Jesus ministry. PPP serves as a publishing house and distribution centre for books, music, videos and Judaica items. Their online catalogue features resources to assist Christian witness to Jewish people by providing tools for direct evangelism and resources to increase understanding of Jewish culture and the roots of Christian faith. Their catalogue is at http://store.jewsforjesus.org.

Messianic Jewish Publishers is a division of Lederer/Messianic Jewish Communications also in the USA. In 1941, a Jewish Christian named Henry Einspruch published *The Yiddish New Testament* as an evangelistic tool to reach Jews of Europe with the gospel in the midst of the Holocaust. From that single publication came the founding of a publishing ministry based in the United States that continues to print and distribute books, videos, CDs, educational computer software and Judaica. They provide evangelistic resources for Jewish evangelism and Jewish background information of the New Testament. Their website features a *Messianic Jewish 'Web Store'* and a catalogue at www.messianicjewish.net.

Media

A new genre called Jewish gospel music was first heard in the early 1970s. Since then the volume of media resources that are available for evangelistic ministry to Jewish people has grown rapidly. International productions of messianic music and videos have dramatically increased in styles and in subject matter over the last two decades.

Since the late 1980s, there has been an increase in musical expressions of Jewish Christian or Messianic Jewish music for praise, worship and liturgy. Sufficient examples can be found on any of the previous mentioned publication websites and online through most of the missions. American groups were producing the first Jewish gospel music in the early 1970s. However, indigenous expressions of messianic music culture and language are now being produced in almost every country where Messianic Jews are found today including new original messianic praise music from Israel in Hebrew.

We can also find a small but growing volume of training materials on video to prepare mission workers and others who are interested in learning about direct evangelistic outreach to Jewish people. Many of the Jewish missions and congregations now produce and feature a small library of Jewish testimonies by those who have come to faith in Jesus. These audio and video files are available online and through catalogues in relevant languages.

The 'You Tube' generation is quick to notice resources that are available on international media outlets and are available for evangelistic purposes. When an Israeli Jewish believer in Jesus was interviewed live on a secular and national morning talk show in Israel, 'HaOlam HaBoker' (Hebrew: 'The World This Morning'), it was posted on You Tube. The testimony has been circulated widely and featured as a link by evangelistic and congregational ministries. It can be found with English subtitles at www.youtube.com/watch?v=DKzZgNlh4sM.

Various evangelistic ministries and congregations have utilized radio and television, both on secular and Christian stations, to produce evangelistic materials as regular features. The list is too numerous to attempt a compendium here, but most are easily found in local settings online and through mission or congregational newsletters where Jewish population is found in significant numbers. In the next section, we will see how media advertising has been used for evangelistic purposes too.

One more resource for Jewish evangelism missiological planning is found online from the *Jewish People Policy Planning Institute*. Jewish community professionals, who plan programming and distribution of Jewish Federation resources, annually prepare excellent reports, analysis and demographic information about world Jewry.

This agency has met each year since 2004 and published preliminary findings and then an annual report in PDF format. The reports are valuable for missiological study. Charts provide information like world Jewish population data and intermarriage rates. They are found online through the JPPPI sites for the years 2004–2008 at www.jpppi.org.il.

Having provided a sample of some resources that are available for Jewish evangelism ministry, we now turn our attention to listing some contemporary practices in the field.

Practices

The (LCJE) *Bulletin* provides some of the best reports of current Jewish evangelism practices. The following information was previously prepared for an article published in the *LCJE Bulletin*.[13] It includes additional material from mission newsletters, reports and further updates in the *Bulletin*.[14] Three categories are identified for summarizing some current evangelistic practices: outreach practices, social structures utilized for evangelism and examples from Diaspora missiology.

Outreach practices

Events: liturgical and non-liturgical

Holy Days on the Jewish calendar present culturally appropriate opportunities for evangelistic outreach to Jewish populations. Jewish missions and messianic congregations have effectively offered liturgical services around the High Holy Days of Rosh Hashanah and Yom Kippur. In many cases, missions and congregations cooperate to provide High Holy Day services with the intention of outreach evangelism. The Jewish community is invited through public notice on street banners, newspaper advertisements and organizational newsletters along with personal invitations.[15] Jewish seekers attend those events and some of them return in subsequent years to give testimony of their journey to faith in the Messiah Jesus. Yom Kippur lends itself easily to discussion of the forgiveness of sin through the blood atonement of Jesus, messianic Suffering Servant.

---

[13] 'Jewish Diaspora Missiology', *LCJE Bulletin* 91 (February 2008).
[14] *LCJE Bulletin* 92 (May 2008).
[15] Congregation Adat Y'shua HaAdon, Chosen People Ministries and Jews for Jesus cooperate annually for High Holy Day services in Los Angeles County.

Passover banquets are also appropriate cultural occasions through which to present the gospel to Jewish seekers. Passover celebrations are hosted in homes. Just as often they are held as banquets and are conducted by messianic congregations or mission agencies; occasionally they are held as cooperative services with local churches. The gospel is easily presented in the context of the redemption story, salvation through the blood of the Lamb and appropriate liturgical elements of a traditional Passover *Seder*.

Often at such liturgical programmes, and at other public outreach events, personal testimonies by Jews who have come to faith in Jesus are commonly featured. An interesting report came from a Passover banquet that was hosted by a messianic congregation in Cape Town, South Africa, in spring 2008. A German Christian reportedly confessed in prayer 'the sins of his people against the Jewish people'. The Messianic Jewish leader of the Seder, representing the congregation, then publicly embraced his German brother and prayed thanks to God for the forgiveness that they share together in Jesus. The report went on to note that a Jewish unbeliever, a guest at the event, was so moved by the power of the gospel in the reconciliation between a Jew and a German, that she 'received Messiah Yeshua into her life'.[16]

Jewish mission agencies and congregations have made wonderful use of creative arts to communicate the gospel among Jewish people. Music concerts and festivals have been produced in major Jewish population centres of the world. Jewish audiences have been attracted to events through distribution of handbills, publicity on radio and television, posters and billboards, organizational publications and advertisements and by word-of-mouth personal invitation. The actual events are presented in churches, messianic congregations, public parks and in secular public cultural venues. Music is a cultural and linguistic tool that is appropriate to reach segments of world Jewry in each region. Concerts often feature a testimony by a Messianic Jew regarding their journey to faith in Jesus.

Music, drama and art have all been used to attract Jewish audiences, communicating spiritual truth or just provoking spiritual discussion. One ministry has effectively used an art show of original pieces with lectures on the work of renowned Jewish artist Marc Chagall as a basis for discussing the gospel.

---

[16] Report by Cecilia Burger, LCJE coordinator for South Africa, *LCJE Bulletin* 92 (May 2008): 3.

Apologetic forums

Today, debates, evangelistic ads and specialized literature have been used to present the gospel among Jewish people in apologetic forms and forums. Jewish-Christian disputations had a deleterious effect on Christian evangelism in the thirteenth century.[17] However, in recent years, respectful discussions and even debates have been conducted successfully around differing perspectives on Jesus and Jewish people.

One of the more successful pairings has been between Orthodox Rabbi Shmuley Boteach and Messianic Jewish scholar Dr. Michael L. Brown. Debates have been hosted at the Harvard Club in Boston, Massachusetts, around the theme, 'Can Jews Believe in Jesus?' In Scottsdale, Arizona, they debated the question, 'Can Jews Accept Jesus as the Messiah?'[18] It is reported that five Jewish missions in England cooperated to bring Boteach and Brown together again for a series of debates in England on the subject, 'Is Jesus the Jewish Messiah?' in 2008.[19] Public interactions between Boteach and Brown have produced a healthy airing of issues without stumbling into manipulative coercion or personal defamation.

Evangelistic media

Over the last thirty years, Jewish missions have effectively used newspaper and magazine advertisements and all forms of outdoor advertising for evangelistic advertising. They need not necessarily be event-driven, but focused entirely on making gospel statements to Jewish and Gentile audiences. Evangelistic advertising has been found to be effective and appropriate for direct outreach evangelism.

For example, in 2006 one mission used 'Jesus for Jews' as an evangelistic slogan on thirty subway station kiosks in New York City. An axiom of advertising is that good ads beget more media. That slogan created enough *ad buzz* to prompt significant added radio and television news coverage, which only served to amplify the message to an even broader audience.

---

[17] H.H. Ben-Sasson, *The History of the Jewish People* (Cambridge: Harvard University Press, 1976), 385–8.

[18] Benjamin Leatherman, 'Rabbi, Evangelist Debate Jewish View of Messiah', *Jewish News of Greater Phoenix* (15 April 2005).

[19] Jean-Paul Rempp, 'Annual Report 2007 for LCJE Europe', *LCJE Bulletin* 91 (February 2008): 11.

In March 2008, the LCJE network in Israel convened a seminar specifically to explore new innovations and resources on uses of media for evangelism.[20] Radio and television have provided limited opportunity in Israel. However, the Internet is offering excellent means to promote the gospel of Messiah. Web-based radio is also a way to get around government control of radio and television broadcasts. Plans are underway for radio broadcast from Israel in Hebrew and in Arabic. Several ministries are conducting radio programming in Russian for ministry to Russian Jewish people.[21]

Another innovative use of media is through billboards for the purpose of evangelistic outreach and to introduce culture change in Israel. A 2008 social research study in Tel Aviv found that only 8 per cent of Israeli Jews know the correct name of Jesus in Hebrew as *Yeshua* while 72 per cent commonly know his name by the rabbinic corruption in Hebrew as *Yeshu*. Only 2 per cent knew that *Yeshu* is an acronym for a curse.[22] So, in response, Jews for Jesus used metropolitan buses and electronic billboard ads to focus attention on Jesus by effectively using a play on words in Hebrew to say that *Yeshu* (the curse) = *Yeshua* (Jesus) = *Yeshuah* (Salvation).

Literature distribution

Evangelistic literature that is created specifically for distribution is produced as pamphlets, booklets, books and the Scriptures in whole and portions. Outreach and discipleship information is available for Jewish readers in Hebrew, English, Russian, Ukrainian, German, Romanian, Farsi, French, Amharic, Spanish and more.

We listed earlier some of the publishing houses that are producing very fine evangelistic materials for Jewish people. Some of the Israeli publishers also create evangelistic advertisements that offer their books to Jewish seekers through the mail. Literature is also made available by hand-to-hand offers in public areas, by workers going door-to-door, through portable bookstalls or tables in farmers markets and at Bible shops.

Often, the evangelistic literature features the name of an organization with e-mail, street address or phone number where a seeker can call for further information. When literature is distributed in public

---

[20] David Zadok, 'LCJE Meeting in Israel', *LCJE Bulletin* 92 (May 2008): 5–6.

[21] Zadok, 'LCJE Meeting', 5–6.

[22] David Brickner, 'New Opinion Poll on What Israelis Think About Jesus', 15 May 2008. Online: http://jewsforjesus.org/publications/realtime/59/01.

forums, outreach workers are able to have personal interaction on the spot with Jewish enquirers. They can also collect contact information to arrange for follow-up visits.

Social structures

Various existing social structures are appropriate for missionary practice. Congregations like synagogues and youth groups for children or young adults are the main examples.

Messianic congregations

A 1999 survey reported on more than eighty-one messianic congregations in the State of Israel.[23] It is safe to say that congregations of Jewish believers in Jesus are functioning in every Jewish population centre of the world today. Congregational ministry is an appropriate method for Jewish evangelism. Some congregations are strategically placed for outreach to Jewish subcultures in home communities and the Diaspora. For example, Russian language congregations have developed for ministry to Jews of the Former Soviet Union (FSU) who are living in Australia, Canada, Germany, Israel and the United States.

Congregational ministry is centripetal, focused on bringing Jewish seekers into the congregation. In that community setting, Jewish people may easily be introduced to the knowledge of Messiah Jesus. One recent congregation reported its purpose is 'to bring Jewish people to God through Messiah Yeshua and into this Jewish congregation.'[24]

A unique challenge within the messianic congregational movement is the attention given to emphasizing cultural elements of Jewish ritual or even mandated observance as defined by traditional Judaism. On few occasions is the gospel of grace in Messiah Jesus compromised, but implications of the debate bear more than uncritical observation.

Children and young adults

Children's ministry is another area where good models for ministry practice exist. Whereas evangelization of Jewish children is a sensitive subject, several messianic congregations and missions, in Israel and in

---

[23] Kai Kjær-Hansen and Bodil F. Skjøtt, 'Facts and Myths About the Messianic Congregations in Israel', *Mishkan* 30–31 (Jerusalem: 1999).

[24] Gliebe Kirk 'A Call for Clarity in Messianic Jewish Community Development', *LCJE Bulletin* 92 (May 2008): 13.

the US, have sponsored summer youth camps. One has been in existence for more than thirty-five years. Jewish children, with the consent of their parents, are exposed to the message of Jesus and some do come to faith in Messiah.

Ariel Ministries has hosted *Camp Shoshanah* as a conference centre and Bible study programme for youth and families in upstate New York. The Jews for Jesus mission has hosted *Camp Gilgal* programmes for children and teens ages 8-18 each summer at three US locations for eighteen years.

Weekly daytime Bible clubs are also being used to reach Jewish children in Israel and elsewhere. Parents are informed that children are receiving instruction in the Bible, including the New Testament and teachings of Jesus. Messianic ministries and congregations in places like Chicago have originated children's clubs with curricula to strengthen Jewish identity and provide evangelistic outreach to Jewish children.[25]

Campus outreach to university students is a familiar format. However, a new phenomenon is the outreach efforts to Jewish students in the cause of Christ. *Beit Eliahu* congregation in Israel has started Israeli student groups on college campuses in Haifa during the last few years. They host open house parties at various apartments that feature a discussion around film clips or songs that lead into biblical truths and the gospel. They have also developed a provocative and thoughtful Hebrew website for reaching Israeli college students at http://www.igod.co.il.

Diaspora missiology

The term *diaspora* refers to the phenomenon of 'dispersion' or the 'movement of any ethnic group' as a people in transition.[26] Diaspora missiology is a missiological study of the group scattered and the strategy of gathering or reaching them for the kingdom of God.[27] Three practices are cited in this regard: outreach to seekers and trekkers, New Age festivals and Jewish-Gentile couples.

---

[25] Kirk Gliebe, 'Children's Outreach: Past, Present and Future', *LCJE Bulletin* 65 (September 2001): 17–25.

[26] Luis Pantoja Jr., Sadiri Joy Tira and Enoch Wan, (eds), *Scattered: The Filipino Global Presence* (Manila:LifeChange Publishing, 2004).

[27] Joy Sadiri Tira and Enoch Wan, (eds), *Missions in Action in the 21st Century* (Portland: Filipino International Network and Institute of Diaspora Studies – Western Seminary, 2008) pre-publication copy, 30.

Seekers and trekkers

Young Israelis trek in groups to places like Thailand, India, Europe, America and Brazil after fulfilling three years of required military service between the ages of 18 to 21. In these places, they sometimes engage in hedonistic indulgence and are often open and approachable to consider new spiritual perspectives.

Some missions have developed successful strategies to encounter and engage these Israeli post-army trekkers in order to offer a hope in the gospel. In 2001 and 2002, the Danish Israel Mission organized project 'Jews in the East'. They brought together teams of youth that ventured to Thailand and India in order to engage Israeli young people in spiritual dialogue and meaningful communication around the gospel. Other mission efforts continue to follow that strategy to India, Thailand and elsewhere.

New Age outreach

Diaspora studies show that populations in transition signal openness to culture change and an opportunity for mission outreach. Israeli society, and particularly its youth, are quite open to New Age ideas. Followers are already in the midst of culture change from traditional spiritual beliefs. The New Age Movement (NAM) arrived in Israel with a syncretistic amalgamation of pantheism, the esoteric, the occult, magic, pop psychology and Gnosticism. Two common expressions in Israeli society are Kabala Judaism and a fascination with Tibetan Buddhism.[28]

New Age festivals have been hosted in Israel for more than a decade. *The Beresheet Festival*, held during the fall season corresponds with the Feast of Tabernacles. More than 25,000 annually attend the festival in the Galilee. The *Boombamela New Age Festival* is held near Ashdod, Israel, coinciding with the Passover holiday and modelled after a Hindu festival.

Mission workers have responded with outreach efforts at these festivals. They purchase booth space where teashops welcome Israelis offering an opportunity for non–judgemental discussion about the gospel.[29]

---

[28] Heinrich Pedersen, 'New Age Judaism', *LCJE Bulletin* 67 (February 2002).
[29] Lisa Loden, 'The New Age in Israel at the Beginning of the 21st Century', *Mishkan* 38 (2003): 24–39.

Ministry to Jewish-Gentile couples and families

Jewish–Gentile couples, intermarried, cohabiting or dating, signal a major demographic shift of world Jewish population. For the past twenty-five years, world Jewry, especially in the Diaspora, has experienced some shifting towards assimilation and intermarriage. During that period more than half of all Jewish people marrying in the United States have married non-Jews. Demographic data on Jewish intermarriage rates in Europe (40–60 per cent), the Former Soviet Union (80 per cent) and Latin America (45 per cent) are similar.[30]

An ethnographic missiological study in the US during 2004 sought to understand the challenges that Jewish-Gentile couples face in order to better formulate mission strategy to reach them.[31] Some missions and congregations are employing culturally appropriate Jewish social structures, like small group *havurot*. These are fellowships where marriage and family life issues can be discussed in practical terms and spiritual resources may be shared. Jewish-Gentile couples present a clear missiological opportunity where new efforts are providing resources for cross-cultural marriage tensions and hope for spiritual family harmony.[32]

Conclusion

We have introduced some of the excellent resources that are available for the support of Jewish evangelism. We hope that the reader will be encouraged to contact these missions and support agencies to seek ways to partner with or become involved in some of these suggested practices for reaching Jewish people with the gospel of Messiah Jesus.

---

[30] Sergio DellaPergola, Yehezkel Dror and Shalom S. Wald, *Jewish People Policy Planning Institute Annual Assessment 2005* (Jerusalem: Gefen Publishing House, 2005), 12.

[31] Enoch Wan and Tuvya Zaretsky, *Jewish-Gentile Couples: Trends, Challenges and Hopes* (Pasadena: William Carey Library Publishers, 2004).

[32] Online: www.jewishgentilecouples.com.

ND - #0076 - 270225 - C0 - 229/152/16 - PB - 9781842276693 - Gloss Lamination